WOMEN IN NEW WORLDS

Historical Perspectives on
the Wesleyan Tradition

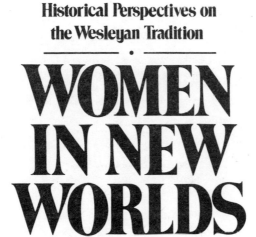

WOMEN IN NEW WORLDS

Editors:
HILAH F. THOMAS
ROSEMARY SKINNER KELLER

ABINGDON

NASHVILLE

Women's History Project

General Commission on Archives and History
The United Methodist Church

Women in New Worlds
Copyright © 1981 by Abingdon

Library of Congress Cataloging in Publication Data

Main entry under title:

Women in new worlds.
    Selected papers presented at the Women in New Worlds
Conference held in Cincinnati, Ohio, Feb. 1–3, 1980.
1. Women in church work—Methodist Church—Congresses.
2. Methodists—United States—Congresses.
I. Thomas, Hilah F. (Hilah Frances), 1941– . II. Keller,
Rosemary Skinner. III. Women in New Worlds Conference
(1980: Cincinnati, Ohio)
BX8207.W48   287'.088042   81-7984   AACR2

ISBN 0-687-45968-0 (v.1)

All Scripture quotations are from the King James Version of
the Bible.

MANUFACTURED BY THE PARTHENON PRESS AT
NASHVILLE, TENNESSEE, UNITED STATES OF AMERICA

CONTENTS

ACKNOWLEDGMENTS............................9

INTRODUCTION.. 13

I. THE LARGER SETTING: WOMEN IN CHURCH AND SOCIETY

1. Women's History/Everyone's History........... 29
   Donald G. Mathews

2. The Last Fifteen Years:
   Historians' Changing Views of American
   Women in Religion and Society.................. 48
   Kathryn Kish Sklar

II. THE SPIRITUAL EMPOWERMENT OF WOMEN

3. Women of the Word:
   Selected Leadership Roles of Women
   in Mr. Wesley's Methodism........................69
   Earl Kent Brown

4. Minister As Prophet? or As Mother?:
   Two Nineteenth-Century Models................. 88
   Nancy A. Hardesty

5. Mary McLeod Bethune As Religionist........ 102
   Clarence G. Newsome

6. Georgia Harkness:
   Social Activist and/or Mystic..................... 117
   Martha L. Scott

III. CONTRIBUTIONS OF WOMEN TO CHURCH LIFE

7. Ministry Through Marriage:
   Methodist Clergy Wives on the
   Trans-Mississippi Frontier........................ 143
   Julie Roy Jeffrey

8. Hispanic Clergy Wives:
   Their Contribution to United Methodism
   in the Southwest, Later Nineteenth Century
   to the Present...161
   Clotilde Falcón Náñez

9. Preparing Women for the Lord's Work:
   The Story of Three Methodist Training
   Schools, 1880–1940................................. 178
   Virginia Lieson Brereton

10. The Social Gospel According to Phoebe:
    Methodist Deaconesses in the Metropolis,
    1885–1918... 200
    Mary Agnes Dougherty

IV. THE STATUS OF WOMEN IN INSTITUTIONAL CHURCH LIFE

11. Laity Rights and Leadership:
    Winning Them for Women in the Methodist
    Protestant Church, 1860–1900....................219
    William T. Noll

12. "A New Impulse":
    Progress in Lay Leadership and Service by
    Women of the United Brethren in Christ
    and the Evangelical Association,
    1870–1910... 233
    Donald K. Gorrell

13. Creating a Sphere for Women:
    The Methodist Episcopal Church,
    1869–1906... 246
    Rosemary Skinner Keller

14. The Laity Rights Movement, 1906–1918:
    Woman's Suffrage in the Methodist
    Episcopal Church, South........................... 261
    Virginia Shadron

15. Nineteenth-Century A.M.E. Preaching
    Women: Cutting Edge of Women's
    Inclusion in Church Polity........................ 276
    Jualynne Dodson

V. THE MOVEMENT OF CHURCH-WOMEN INTO SOCIAL REFORM

16. Evangelical Domesticity:
    The Woman's Temperance Crusade of
    1873–1874... 293
    Susan Dye Lee

17. For God and Home and Native Land:
    The W.C.T.U.'s Image of Woman
    in the Late Nineteenth Century.................. 310
    Carolyn DeSwarte Gifford

18. Korean Women in Hawaii, 1903–1945:
    The Role of Methodism in Their Liberation
    and in Their Participation in the
    Korean Independence Movement............... 328
    Alice Chai

19. Shaping a New Society:
    Methodist Women and Industrial Reform
    in the South, 1880–1940........................... 345
    Mary E. Frederickson

20. Winifred L. Chappell:
    Everybody on the Left Knew Her...............362
    Miriam J. Crist

NOTES..379

CONTRIBUTORS.......................................437

OTHER PAPERS DELIVERED
AT THE CONFERENCE...........................443

ACKNOWLEDGMENTS

The General Commission on Archives and History of The United Methodist Church owes an enormous debt of gratitude to numerous individuals, to church agencies, and to other organizations for the support and assistance which enabled the commission to convene the national conference, Women in New Worlds: Historical Perspectives on the United Methodist Tradition, held in Cincinnati, Ohio, February 1–3, 1980. This volume makes available to the general church, and to women's, social, and religious historians, twenty of the papers presented at that conference.

Following a recommendation from the National Seminar of United Methodist Women at Norman, Oklahoma, in 1975, the directors of the Women's Division, Board of Global Ministries, sent a petition to the 1976 General Conference, calling for the General Commission on Archives and History to "appoint a special committee to research and publish a history of the contribution of women to The United Methodist Church." The petition was adopted and the mandate handed to the commission without funding.

The General Commission is particularly indebted to Norma Taylor Mitchell, who served as chairwoman of its standing committee on the Status and Role of Women (later to be called the Women's History and Status Committee) for 1976–80. Dr. Mitchell gave generous, strong, and farsighted leadership to the implementation of the 1976 mandate. As a member of the commission for two quadrennia and with a background of involvement in women's organizations of the church, she brought a special expertise to this responsibility. She was able to blend the talents and abilities of committee members Emora T. Brannan, Kenneth E. Rowe, Eula Pryor, and Sonia Shinn Sunoo; John H. Ness, Jr., general

9

secretary of Archives and History, and Louise L. Queen, assistant general secretary; Barbara E. Campbell, liaison from the Women's Division, Board of Global Ministries, and Marilyn Owen Robb, representative of the General Commission on the Status and Role of Women, channeling their gifts into a comprehensive proposal which responded to the mandate in an affirmative way.

Building on the advice of Dr. Margaret E. Crahan of New York City, a scholar of Latin American missions with considerable experience in funding historical enterprises, the General Commission on Archives and History applied to and received from The United Methodist General Council on Ministries the initial resources to launch its Women's History Project. In the fall of 1978, Hilah F. Thomas was employed to serve as coordinator of the project and as a temporary member of the staff. She assumed responsibility for further funding and for program development and interpretation, with the advice and guidance of the committee and its adjunct members. Subsequent grants from the Women's Division and from the Lilly Endowment, Inc. were obtained for the project, in addition to a second subsidy from the General Council on Ministries. Special appreciation is expressed for the support and guidance of Martha Boyd Watson and Norman E. Dewire of the General Council on Ministries; to Theressa Hoover and Mai H. Gray of the Women's Division; and to Robert W. Lynn of the Lilly Endowment.

The Cincinnati conference itself, other programs of the Women's History Project, and the operation of the project office over a period of more than two years could not have been realized without the help of other persons and organizations: Sharon Abner, Emora and Nancy Brannan, Louise Branscomb, M.D., Henrietta W. Bryan, Eugene M. Decker III, Hazel M. Decker, Mary Charlotte Decker, Mrs. Joe A. Hale, Diane E. Kenty, The Edwin Mellen Press, F. Joseph and Anne Virginia Mitchell, Jeanne Audrey Powers, Thelma Stevens, the United Methodist Women of St. Luke's Church in Houston, Texas, the Oregon-Idaho Annual Conference United Methodist Women, and a generous anonymous donor.

ACKNOWLEDGMENTS

The General Commission on Archives and History gratefully acknowledges the contributions of hospitality, labor, information, and counsel received from the more than three-score additional persons recognized individually in the printed conference program—especially the chairman and vice-chairwoman of the commission at that time, Bishop John B. Warman and Carroll Hart, and the consultants at the planning session at United Theological Seminary (Dayton) in May 1979. The commission also acknowledges the meaningful support given by the General Commission on the Status and Role of Women and its secretariat, Lovely Lane United Methodist Church in Baltimore, other staff of the Women's Division, the Anna Howard Shaw Center at Boston University, Frances S. Smith of United Methodist Communications, and artists Margaret R. Rigg and Janet Pearson Roth.

Special recognition is owed to other staff members of the General Commission on Archives and History as well, for the support they have given to the Women's History Project in addition to their other duties: Evelyn M. Sutton, Catherine Jones, and William C. Beal.

From among the fifty-eight essays delivered at the Women in New Worlds conference, final selection for this volume was made by a screening committee of nine persons representing the ethnic and racial diversity of this church, and their dedication has contributed to the broad and scholarly coverage of church women's history found within these pages. They are Jualynne Dodson, Rosemary Keller, chairwoman, Glenda E. Morrison, José Palos, Louise Queen, Sonia Sunoo, and Hilah Thomas.

The essays were compiled and given final editing by Louise Queen, without whose skill, time, and dedication the publication of this volume would not have been possible. Her insights and assistance were indispensable to the Cincinnati conference and to the entire project.

The commission is indebted to Rosemary Skinner Keller, chairwoman of its Women's History and Status Committee for 1980–84, and to Mamie Ratliff Finger, a member of that committee, for their leadership in carrying out the intent of the committee for the promotion of this volume.

INTRODUCTION

The New Woman who advocated suffrage, entered professions, and wore practical clothing was a controversial figure in late nineteenth-century America.

Simultaneously, debates on the "woman question" raged throughout the churches. Women presented their cases for ordination before high officials and some were elected lay delegates to national governing bodies—usually to have their petitions denied. Single women journeyed to Africa and Asia as foreign missionaries while their sister deaconesses walked the streets of inner-city slums in the United States, spreading the "gospel message" of evangelism, education, and social uplift. Other women entered and prayed in saloons and picketed to have their doors permanently closed. Claiming the fire of Pentecostal baptism, Christian women placed reform of society at the heart of the gospel imperative.

Lucy Rider Meyer was one of many colorful predecessors in the United Methodist tradition who worked for both women and the church in the late nineteenth and early twentieth centuries. As founder of the Chicago Training School, the first Methodist Episcopal preparatory school for deaconesses, she edited its journal, *The Deaconess Advocate*.

An article she printed in 1895, "A 'New Woman' of Ye Olden Time," sets the stage for the stories of United Methodist women contained in this volume. The debate regarding admission of women to the ministry is not confined to modern Methodism, Meyer wrote. She pointed to Hilda, Abbess of Whitby, born in A.D. 614, as a role model for turn-of-the-century women who sought full and equal status with men in the church. Hilda founded Roman Catholic monasteries for men and women in England and was active in the councils of the church. Meyer concluded her article with these arresting words: "I closed the life of this noble Abbess of Whitby, wondering if God sent a St. Hilda to Methodism *what should we do with her.*"[1]

In truth, since the early days of the republic, countless women in the United Methodist tradition have practiced the ministry exemplified by St. Hilda. Their rich and varied stories begin to unfold in these pages. Through the organizations and movements they represented, the women come to life in a score of ways—as committed, courageous, powerful, controversial, or innovative pioneers of the expanding role of women in church and society.

This volume begins by analyzing the larger context of women in American church history and the way that history has been written to date. Then, turning directly to United Methodist women, we trace episodes in the spiritual empowerment which led females beyond silent participation in the established church of John Wesley's day to their rightful place beside men as ministers and preachers. Through their contributions as pastors' wives on the frontiers and as deaconesses in the inner cities, women in the United Methodist tradition expanded the boundaries of their own lives and brought new dimensions to the work of the church. The status of females was an explosive issue as women sought to be ordained, to gain lay voting rights in the governing structures of their denominations, and to develop home and foreign missionary societies. Our United Methodist foremothers moved outside the official church bodies as they sought to reform society through specific causes, ranging from temperance to labor to peace.

Through these pages, we begin to touch the rich fabric of the heritage of United Methodist women, conceived in faith and in the bonds of sisterhood. It is a complex, multifaceted tradition. The United Methodist Church itself was born in 1968 through a merger of the Methodist and the Evangelical United Brethren denominations. Its antecedent denominations go back to the founding of the nation and include the Methodist Protestant, Evangelical, United Evangelical, United Brethren in Christ, Methodist Episcopal, and Methodist Episcopal, South. It is a story of black and white;

of Asian, Hispanic, and Native American. From these essays themes emerge which interrelate the experiences of women and the church in this broad tradition; the divergence of racial, ethnic, and denominational experiences is also demonstrated.

The twenty essays included in this volume were selected from fifty-eight papers presented at the Women in New Worlds conference. That historic conference was the first to focus on the heritage of women in a major American denomination, and the first to be sponsored by the historical agency of a mainline Protestant church—the General Commission on Archives and History of The United Methodist Church.[2] Soon Abingdon will publish a second volume of *Women in New Worlds,* drawing primarily from other papers delivered at the conference. That volume will recover further the denominational, racial, and ethnic streams of United Methodism and their relationship to wider church and social history.

The essays in these volumes are lively and provocative, each documenting a little-known story that should be recovered and shared. A larger significance, however, is the introduction of denominational history as a major facet in the history of women and in the broader heritage of women in American society. It is hoped that these books will stimulate other historians, lay and professional, female and male, to probe more deeply the subjects introduced here and to venture forth into these obscure aspects of denominational history. We simply open the door and point a way, hoping others will seek to discover and analyze these rich traditions.

The two articles in Section 1, featured as keynote addresses at the Women in New Worlds conference, introduce this volume and set the broader context for women in the United Methodist heritage. Donald Mathews, in his opening essay, "Women's History/Everyone's History," voices the challenge created by women's history today and by the articles in this volume. Because women are now part of our historical consciousness, everyone's history must be rewritten, Mathews contends. The recovery of little known information regarding women has not substantiated the information we already possessed. Rather, it has consequentially changed traditional interpretations of the past. Resistance to the movement of women into power structures has been caused partially by recalcitrant males. But habits of mind and rules of propriety have formed women's own consciousness and led them to war with themselves. What begins as a search for women in history leads to an exploration of the complex world of human experiences. The goal of "everyone's history" is inclusiveness—of races, classes, and sexes—which will enable persons and groups to understand their own place in history, not exclusively, but in relationship to others.

In a second contextual article, Kathryn Kish Sklar explores "Historians' Changing Views of American Women in Religion and Society." She parallels five stages in historical writings about American women and religion, and about women in the background of United Methodism. Sklar projects that historians of women in the 1980s will continue to investigate the ways females benefited personally and socially from their religious beliefs. Further, they will research in greater depth the effect of classes, ethnicity, and race on women's experience. Essays in this volume focus on these areas. They also probe the methods by which women sought to change the nature and scope of institutional church life, and in some ways succeeded.

Before we turn to the four sections on women in United Methodism, it is well to gain some perspective on the role of women in the church and how it has changed. The antecedent denominations of United Methodism, in the mainstream of Protestantism, have been broadly inclusive of diverse groups and viewpoints. Change, therefore, has not taken place in wrenching and dramatic upheavals. The expansion of women's roles and rights has been an evolutionary process, faltering and uneven. This has been true both in the increased status of women in the church and in the contribution females have made to institutional church life and social reform.

Two basic understandings of the relation of women to religion have undergirded the role of females in the church and the response that both women and the church have made to the female presence. First, the church has been the social conservator, reinforcing the traditionally approved place of females in society. In keeping with Alexis de Tocqueville's understanding of the influence of religion in early nineteenth-century America, churches have exerted supreme influence over the minds of women.[3] Females have been elevated over males as the protectors of morals within society. In her already classic article "The Cult of True Womanhood," written in 1966, Barbara Welter demonstrated the strong religious foundation of this traditional view of woman's place.[4] Women and men of religious persuasion have been among the sternest advocates of the four cardinal virtues of womanhood: domesticity, submission, purity, and piety. Religion often has served as a lid to confine women within the home, submissive to men, untainted by the outside world, and pious before God and "man."

Second, the church has been called to be the social pioneer. It is called to act on behalf of the wider community, to repent for the sins of society and for its own. Thus oppression has been a part of female experience in the church. Throughout the history of United Methodism, however, women and men have stood out as social pioneers, recognizing the sexism so deeply embedded in its life. They have understood sexism not simply as a "woman's issue" but as part of the whole human experience, calling forth the judgment of God on church and society alike.

These forces of constriction and of liberation, part of the whole story of women in the church, are analyzed in the four sections on women in the United Methodist tradition. Findings of these authors indicate that processes of change which often look highly traditional on the surface have been at work. Sometimes to gain their ends as social pioneers, women have employed ideology and procedures more commonly associated with the "cult of true womanhood" and with the church as social conservator. In the process, however, they have altered, sometimes radically, their own roles, and the United Methodist heritage as well.

The Spiritual Empowerment of Women, Section 2 of this volume, provides a useful beginning for the understanding of this movement in the lives of United Methodist foremothers. We labor under the false assumption, states Earl Kent Brown in "Women of the Word," that females simply were present but silent in the early class meetings of the Wesleyan movement in England. In practice, however, they prayed and spoke freely of religious experience, "not loud, yet fervent," exhorted others to respond, and expounded on Scripture. The effectiveness of their witness led Wesley to conclude that God was owning the ministry of these women with a harvest of souls, to the point that Wesley no longer labored distinctions between testimony, exhortation, and preaching. In extraordinary cases, he even permitted women to preach, because of their effectiveness in converting sinners to Christ. Though Wesley never appointed women as itinerants, a number "travelled the connection" with his approval, being invited by laity and clergy who were eager to hear their messages.

In nineteenth-century America, women began to seek the legal sanction of the churches to preach and to be ordained. The strongest defenses sanctioning the ministry of women grew out of long-accepted understandings of the role of women and the way in which Christ calls persons to discipleship, states Nancy Hardesty in "Minister As Prophet? or As Mother?: Two Nineteenth-Century Models." Phoebe Palmer, powerful evangelist of Methodism and the Holiness movement, based her convincing argument on the fulfillment of the prophecy at Pentecost, "Your sons and your daughters shall prophesy." Frances Willard, who received "entire sanctification" at the hand of Phoebe Palmer, became the second president of the Woman's Christian Temperance Union (W.C.T.U.), built directly on the cult-of-true-womanhood argument. As ministers, women could extend their mothering roles into all society, to make the whole world more homelike. Through the W.C.T.U., Willard took women into the marketplace to advocate suffrage "for home protection," and prohibition "for God and home and native land."

The personal religious journeys of Methodist women provide another way to understand the spiritual empowerment that led them to active public ministries, as seen through the articles of Martha Scott, "Georgia Harkness: Social Activist and/or Mystic," and Clarence Newsome, "Mary McLeod Bethune As Religionist." Harkness was the major female theologian, author, and seminary professor of Methodism through the mid-twentieth century. Bethune was one of the first black women to serve as lay delegate to a General Conference of Methodism. She also founded Bethune-Cookman College and the National Council of Negro Women. Scott interprets Harkness as a mystic who sought to practice the presence of God at all times; Newsome describes the evangelical training which molded Bethune's development. Conventional interpretations would stress the individualistic nature of religious encounters which mystics and evangelicals have with God, but our writers develop the radical social accountability which grew out of the spiritual empowerment of Georgia Harkness and Mary McLeod Bethune.

Contributions of Women to Church Life, Section 3, recognizes the pioneer efforts of women on the western frontiers and in the inner cities of the nineteenth century. In both cases, the expansion of home and mothering responsibilities brought qualitative changes to the lives of women themselves and to the nature of the church.

Advice literature addressed to wives of Anglo-American and Hispanic pastors admonished them to adapt the typical cult-of-true-womanhood understandings to their newly defined role on that narrow line between the wilderness and civilization. Duties of wife and mother were to be placed above all others. Their reward would be the knowledge that they had served their husbands well, according to Julie Roy Jeffrey in "Ministry Through Marriage: Methodist Clergy Wives on the Trans-Mississippi Frontier," and Clotilde Falcón Náñez in "Hispanic Clergy Wives: Their Contribution to United Methodism in the Southwest."

When ordination was not a possibility, marriage to a minister became the next-best opportunity to proclaim the gospel, a fact of life widely recognized by wives on the frontier. Such motivation may have played a significant part in their decision to marry. The qualities of women in the unsettled land on the frontier were neither typically feminine

nor consistent with those of people who continually played
subordinate roles. Broad new "fields of usefulness" opened
to pastors' wives, who made most of the same contributions,
though lacking the status of their mates. Traveling circuits
with their husbands, the wives facilitated conversions,
established schools and Sunday schools, and cared for the
sick and dying, even preparing bodies for burial.

By the late nineteenth century, when urbanization and
immigration created new frontiers in the inner cities, single
women deaconesses became instruments of service to meet
pressing needs. Recognizing the necessity for consecrated
lay service in what was deemed a religious emergency, the
church initially termed such workers "gap men" or
"irregulars." Unprecedented needs demanded new institutions. Deaconesses developed settlement houses and industrial schools in the slums and took their message of salvation
directly to depressed immigrants. While creating radically
new institutions, the churches and the deaconesses themselves based their vision on earlier nineteenth-century
models of life. They hoped to reconstruct the burgeoning city
on the model of small town or rural life, with a neighborly
atmosphere for the inhabitants, newly arrived from Europe.

New models were brought forth, however, which sub-
stantively changed the lives of deaconesses and the nature of
training for religious vocations. In her article "Preparing
Women for the Lord's Work: The Story of Three Methodist
Training Schools," Virginia Brereton describes the respect
for education and the practical orientation which characterized this new form of religious academic institution. Mary
Agnes Dougherty's "Social Gospel According to Phoebe:
Methodist Deaconesses in the Metropolis," is a fitting
complement. Dougherty posits that the origins of the social
gospel lay in the deaconess movement. A new breed of
churchwomen, deaconesses were the earliest trained experts
in the new field of social service which came into its own at
the turn of the century.

Significant efforts to raise the status of women in the
church were initiated during the late nineteenth century in
each of the antecedent denominations of United Methodism, as well as in the African Methodist Episcopal (A.M.E.)

Church. Women sought entrance into mainstream structures of power and service in the church through efforts to gain ordination and lay voting rights in conferences and national legislative bodies. During the same period, widespread movements resulted in the creation of women's missionary societies, constituting a separate sphere for women's work. While these alternative forms of leadership isolated female service outside the established denominational structures, they also enabled women to concentrate their energies and, in some cases, to create powerful autonomous organizations "for women only."

The complex interweaving issues which affected The Status of Women in Institutional Church Life are compared and contrasted in five case studies in Section 4. Taken as a group, the essays introduce most of the issues involved in the expansion of the roles of women across the spectrum of Protestantism. The first four essays focus on the preceding denominations of The United Methodist Church and the fifth, on the African Methodist Episcopal Church.

The findings of William Noll in his article "Laity Rights and Leadership: Winning them for Women in the Methodist Protestant Church," indicate that this smallest of the Methodist denominations proved the most flexible in relating to women's petitions. As was characteristic of other denominations, its female missionary society concentrated on efforts to evangelize, educate, and uplift women and children. After overcoming mutual distrust between the women's group and the larger denominational mission board, the women's missionary society maintained its autonomy, simultaneously spurring successful drives for ordination and lay voting rights.

The second article, " 'A New Impulse': Progress in Lay Leadership and Service by Women of the United Brethren in Christ and the Evangelical Association," by Donald Gorrell, compares the response to women within two denominations which merged in 1946. The author began his work as a study of one tradition, the Evangelical United Brethren Church. He found, however, that contrasts, rather than likenesses, predominate in comparing efforts of the uniting denominations to raise the status of women. The essay traces ways in which the United Brethren were more open to the creation of women's societies, as well as to the admission of women as lay delegates, than was the Evangelical Association.

The two larger uniting denominations, the Methodist Episcopal Church and the Methodist Episcopal Church, South, which, with the Methodist Protestant Church, formed The Methodist Church in 1939, present further notable examples of contrast. Rosemary Keller's essay, "Creating a Sphere for Women: The Methodist Episcopal Church, 1869–1906," demonstrates that movements to enter mainline power structures and to create autonomous women's societies occurred at virtually the same time in that northern-based denomination. The result was a consciously created "separate sphere" for women's work. While clergy and lay voting rights were denied women by the General Conference, it heartily endorsed an autonomous Woman's Foreign Missionary Society. Maintaining administrative and financial control until, from a position of power, it merged with the larger denominational mission board, the Woman's Foreign Missionary Society left a legacy of strong and forward-looking leadership.

Virginia Shadron's "The Laity Rights Movement, 1906-1918: Woman's Suffrage in the Methodist Episcopal Church, South" provides a notable contrast. She, too, recognizes the significance of strong autonomous organization through the Woman's Home Missionary Society. After the society was absorbed into the larger General Board of Missions of the southern denomination, however, leaders of the Woman's Home Missionary Society redirected their energies toward gaining lay rights for women in the governing structure. Shadron explores the means of confrontation and compromise employed by these women and the tensions which surfaced among female leaders, as well as the opposition by males in the established power structures. Though lay rights finally were gained for women within the mainline legislative body of the denomination, this did not compensate for the autonomy and organizational vigor that females previously had had in separatist missionary societies.

In the final essay of this section, "Nineteenth-Century A.M.E. Preaching Women: Cutting Edge of Women's

Inclusion in Church Polity," Jualynne Dodson analyzes the result of another attempt to gain entrance into power structures of the church. She traces the efforts of a select number of black women who sought and were denied licenses to preach and ordination in the African Methodist Episcopal Church. Dodson posits that an alternative separate structure for stewardesses and deaconesses was created to function on a basis of equality with men. Female deaconesses and stewardesses were "helpers," in subordination to men. It was only because preaching women pierced the consciences of A.M.E. men, however, that the structures were expanded to include women even to this degree, according to Dodson.

Throughout the nineteenth and twentieth centuries, United Methodist women have been leaders in The Movement of Churchwomen into Social Reform, as demonstrated in the fifth and final section. Wesleyan theology, with its emphasis on perfectionism, blended easily with belief in the moral superiority of women. These primary motivations provided powerful momentum in the nineteenth century, leading females into frays for abolition of slavery, women's rights, prison reform, and educational advancement. No reform issue is more illustrative of the zeal and significance of United Methodist foremothers in the last quarter of the century than was temperance, as seen through the companion articles by Susan Dye Lee, "Evangelical Domesticity: The Woman's Temperance Crusade of 1873–1874," and Carolyn Gifford, "For God and Home and Native Land: The W.C.T.U.'s Image of Woman in the Late Nineteenth Century."

Temperance crusaders aimed to purify society by making it more "homelike." They proclaimed that God had ordained women to bring sobriety to the community. When attempts to close saloons by moral suasion were unsuccessful, their tactics became distinctly political, as Susan Lee demonstrates. Women circulated petitions, took saloon keepers to court for violation of local temperance laws, and supported temperance candidates. It did not occur to them, however, that without the vote, they lacked the political power commensurate with the moral power they attempted to exert.

Carolyn Gifford contends that one of the most important accomplishments of the W.C.T.U. was to help redefine the cult of true womanhood. The belief in "cultural mother-hood" is central to her thesis. Frances Willard, second president of the W.C.T.U., advocated a new and promising profession of women in reform work and philanthropy—the world itself was to be woman's "sphere."

That wider world of the twentieth-century New Women of Methodism who have taken strong political-action stands on social issues is the subject of the final three essays in this section, and in the book. Alice Chai's article, "Korean Women in Hawaii," demonstrates how the church enabled Korean women, both in Hawaii and in their native land, to become political forces for Korean independence. Through American female missionaries, Korean women gained education and organizational ability which they used to organize relief societies when later threatened by Japanese domination. Once activated, women were at the center of all areas of resistance, caring for political prisoners and their families, collecting funds to aid the exiled government in Shanghai, and even being imprisoned as political activists.

In the last two essays, we return to the mainland. Virginia Shadron has mentioned the short-lived autonomous exis-tence of the Woman's Home Missionary Society in the Methodist Episcopal Church, South, but has indicated that the Woman's Missionary Council, even after being reorgan-ized under the General Board of Missions, maintained a strong and even radical ministry of social action. Mary Frederickson captures the significance of the witness to social justice effected by those two organizations in "Shaping a New Society: Methodist Women and Industrial Reform in the South, 1880–1940." Her article provides notable comparisons to the missionary societies described in Section 3. Beyond the similarities with other societies in expanding the vision of its members, the home missionary work of southern women was an important force in leading the church to adopt a stronger social creed and in fighting for greater justice for southern women and children in industry.

INTRODUCTION

"Winifred L. Chappell: Everybody on the Left Knew Her," writes Miriam Crist in the final essay. A deaconess educated at the Chicago Training School, Chappell became a religious journalist and editor of the *Social Service Bulletin* for the Methodist Federation of Social Service (M.F.S.S.), championing causes of the working class from the 1920s through the 1940s. Chappell challenged the churches to open their doors to the poor during the depression and to face up to an industrial order which she joined the Methodist General Conference of 1932 in deeming "unchristian, unethical, and anti-social." Her strong statements questioning the ability of the economic system to generate real improvement in the quality of life contributed to allegations of Communist infiltration of the M.F.S.S. and led to tensions within it. After a temporary release from the staff for health reasons in 1936, she never returned in an official capacity, but organized sharecroppers and taught in Arkansas until her retirement.

Winifred Chappell's story provides a fitting conclusion to *Women in New Worlds*. Her life and work cap the broad spectrum of women who have been a part of United Methodist tradition, and the variety of ideologies and movements they have represented. They introduce us to a revised picture of women in the churches who stepped forth more boldly than heretofore had been recognized to seek justice and rights for themselves and for others and to qualitatively change the nature of institutional church life.

The essays detail the expanding circles of women's lives, from their spiritual empowerment, to their relationship to institutional church life, to their contribution to society at large. The circles are concentric, however, growing out of commitment to a more faithful Christian witness. Finally, the essays take us full circle, back to the challenge of rediscovering and rewriting everyone's history. We submit this volume as an impetus toward deeper investigation and a fuller vision of the significance of women in the American religious tradition.

—Rosemary Skinner Keller

Evanston, Illinois

I

THE LARGER SETTING: WOMEN IN CHURCH AND SOCIETY

WOMEN'S HISTORY / EVERYONE'S HISTORY*

Donald G. Mathews

Women in New Worlds: Historical Perspectives on the United Methodist Tradition—the theme of the conference held in February, 1980, puts in bold relief the irony of historical experience. Our newest worlds are sometimes in the past. This is as true for historians as it is for their audiences. It is as true for those who assume a history of national innocence as it is for those who celebrate a history of turmoil and resistance in the dramatic search for personal roots. In the United States today, both chauvinistic myth and family genealogy challenge us to test our present experience against historical evidence to discover what we have been as a people, as families, and therefore as persons-in-time, and in the process to discover new worlds. When seen against the pluralism of our diverse origins, a simple uncomplicated past of "Americanism" can become many pasts. When reconstructed from lifeless documents, the lost memory of persons, families, and peoples can place us in a living past of relationships and anchor us in time with the maturity that comes from self-knowledge. A richly textured historical identity can create a new world because it reveals something about ourselves that we did not know.

The women in United Methodist history whose work and ideas provided substance for the conference in Cincinnati created new worlds for themselves as well as for us. They are

*Closing keynote address presented at the national conference convened by the General Commission on Archives and History of The United Methodist Church, Women in New Worlds: Historical Perspectives on the United Methodist Tradition, Cincinnati, Ohio, February 3, 1980.

part of a new world for women who did not know their own past; a new world for historians who did not study that past; a new world for men who, despite being sons, husbands, friends, and brothers, did not know that they were part of this world of women; a new world for men who, reading backward through time, have been the oppressors, masters, and adversaries and are now faced with a history which they, too, did not know. The words *oppression, master,* and *adversary* are offensive, freighted with disturbing emotions, but they express a historical reality which confronts us as students and subjects of history, whether we like it or not.

To emphasize the new world of women's history is not to suggest that men should apologize for the past. That would be no more appropriate than if the new world of black history had elicited only a wailing confession of sin from whites. For if the histories of women and black people teach us anything, it is that men are not the subjects of women's history and that whites are not the subjects of blacks' history. We are not searching for guilty parties and scapegoats, any more than we are searching for heroines and villains, although all these characters populate the past in more than modest abundance. The importance of women's history is not that men should know it—although they certainly should; nor is it that historians who write books should now mention "the ladies," because that is what they certainly should *not* do. The significance of women's history is that the injection of women into our historical consciousness demands a rewriting of everyone's history.

Whenever we encounter new information about the past, we must ask if the discovery essentially changes anything or whether it merely underscores what we already knew. Probably every historian has at one time or another daydreamed about finding a lost trunk of letters, which when opened would almost automatically revolutionize our historical understanding. What most of us did not know is that we have had that trunk in our intellectual attics for a long time and never have thought to look inside. Historians of women, having pried open the lid, invite us now to think in new terms, leading to new perspectives and therefore to a new past.

WOMEN'S HISTORY / EVERYONE'S HISTORY

The process of discovery begins in a formidably simple way: *Cherchez les femmes.* Papers at the Cincinnati conference discussed individuals, as well as women's groups, movements, and institutions. Some of the individuals explored were familiar to us as innovators, or as mythic figures of the Wesleyan tradition, or as both: Susanna Wesley, Frances Willard, Mary McLeod Bethune, Phoebe Palmer, Jessie Daniel Ames. The studies of groups and movements showed us how women have expanded their social roles by perfecting and diversifying their roles within the church. And the analyses of conflicts between women and those who resisted their movement into the latticework of power suggested the creative tension through which women frequently have been able to induce change. In this search for women, we have discovered who and what they were up against—men, yes, but in addition, habits of mind and rules of propriety which shaped their own consciousness and placed them at war with themselves. They faced not only flagrant abuse and the refusal to allow them to be the persons they wanted to be, but also myths and ideologies inadequate to enable them to understand the particulars in their own experience that prevented their articulation and justification of the persons they wanted to be.

The papers presented at the conference showed that women have faced the circumscription of their lives by ideas about appropriate role and place, but also have grasped the opportunity, when ideal female roles were self-contradictory enough, to create intellectual and psychological means of molding new models of thought and practice. In discovering the creativity of women in the process of cultural change, we also have uncovered the historical creativity of women in the maintenance of their own worlds, which have been closed to men and therefore to male historians. In the exploration of the past of United Methodism, as of other pasts, what begins as a simple search for women soon becomes the discovery of a complex world of human experience.

To understand this complexity, two things should be clarified. First, we must explain why we are making a special effort to look for women in history; second, we must explain why this enterprise will teach us something new about all human experience—why women's history is everyone's history.

Why Study Women in History?

The most obvious reason for studying women in history is that they are there. The problem has been, however, that despite their presence, historians did not see them. They saw Queen Elizabeth, to be sure, and perhaps Martha Washington. They remembered a few women who agitated for reform and equal rights and eventually, the vote. They could even recall the exceptional women who were either so outrageous or so effective that no one could ignore them. Victoria Woodhull and Carrie Nation were always good for a laugh, and we all recognize the public images of Frances Willard, Susan B. Anthony, and Eleanor Roosevelt. (As a child, I can remember thinking that Susan B. Anthony must have been important because, like my father, she had a middle initial.) But historians saw these very visible women from the perspective of those who possessed power—that is, those who were in a position to change the course of events. Elizabeth Tudor was the perfector of her father's vision of the English state. Her sex was a matter of statecraft. Woodhull and Nation were fanatics from the vantage point of power and position, and Willard, Anthony, and Roosevelt were remarkable women who emerged from the anonymous powerlessness of "woman's place" to become part of the world of public affairs. In reality, historians judged women by how far they were allowed to come into the arena of power where most of the protagonists were men. Their accomplishments were evaluated by the extent to which they provided women with the trappings and appearances of traditional power. They never were seen as significant representatives and leaders of constituencies quite unlike those that comprised the male political world.

If women were visible to historians, therefore, it was only as they entered the limelight of traditional power or as they appeared in close association with their husbands. Historians did not make a special effort to seek out other women, since they already saw all those who were important. The vast majority remained invisible because they were not important—that is, they were not powerful.

What flawed this perception was that importance, like beauty and evil, is in the eye of the beholder. To underscore this caveat, we need only recall that in the history of American religion, the full significance of Mistress Anne Hutchinson's challenge to the Puritan patriarchy was obscured for years by calling it the Antinomian controversy. Within the traditional framework of church history, which defined religious life and explained controversy in theological terms, this conflict was simply another example of the persistent tension between law and grace, works and faith, sanctification and justification within the Christian ethos. When it cropped up in 1636 in Puritan New England, the controversy became a dangerous challenge to public order, because in that particular society, theology was politics. Now this was of course true, but Anne Hutchinson's gender—with all its cultural implications—is as relevant in studying this episode as was the theology she espoused. Although her sex did not transform theological debate into a conflict over women's rights, it did underscore her potential threat to a social order authenticated in part by the subordination of women. The identification of Antinomianism with issues of sexuality and with the confusion of women's traditional role even before the Great Migration to Massachusetts, suggests that the heresy was always more than a dispute about grace and works. Once the contagion spread beyond Hutchinson's intimates, both men and women heretics were attacked for behaving in ways unnatural to their sex. The "unnaturalness" of their behavior was so much at odds with traditional views of status and power that Hutchinson's accusers charged her and another woman with having given birth to monsters, an indisputable evidence of the demonic.[1] The Antinomian debate was not, therefore, just a disagreement about theology, but a dispute concerning a social order maintained by strict rules of behavior associated with sex, by patterns of deference associated with social rank, and by orthodox religious views which favored communal solidarity over individual expressiveness. Anne Hutchinson's rebellion could never be fully understood until her sex became as important to historians as it had been to Puritans.

Since historical perception is so susceptible to mythic and ideological shading, the not-so-simple search for women in our past has been necessarily propelled by developments in politics as well as in scholarship—specifically, by the movements for the liberation of blacks and women, and the development of a new social history which has tried to free the historically "inarticulate" from their traditional anonymity. Pushing back cultural and social restrictions on the free development of black people, the first movement challenged the history whites had written about them. Blacks did not want to be integrated into a white culture more concerned with its retrospective guilt than with the historical experience of Afro-Americans. They did not want to be integrated into a white-defined history which demanded that they accept slaveholders such as Thomas Jefferson and George Washington as their heroes. On the basis of their own experience, they could not believe that blacks had been only the victims and never the formulators of history. They found, in sources as open to whites as to themselves, that black people had developed experiences and heroes of their own. They found that their history reached back into Africa, grew through the struggles of Richard Allen and Frederick Douglass, and unfolded in the words of James Weldon Johnson, Richard Wright, W. E. B. DuBois, Malcolm X, and Martin Luther King, Jr.[2] It was a new history which defined a people. The 1960s witnessed a powerful emotional bonding with a new past—new not in the sense that it had just been created, but that it had just been discovered. Once the political point was made and the excitement of discovery communicated, this new world of black history was offered to all, challenging us to seek all people who were invisible to traditional history.

The movement for women's liberation, rising out of the social upheaval of the 1960s, had much in common with the black liberation movement; the social experience of the two groups was in some ways analogous: Both blacks and women, insists William H. Chafe, have had to deal with the imposition of social controls by white men;[3] both have been assigned subservient positions according to ascriptive characteristics. The race and class privileges of white middle-class women did partially sedate them from feeling wronged, to be sure; but like blacks, they have been subject to the physical intimidation, economic control, and psychological power of white men who set limits on their activities. Inside these limits, women were taught values which reinforced their own sense of propriety within this subordinate position. Long-term changes in education, employment, economic distribution, and sexual behavior, which reached a critical mass in the 1960s, undermined these limits, however. Then women began to ask: In what ways are we a group like other groups? How are we bonded together as women? How do we think of ourselves? How *should* we think of ourselves, and what keeps us from being who we want to be? To answer these questions, they began to study their culture, their psychology, their roles in the economy, and their past.

Women discovered their past at a time when an increasing number of United States historians were beginning to participate in a modest movement of their own. Today this group is writing a "new social history," characterized by an interest in everyone's history. They have been influenced and emboldened by the impressive work of French and British colleagues to study the way people actually lived in the past. That this is an innovation may come as a surprise to nonhistorians, who may have thought that that was what historians were doing anyway—but not so! Historians were writing biographies of famous people, analyzing the ideas of prominent thinkers, and tracing public political debate in terms dictated by politicians; we were dividing our history according to the years wars were fought, presidents elected, institutions developed (or destroyed), and laws passed. The limitations of this kind of history are suggested by the traditional view of the so-called Age of Jackson: "With the achievement of universal, white, manhood suffrage, America was now a Democracy."

Some people were left out of this history, and out of this "democracy." Indeed, *most* people were left out. The new social history attempts to include them all. Although agreeing neither on method or theory, contemporary social historians in the United States do agree that we will never understand the past until we include everyone in it—the powerless, the dissidents, the deviants, the workers, the criminals, the saints, the elite, the poor, the rich—and establish their relation to one another. We need to know what divides all these people into aggregates, collectives, groups, or classes. Social historians are agreed that we will not understand the past until we look at the evidence of everyday life of all the people, in petitions, wills, marriage bonds, church books, trial records, census reports, and tax lists. They are agreed that the framework of our past must be exposed by examining health care, birth rates, families— both internal structure and external place in the social system—and the nature of the population, its density, ecology, and volatility. They are agreed that collective behavior such as riots, strikes, revivals, and social movements is just as important as a political tract in expressing what people believe about themselves and about those in power. Since women's role, work, fertility, and behavior are so important to these new inquiries, it is not surprising that the history of women should have gained rapidly in adherents, quality, and recognition since the late 1960s.

In answer to the first question, then, we should make a special effort to look for women in history because they are there. We do not yet know very much about them, because they have been ignored; and the folly of this fact is being driven home to all of us both in politics and in scholarship.

Why Is Women's History Everyone's History?

The second question, Why do we say that women's history is everyone's history? requires a brief explanation of "everyone." The concept is familiar enough, even if amorphous. Indeed, its lack of precise meaning has made it so popular: "Uncle Donald, don't be a drag; *everyone* is doing it!" "*Everyone* says that I should run for public office to serve the people." "I don't see why you should stop me, officer, *everyone* is going over 55!" In a democracy, the idea of "everyone" conveys a commonality which justifies action

36

and thought. Thus for many of us, "everyone's history" would be the attempt to portray the historical experience of all groups—the lambs as well as the lions, the rabbits as well as the foxes—as if their commonality would one day unite them all in an idyllic and vegetarian peace. But it is not commonality that we seek in social history, nor is it typicality or a reductionist personification of androgynous unity. The goal is inclusiveness: to count no historical understanding as authentic until all groups and beliefs are included in our analysis. To put the matter into subjective terms, "everyone's history" enables persons and groups to place themselves in the historical process without excluding others.

Women's history, therefore, is not exclusive in retaliation for the tradition of male-oriented history, but aims for inclusiveness through the introduction of women into the historical consciousness of both sexes. This is currently being accomplished by studying women in three major ways—in the work force, in the private sphere, and in the public sphere. These are the large historiographical divisions suggested by the report on United States scholarship in women's history submitted to the Fifteenth International Congress of Historical Sciences at Bucharest in 1980.[4]

Women have always worked, although they have not necessarily been honored or paid for it. Women's history is showing that the modern assumption that the working woman is a recent innovation is false; so is the idea that work outside the home can automatically raise the status of women. Most of woman's work before industrialization was confined to domestic tasks, farm work, or the pursuit of trades within the home. After 1800, a few began to enter industrial production, but until 1850, half the women wage earners in the United States were in domestic service, from which they moved into other forms of service or into industrial production. Women wage earners prior to 1870 tended to be lower class, young, and single, enjoying "few opportunities for advancement or permanent employment." Married women usually did not work outside the home, but when they did, "their jobs tended to be episodic and improvised." After 1890, the pace of women's entrance into the labor market accelerated, but their position continued to be marginal. Even when improvements in education enabled them to enter the professions, prejudice reversed the trend after 1920. During the Great Depression there was an upward swing in the employment of married women in the total labor force, but not as the result of conversion to the ideal of equality. "Women's low wages and the extreme sex segregation of the labor force operated in favor of female work during a period of high unemployment."[5] In other words, women were valued as laborers because they could be paid less than men were paid. Entering the wage-labor force, therefore, in many ways was no more beneficial to the status of women than had been their entry into the professions. Indeed, certain paid jobs came to be identified as women's jobs, a fact which diminished the status of the jobs rather than enhancing the status of the women.

Perhaps the most important impact of women's history will result from its sustained focus on the private sphere of "reproduction, domesticity, and family relations."[6] Women's progressively greater ability to "control their own fertility is," many feminist scholars believe, "one of the central facts of their history." The technological, ideological, and personal ability to regulate the bearing of children grants women the ability to decide whether they want to be thought of primarily as baby-making machines. The new capacity of social and women's historians to see this as a problem helps them in turn to appreciate that issues of power—the ability to control events—are not issues of electoral politics alone, but of domestic life as well. To take an example from religious history, the traditional debate between freewill Arminians and predestinarian Calvinists never so clearly defined the issue of freedom in the historical process as has the problem of birth control. The sovereign will of Almighty God in directing his mysterious providence has never seemed so restrictive of helpless human beings as in the condemnation of women across the centuries to unwanted pregnancy and the terrors of disease and death. In recent history, however, women have learned to control their bodies and, in that sense, their fate.

Studies of changing birth rates and marriage patterns,

and of birth control, reveal that the framework of human reproduction has shifted dramatically since 1800. Accompanying this change for much of the nineteenth century was the Victorian ideal of sexual restraint, which has been interpreted in widely different ways—as opportunity for women to be more free of biological motherhood; or as a restriction of their ability to express and celebrate their inner selves.[7] Whether formulated consciously or not, the Victorian ideal helped to shape an ideology through which women could assume responsibilities they had not had previously. Most dramatic may have been the shift from father to mother of the responsibility for raising children, a change which put women, especially in middle-class households, in a position of control over future generations. The mother increasingly became the conduit of civilization. Gradual though it was, this shift altered the way women could be seen and the way they would think of themselves, away from being men's "helpmeets or ornaments"—the position to which they had been consigned in the previous century.[8] Against this background, the responsibilities of motherhood ceased to be a mere extension of the responsibilities of wifehood and became, in addition, an avenue for women's development of a sense of autonomy and self-esteem.

Tracing such change in the past reveals that what today's traditionalists believe to be basically natural because it is biologically established, in reality is created by historical circumstances. That is, by the nineteenth century, the identification of women primarily as mothers ceased to lie in the biological fact of their giving birth and came instead to rest on a fabric of ideas that explained the meaning of motherhood and its requirements of women—to be nurturers, teachers, religious preceptors.

Acceptance and eventual perfection of these roles within the family helped women change their role in society, the third major area of study in women's history today. The Victorian ideal of motherhood did not necessarily restrict the activity of women to the domestic sphere. When they encountered things in the world that they would never have allowed in their homes, they began to organize to expand their control. The ideals they tried so hard to teach their children were very frail indeed, when compared to the tastelessness, injustice, and vice of the public sphere. But rather than cowering in their cages like frightened canaries, they launched out into new forms of social activity—not all the women and not all at once, but gradually and with considerable success by the early twentieth century.

Many of the papers presented at Cincinnati demonstrated the political astuteness and persistence of the new women who were determined to make their world a better place to live, just as they created order in their homes. Through social work, reform agitation, and political lobbying, women enlarged their sphere by making themselves into a militant public constituency, with leaders, strategists, tacticians, and troops. To be sure, the women's clubs, missionary societies, temperance unions, and mothers' associations were not especially radical by today's standards; and reformers could not, even as suffragists, strike a deathblow to the persistent strain of inequality, prejudice, and discrimination in American life. But feminist and nonfeminist women alike were attempting to define the meaning of womanhood and to create among women a sense of social solidarity which would be personally satisfying and publicly beneficial. They were attempting to create a world that would be better for women as a whole.

If women's history can help to provide a collective identity for women, we might conclude that that would be its only impact, and that women's history therefore is socially divisive, separating women from men. If this were true, it would make absolutely no sense to link women's history with everyone's history. But one of the fundamental contributions of women's history is to add gender as an essential part of our historical consciousness—in work, in the private sphere, and in the public arena. One of the results of this innovation could be the examination of all forms of work to see whether they have been sex specific by virtue of real biological differences or because of culturally imposed constraints. Or, consider the historical analysis which has stripped motherhood of its credibility as a biologically defined status. Women's history has raised questions concerning many of our common assumptions about gender roles. Are they based on ideas we can change, rather than on immutable "givens" which we cannot? Or, if we probe the private sphere of the family with as much concern for male behavior as for female, and if we pay special attention to all the possible matrices of interaction, we may possibly begin to understand the real significance of placing sex and the family in history. The study of women's history, in other words, opens new possibilities of historical research which may elicit the response from both sexes: I can see myself in this history!

There is something else that should be considered in evaluating the impact of women's history upon our historical consciousness in the United States and in evaluating the importance of the Women in New Worlds conference. Let me illustrate by sharing with you part of my own intellectual biography. For a number of years, I have been studying the way religion has affected southern society in the United States. As preparation for a book on this topic, I accepted an invitation to write a preliminary interpretive essay, which has been published as *Religion in the Old South*.[9] Previous study of church records had shown the significant role played by local churches in the organization of society beyond the family and the kinship systems of the early republic. These churches—most of them evangelical—extended the emotional bonds of kinship into a community of people who belonged to one another not only by geographical proximity or economic position, but also by a common commitment to specific behavior patterns, goals, and ways of explaining self and God. In acknowledging this commitment, evangelicals self-consciously had rejected certain beliefs and ways of doing things, and in so doing had established invisible but nonetheless substantial boundaries between themselves and other people. In the process of historical elaboration, my perception of these religious folk became fairly abstract; their experience became sometimes elusive. It was essentially disturbing, because there was something in this record that was easy to see, but not easy to understand. A fair majority of church members were women. Whether in Alabama or South Carolina or Virginia, about 64 percent of each congregation was female.

But in the words of the anonymous sage, So what? Lists of names scribbled in an almost indecipherable hand on paper bleached yellow by time and dust can have a depressing effect. There was nothing self-evident about the lists; they represented completely anonymous people, scarcely visible at all except for their names. And it was very simple to leaf through the records and ignore the names; in fact, I had read one set of records three times, over a period of ten years, before I took any notice of the names and therefore of the women. Christian and family names were then checked and traced, defining family ties, seeking them out in census lists and tax receipts. Had the women come alone into the church? Or had they led their families? Were they the dutiful daughters of pious parents? Or were they courageous if mild dissenters who entered the church for support and self-esteem? It was not as important, however, that I find answers to all my questions as that I had been arrested by the presence of women in the first place; that I had been compelled by some change in perception, by some insistence of the social historians, to look at everyone—especially at those who are difficult to recognize. Eventually, with the aid of literary sources, it became easier to see these women, first in the context of kinship and then of female bonding. Gradually, it became clear that women were the very people through whom the churches were established. And gradually, the fact which their names on church lists had suggested in the first place became obvious: *churches were organizations of women.* No more than Anne Hutchinson's Antinomianism should have concealed her sex, should the fact that churches were religious organizations have obscured their significance as female organizations.[10]

What was true in explaining the social constitution of local churches is also true in explaining the sweep of American history: The obvious presence of women must affect the way we understand our past. Women's organizations, whether specifically religious or not, have been the channel through which the private sphere of the home became part of the public sphere. But the role of women's organizations in the process has been ignored because of traditional infatuation with electoral politics. If, however, this bias were to be complemented by studying the gradual entry of women into the public life of our society, with their domestic-oriented subculture accompanying them, we might begin to perceive a new history which has affected everyone.

For the sake of argument, we could call the process *feminization,* a concept which Barbara Welter identified with change in nineteenth-century American religion, and which Ann Douglas identified with the sentimental impoverishment of nineteenth-century American culture.[11] Without either the religious or the pejorative connotations, however, the process could well be identified as the impact upon our public life of changes in women's institutions, consciousness, and action. The beginning of this long process is suggested by Mary Maples Dunn, who has pointed out that during the middle years of the seventeenth century in New England, women became the preponderant constituency of the church population "even after their attempts to share in governance were defeated and male membership shrank." The explanation, Dunn argues, may reside in the conclusion of anthropologists that "all societies tend to esteem male roles more than female ones," to judge male action as a matter of public importance and female action as a "domestic matter, carrying less status." Anne Hutchinson's challenge had revealed a serious conflict over social goals, resolved in part by assigning "one set of goals to men and another to women." In this conflict, the clergy had resisted "all claims to lay prophetic power" and gradually had "enjoined silence on the men." By the end of the seventeenth century, men were moving out of the church and the clergy was defining the church through celebration of virtuous and Christian women. A new role for women seems to have been created: They "became the keepers of the covenant and protectors of the idea of mission. Put historically, women accepted the burdens of the past, and men the burdens of the future. Put politically, gender differentiation could in this way be seen as a stage in the separation of church and state."[12]

Dunn's insight and her imaginative restatement of the process traditionally called "separation of church and state" suggest one significant way in which women's history can become everyone's history. The institutionalization of separate spheres achieved by the late eighteenth century has persisted throughout United States history, but through major changes in the roles of middle-class women, it also has provided a social base from which to bring the two spheres closer together. These changes and the institutional arrangements associated with them can be limned as falling into five hypothetical periods: 1780–1820, 1820–1880, 1880–1920, 1920–1960, and 1960 to the present. The first period after institutionalization of the private and public spheres could be called that of "Republican motherhood," when the role of the mother as nurturer, teacher, and moral preceptor in the homes of the new American republic supplanted the rule of the father.[13] In her domestic sphere, the mother assumed a public role by shaping the next generation of citizens and teacher-mothers. Developments during the second period, from 1820 to 1880, did not negate the maternal ideal projected in the first, but added to it the ideal of "reformist motherhood" as women enlarged their sphere of home and church through missionary societies and moral reform societies, beginning to impose their ideals upon the reluctant world of male business and politics.[14] In the third period (1880 to 1920) a new set of roles which we may refer to as "political motherhood" was characterized by the increased activity in reforming society through such organizations as the Y.W.C.A., W.C.T.U., settlement houses, and social reform agencies, as well as in demanding the vote through the National American Woman Suffrage Association and the suffrage movement as a whole. The next change took place between 1920 and 1960 in the world of work outside the home.[15] This shift in the experience of women was also additive, rather than completely transformational. Women who were mothers began to enter the paid labor force in ever greater numbers. Against the background of past achievements and cumulative changes in the technology and ideology of birth control, this change enabled women in the dissenting culture of the 1960s to divorce both their private and their public roles from motherhood altogether.[16]

The trend through these two hundred years has been for

women to move out from the private sphere in stages. The impact upon women has been to produce a crescendo of sensitivity to their "rights." The impact upon public life in the United States has been to bring the values of traditional Protestantism into the public sector by applying the values of the domestic sphere to the public sphere. This process has not been characterized by radical changes; that is not the essence of cumulative process. And to be sure, in each stage, a relatively small number of women moved through the dynamic of introducing the values. In each stage, vanguards urged further advances than constituencies were willing or able to make, and activists could be distinguished from those who wished to remain in what were for them perfectly acceptable positions. It could be argued, however, that even those "places" were further advanced than previous places for women had been. In each of the five stages, male reformers were obviously active in the new synthetic sphere of public-domestic activity, but unlike men in traditional electoral politics, they had a constituency of women activists who were using the tools of the home—moral suasion, influence, and what could be called "nagging"—to get things done. This constituency of women, developing over a long period of time, may have been the crucial social fact upon which a reform tradition could be built.

The implications of this way of looking at the entire reform tradition in the United States can be suggested by a brief glance at Progressivism, which often has been explained through studies of men.[17] If the focus is shifted to women, our understanding of the Progressive experience is altered and enriched. Moreover, the issue of woman suffrage is placed in its appropriate historical context. Women suffragists recently have been criticized for extending the privatistic categories of home and motherhood into their politics in order to justify enfranchisement. There are good historical and logical reasons for their doing so; "home" and "motherhood" were part of their opponents' political lexicon which they could adapt to their own purposes. These evocative symbols were not boundaries of limitation, but the channels of opportunity. Winning the vote was part of a long

45

and cumulative process affecting the whole of American society, and no serious woman believed it was complete by 1920; in the long process of feminization, it represented the *pen*ultimate entry of women into the public sphere.

In explaining woman suffrage, historians traditionally have placed it within the framework of Progressivism. But for the sake of argument, let us reverse the categories and place Progressivism in the framework of feminization. The switch makes sense if one recalls what Progressives wanted. They wanted expanded social services or welfare systems: better health care, better penal facilities, better laws governing work. They wanted cleaner, safer, and more honestly governed cities, and they wanted laws to control business. They wanted woman suffrage as part of their vision of a perfected democracy. All these reforms are inherent in the American Protestant reform tradition, in which women had been so prominent over such a long period of time, and to which, indeed, women were indispensible. All these reforms were justified by an ideology based on motherhood—not biological motherhood, but cultural motherhood, an ideology emphasizing nurture, education, instruction in values, and general welfare. In this context, temperance reform makes a great deal of sense because it was an integral part of the feminized moral imagination which saw "drink" as a drug-related problem and as a woman's issue, to use the jargon of a later day. If temperance is placed within the activist tradition of Protestant churches —which were, after all, organizations of women—it is easily seen as a basic part of the process of feminization and therefore scarcely as an aberration of Progressivism.

If the hypothesis of feminization has any validity at all, the study of women's history will have revitalized everyone's history in the United States by suggesting a new historical perspective. To be sure, this historiographical trail is not Interstate 75, but it has a logic which should be pushed, and it would not have been pushed except for recent studies in the history of American women. The idea of feminization is not suggested without some uneasiness at its hyperbole. Possibly the major problem with the hypothesis is that it might replace the image of Big Brother with that of Big Mama. But it is necessary to introduce into holistic historical analysis the previously unevaluated role of women as a force in American history. The empirical evidence will not reveal its secrets to historians and to other students of society without a conscious search for women within the total ethos—the *total* ethos. There are no answers in history until questions are asked. The androcentric bias of our culture has prevented our writing everyone's history because we could not ask the right questions, those now suggested by women's history—not until politics and scholarship shocked us into awareness. Those of us who are not historians of women, as well as those who are, have had a new world opened to us. It reminds one of the Bible verse which captured the imagination of the Woman's Missionary Society of the North Carolina Conference in 1920: "Behold, I have set before thee an open door, and no man can shut it."[18]

2

THE LAST FIFTEEN YEARS*

Kathryn Kish Sklar

Ours is a time of unprecedented change and uncertainty. In order to understand our own epoch we urgently need to improve our comprehension of the past. The conference on the history of women in the United Methodist tradition was an important contribution to that effort. As the first women's history conference to be sponsored by the historical agency of a major American denomination, Women in New Worlds and the publication of selected papers from the conference mark an important moment in the history of scholarship on American women and religion.

For many of us who participated, it provided a rich exposure to the vital example of church people who are writing the histories of their women's groups and of their own spiritual foremothers. This essay attempts to convey some of what I, as an outsider to the church, have learned from them and from their work. The conference brought together two kinds of scholars who have much to offer each other: historians within the church who view their history from the perspective of their own religious wrestling and commitment, and historians who approach the history of women and religion from a secular perspective. This blend of scholarship unfortunately has been rare; it in part accounts for the vitality of sharing that was felt at the conference. I salute the women and men of the United Methodist tradition who helped make the conference and this volume of papers a reality.

*A revised version of the opening keynote address delivered at Women in New Worlds: Historical Perspectives on the United Methodist Tradition, Cincinnati, Ohio, February 1, 1980.

The enrichment of our understanding of the past afforded by the Women in New Worlds conference was closely linked to its second important purpose: to deepen our sense of present and future possibilities for churchwomen and historians alike. The present volume should be understood as just a beginning; I call on historians of both secular and religious perspectives to find ways in the future to continue the exchange of ideas and information that was so fruitful at Cincinnati. Without further concerted steps, the conference and publication will have achieved only a portion of their potential value.

To set the context of that effort, this essay surveys the history written about American women in religion and society during the last fifteen years and interprets the way the historiography of the United Methodist tradition fits into this larger history. How have historians' views of American women in religion and society changed? How does the written history of women in the United Methodist tradition seem to fit into those changes?

Historians' views of women in American religious life have changed in two basic ways. First, the feminist movement has prompted historians to ask new questions and has enabled them to see historical issues from new perspectives. Second, broader changes in historical methods have encouraged historians to seek out new kinds of evidence and to use it in new ways in reconstructing the past. In other words, the field of United States women's history has been parented and nurtured both by feminism and by the "new social history."

Relatively few historians have explored the recent history of United States women and religion at any length. Therefore, since they focus primarily on the nineteenth century, I will do so here as well.

Five major stages of history writing about American women and religion can be identified and described. Please imagine these stages to be fluid rather than solid entities. I envision them as four streams which come into existence in chronological order and eventually combine to form one river.

Stage one has been in existence longest. It extends from the beginning of the historical profession in the United States in the 1880s, to the mid-1960s. This stage might be characterized as "prehistory," preceding the development of the field of women's history as we know it now. Some very concrete depictions of women in religion were made during that early period, but with rather primitive tools. Having no conceptual framework for the interpretation of their data, historians from that era left us chiefly a disparate body of specific facts.

Stage one is best exemplified by Julia Cherry Spruill's *Women's Life and Work in the Southern Colonies,* first published in 1938 and reprinted in 1972, with a new introduction by Anne Firor Scott. Almost half the chapter on women's "Participation in Public Affairs" was in fact devoted to female involvement in church affairs. Spruill wisely concluded that "in church affairs as in those of government, while women were generally supposed to be meek and quiet onlookers, they were sometimes persons of influence."[1] The chief attraction of Spruill's book is its piling up of facts about women. Gathered from widely varied primary and secondary sources, few pertinent facts available to Spruill escaped inclusion in her book. The chapter mentioned contains only one paragraph on Methodist women, but it is a very capable sketch of their history in the colonial period, and worth quoting.

Women are among the most active leaders among the early Methodists. In England, Wesley's female converts went about the country speaking in cottages and in the open air, organizing societies, and sometimes addressing large assemblies of men and women. The distinction of founding Methodism in America belongs to Barbara Heck, who came to New York in 1760 with her cousin Philip Embury, a lay minister, and several other Methodists. Mistress Barbara apparently did not preach herself, but was responsible for the first Methodist church in this country. We find no women preachers among the Methodists in the southern colonies, probably because the movement was already well established in England before it began to take root here. Wesley had encouraged the ministry of women in the early years, explaining that the extraordinary circumstances attending the whole Methodist movement justified an exception to St. Paul's injunction, but after his followers were better organized and a sufficient number of masculine preachers became available, women were discouraged from ascending the pulpit. They were, nevertheless, the most ardent converts to Methodism. The Reverend Francis Asbury found here many "heroines for Christ," who opened their houses for preaching, entertained itinerant ministers, gave testimonies at love feasts, and as class leaders, traveled about the country conducting prayer meetings and teaching and exhorting members of their own sex.[2]

Beyond this paragraph on Methodist women, Spruill's study devotes two paragraphs to Catholic women and six pages to Quakers. She gives, however, no justification for her inclusion of these three denominations and the exclusion of others, nor does she compare the experience of women in these three groups. *Women's Life and Work in the Southern Colonies* is like a series of impressive neolithic cave drawings, each paragraph aesthetically satisfying, but the whole leaving questions. How are the parts of this work related to one another? What interpretation are we to draw from these facts?

We now move northward to look at a second book from this prehistoric stage, Whitney R. Cross's *The Burned-Over District*, published in 1950. Properly speaking, Cross concluded, women "should dominate a history of enthusiastic movements, for their influence was paramount," but unfortunately this was not possible, he said, since "little satisfactory direct evidence about [women] has survived."[3] Nevertheless Cross managed to convey a great deal of evidence about women in the revivals he studied. His index contains more than one hundred references to individual women or to topics related to women, such as the women's rights movement. It was not evidence that Cross lacked. Rather, we see with hindsight, he lacked a theoretical perspective from which to integrate and interpret the rich evidence he had found concerning the religious activities of women in the Burned-Over District.

Such a theoretical perspective can be found in Timothy L. Smith's *Revivalism & Social Reform*. There Smith links evangelical religion, social reform, and women's rights, showing how they were mutually supportive in the 1840s and 1850s, especially within the Holiness movement of early Methodism under the leadership of Phoebe Palmer, editor-in-chief of *The Guide to Holiness,* a monthly newspaper with 30,000 subscribers. Smith notes that under Palmer's leadership, women of all sects gathered together under female direction for the propagation of perfectionist religion and by 1886, had formed 238 groups, including 15 in Philadelphia, 14 in Boston, and 12 in Baltimore.[4]

Stage two in the development of historical writing about American women in religion and society came into being in the 1960s, when historians began to see their material through feminist eyes—that is, to probe the history of women's rights and interests. I would characterize stage two as the "birth and infancy" of the field of United States women's history. The number of historians working on topics about women and religion increased in the middle and late 1960s, and they asked new kinds of questions. This stage is exemplified by Barbara Welter's well-known article, "The Cult of True Womanhood," published in 1966.[5] Based on a survey of American women's magazines in the era between 1820 and 1860, her essay showed how those magazines both articulated and shaped contemporary social and religious ideas about women. Welter's article appeared just three years after Betty Friedan's celebrated book, *The Feminine Mystique.* In some ways, "The Cult of True Womanhood" did for the historical study of women in American religion and society what Friedan's book did for the development of feminism. Like Friedan, Welter provided a *name* for the source of women's oppression—in this case, The Cult of True Womanhood. Her term has been widely adopted by other historians and has helped many people analyze the cultural sources of sexual inequalities.

In another sense, however, Barbara Welter's article was not like Betty Friedan's book, for *The Feminine Mystique* viewed the home as a cage containing women as passive victims, while Welter presented nineteenth-century women as historical actors who helped shape their own destinies. This was evident in Welter's conclusion that "the very

52

perfection of True Womanhood carried within itself the seeds of its own destruction. For if a woman was so very little less than the angels, she should surely take a more active part in running the world, especially since men were making such a hash of things."[6]

This second stage of women's history introduced both female and feminist perspectives on the past. Insofar as she focused primarily on female experience and female protagonists and was interested in them for their own sake, Barbara Welter offered a female perspective on the past. While Whitney Cross introduced women into a study about religion, Welter introduced religion into a study that was basically about American women. Insofar as it asked questions about women's struggle against the limiting circumstances of their lives, however, Welter's article may be said to have adopted a feminist, as well as a female perspective. It implied, more than declared, those struggles, perhaps reflecting her nineteenth-century magazine sources. In a footnote, however, Welter signaled that "rebellion" could be found "in the diaries and letters of women. . . . The death of a child seemed consistently to be the hardest thing for them to bear and to occasion more anguish and rebellion, as well as eventual submission, than any other event in their lives."[7]

One other important work from this second period is Gerda Lerner's *Grimké Sisters,* which focuses on two Quaker women. Here too the author wrote from both female and feminist perspectives—that is, she was concerned primarily with female experience, and she also asked questions about women's struggle.[8]

In the 1970s, a third stage emerged. This was an "adolescent" stage of rapid growth, following the beginnings established in the 1960s. Now scholars paid less attention to the question, How did religion and society oppress women? and more to, How did women benefit, personally and socially, from their religious beliefs?

Three characteristic works from this adolescent stage are Carroll Smith-Rosenberg's article on the antebellum American Female Moral Reform Society; my biography of Catharine Beecher; and Nancy F. Cott's book, *The Bonds of*

Womanhood. Stage-three historians benefited from their predecessors' work in the 1960s. They began to look more closely at the positive aspects of the relationship between American women and religion. Carroll Smith-Rosenberg, Nancy Cott, and I all emphasized the positive benefits derived by white, middle-class women from their participation in evangelical religion. After describing the militancy and effectiveness of the American Female Moral Reform Society in the 1830s, Carroll Smith-Rosenburg concluded that as these women began "to create a broader, less constricted sense of female identity, they were naturally enough dependent upon the activist impulse and legitimating imperatives of evangelical religion. This was indeed a complex symbiosis, the energies of pietism and the grievances of role discontent."[9]

In stage three of the historiography of United States women and religion, therefore, the plot thickened. Evangelical religion now emerged as an important agency through which women entered the public domain of American society and politics. As Nancy Cott wrote:

Female converts in the New England Great Awakening between 1798 and 1826 (before the Methodist impact) outnumbered males by three to two. Women's prayer groups, charitable institutions, missionary and education societies, Sabbath School organizations, and moral reform and maternal associations all multiplied phenomenally after 1800, and all of these had religious motives. Women thus exercised as fully as men the American penchant for voluntary association noted by Tocqueville in the 1830s, but women's associations before 1835 were *all* allied with the church, whereas men's also expressed a variety of secular, civic, political, and vocational concerns.[10]

Since her study ends in 1835, Cott did not explore "the Methodist impact" to which she refers, since it occurred after that time, but she noted that "Methodist evangelists adopted the unorthodox tactic of encouraging women to pray aloud in public, but ministers of opposing denominations strengthened their prohibition against women's preaching." And to her question, Why did women support religion so faithfully? she answered:

No other public institution spoke to women and cultivated their loyalty so assiduously as the churches. . . .

No other avenue of self-expression besides religion at once offered women social approbation, the encouragement of male leaders (ministers), and, most important, the community of their peers. . . .

Church-related voluntary associations commanded a much larger membership through the nineteenth century than did the women's rights movement proper.[11]

In my biography of Catharine Beecher, I showed how Beecher relied on the institutional leverage and rhetorical clout of evangelical religion to assist her work. For example, at one point in her career, needing to justify her opinion that women were better schoolteachers than men, Beecher wrote, "It is ordained by infinite wisdom, that, as in the family, so in the social state, the interests of young children and women are one and the same."[12] Aware of the limits that religion ultimately enforced on women's lives, stage-three historians also have been aware that the interests of women, evangelical religion, and the United States middle classes were mutually reinforcing in the first half of the nineteenth century.

Impressed by the enormous range of women's activities that sprang from religious roots, Barbara Welter concluded that American religion itself became "feminized" in the nineteenth century—not only because a majority of revival converts and church members were women, but also in the sense that a more genteel theology now replaced the harsher religious styles of colonial Puritanism.[13] In *The Feminization of American Culture,* Ann Douglas built on this idea by examining the symbiosis between male ministers and female authors between 1820 and 1875, and concluded that it did much to shape American culture and literary ideals (in her view, with highly questionable results).[14]

One of the most significant notions advanced in this third stage is that of the historical existence of a cultural experience peculiar to women—a "female culture"—called homosocial by Carroll Smith-Rosenberg.[15] In *Religion in the Old South,* Donald Mathews incorporated this view of female culture in his description of white women's participation in religion in the antebellum South.

> By projection of their shared experiences into associations, such as the churches and related organizations, women built a world which was theoretically acknowledged and valued by men, but which men could never penetrate. Evangelicalism, through bringing women together in churches, academies, seminaries, and societies and providing the framework within which to form this homosocial network and the language in which to explain it, made a profound impact upon southern women, the effects of which still persist in many parts of the twentieth-century South.[16]

Mathews concluded that churches were "the chief means of establishing a public life for women." This was an outstanding achievement. It was as true in the North as in the South, and it is an important reason historians of American women will continue to rely on religious sources.

A new fourth stage of written historical scholarship about women recently has emerged, using new methods ranging from oral history to computers to take a closer look at the effects of class, community, ethnicity, and race upon women's experiences in religion and society. This current stage might be characterized as "mature," one in which the thrusts of stages two and three continue, but with the work of all scholars in the field being enhanced by a heightened awareness of these effects. For the forseeable future, historical writings about American women and religion probably will combine the approaches developed in stages three and four.

Studies closely examining class, ethnic, or racial identity were strongly represented in a special issue of the *American Quarterly* entitled *Women and Religion,* edited by Janet Wilson James. They included a study by Mary P. Ryan, showing how female religious experience varied by denomination and class, and how it helped shape family life. Ryan's conclusions pointed to the importance of mature women as agents of change in the wider society.

> The success of this woman's evangelism contradicts the interpretation of the Second Great Awakening as a rite of youthful independence. Quite the contrary, maternal evangelism in

particular led scores of young men and women to an active, intensive, and deeply personal affirmation of the faith of their parents.[17]

"Maternal evangelism" was created in the first half of the nineteenth century, partly as a result of the increased authority of women in family life and partly because of the rapid increase in lay power in American Protestantism after the disestablishment of American religion following the Revolution. Whereas men controlled family religious devotions in the eighteenth century, women generally assumed that responsibility in the first half of the nineteenth century.

Ryan's quantitative work at the community level shows that membership in female religious associations varied by class. For example, in Utica, the Female Missionary Society was more likely to attract women from the merchant and professional classes, while the Maternal Association drew women whose families were artisans, shopkeepers, and farmers. New quantitative methods also allowed Ryan to show that some aspects of women's lives transcended class. Women of all classes tended to draw the men of their families into church membership, for example. Ultimately, Ryan had to rely on qualitative judgment to interpret the significance of her quantitative data, of course.

A recent history of American women in religion and society that has paid particular attention to the effects of racial identity on women's religious experience is Jacquelyn Dowd Hall's *Revolt Against Chivalry*.[18] This study of the Association of Southern Women for the Prevention of Lynching emphasized the critical role played by the leadership of southern women's religious associations in social change. Hall found Methodist women particularly important, and underlined their singular part.

In October 1920, these strands converged in a historic meeting of black and white southern women in Memphis, Tennessee. Jointly initiated by the Methodist Woman's Missionary Council and black YWCA members . . . the Memphis Conference marked the beginning of interracial women's activities in the region.[19]

In this study, Hall's innovative questions focus on the relationship between black and white southern women. For the most part, her methods are those of traditional political history, investigating the way interest groups combined to effect change in the public domain, although she has presented quantified data on the incidence of lynchings in the South and the accusations against persons who were lynched.

The new mature fourth stage of religious women's history includes investigations of the religious experience of American Catholic and Jewish women, as well as those in Protestant denominations. Mary J. Oates's article in the special *American Quarterly* issue is one recent example. Through quantitative methods, Oates has shown that "while [Catholic] women in full-time church work in 1870 were well distributed over a range of occupations, by 1940 that variation and flexibility of choice were gone."[20] The fourth stage of scholarship makes it possible to analyze American women's experience in religious life in greater detail and with much greater accuracy than was possible in the past.

How does the writing of the history of women in the United Methodist tradition mesh with these four stages in the historiography of American women in religion and society? It would seem that secular and religious perspectives on the topic have changed in comparable and complementary sequences, since historical writing about United Methodist women appears to have proceeded through its own version of the four stages.

A long first period stretched from the late nineteenth century to the middle of the 1960s and was characterized by Methodist equivalents of Julia Spruill's book—compendiums of facts about women's organizations in the United Methodist tradition. Some examples are Frances J. Baker's story of the Woman's Foreign Missionary Society of the Methodist Episcopal Church, Mrs. T. L. (Laura E.) Tomkinson's history of women's home mission efforts, and Christian Golder's history of the deaconess movement.[21] These works contained much valuable information, but their interpretive scope was extremely narrow. They made little effort to explain how and why Methodist women's lives were changing, and offered no overall interpretive framework capable of linking the particular experience of Methodist women to the general experience of American women.[22]

After the mid-1960s, with the emergence of the twentieth-century women's movement and the effort by social historians to enlarge the perimeters of historical inquiry, this changed rapidly and stage two opened. An early sign was Theodore L. Agnew's article in the quarterly review *Methodist History,* published in January, 1968, by the same commission that has sponsored this conference.[23] In "Reflections on the Woman's Foreign Missionary Movement in Late 19th-Century American Methodism," Agnew examined the relationship between Methodist women and American society in general, finding that Methodist women conformed to the general social characteristics of American optimists. Agnew's attention was drawn to "the woman question" as discussed by Methodist women in the nineteenth century—Frances Willard and Jennie Fowler Willing being more advanced in their thinking on the topic than most Methodists, United Brethren, or Evangelical Association members of either sex.

Stage-two developments in the written history of Methodist women were part of larger shifts then taking place in writings about women and religion in general. Valerie Saiving's article, "The Human Situation: A Feminine View," originally published in *The Journal of Religion* in 1960, was an early harbinger of critical changes ahead. Writing before the publication of Friedan's *Feminine Mystique,* and anticipating its message, Saiving reflected:

Today when for the first time in human history it really seems possible that those endless housewifely tasks—which, along with the bearing and rearing of children, have always been enough to fill the whole of each day for the average woman—may virtually be eliminated; today, when at last women might seem to be in a position to begin to be both feminine and fully developed, creative human beings; today, these same women are being subjected to pressures from many sides to return to the traditional feminine niche and to devote themselves wholly to the tasks of nurture, support, and service of their families. One might expect of theologians that they at least not add to these pressures. One might even expect them to support and encourage the woman who desires to be both a woman and an individual in her own right, a separate person some part of whose mind and feelings are inviolable, some part of whose time belongs strictly to herself, in whose house there is, to use Virginia Woolf's marvelous image, "a room of one's own."[24]

It was in this climate of altering attitudes toward the present possibilities that historians began to take a new look at women's past achievements. In particular, in 1968 R. Pierce Beaver published a sensitive exploration of the wider meanings of American churchwomen's avid participation in the foreign mission movement in *All Loves Excelling*.[25]

As represented by Theodore Agnew, stage-two writings about women in the United Methodist tradition were the equivalent in many ways of Barbara Welter's "Cult of True Womanhood." Both Welter and Agnew analyzed the effect of social values on American women's behavior and attitudes. While Agnew did not share Welter's view that American values oppressed women, his article paralleled hers in looking more closely at the way Methodist women were acted upon by their social environment than at the way they acted to change that environment. Like Welter's 1966 article, Agnew's, in early 1968, acknowledged the threat that nineteenth-century feminist ideas about women's rights posed to the status quo, but it did not study that threat directly.

We find historical writing with stage-three characteristics emerging about women in Methodism and related movements in the 1970s. Several articles published in *Methodist History* between 1974 and 1977 paralleled the secular work of Ryan, Cott, and Sklar. They were: Kenneth E. Rowe, "The Ordination of Women, Round One: Anna Oliver and the General Conference of 1880" (1974); Norma Taylor Mitchell, "From Social to Radical Feminism: A Survey of Emerging Diversity in Methodist Women's Organizations, 1869–1974" (1975); Lucille Sider Dayton and Donald Dayton, " 'Your Daughters Shall Prophesy': Feminism in the Holiness Movement" (1976); and William T. Noll, "Women as Clergy and Laity in the 19th-Century Methodist Protestant Church" (1977). Other stage-three scholarship on Methodist and related women emerged in dissertations and conference papers.[26]

While these works in many ways paralleled the studies by Smith-Rosenberg, Sklar, and Cott quoted earlier, there was a difference, in that the secular authors more frequently analyzed the way religious beliefs and activities benefited women than did scholars in the United Methodist tradition. The latter tended to take these benefits for granted and therefore did not explore them as thoroughly. However, both sets of stage-three historians studied church women's struggle against the limiting circumstances of their lives, and in the process they not only helped shape their own destinies, but also became active agents of social change on a far wider scale.

Stage-three essays on the history of United Methodist women are related as well to wider changes in 1970s writing about the history of women, composed from a religious perspective. An exemplary case was Donald W. Dayton's *Discovering an Evangelical Heritage*.[27] This essay on the founding of Oberlin and the involvement of evangelicals in abolition contained an excellent chapter on "The Evangelical Roots of Feminism," arguing that the women's rights movement of the antebellum years was strongly felt and partly led by evangelical women. Dayton noted, for example, that the Seneca Falls convention of 1848 was held in a Wesleyan Methodist church. He also mentioned the activism of Mrs. Amanda Berry Smith, an ex-slave and Methodist evangelist who preached around the world in the second half of the nineteenth century and won an especially large following in India.

Indications of the emergence of a new fourth stage in historical writing about women in this denominational tradition appeared on the program of the Women in New Worlds conference early in 1980.[28] Attention to the effects of race and ethnicity on women's religious experience and participation characterize this stage, and the conference offered many initiatives along those lines—thirteen papers in all.[29]

This is consonant with current trends; for religious scholars as well as secular, differences in religious women's social and cultural circumstances have become increasingly important. Exemplifying stage four, for instance, is Dorothy C. Bass's article " 'Their Prodigious Influence': Women, Religion and Reform in Antebellum America," in an important anthology edited by Rosemary Ruether and Eleanor McLaughlin. Emphasizing diversity in female religious experience, Bass concluded that "different women responded in different ways to the variety of opportunities . . . for female activism" in the antebellum era. The increasingly strong interest in women's cultural specificity can also be seen in a study by Nancy Auer Falk and Rita M. Gross, *Unspoken Worlds,* which while more anthropological than historical, typifies trends found everywhere today in the study of women and religion.[30]

Within the next decade we might expect the development of a new fifth stage in historical analysis about women and American religious life. Although it is impossible to predict the specific content of the next stage, a period of synthesis and larger interpretation is needed. Ideally, historians first would combine the knowledge gained from both secular and religiously oriented scholarship in the first four stages, and then in the light of new data, would revise a number of major hypotheses about the history of the United States and American churches.

Although forecasting the future is risky, we may safely predict that the pathfinding national conference on church women's history sponsored by the United Methodist General Commission on Archives and History, and the publications that flow from it, will multiply the links between students of women in the United Methodist tradition and scholars who are researching women, religion, and society from alternative perspectives. The conference provided these diverse groups not only a forum for personal interaction, but also a common reference point for the future. The expansion of historical knowledge represented by that conference will itself attract historians to further investigation of women in Methodism and related movements, since it is easier to progress where significant work has already been undertaken, especially research as promising as that represented by the Cincinnati papers.

Increased communication between secular and religious historians working in this field is the best possible basis for new syntheses in women's religious history in the future. What was the Methodist impact on American women's lives in the nineteenth century? How did religion assist the growth of women's education in the nineteenth century? How did nineteenth-century evangelical religion contribute to women's participation in social reform movements in England, Europe, and the United States? We need to join forces to do comparative research on these issues, which remain largely unaddressed. They merit the attention of historians from both secular and religious perspectives, and they require a great deal more work before they can be properly answered. Increased communication and the pooling of our resources will help us make significant progress on these questions in the 1980s.

Secular and religious historians stand to benefit from working together more closely; since they have tended to emphasize different aspects of women's religious experience, they need each other to redress their own imbalances. Secular historians have used religious sources primarily to chart and illustrate women's participation in reform movements, for example. They have less frequently explored religious materials in order to understand American women's consciousness or to measure their access to leadership and authority within the churches. Secular historians have been more interested in assessing the impact of religiously motivated reformers on society than in studying their motivations or the ecclesial institutional changes that facilitated women's entrance into church government. As secular historians become alert to what they can learn about women's cultural values by studying their religious motivations, and about women's changing social status by studying their status within American churches, this balance may tip.

Students of the religious experience of American women have established this topic as extremely important within United States women's history and within United States history as a whole. During the last decade, historians of many sorts have turned to religious sources about women—

diaries, church records, and the records of religious associations—because these materials help them understand three basic aspects of women's lives: women's interior lives—that is, their consciousness about and attitudes toward the world and their own experience of it; women's social status relative to men, as measured by their comparative access to leadership and authority within the church; and women's participation in social movements, so often inspired by religious beliefs and so closely related to their religious associations.[31] It is possible, then, to depict a very full range of female experience through religious sources, and it is clear that we cannot understand the meaning of those women's lives apart from these sources.

In any historical period, full consideration of women's lives requires attention to their family and work in addition to their religious faith and activity, and scholars have discovered that investigation of religion often provides a framework for studying family and work as well. For example, in her article on the American Female Moral Reform Society, Smith-Rosenberg has examined the economic alternatives to prostitution for poor women and also the reformers' attacks on male domination of family life. An 1838 editorial in the society's newspaper, *The Advocate,* is quoted:

A portion of the inhabitants of this favored land are groaning under a despotism, which seems to be modeled precisely after that of the Autocrat of Russia. . . . We allude to the tyranny exercised in the HOME department, where lordly man, 'clothed with a little brief authority,' rules his trembling subjects with a rod of iron.[32]

My study, "The Founding of Mount Holyoke College," shows the way American women's religious beliefs, their work, and their family life all contributed to the establishment of this singularly important female seminary in 1837.[33]

Ecclesial and other religious sources give the best access to important data about American women, especially to their role as reformers, through the first half of the nineteenth century. After about 1880, however, as reform activity slowly shifted to a more secular foundation, and religion gradually came to stand less at the crossroads of American experience, those sources begin to decline in importance. There are exceptions to this trend, however, and these deserve careful study. Reform activity by women in The United Methodist Church continues strikingly unabated today.[34] This suggests that when historians analyze the motive forces and channels of later twentieth-century women's history, religious source material will continue to be valuable.

Concerning a future fifth stage of synthesis, a synthetic treatment of religious women in the United States necessarily will prominently include women in the United Methodist tradition. If historical writings on such women continue to increase at the rate exemplified by this conference, a future synthesis might well be dominated by this perspective. Since, beginning in 1850, Methodists were for many decades the largest Protestant denomination in the United States, there would be a degree of historical justice in such an outcome.

II

THE SPIRITUAL
EMPOWERMENT OF WOMEN

3

WOMEN OF THE WORD*

Earl Kent Brown

Methodism began in the personal religious experience of John Wesley of Epworth. For that reason, and because he left such extensive manuscript and published resources on his own life, Methodist historians writing on the eighteenth century frequently have focused on the deeds and thoughts of Mr. Wesley. This is natural enough, even though it tends to hide the large leadership cohort of associated ministers and lay people who accounted for much of the success of early Methodism. Most of Mr. Wesley's male associates are little more than names to United Methodists today. With the exception of his mother, Susanna, his female associates are almost totally unknown to our generation.[1] This is unfortunate, because women made up a majority of the early Methodists—perhaps a rather substantial majority. Moreover, Mr. Wesley's letters to those women strongly urged that they be active within the societies.

Women responded to Mr. Wesley's invitations with activities remarkable for religious women of the eighteenth century, and most other centuries as well. Their role evolved as they felt God's call to particular kinds of service. Sometimes Mr. Wesley guided the evolution closely; at other times he seems to have blessed a given female activity after the fact. But certainly the Methodist women of the first generations transcended the stereotype of attendant at meeting, listener, helpmate, and mother, to which female

---

*The research undergirding this article was done in 1979 in various libraries in England, with the aid of a research grant from Boston University Graduate School. Eighteenth-century courtesy titles usually will be observed in the essay.

participation in church life often has been limited. In Mr. Wesley's Methodism—the Methodism of the eighteenth century—women became public speakers, class and band leaders; intimate advisors to the Wesley brothers and other male leaders; school founders and teachers; visitors to the sick, the prisoner, and the backslider; ministers' wives; leaders in female support-groups; itinerants; patrons; and models of the Christian life for male and female alike. Three particular roles of early Methodist women are selected for special attention in this essay: speakers of the Word; itinerants; and support-group leaders.

Speakers of the Word

A considerable number of the women of early Methodism felt themselves called to give public utterance to their Christian conviction. That fact has been well documented by Leslie Church in his famous chapter on the women preachers.[2] These Methodists were, of course, acting in contravention of the popular understanding of "woman's place" and the conventional interpretation of I Corinthians 14 and I Timothy 2—the famous Pauline prohibitions. Therefore these questions arise: What forms did their public speaking take? and, How did they defend themselves against male attack?

The sources reveal several modes of public speaking used by early Methodist women, ranging from informal casual conversation with friends, to formal preaching—that is, biblical exegesis and application. The women who spoke publicly always did so under the threat of disapproval, for they knew the traditional attitude of society that any speaking by females on matters religious might be questioned. To avoid giving possible offense, some, like Margaret Davidson, were careful never to "presume to stand up as an exhorter, lest any should take an occasion to say that I assumed the character of a preacher, which might have hurt the cause of God."[3] Similarly, Mary Bosanquet Fletcher customarily did her speaking from the steps leading to the pulpit rather than from the pulpit itself.

Early Methodist women's modes of public expression might be listed as follows, proceeding from informal to the most formal: casual conversation, talks or prayers in band and class meetings, prayer in society or other public meetings, testimony, exhortation, expounding, biblical exegesis and application. Our era would call the last four preaching. Encouraged by Mr. Wesley, however, the women tended to restrict that term to the final mode, biblical exegesis and application. These careful distinctions served to distinguish those practices appropriate for women, and seem to have emerged, at least in part, from the Methodist effort to avoid criticism. It will surprise none to learn that it only partially succeeded.

The mode of casual conversation needs little elaboration. Margaret Davidson described her approach as follows: "The method that I generally used was, to draw inferences from their own catechism and from the hymns with which they were affected."[4] Here she was dealing with persons new to Methodism, who attended preaching or were considering doing so. She drew on the familiar to lead them to further discussion.

Classes and bands were not unique to Methodist circles in eighteenth-century England; however, Methodists used them very widely. New members of the society were "classed"—that is, placed in small discussion groups. Those spiritually more advanced often "banded" together with others of similar accomplishment and aspiration. In those meetings, women spoke and prayed freely. The subject might be reproof, confession, or spiritual counsel, or it might be a more formal type of exposition. Apparently Hester Ann Roe was reporting such a discussion when she wrote to Mr. Wesley on April 7, 1782: "On Tuesday, last, as I was *repeating and enforcing* some of the passages in your last Sermon, and a *few parallel promises,* another young woman . . . was by faith brought into full liberty."[5] Here Miss Roe not only read the sermon aloud, but "enforced" its meaning by enlargement, particularly by citing a "few parallel promises" which *she* had extracted from the Bible and the tradition.

Public prayer, for many Methodist women, was their first

71

experience in public speaking. It was the least threatening entry into such activity, since prayer is to some degree a charismatic activity—one inspired by the Holy Spirit. Frances Pawson later recalled Sarah Crosby's prayers: "She used to begin prayer with the simplicity of a little child, and then rise to the language of a mother of Israel. Thus she prayed with the Spirit and with the understanding."[6] Ann Cutler was so noted for her prayers that she was nicknamed Praying Nanny. She wrote, "I think I must pray, I cannot be happy unless I cry for sinners. . . . I see the world going to destruction, and I am burdened till I pour out my soul to God for them."[7] Her prayer life centered in frequent private prayer each day, some of those periods lengthy; her biographer reports twelve to fourteen such times a day. When asked to pray for others, she sought to learn as much about the condition of the persons as possible in order to sense what they required, and then she would pray out of a firm conviction that God would do what was needed. Miss Cutler's public prayers were shorter, but they are also reported to have been very loud, which occasioned considerable criticism. Mr. Wesley's blunt advice to Sarah Mallet comes to mind: "Never scream. Never speak above the natural pitch of your voice; it is disgustful to the hearers. It gives them pain not pleasure."[8] "Nanny" Cutler recognized that there was some justice in the complaint, but she wrote, "I have tried to pray differently, but am always less confident. I would do anything to please if it did not hurt my own soul; but I am in this way the most free from wanderings [of mind], and have the greatest confidence. I dare not strive against it [the loudness] anymore."[9] Isabella Wilson probably pleased Mr. Wesley more. Her public prayers are described as "not loud, yet fervent."[10]

Testimony was perhaps the second most common mode for women's public statements. Mr. Wesley found such witnessing abundantly appropriate. In a journal entry on March 18, 1787, he spoke of a love feast at which "Mrs. Fletcher simply declared her present experience." He praised her manner of speaking, which he found "smooth, easy and natural, even when the sense is deep and strong."[11] Mr. Wesley also recommended such testimony to Sarah

Crosby when she was attacked for speaking publicly in Leeds: "When you meet again . . . tell them . . . 'I will just nakedly tell you what is in my heart.' "[12] Mr. Wesley clearly felt that women's witnessing was not "preaching, properly-so-called." Hence he hoped the women would not be criticized for such activity.

Exhortation, too, was a kind of public speaking that fell short of true preaching. Fervent urgings to hear the gospel message, repent, and be saved constituted exhortation. The speaker did not actually take a text and proclaim the good news; rather, she urged persons who had already heard the gospel message to respond to it. Thus exhortation frequently followed preaching by one of the itinerants. In 1825, Mrs. Mary Holder wrote to Mr. Taft, "My method, as you know, was to give a word of exhortation after my dear husband had finished his sermon, or to pray, as I felt led by the Spirit of God." Elizabeth Tonkin Collett is also reported as "usually exhorting without taking a text."[13]

"Expounding" had a rather special meaning in circles of Methodist females, and it took various forms. Mrs. Mary Bosanquet Fletcher makes its meaning clear in a letter to Mr. Taft, written shortly before she died in 1816.

For some years I was often led to speak from a text. Of late I feel greater approbation in what we call *expounding,* taking a part or whole of a chapter and speaking on it. . . . Miss Sally's [Crosby] usual way was to read some pious author, and stop and apply it, as the Lord gave her utterance. But everyone must follow their own order, and the Lord hath promised, *"I will instruct thee in the way thou shall go."*[14]

Thus expounding might be based on Scripture, or on some uplifting book or article. Mrs. Fletcher's choices included biographies of outstanding Christians, sermonic material, church historical excerpts, and works of spiritual counsel. She notes that her beloved younger companion Sarah Lawrence followed the practice of expounding upon "some life experiences or some awakening author."[15] Mrs. Fletcher's own expounding often took on the flavor of catechesis, as she would ask questions after reading a passage aloud. The answers of those present or the questions they asked became the departure points for further instruction.[16]

Several of the women in Mr. Wesley's circle even were willing to undertake the kind of biblical exegesis and application considered "preaching" within the narrow definition noted above. Sarah Mallet wrote to Mr. Taft, "My way of preaching from the first is to take a text and divide it, and speak from the different heads." Mary Harrison also felt free to take a chapter or a few verses and then "explain" or "apply" them as the "spirit gave her utterance."[17] As noted above, in her later days, Mrs. Fletcher moved away from such textual sermons in favor of "expounding," which seemed to provoke less resistance. However, her only extant sermon is built on a textual analysis of Acts 28:29.[18]

It was perhaps inevitable that women's public speaking would provoke strong opposition both within and outside the Methodist movement. I Corinthians 14:34 and I Timothy 2:12 were quoted repeatedly. Because Quaker women also preached, the Methodists sometimes were called Quakers, not a complimentary term in the eighteenth century. Initially Mr. Wesley himself was conservative on the subject. On February 10, 1748, he wrote Thomas Whitehead about the differences "between Quakerism and Christianity." Commenting on the preaching of Quaker women, he rejected the practice, citing exactly the biblical passages above;[19] but he believed the prohibitions applied only to preaching in the full church assembly. Women were already speaking freely in Methodist bands and classes.

But the number hearing them gradually enlarged, because the folk attending found their message "enlivening," and Mr. Wesley's attitude began to liberalize under the impact of the evangelical success of several women friends. He was a pragmatist when it came to institutions through which the gospel was spread. What most impressed him was that God was blessing the women's work with a harvest of souls. In light of the way God was "owning" their ministry, Mr. Wesley began to modify his own stand.

Early in February 1761, he heard from Mrs. Sarah Crosby that some two hundred people were attending her class meeting and expecting her to address them. His advice was that she preface future remarks with the words, " 'You lay me under a great difficulty. The Methodists do not allow of women preachers; neither do I take upon me any such character. But I will just nakedly tell you what is in my heart.' This will in great measure obviate the grand objection." In September he wrote to Grace Walton, "If a few more persons come in when you are meeting . . . enlarge for a few minutes . . . with a short exhortation."[20] Thus Mr. Wesley justified their speaking by distinguishing testimony and exhortation from true preaching. Only "preaching" was prohibited. A similar distinction appears in a letter of 1769 to Mrs. Crosby.

In public you may properly enough intermix *short exhortations* with prayer; but keep as far from what is called preaching as you can: therefore never take a text; never speak in a continued discourse without some break, about four or five minutes. Tell the people, "We shall have another *prayer-meeting* at such a time and place."[21]

Mr. Wesley's confidence that such nice distinctions would "obviate the objection" proved mistaken. Sarah Crosby tells us that Mr. Wesley himself was excluded from a given parish church because the congregation thought he had allowed her to speak at Huddersfield. Wesley apparently advised her that he did not mind, since "he had Places enough to preach in."[22]

Mr. Wesley's view was still in process of evolution, for by the time he wrote to the then Miss Bosanquet on June 13, 1771, he had changed the grounds on which he defended women's speaking.

I think the strength of the cause rests there—on your having an *extraordinary* call. So I am persuaded has every one of our lay preachers. . . . The whole work of God called Methodism is an extraordinary dispensation of His providence. Therefore I do not wonder if several things occur therein which do not fall under the ordinary rules of discipline. St. Paul's ordinary rule was, "I permit not a woman to speak in the congregation." Yet in extraordinary cases he made a few exceptions; at Corinth in particular.[23]

In 1777, he again discussed Methodist and Quaker practice. The difference, he asserted, was "They flatly deny the rule itself [excluding women from preaching], although it stands

75

clear in the Bible. We allow the rule; only we believe it admits of some exceptions."[24] By that date, the distinctions between testimony, exhortation, and preaching were no longer labored. Even formal preaching was permitted to women in "extraordinary cases." Mr. Wesley had found his biblical precedents—presumably Priscilla in Acts 18 and the "prophetesses" in I Corinthians 11:15—and was willing to grant that such exceptions existed in the eighteenth century as well. He would examine each woman as to her call to preach, but once convinced she was indeed an extraordinary case, he would give her every assistance.

When the women defended themselves, it was usually on one or more of the following grounds. (1) *The Inner Witness.* Mrs. Crosby confided to her journal in October 1774, "I was so sensible when praying alone that I was doing my master's blessed will, in going among the people, that no outward voice could have strengthened the conviction."[25] Miss Bosanquet speaks in her journal entry for September 10, 1775 of the "clear conviction that God brought me to Yorkshire and that I had a message to his people."[26] Though initially "no friend of women's preaching," Sarah Mallet felt the call "continually before me, Reprove, rebuke, exhort!" So intense was this call that she first preached in "fits" or in a trance.[27] (2) *Success.* Methodist women defended their ministry because, as Ann Gilbert put it, "God owned my poor labors in the conversion of many sinners."[28] There are dozens of similar references in the writings of Mrs. Fletcher, Mrs. Crosby, Miss Roe, and others. (3) *Biblical Exegesis.* The women dealt capably with relevant scriptural passages, employing an exegesis that allowed female public discourse. In a long letter to Mr. Wesley, Miss Bosanquet carefully considered I Timothy 2 and I Corinthians 14. She concluded that these passages mean only that a woman shall not take authority over her husband and shall not meddle in church discipline. The scriptural ban on speaking thus related only to disciplinary considerations. She continued, "I do not apprehend it means she shall not entreat sinners to come to Jesus."[29] Indeed to take the words literally would contradict I Corinthians 11:5, since a woman cannot prophesy or pray publicly without speaking. Miss Mallet dealt with her critics by quoting other Scripture. She warned them that they must "quench not the spirit" and "despise not prophesyings."[30] (4) *Reference to Mr. Wesley.* A final female defense was to cite Mr. Wesley's support. Miss Bosanquet wrote in 1776, "I do nothing but what Mr. Wesley approves."[31]

Mr. Wesley liked to believe in his later years that prejudice against woman preachers was declining—at least among the male preachers of the Methodist connection.[32] The women themselves expressed such confidence from time to time, but they were mistaken in this belief. Antifeminist prejudice hardened in the decades following Mr. Wesley's death, and nineteenth-century Methodism was far less liberal than Mr. Wesley had been.

Itinerants

In Methodist usage, *itinerant* has a very specific meaning. In Mr. Wesley's day, it referred to the preachers assigned to "travel the connection" in the particular circuits to which they had been appointed at the annual conference. A primary and early duty was to set up the "preaching plan" for the circuit, announcing the services for each society for the quarter. The itinerant would visit all groups in the circuit regularly. When he was scheduled elsewhere, local preachers or the second itinerant on the circuit, if there was one, would fill the pulpit. Normally a traveling preacher remained no longer than two years in a given appointment. It was a hard life, particularly for a married man. But the itinerants knew that Mr. Wesley was traveling as much or more than they. His "circuit" was the whole of England, Scotland, and Ireland.

Mr. Wesley never formally appointed a woman as a regular itinerating minister, so perhaps it is a misnomer to call any of the women itinerants. Yet a number did in effect "travel the connection" with Wesley's approval. The earliest was probably Grace Murray (later Mrs. Bennet). Her travels began in the immediate area of Newcastle, where her particular skill in leading women's classes was discovered. Mr. Wesley encouraged her to visit the societies in the surrounding areas, and she later went to Ireland in a group with Mr. Wesley, where she performed a similar function. On her return to Britain, she traveled extensively in the southern and eastern counties on her own, eventually returning to Newcastle. All this was done "by Mr. Wesley's direction," according to the memoir written by her son. On an Easter Sunday when she was seventy-seven, she recalled her activities fifty years before. "I have known the time, when I have been joining in the praises of my Lord with his people at *four* o'clock in the morning; and continued all day from one place of devotion to another, without faintness."[33]

Sarah Mallet, too, traveled with Wesley's approval. In March 1788, he wrote to her, offering funds to finance her "traveling up and down," preaching as she went.[34] He gave her advice, also, which she remembered thirty years later when she wrote to Mr. Taft of her ministry.

When I first travelled, I followed Mr. Wesley's counsel, which was to let the voice of the people be to me the voice of God;—and where I was sent for, to go, for the Lord had called me thither. . . . But the voice of the people was not the voice of some preachers. But Mr. Wesley soon made this easy by sending me a note from the Conference.[35]

There are similar letters to Hannah Ball, Sarah Crosby, Elizabeth Ritchie and others, giving encouragement in their travels. In some circuits, women even appeared on the preaching plan. After Miss Mallet married Mr. Bryce, her husband regularly listed her name—several times a month she would be the announced preacher at a given meeting. Mr. Taft was somewhat more discreet: "I have generally adopted the plan of one of my former superintendents, of putting a star in the plan where she [Mrs. Taft] is expected; taking care never to appoint her to any place where she is not properly invited."[36]

Sometimes the ladies became involved in preaching or special meetings on occasions of casual personal travel. Miss Hester Ann Roe wrote of a visit to Nantwich, where the people "flocked around me with eagerness and I had a prayer meeting with twelve or fourteen of them."[37] In 1776 Miss Ball went up to London to attend the Annual Conference. She was there for nine days and attended preaching services fourteen times, Wesley being the preacher at six. There were also three sacramental services. But in fourteen meetings, some of which were band meetings, some classes, and some personal interviews, she herself testified or counseled. This was not a formal itineration, but Miss Ball was making a considerable impact on the London Society.[38]

Another example of preaching or speaking while on a trip taken for other purposes involved Miss Bosanquet. It is interesting both for its revelations about the lady and for the serendipitous character of the activity. In 1773 she was ill, and the doctor felt her labors at Cross Hall were frustrating her recovery. He therefore sent her off to rest at the Yorkshire resort town of Harrowgate. Arriving on Saturday evening, she was distressed on Sunday to find several men "profaning the sabbath" by playing horseshoes. She reproved them vigorously. The inn where she was staying, moreover, was full of "frivolous" persons whose talking, swearing, loud laughter, and louder music interrupted her thoughts. Friends nearby asked her to hold a meeting in Pannel, a mile away. The hotel crowd was much amused and after closely questioning Miss Bosanquet's maid, some were sufficiently intrigued to issue her an invitation to lead a meeting in the hotel ballroom the next Sunday. Her inclination was to decline, but she resolved to accept, lest it be thought she was behaving rudely or that she was "a bad woman, or a stage player." She was remarkably well received and was invited to speak again the following Sunday. She confided to her journal, "Much more company came in, even from High-Harrowgate, but the Lord bore me through, and glory be to Him, we had some fruit. The next day I returned home, better in health, and comfortable in mind. All praise be to the Lord."[39]

Probably the most famous female itinerant preacher was Sarah Crosby. She was speaking publicly as early as the 1760s, but her long itinerations apparently began in the 1770s and lasted for about twenty years, until ill health forced some reduction of her travels. In 1774 and 1775, for weeks on end, on many days her diary entries begin by noting a meeting at 5:00 A.M., or occasionally at 5:30 or 6:00 if the local Methodists proved to be slugabeds. On November 22, 1774, in York, she noted she "was pained to find that none in this city rise to meet together to worship God at five o'clock." And when she herself slept unil 7:00 because of illness, she mentioned the fact rather guiltily. The early meetings were just a nice start to the day. If it happened to be Sunday, she would attend an Anglican morning prayer and Communion service, as befit a good member of the established church. But she would soon be speaking again. Four meetings a day, with several hours of carriage or horseback travel between, were not at all uncommon. The groups varied from as few as ten to more than five hundred. She reported that at Bradford there was fear that the galleries in the preaching house might collapse, so many were the "quakers, baptists, church folks and Methodists" who crowded into the pews.[40] She described a typical day in 1774: "We had a lively prayer meeting at five [A.M.], a good band meeting at ten, and another at two; at five, Mrs. C. walked with me to Beeston; at seven, the house was full of people, and they obliged me to get into [sic] their little desk. I had great liberty in speaking, and felt my Lord exceeding precious. . . . Glory be to God."[41] When Mr. Wesley was in the north country, she naturally gravitated to his side. She often rode with him in his carriage, enjoying much "profitable discourse"; the spring and summer of 1774 saw her with him for three weeks.

The other Methodist itinerants were also cooperative. Mrs. Crosby's diary for May 2, 1775, notes a meeting with Mr. James Pawson, the itinerant appointed to the Leeds circuit. "He told me that he had heard that I had meetings at the preaching house at Halifax and Bradford, and that they were filled with people, and said *I was very welcome to have my meetings at the preaching house in Leeds if I pleased.*"[42] Many itinerants invited her to their territories to preach and meet the classes. She also received invitations from local women, particularly the wives of the itinerants.[43] In one year, itinerating out of Leeds, she traveled 960 miles, held 120 public services, led 600 class and private meetings, and wrote 116 letters.[44]

Miss Ritchie also was an active itinerant. For about a decade, from 1780 to 1791, she traveled widely and freely, generally in the north. Her visits resulted from invitations from friends and societies to instruct them, but she did not normally preach. Her genius was with small groups and in private conversation. A Miss March, of Bristol, wrote of Miss Ritchie, "We had a profitable prayer-meeting on Monday morning at eleven o'clock, at Mrs. Pine's. Miss Ritchie is in Bristol, and takes the lead. She is a true disciple, a simple humble follower of the Lord . . . and lives on earth the life of heaven." Seven weeks later Miss March wrote again: "As a ministering angel, she goes about doing good to the bodies and souls of her fellow creatures. She has a rare talent, an equal capacity for usefulness in spiritual and temporal things; a ready hand for all the concerns of life, while her spirit soars aloft."[45]

While Mr. Wesley lived, Miss Ritchie often reported to him. In one such letter, she proved her talent for brief characterizing comments. She found the Liverpool Society "much among worldly people." Macclesfield was "a happy lively people." At Portwood, "my soul was greatly humbled and richly comforted." The members of the Stockport Society "love the whole truth; but as yet, few of them enjoy the full liberty of the gospel." At Bolton, "I had a good time. The Lord blessed me in my own soul, and gave his blessing to the people."[46] Miss Ritchie married Mr. Mortimer in 1791, and thereafter her activity seems to have declined. She lived in the west, near Bristol, still led class and band meetings, and frequently called on the sick and nursed them, but there were few long itinerations.

There were a number of other Methodist women itinerants of whom we know less than we do about Mrs. Crosby and Miss Ritchie. Margaret Davidson had many invitations to preach, and despite her blindness she itinerated a few weeks each year. Elizabeth Harrell also "traveled through many counties of [the] kingdom, preaching the unsearchable riches of Christ." Among her converts were several men who in due time became itinerants themselves. Ann Cutler traveled to Leeds, Bradford, Otley, Oldham, Manchester, Darby, Macclesfield, and Dewsbury, among other places.[47]

Whether or not we call them "itinerants," these women

81

were invited to "travel the connection" in the eighteenth century. Invitations to do so came from folk eager to hear their words. Mr. Wesley fully approved, for it was clear to him that God was "owning" their work. And some letters of appreciation written after their visits suggest that they may have been more welcome than the male itinerants appointed by the conference.

Support-Group Leaders

In contemporary psychological writing there is much discussion of personal "support structures"—the network of interpersonal relationships built through family, friends, and professional contacts. In time of trouble, this network, or group, provides support, encouragement, and undergirding. A member also owes special debts of counsel and support to others of the network when they are in difficulty. The group may not be large, but it plays a major role in enabling the individual to operate effectively in the midst of besetting problems. It often has been suggested that women, who find themselves caught in a world to a large degree controlled by men, especially need a female support-group if they are to function well.

Early Methodist women of the Word certainly felt the need for contact with and support from other women, and in the local society, the women's bands often substantially filled this need. Other women class members frequently became support figures with whom one could reveal fears, share weaknesses, describe aspirations, and be always sure of a sympathetic ear. It is this supportive function to which Mrs. Crosby refers here: "The greatest means of increasing Christian Affection is close conversation concerning the work of God on our own souls; speaking without reserve our trials, temptations, comforts and accordingly pleading with God for each other."[48]

Mr. Wesley clearly belonged to the support groups of many of the women discussed in this paper. He wrote countless letters of spiritual advice and, on his long itinerations, had equally countless personal conferences with women. But also clearly, networks of female friendships existed in local societies, and in addition there was a group of women across the connection who mutually supported one another by their letters, regularly seeking and giving spiritual advice. For example, we are fortunate in having at the John Rylands Library a "letter-book" of Hannah Ball, dated from May 19 to December 6, 1776, and containing copies of thirty-one letters. Three were to Mr. Wesley; the rest were addressed to women friends. Five were to Patty Chapman, who held a position of leadership in the society at Watlington not unlike Miss Ball's at High Wycombe.

Miss Ball's letters are singularly devoid of information about worldly activities. If she still operated the Sunday school she had founded seven years earlier, it would never be guessed from this letter book. But they abound in advice on the growth of the religious life, testimonies of her own experience, and comments upon her spiritual health. From this document it is clear that Hannah belonged to the support structure of a sizable number of other women, and her dependence on them is also clear. A letter to "A. E." is an example.

Having heard by patty wetroup [?] that you are still poorly in body and not happy in soul, I write these fue [sic] lines to encourage you to come afresh to Jesus, who is ready to receive you after all you have dun [sic]. . . . The Lord is still willing to hear and answer your prayers. Don't think nothing hard that the Lord is pleased to permit to befall you, for if it was not destined for your good it would not be permitted.[49]

An even clearer view of such a supportive relationship emerges in the case of Frances Pawson and Sarah Crosby. Of Mrs. Crosby, Mrs. Pawson wrote in her journal, "She has been to me a friend, dear as my own soul, and that from my first setting out in religion."[50] Just how this relationship developed is made clear by a cache of letters from Mrs. Crosby to Mrs. Pawson, dated from 1764 to 1803. Most were addressed to "Miss Mortimer," since they were written before Mrs. Pawson's marriage in 1785. The letters deal with many things but are primarily concerned with the state of Miss Mortimer's soul, particularly the earlier letters. Some contain quite explicit theological instruction to a believer young in the faith. Apparently the relation between faith and reason was bothering Miss Mortimer. Mrs. Crosby wrote, "We are saved by *believing*. Hitherto you have been labouring to *understand* the Gospel truths. Now my Dear, Believe and feel them in your heart."[51] Again she urged:

The Simplicity you want is opposed to *Reasoning*, wich [sic] you are very apt to do; and none can help you against it, but the *Author* and *giver* of *Faith*. Apply to Jesus my dear for the Divine power: Instruction you have had *much;* Now practice looking unto *Jesus*. . . . *Look till* you are saved from Sin. *Believe till* you are clean.[52]

Anselm could not have elaborated more clearly on the principle of *credo ut intellegam* (I believe in order that I may understand).

The letters abound with advice on prayer life and other spiritual discipline. As the years passed, they became less formal and more friendly and relaxed. However, the form of address never slipped from "Dear Miss Mortimer" to "Dear Frances." The relationship remained close, but after Miss Mortimer's marriage the letters became less intimate and less frequent. In 1795, Mrs. Crosby feared she had offended Mrs. Pawson and asked for a visit. The letters clearly were no longer the guidance of a younger by an older woman, but had become a mutual sharing of support as the years progressed. There was more about common friends and the day's activities. There was less theology, but continuing testimony. Unfortunately, Mrs. Pawson's responses in this long exchange are not available.

One of the major support groups for women centered in the Leytonstone School under the direction of Miss Mary Bosanquet. The fellowship of The Cedars in Leytonstone and of Cross Hall in Leeds was itself the product of an uncommonly close and supportive friendship between Mary and her friend Sarah Ryan. In the summer of 1757, while her parents were on holiday at Scarborough, Mary lived at an uncle's home in London. There she met Mrs. Ryan, who was then running a rooming house in Moorfields where a number of pious women—including Mrs. Crosby—lived together in close fellowship and friendship, meeting together regularly for religious discussion. At the age of eighteen, Mary was introduced into this fellowship by Mrs. Crosby; but it was in Mrs. Ryan that Mary found her "mother in the faith." Again in 1758 she stayed with Mrs. Ryan, now the housekeeper at the Bristol New Room, while her parents were socializing in Bath. The relationship was nourished by correspondence and occasional meetings until 1763, when the two women pooled their resources to found Leytonstone School.[53]

Mrs. Ryan was the elder and the leader in this relationship, and Mary customarily referred to her as "mother." Her testimony to the importance of the relationship was deeply heartfelt. "The more I conversed with Mrs. Ryan, the more I discovered of the glory of God breaking forth from within, and felt a strong attraction to consider her the friend of my soul." Again, "Our hearts were united as David and Jonathan's. The spirit of community that reigned in the church at Jerusalem, I felt a taste of; and from that time to her death, the cold words of mine and thine were never known between us."[54] As long as it existed, the institution founded by these women partook of this "spirit of community." It provided a world of support both to those who lived within it—women such as Sarah Lawrence, Sarah Crosby, Ann Tripp, and Mary herself—and to those who came occasionally, when the outside world had bruised them. The refugees were many, and they found both physical and spiritual healing at Leytonstone.

One who came to Cross Hall frequently in the late 1770s and who remained an intimate of Mary Bosanquet as long as the latter lived, was Elizabeth Ritchie, who in 1791 became Mrs. Mortimer. Mr. Wesley may have introduced the two women, since Elizabeth first visited Cross Hall after meeting Wesley. In a letter written March 23, 1775, he expressed his pleasure that she had done so; he was sure that her time with Miss Bosanquet "has been a blessed means of increasing your spiritual strength."[55] Paradoxically enough, sixteen years later, when Elizabeth Ritchie was exhausted from nursing Mr. Wesley through his last illness, it was to Miss Bosanquet (by then Mrs. Fletcher) that she retired for comfort and recovery. She wrote from Madeley, September 11, 1791, "This visit has been a real blessing to me. I have caught fervour from a kindled fire; and long to follow my

Lord as closely as my friends here do. Dear Mrs. Fletcher's love, zeal and humility make me feel most sensibly that I am far behind."[56]

Few persons had a larger circle of female relationships than did Elizabeth Ritchie Mortimer; everywhere she went she made friends. She traveled widely and wrote more widely still. She had a particular genius in band and class meetings; thousands heard her and were inspired by her words. Doubtless more than our limited sources reveal felt free to seek her private counsel and to write to her for advice. She was speaking about those relationships when she wrote in April 1798, "The office of friendship is to sweeten life, and accelerate the movements of our friends heaven-ward. . . . Life is the dressing room for eternity. We are called to put off the old man . . . and put on the Lord Jesus Christ; to put on the whole armour of God." Clearly, friends were to be aides in that armouring. When Mrs. Crosby died, she wrote, "I have lost a friend who . . . watched over me from the time of my first setting out in the heavenly race. Our souls were knit together in the bonds which death cannot dissolve." Of Miss Roe, she said, "I feel towards Miss Roe, what I have seldom felt towards anyone. I believe, as Dear Mr. Wesley expresses it, we are 'twin souls.' "[57] There are similar expressions about Lady Maxwell, Sarah Wesley (Charles' daughter), Lady Mary Fitzgerald, and others.

One wishes for recorded reactions from Miss Ritchie's contacts over the years of her active life. Unfortunately there are no extensive files of letters *to* her, but we do have the reaction of Hester Ann Roe, who first contacted Miss Ritchie, apparently at Wesley's urging.[58] According to her own journal, Miss Roe received a remarkably moving letter in response: "I received a letter this morning . . . from Miss Ritchie. . . . I never felt such love for one Unseen before. My soul is knit to hers and I believe my precious Lord means to make her a blessing to me."[59] The relationship matured over the next decade, and the two women were close friends until Miss Roe's death in 1794.

Mary Bosanquet Fletcher, Elizabeth Ritchie Mortimer, and Sarah Crosby each made substantial contributions to early Methodism. They were intimate supportive friends. If one uses these three women as a core and creates a scatter diagram (see below) of the persons with whom they in turn apparently established close supportive relationships, one brings into much sharper focus the role of women as support groups for other women in Mr. Wesley's Methodism. Of course, data about these relationships are fragmentary. But it is probably safe to assume that similar diagrams could have been made in most eighteenth-century Methodist societies by someone who knew the local women well. Written documentation for these latter relationships does not exist, since they were expressed primarily in conversation in the bands or in private meetings. Only because the three women above traveled widely and established a network of close friendships across the connection does documentation exist for them.

Writing in 1813, Joseph Sutcliffe opined, "The history of Methodism is not less distinguished than the other revivals of religion by women of extraordinary piety and zeal, who have stood forth for the help of the Lord of Hosts."[60] Because this is stated negatively, it is an understatement. Methodist women in the earliest days played roles so remarkable, so fruitful, and so diverse in accomplishment that the historian will look far indeed to find their like in all the history of Christianity.

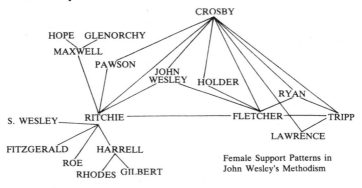

Female Support Patterns in John Wesley's Methodism

87

4

MINISTER AS PROPHET?
OR AS MOTHER?

Nancy A. Hardesty

Woman's role in the church, and particularly her right to preach the gospel, was the topic of much discussion in nineteenth-century America. Men and women of various denominations wrote books and articles on the subject, and we find that representatives of the Wesleyan tradition were predominant among advocates of the expansion of woman's sphere.[1]

This essay analyzes and compares two works which offer alternative models for ministry: Phoebe Palmer's *Promise of the Father; or, A Neglected Speciality of the Last Days* and Frances Willard's *Woman in the Pulpit*.[2]

Palmer, who lived from 1807 until 1874, has been called the mother of the Holiness movement. She was a lifelong member of Methodist Episcopal churches in New York City, and in 1850 she founded the famed Five Points Mission, sponsored by the Methodist Ladies' Home Missionary Society. As a theologian, Palmer redefined John Wesley's doctrine of sanctification in such works as *The Way of Holiness,* first published in 1843, and *Faith and Its Effects.*[3] Her discovery of a "shorter way" to holiness or Christian perfection involved simply "laying one's all on the altar," believing God's Word, and claiming the "second blessing." She spread her teachings through the Tuesday Meeting for the Promotion of Holiness for more than sixty years; through *The Guide to Holiness* which she edited; and through evangelistic tours with her husband Walter in the United States and Canada, and in the British Isles.[4] Although her ministry changed the lives of thousands, Mrs. Palmer never sought or received a preaching license. She began *Promise of the Father* with a disavowal of any intention to discuss "the question of 'Women's Rights' or of 'Women's Preaching,' technically so called."[5] In reality, however, her book is a 421-page defense of woman's right to minister.

Frances Willard, who was born a full generation after Palmer and died in 1898, experienced the "filling of the Holy Spirit" in 1866, under the ministry of "Dr. and Mrs. Phoebe Palmer," in Evanston, Illinois.[6] After a career in education, Willard became president of the Woman's Christian Temperance Union (W.C.T.U.) in 1879, a post she held for twenty years. In 1888, she was one of the first five female delegates elected to the General Conference of the Methodist Episcopal Church. When the conference denied the women seats, Willard became an outspoken advocate of laity rights, particularly of lay women's rights within the church.[7]

In several of her writings Frances Willard admitted longings to enter the ministry: "The deepest thought and desire of my life would have been met, if my dear old Mother Church had permitted me to be a minister. The wandering life of an evangelist or a reformer comes nearest to, but cannot fill, the ideal which I early cherished, but did not expect ever publicly to confess."[8] In *Woman in the Pulpit* she wrote, "I was too timid to go without a call; and so it came about that while my unconstrained preference would long ago have led me to the pastorate, I have failed of it." Indeed, *Woman in the Pulpit* was her attempt to help others succeed where she failed.

Let me, as a loyal daughter of the church, urge upon younger women who feel a call, as I once did, to preach the unsearchable riches of Christ, their duty to seek admission to the doors that would hardly close against them now, in any theological seminary, save those of the Roman, Episcopal, and Presbyterian churches; and let me pleadingly beseech all Christian people who grieve over the world's great heartache, to encourage every true and capable woman, whose heart God has touched, in her wistful purpose of entering upon that blessed Gospel ministry.[9]

While *Promise of the Father* and *Woman in the Pulpit* deal similarly with much of the same material, they offer two distinct models of ministry.

Biblical Arguments

Both Palmer and Willard confront the biblical issues straightforwardly. Although Willard remarks that "the plain wayfaring woman cannot help concluding that exegesis thus conducted [by those who would teach woman's subordination], is one of the most time-serving and man-made of all sciences, and one of the most misleading of all arts," she does not reject scriptural exegesis but pleads for revised methods and less narrow, more universal interpretations.[10] Both Palmer and Willard counter Paul's "Let your women keep silence in the churches" (I Cor. 14:34) and "I suffer not a woman to teach" (I Tim. 2:12) with evidence that women did indeed preach or prophesy (I Cor. 11:5) and teach (as in the example of Priscilla, Acts 18:26) in the New Testament church. They also call attention to female prophets such as Deborah (Judg. 4:4), Miriam (Exod. 15:20), Huldah (II Kings 22:14), Isaiah's wife (Isa. 8:3), Anna (Luke 2:36), and Philip's daughters (Acts 21:9); and church officials such as Phoebe the deacon (Rom. 16:1-2), Euodias and Syntyche, Paul's co-workers (Phil. 4:2-3), the women deacons in I Timothy 3:11, and the female elders in Titus 2:3.

Both writers ridicule, sometimes sarcastically, many churches' absurd inconsistency in applying the biblical injunctions against women's participation. Palmer asks, "Does not every woman that opens her mouth in the church in the presence of a man, to sing or to cough, or, if fainting, to say, I am ill, render herself liable, on this principle to be silenced? In either of these she breaks silence."[11] Willard begins *Woman in the Pulpit* with the story of the pastor of a Congregational church in New Jersey who, in his attempt to be consistent, ordered the church's "chorister" not to allow women in the choir! After ridiculing those who take Scripture too literally, Willard attacks another category of exegetes who employ "the method of playing fast and loose."[12] They would like to enforce women's subordination literally but ignore injunctions in the Sermon on the Mount against striking back, going to court, or allowing divorce. They refuse to permit women to teach, yet ignore Paul's comments against braided hair, gold jewelry, and expensive clothes (I Tim. 2:9). In the story of Cain and Abel, they do not see the verse "And unto thee shall be his desire, and thou shalt rule over him" (Gen. 4:7) as a mandate for the supremacy of elder brothers, yet they argue that Genesis 3:16, "Thy desire shall be to thy husband, and he shall rule over thee," is a sanction for male supremacy.

To assist the reader, Willard charts the arguments for and against women's right to minister, balancing such passages as "Let your women keep silence in the church" (I Cor. 14:34) with "Your daughters shall prophesy" (Joel 2:28; Acts 2:17) and "There is neither male nor female" (Gal. 3:28). She concludes emphatically, "There are thirty or forty passages in favor of woman's public work for Christ, and only two against it, and these not really so when rightly understood."[13]

Male Endorsements

Both Palmer and Willard support their biblical defenses of women's right to minister with more modern endorsements. As Methodists, both appeal to John Wesley. Palmer notes that as a Church of England priest Wesley at first did not favor any lay preaching but later was persuaded of its appropriateness by his mother Susanna, who cautioned, "I charge you before God, take care what you do, for that man is as truly called of God to preach the gospel as ever you were." Thus was John Wesley forced to acknowledge and honor the Spirit's gifts to laymen—and women. Phoebe Palmer cites his letter to Mary Bosanquet Fletcher: "My dear sister, I think the strength of the cause rests here—in *your* having an extraordinary call; so I am persuaded, has *every* one of our lay preachers; otherwise I could not countenance their preaching at all." In both *Promise of the Father* and *The Way of Holiness,* Palmer declares that Wesley himself licensed Sarah Mallet to preach at the Manchester Conference in 1787, by giving her a written note saying, "We give the right hand of fellowship to Sarah Mallet, and have no objection to her being a preacher in our connexion, so long as she preaches the Methodist doctrine, and attends to our discipline."[14]

Willard refers to another letter from Wesley to one of his women preachers: "But it [conscience] will not permit you to be silent when God commands you to speak."[15] In answer to the question, Shall women ordain themselves? Willard, with full appreciation of its import, cites Wesley's own ordination of Thomas Coke after the Bishop of London had refused to act.

That decision of the intrepid founder of Methodism cost the Episcopal Church its future in the New World, as time has proved. . . . We stand once more at the parting of the roads; shall the bold, resolute men among our clergy win the day and give ordination to women, or shall women take this matter into their own hands?[16]

Both Palmer and Willard are fond of the work of Methodist biblical scholar Adam Clarke. Palmer notes that he calculated the influence of one woman as equal to seven and a half men![17] Almost without exception, nineteenth-century defenses of women's ministry quote Clarke's comment on Galatians 3:28: "Under the blessed spirit of Christianity they [women] have equal *rights,* equal *privileges,* and equal *blessings,* and, let me add, they are equally *useful.*"[18] Palmer uses his commentary to buttress her argument that women did preach in the New Testament, quoting him concerning Tryphena, Tryphosa, and Persis in Romans 16:12: "We learn from this, that Christian *women,* as well as *men,* labored in the ministry of the word. In those times of simplicity, all persons, whether men or women, who had received the knowledge of the truth, believed it to be their duty to propagate it to the utmost of their power."[19]

In addition, Palmer's *Promise of the Father* is prefaced with supportive letters from Alexander McArthur, a Presbyterian minister from Nova Scotia; William McDonald, a Methodist minister from Portland, Maine; and Henry Belden, a Congregationalist from Brooklyn. In the same manner, Willard's fourth chapter in *Woman in the Pulpit,* "The Testimony of Preachers Who are Men," includes corroborating letters from "a Methodist minister in New England" and "a Methodist D.D. from New York state"; a reference to an article by "Dr. Thoburn," bishop of India; and a letter from the late Bishop Gilbert Haven's son, affirming that though he failed to find any printed evidence, he was sure his father believed that "women whom God calls to preach should be licensed and ordained by the Church."[20]

Female Examples

Both Palmer and Willard further buttress their arguments with examples of effective women in ministry. The majority of Palmer's examples come, of necessity, from the circle of Wesley's co-workers. She clearly reveals that such books as Taft's *Memoirs of Eminently Holy Women,* Burder's *History of Pious Women,* and Moore's *Life of Mrs. Mary Fletcher* influenced American women to follow in the footsteps of their British "mothers in Israel," the "nursing mothers" of early Methodism.[21] She devotes many words to the stories of Mary Barritt Taft, Mary Bosanquet Fletcher, and Sarah Mallet Boyce. Palmer finds Mallet's story particularly apt in supporting her argument for women's ministry. At an early age Mallet felt a strong call from God to preach, but she resisted for some years, Palmer relates. Then she began to have "fits," or trances, during which she would see herself before congregations, praying and preaching. Over the course of several years, Mallet experienced about eighteen such episodes, until she finally told God she would preach. When she began to do so, the trances never recurred.

Frances Willard's fifth chapter, "Testimony of Women Preachers," quotes "Mrs. Phoebe Palmer, of sainted memory"; Catherine Booth, "joint-chief" of the Salvation Army; and finally a woman minister from the Court Street Methodist Church, Rockford, Illinois, who was national superintendent of the W.C.T.U.'s Evangelistic Department. Willard also recounts the pointed and poignant story of a young woman who was studying theology at Garrett Biblical Institute, but who previously had held a pastorate. Over a two-year period, the young woman had preached 163 sermons and ridden 4,460 miles on her circuit. Though she lived 18 miles from one church and 25 from another, she missed only one appointment while temperatures ranged from 10 to 42 degrees below zero, and snow drifted to heights

of three and four feet. "Being always provided with a shovel
. . . she could dig herself out of deep snow as she was often
obliged to do." A neighboring male minister, however, who
lived only eight miles from his church, missed six straight
Sundays that winter.[22]

Minister As Pentecostal Prophet

Despite their similarities, Phoebe Palmer and Frances
Willard offer two distinct models of ministry. Though these
are not the only models found in nineteenth-century
defenses, they do represent two strands of thinking also
apparent in other works.

Phoebe Palmer's primary model for women in ministry is
the *prophet*. Although she initially declares that it is not her
intention "to set forth the expediency of woman's preaching,
technically so called," she finds "the scriptural idea of the
terms *preach* and *prophesy* . . . inseparably connected as one
and the same thing."[23]

Palmer's predominant biblical motif is Pentecost, the
fulfillment of the "promise of the Father" that the church
would be "endued with power from on high" (Luke 24:49).
She begins her second chapter with an "IMPORTANT
QUESTION": "Has not a gift of power, delegated to the
church on the day of Pentecost, been neglected? Or, in other
words, has not a marked speciality of the Christian
dispensation been comparatively unrecognized and kept out
of use?" Palmer then analyzes Acts 1–2, arguing that "the
women, and Mary the mother of Jesus" were present in the
upper room at Pentecost and "continued with one accord in
prayer and supplication" (Acts 1:14). In light of this, "from
whence has the doctrine obtained that women may not open
their mouth in supplication and prayer in the presence of
their brethren?" Palmer asks. These were the very women
who had been "last at his cross, and earliest at his grave";
who had received from the lips of a mighty angel "the first
commission ever given to mortals, to proclaim a risen
Christ"; and had received from Jesus himself "the first

94

commission ever given to mortals, direct from the newly risen Head of the church."[24]

Palmer begins chapter three with another question: "Did the tongue of fire descend alike upon God's daughters as upon his sons, and was the effect similar in each?" Her key text here is Acts 2:3-4: "And there appeared unto them cloven tongues like as of fire, and it sat upon *each of them.* And they were *all* filled with the Holy Ghost, and began to speak with other tongues, as the Spirit gave them utterance" [emphasis Palmer's]. "Was it designed that these demonstrations of power should cease with the day of Pentecost?" asks Palmer. No, is her answer. When the men and women of Jerusalem were scattered by persecution, they went "everywhere preaching the word" (Acts 8:4). As the prophet Joel had foretold, "your daughters shall prophesy"; this was to be a *"speciality* of the last days."[25] She includes in this chapter "a supposition," speculating as to how the apostles, the Twelve, might have responded to the sight and sound of the preaching of their sisters from Galilee. If an apostle had interfered with a sister's proclamation or questioned her right to testify concerning Christ before a "mixed assembly," asks Palmer, "Would not such an interference look worse than unmanly? And were her testimony, through this interference, restrained, or rendered less effectual, would it not, in the eye of the Head of the church, involve guilt?"[26]

Palmer argues that a woman of her own day who has received the "baptism of fire," who has been "filled with the pentecostal flame," who is a "Spirit-baptized Mary . . . on whose head the tongue of fire rested," who has "intelligently and consciously felt the constrainings of the Spirit to open her lips in the presence of her brethren," must do so.[27]

Simply stated, Palmer argues that women who have been "endued with Pentecostal power" are often impelled by the Holy Spirit to speak out about what they have experienced and to urge others to a more heart-felt faith. In fact, testimony to the experience is requisite for its retention. If these women are rebuked or silenced, the Holy Spirit is grieved and the church will suffer. In *Promise of the Father,* Palmer tells story after story in which the "ancient fire" in the community was merely smoldering, when a few women received the "baptism of fire" and felt a "burning desire" to "spread the pentecostal flame" which "might have resulted in the flame of revival spreading throughout that church community." But the women were denied their ministry, and the church declined. Holiness "is the ordination which Christ gives his disciples, by the reception of which they are empowered to go forth and bear much fruit." To reject the use of this gift of prophecy bestowed on God's daughters is to withstand the Head of the church.[28]

The experience of that pentecostal encounter and the logic of this scriptural argument account for the fact that the ordination of women was taken for granted and women ministers sometimes even outnumbered men in such early Holiness denominations as the Salvation Army, the Church of the Nazarene, and the Pilgrim Holiness Church, and also in such Pentecostal churches as the Pillar of Fire and the Assemblies of God.

Minister As Mother

Frances Willard's defense of women's ministry is grounded in an entirely different image and motif. Her argument undoubtedly owes much to the "Cult of True Womanhood" and the shift in definition of woman's nature and role which had taken hold in the thirty years since the appearance of *Promise of the Father*.[29]

Willard's thinking was anticipated in Anna Oliver's eloquent plea for ordination at the 1880 General Conference of the Methodist Episcopal Church. Oliver asserted that the church was caught in self-contradiction when it denied pastoral ministry to women while granting them licenses to preach as evangelists. "The work of an evangelist is unsuited to women," argued Oliver.

The evangelist has no home, is tossed from place to place. Women are said to be timid and shrinking, and will our good mother Church take these shrinking, delicate, modest, sensitive, home-loving, nestling, timid little things, and toss them about from Maine to California, or send them as missionaries to wild and naked barbarians, at the same time forbidding them to engage in the motherly work of the pastorate? . . .

Pastoral work is adapted to women, for it is motherly work. The mother has her little group, the pastor the flock. As a mother spreads her table with food suited to the individual needs of her family, so the pastor feeds the flock.[30]

In the role of evangelist, Oliver declared, she felt "as though a whole nursery full of my own little ones were being turned over to the care of strangers." Her desire, as she told the assembled clergy, was to "toil quietly in a corner with a handful of persons, seeing believers sanctified, and families transformed." But the General Conference was unsympathetic. Despite her eloquent plea, it denied her ordination and also revoked the licenses to preach already given other women.[31]

Willard picked up Oliver's theme of the pastorate as "motherly work," and it became her rallying cry. The slogan of the W.C.T.U. was and still is "For God and Home and Native Land." Willard fought for woman's suffrage as a part of her "home protection" campaign. Her goal was to make "the whole world homelike" because "what the world most needs is mothering." She exhorted her followers, "Mother-love works magic for humanity, but organized mother-love works miracles. Mother-hearted women are called to be the saviors of the race."[32]

According to Willard, some opponents of women's ministry had abandoned arguments based on biblical exegesis and were resorting instead to what she called the earth-born argument that ministry and motherhood were incompatible. In *Woman in the Pulpit,* she devotes a whole chapter to a "Counter Argument" by Presbyterian Henry J. Van Dyke, Sr., in which he opines that "motherhood, with all its burdens and blessings is her [woman's] divinely appointed destiny" and that subordination of women is "written upon the constitution of her nature, in the history of her creation, and in all Christian theology." Says Van Dyke, *"Women have no special qualifications for the work of the ministry.* They are not holier by nature than men, and if they were this would not make them better ministers."[33]

Willard counters by using all the "cult of domesticity's" rhetoric in support of women's ministry.

If the refinement, sympathy, and sweetness of the womanly nature, as men describe it, fit women especially for the sacred duties of the pastoral office, and these qualities are raised to their highest power by the relationships of wife and mother, as all must grant who have not forgotten the priestesses of their own early homes and present firesides, then, other things being equal, that woman who is a mother and a wife is, above all others, consecrated and set apart by nature to be a minister in the household of faith. Viewed without prejudice, this position is invulnerable.[34]

Willard also gives L. T. Townsend a chapter in which to reply to Van Dyke. He declares that "women *have* special qualifications for the ministry"; these are "the ground of their peculiar endowments and of the work which they have already accomplished." Women have "more accurate and quicker intuitions than those of men; . . . they have quicker and tenderer sympathies." In fact, according to Townsend, these "gifts of Spirit" and "their mother-nature [give women] peculiar advantage in winning souls to Christ and in building up Christian character."[35]

Willard also quotes at length from Catherine Booth on the danger of confusing "nature with custom." Booth asserts that "God has given to woman a graceful form and attitude, winning manners, persuasive speech, and, above all, a finely toned, emotional nature, all of which appear to us eminent *natural* qualifications for public speaking." And again, Willard quotes a Universalist minister, in the pastorate twelve years, who declares, "The strongest argument in favor of a woman ministry [sic] is found in woman herself, in her sympathetic and intuitional nature, in her high moral sense, in her deep and fervent religious spirit. The mother element in woman's character gives her a peculiar power in religion."[36]

Willard herself notes that rather than worrying about the unsuitability of mothers in the ministry, "we can trust the delicate instincts of a Christian mother to guard herself and her audience alike from the least unseemliness." She goes on boldly to assert that the depths of meaning in the Incarnation and the vicarious sacrifice of the Atonement "can never be so convincingly borne to the world's heart as from the lips that have blanched with agony" in childbirth. "Our holy faith can have no human ally so invincible as she who, with strong crying and tears, has learned the sublime secrets of pain and pathos that only mothers' hearts can know." If clergymen are worried about upholding the honor of the profession, Willard responds in irony that "if the purest should be called to purest ministries, then women, by men's own showing, outrank them in actual fitness for the pulpit, and the fact is that woman's holiness and wholesomeness of life, her clean hands and pure heart, specially authorize her to be a minister of God."[37]

To both Willard and Palmer, the perfect example of the acceptability of women's authority is Queen Victoria,

a woman of high character and great common-sense . . . whose discharge of the highest political functions never impaired her womanliness, and who has been able to show, day by day, for fifty years that the affairs of state, even when most engrossing, never interfered with the ideal of the wife and the mother, or destroyed the homeliness of the home.[38]

The contrast between distinctive male and female "natures" involved in the motif of minister as mother inevitably sets up a battle of the sexes and invites invidious comparisons. In her determination to liberate her contemporaries from misplaced concerns and images, however, Willard presses ahead. In a fine example of her rhetorical gifts, she declares:

It is *men* who have defrauded manhood and womanhood, in the persons of priest and monk and nun, of the right to the sanctities of home; men who have invented hierarchies, enthroned a fisherman as God's vice-gerent, lighted inquisitorial fires, and made the Prince of peace a mighty man of war. It is men who have taken the simple, loving, tender Gospel of the New Testament, so suited to be the proclamation of a woman's lips, and translated it in terms of sacerdotalism, dogma, and martyrdom. . . . Men deal in formulas, women in facts. Men have always tithed mint and rue and cummin in their exegesis and their ecclesiasticism, while the world's heart has cried out for compassion, forgiveness, and sympathy. Men's preaching has left heads committed to a catechism, and left hearts hard as nether millstones.[39]

And in characteristic idiom, she asserts on women's behalf, "It is men who have given us the dead letter rather than the living Gospel. The mother-heart of God will never be known to the world until translated into terms of speech by mother-hearted women."

Conclusion

Thus we see two distinct models emerging in the nineteenth-century defense of women's right to minister. Both Phoebe Palmer and Frances Willard rightly realized that while it was important to adduce positive scriptural examples of women's ministry to counter the arguments which prohibited women's participation, it was necessary to reach beyond this to find ways to encourage women to participate in ministry and to encourage men to allow women's participation. Both their models of ministry do this effectively.

Palmer's argument continues to be attractive to those who emphasize Pentecost as a decisive event, paradigmatic for the lives of all Christians. In her lifetime, Palmer's model of minister as charismatic prophet exerted a strong influence on a number of Christian groups, inspiring both women and men to ministry in church pulpits, urban slums, and foreign missions. In our day, as we attempt to move from hierarchical models to more collegial ones, Palmer's emphasis on ministry as the exercise of the Spirit's gifts, distributed to all Christians as the Spirit wills (I Cor. 12:11), is helpful.

By contrast, while today we may admire Willard's inversion of her culture's antifeminist arguments so as to cleverly support women's rights, her model of minister as mother ultimately raises serious theological and sociocultural problems.[40] It is based on and perpetuates cultural stereotypes of women's role as derived from biological differences. Though Willard herself was not married or a biological mother and thus interpreted the concept of motherhood quite broadly, that concept obviously tends, for the majority of women, to circumscribe their sphere to marriage and maternity within the confines of the home and the nuclear family.

Traditionally, Christian theology, while revering motherhood, has not specified it as woman's only or supreme role. Within Scripture, the Old Testament makes it clear that God does not particularly favor married women and mothers, even though that tendency pervaded Hebrew culture. God is also on the side of the barren and the widowed. In the New Testament, one is first to be a member of the family of God and only secondarily, a member of an earthly family. Marriage is upheld, but according to Paul, singleness may be better suited to the demands of the Kingdom. Jesus honored his mother but would not let others unduly glorify her maternity (Luke 11:27-28).

An admirer notes with relief that Frances Willard herself sometimes employs more egalitarian, androgynous images in speaking of the relationship between the sexes. One is tempted to ask whether her use of motherhood and the rhetoric of "true womanhood" was not simply polemic expediency. In *Woman in the Pulpit,* she approvingly quotes a "Methodist D.D. from New York state":

There is no marked difference between the sexes. The Bible does not represent Adam and Eve as separate species. The highest qualities belong to humanity in common. Christ is as much the typical woman as the typical man of the race.[41]

5

MARY McLEOD BETHUNE AS RELIGIONIST

Clarence G. Newsome

Mary McLeod Bethune, outstanding educator, prominent Negro clubwoman, advisor to four Presidents, and active laywoman was born July 10, 1875, and died May 18, 1955.* Less than a year before her death she wrote, "My life has been a spiritual thing, a religius reality, creative and alive. Whatever 'works' I have done have 'justified' my faith . . . for I have daily felt the presence of God in the tasks he has set before me in visions, and I have known his divine guidance and presence through all the years."[1]

Although she was a consummate organizer and politician, garnering her share of critics across her active career, all who knew Mary McLeod Bethune acknowledged that she was a person of great faith. The way her faith in a divine reality informed and distinguished her style of leadership remains an open question, however. How did her faith inspire her vision of leadership, and to what end? What does her career suggest about the nature of religious leadership among blacks and among women during the first half of the twentieth century? How does an elucidation of her faith shed light on the realities of history as seen, as lived, and as created by the oppressed in American society? Any resolution of these questions is contingent upon some preliminary understanding of Christian faith as a concrete reality.

*In keeping with Mary McLeod Bethune's own language and the usage of her contemporaries, the term *Negro* usually will be used for black Americans in this essay. However, sometimes Mrs. Bethune herself employed the word *black,* in a style bold for her day.

In pursuing reality of faith in relation to the quality of Mary Bethune's leadership, this discussion takes the position that "faith is inseparably connected with experience."[2] As the study of biblical history shows, revelation was given through a series of disclosure experiences, peculiar in that they involved discernment of total meaning with a simultaneous call to complete commitment "and trustful reliance on the power and goodness of that to which one stands committed."[3] This discernment is not logical in the rational sense but is felt as a deep conviction about the nature of ultimate meaning and value; it is intelligible in that in any life there are, as H. Richard Niebuhr asserted, two histories: the "external," an event or a series of events taken objectively, and the "internal," the assessed meaning attached to a particular event or sequence.[4] Within the realm of internal history, events are experienced and understood as disclosing the personal reality of God. As the biblical disclosures suggest, within this realm religious faith is "reasonable" in terms of the pattern of God's dealings with an individual or community as the source of "ultimate power by which our lives are ruled" and sustained.[5]

Any examination of Mary Bethune's faith must be pursued through the consideration of the meaning of divine revelation in her life. Such a study must be made in the context of her own understanding that her rise to prominence as an international leader during a period of widespread social unrest was due to the involvement of providence in her personal history.

The significance ascribed to religious faith by Mary McLeod Bethune was integrally connected with her experience of Deity. Viewed in light of the circumstances of her birth and the time in which she lived, Bethune's belief and commitment to a divine reality was characterized by a profound sense of destiny, underscored by a need for self-fulfillment and the experience of freedom.

The fifteenth child of former slaves, she was born into abject poverty five miles outside rural Mayesville, South Carolina, two years before the Compromise of 1877 sounded the death knell to Reconstruction. She was confronted with every conspicuous disadvantage. She lacked the family

103

status, the educational background, and the economic advantages of a Mary Church Terrell, pioneer Negro clubwoman and lecturer. She had neither the class status of an Eleanor Roosevelt or the sexual advantage of a Booker T. Washington. As a champion of the Negro's cause, however, she became as potent a force in diverse sectors of American society as did those friends and associates.

The strong personal presence of God was deeply felt in the home in which Mary Jane McLeod grew up. Both Samuel and Patsy McLeod had been converted during slavery and after emancipation they became leaders in the local all-black Methodist church. For them God was the "Keeper of the field, the Watchman of the household and the Intimate friend" with whom the family conversed through prayer around the fireside at the end of the day.[6]

Patsy McLeod, in particular, was a model of faith. Her indomitable spirit, which Mary Bethune later recalled so often, transformed the family's three-room log cabin into a home. Like most who emerged from slavery, Patsy was illiterate. But as Mary Bethune once expressed it, her mother had another sort of education—a grand vision of the world and of what life was about.[7]

A tradition in Patsy's family held that they were descended from African royalty.[8] While the particular tribe was unknown to her, she exuded evidence of her African inheritance. Living was a religious celebration in which reason and emotion, mind and body, were fully joined. As a result, her ethical convictions stemmed from and were confirmed by her life experiences. Acutely sensitive to the needs of her own family, "Aunt Patsy," as she was called in the community, also gave unselfishly of her time and resources to others in Mayesville and its environs. She was quick-tempered but could be easily approached; for this reason she was frequently called upon for advice and counsel, sometimes in legal matters. As a midwife, she delivered many babies, both black and white, born before, during, and after Mary's childhood.

Mary McLeod learned early to perceive providence as an ally. Near the time of her eighth or ninth birthday she experienced "the first real wound . . . in soul and mind." It was "the realization of the dense darkness and ignorance" in which she found herself, "with the seeming absence of a remedy."[9] One day while playing with the grandchildren of her mother's former master, she was ruefully awakened to the fact that she could neither read or write. She had not been altogether unaware of her inability prior to that time, but to be reminded by her white playmates made it a badge of inferiority, particularly since there was no school for Negroes in the vicinity. In the days that followed, Mary kept up a constant prayful intercession for an opportunity to attend school, and God became increasingly personal and intimate as prayer became the central activity of her life.[10]

In about 1884, a mission school for Negroes was established in Mayesville by the Presbyterian Board for Freedmen. It was the answer to Mary McLeod's prayers! Creation of the school reinforced a nascent notion that parity between the races could be achieved through education. One of the first lessons taught greatly helped her to overcome her sense of inferiority; it was drawn from John 3:16: "For God so loved the world, that he gave his only begotten Son, that whosoever believeth in him should not perish, but have everlasting life." That God loved the world in this way meant that all are equal in the eyes of God, and throughout the years this interpretation was the foundation of Mary McLeod's self-understanding as a black woman.[11]

Of the seven or eight children at home during her childhood, Mary was the one selected by her parents to attend school. She was the first in her family to be educated, and she perceived that God had set her aside for a particular purpose. She first glimpsed what that purpose might be through Miss Emma Wilson, the Presbyterian missionary sent to conduct the school. Mary never before had known a Negro called "Miss." As she did with all her students, Miss Emma took Mary under her wing, guiding her with meticulous care through her early intellectual and spiritual growth. She conveyed to Mary an image of womanhood that was an extension of her mother's, combining a nurturing style of leadership with a vision of service grounded in the Golden Rule.[12]

At the age of twelve, Mary had a revelation after attending

105

a lecture in Sumter, South Carolina. She sensed that the course of her life would lead to a missionary post in Africa. Throughout the years of her formal training, this initial understanding of her destiny was seemingly confirmed in a variety of ways. For example, when there was little hope that she might extend her education beyond the mission school in Mayesville, a scholarship was unexpectedly made available through the beneficence of a white schoolteacher in Denver, Colorado, making it possible for her to attend Scotia Seminary in Concord, North Carolina. Although Mary was one of the least prepared students when she entered Scotia, she graduated in 1894 as a leader of her class. When she entered Moody Bible Institute the following year, she was one of the first Negro Americans, if not the first, to be enrolled.

Mary McLeod spent two years at Moody Bible Institute, bridging the gap between intellectual training and spiritual understanding. At the institute she came into contact with the world-famous evangelist, Dwight L. Moody. Under his influence she experienced for the first time "the baptism of the holy spirit." Hearing Moody lecture on the power and reception of the Holy Spirit, Mrs. Bethune recalled that "I realized a quickening and an awakening that I had not words to express." As part of the graduation exercises at the mission school in Mayesville years earlier, she had been baptized into the Presbyterian Church, but baptism had preceded conversion. Throughout her career, she drew on her conversion experience at Moody Institute for the power to give "effective service."[13]

Upon completing her evangelistic training at Moody Bible Institute, Mary McLeod applied to the Presbyterian Board of Missions for a missionary station in Africa. She was greatly disappointed and utterly amazed when she was told that there were "no vacancies at that time for colored missionaries." Not once had she entertained the possibility that she might not spend her life in Africa introducing the tenets of Christianity to her kinsmen. From the time she was twelve years old, "No thought," she once expressed, "of serving my people here in America entered my mind."[14]

The summer following her graduation from Moody

Institute was a cruel time for Mary McLeod. She was bitterly disappointed and took the board's decision personally. "I was anxious to go back to the land of my ancestry," she wrote years later. Up to that point in her life, she had always been close to Africa in spirit. "The drums of Africa had beaten in my mother's heart during the whole of that beastly, anguish-filled period of slavery and much of her sentiment had been kindled within me. I was my mother's daughter."[15]

Mary McLeod was unsure of the future and aware of the unpredictability of providence, but she was "neither cowered nor beaten" when she left Chicago near the end of the summer of 1896. Returning South, she secured a teaching position at Haines Institute in Augusta, Georgia. At Haines, Mary "came in contact with one of the most amazing and dynamic personalities . . . a Negro woman by the name of Lucy Laney," founder and principal of the institute. Mary McLeod was greatly "impressed by her fearlessness, her amazing human touch . . . an energy that seemed inexhaustible, and her mighty power to command respect and admiration from her students and all who knew her." In Lucy Laney, she was able to glimpse the work that a black woman with a fervent faith in the power of God was capable of accomplishing in this country. Consequently, her passion to serve in Africa waned; she resolved to be a missionary among her people in the South.[16]

While at Haines, Mary McLeod visited Tuskeegee Institute. There she met and talked with Booker T. Washington for the first time. During a tour of the school, she made mental tabulations of "certain aspects" of the institution. "A great realization dawned upon me. I was electrified with a resolution to do on a slightly different scale and in a different manner . . . what Mr. Washington had in mind and what he had already started out to do." She conceived the idea of an institution for Negro girls "in which would be taught the essentials of home making, of the skilled trades . . . [and] courses stressing the importance of citizenship and the duty of the citizen in using his voting power." These courses, she felt, "must be unduly stressed as a measure of realizing citizenship in its entirety." She envisioned as head of the institution a woman who would preside as "a modern matriarch, head of the family."[17]

Mary McLeod spent only one year at Haines Institute. In the fall of 1897, she took a position at Kindell Institute in Sumter, South Carolina, in order to be near her parents. During the year she taught in Sumter, she met and married a fellow teacher, Albertus Bethune, a native of Wedgefield, South Carolina, who was from one of the finest Negro families in the area.

During the summer the couple moved to Savannah, Georgia, where Albertus had the prospect of a better paying job and again, they were there for only one year. But it was an important year, for their only child, Albert McLeod Bethune, was born in February 1899.[18]

Though removed from public service while in Savannah, Mary and Albertus discussed in earnest her hopes for establishing a school. There is some indication that he initially endorsed and even shared in what she regarded as her divine calling. He began to draw back, however, in 1900, when Mary moved to Palatka, Florida, to assist the Reverend Uggams, a Presbyterian minister, in establishing a school in connection with his church. Albertus regarded his wife as too much the visionary when she left Palatka for Daytona Beach in 1904. He followed her to Daytona, but the move resulted in an amicable separation. He did not share her vision of education for Negro girls; she did not share his view that a woman's place is in the home.[19]

At the turn of the century, opportunities for Negroes in Daytona Beach were not substantially improved from the days of slavery. The town had a school for Negroes when Mary Bethune arrived, but she saw it, for the most part, as spiritually, intellectually, and culturally barren. Here she gave birth to her second child—the Daytona Normal and Industrial Institute for Negro Girls, on October 3, 1904.[20]

Mary Bethune's school was a remarkable accomplishment. She began with virtually no funds and without sponsorship. "No man," she wrote during her later years, "commissioned me to come to Daytona Beach to found a school for my people; no board or agency hired me. I have known no employer but God." In the absence of organizational support, she alone had to face her critics in the black and white communities. Opposition among whites came as no surprise; she was altogether dismayed, however, by a Negro Baptist minister who used his pulpit to attack her school. In his opinion, her educational philosophy with its emphasis on manual training skills was too accommodationist. Against such strident opposition, she trained her girls in the virtues of hand, head, and above all, heart, and several Negro ministers did endorse her approach.[21]

Working against tremendous odds, Mary Bethune strove to produce a cadre of black women who could bring the Negro family increased stability and create a vision which would help improve race relations in the South. The school operated on a shoestring budget during its early years. Mrs. Bethune's abiding confidence in the beneficence of providence sometimes bordered on naïvete. As she once admitted, she frequently failed to plan. Her day-to-day manner of living reflected, in part, her understanding of religion—it "is not only a comfort, it is sometimes a cross." Often she found herself on the brink of disaster, without money or supplies. But one of the miracles of Mary Bethune's life was that the needs of her school somehow were met when they were most pressing. Time and again, when the prospect was most bleak, unsolicited funds were provided.[22]

For Mary Bethune, the power of providence enabled her to interest people in her objectives. Basing her appeal on faith in doing the impossible, she enlisted the support of many philanthropists. Had it not been for the backing, counsel, and enduring friendship of wealthy industrialists such as James Gamble and Thomas White, her school might have died a quiet death, as did many Negro academies founded in the South at the turn of the century.

However, in 1923, Mary Bethune was compelled to seek church support in order to keep her school alive. She initially sought help from black denominations, but to no avail. She approached nearly all the major black and white Protestant denominations, and after extended consideration, the Episcopal Church offered aid, but an affirmative response from the Methodist Episcopal Church reached her office first.

In agreeing to sponsor Mary Bethune's school, the church proposed a merger with Cookman Institute, a Methodist-supported coeducational school for Negroes in Jacksonville, Florida. Initially, Mary was quite circumspect about the idea. Merger meant abandoning her commitment to an all-girls' school. Moreover, it seemed to mean relinquishment of her position of leadership. She overcame her reservation, however, when the Methodist Episcopal Board of Education asked her to accept the position as president of the new school, Bethune-Cookman Institute. Mrs. Bethune's standard operating procedure was to compromise when it was advantageous to do so.

For practical reasons Mary Bethune withdrew from the Presbyterian Church and affiliated with the Methodist denomination. Doctrine and church polity were of less importance than being true to her calling. She thought that she could be more effective in advancing the work she was destined to do through involvement with the Methodist church.

Mary Bethune believed in the work of the church. During her early Presbyterian years she was an outstanding Sunday school worker. As a Methodist she was among the first Negro women to serve as a lay delegate to the General Conference and as a member of the Board of Education. While a person of great faith, she did not concentrate the bulk of her time in church work, but expressed her witness in the arenas of education, politics, and women's club work. Many of her projects drew on the strength of church organizations, but they were seldom rooted there.[23]

Mary Bethune worked primarily outside the institutional church because most denominations have denied women equal participation in positions of power and influence.[24] By fostering division along sexual and racial lines, the church, to Mary Bethune's view, faltered in its calling. She felt that the church's important concern should be the welfare of others, but that it too often promoted and reinforced structures of disunity and division.[25] She opposed the organization of the Central Jurisdiction in the 1939 Methodist Plan of Union precisely because it was a divisive act which would strengthen the barriers of segregation.[26]

Mary Bethune was pressed by a need for self-fulfillment, which for her was a way of life; it was living as if all people shared a common beginning and as if the human race were bound together as one family. As a way of achieving self-fulfillment, she sought to be true to herself by exercising the responsibility she felt was hers. To this end she posed as mother to her race. At the risk of forsaking the needs of her own child, she readily claimed and took under wing anyone who dared call her "Ma Bethune," as she was fondly known by many in the Negro community. Characteristically, she once depleted her savings so that Kwame Nkrumah, who later became president of Ghana, might complete his studies in America.[27]

She also deported herself as if she were matriarch of her nation. As director of the Negro Division of the National Youth Administration (N.Y.A.), she represented not only Negro youth but, without formal authorization, other minority youth groups, especially the American Indians.[28] But perhaps her maternal concern for President Franklin Roosevelt during the war years is more illustrative. As a member of the "black cabinet," she functioned as more than an advisor on political and social issues.[29] She assumed the responsibility of serving also as his spiritual counselor, as indicated in a letter written to Eleanor Roosevelt, June 21, 1943.

Mrs. Eleanor Roosevelt
The White House
Washington, D. C.

My dear Mrs. Roosevelt:

These are such difficult days. There are so many very trying problems for us all now. I would like, as soon as possible, to have just a short conference with you on a few things that seem to me to be very important.

I am thinking most sincerely now in terms of strength and guidance for our President. We must all understand that the wisdom we seek from above will not fail us. As soon as it is convenient for us to have a conference, please let me know.

Sincerely yours,
Mary McLeod Bethune
Director of Negro Affairs[30]

By assuming responsibility for the welfare of others and by creating situations of interaction in which people could work together in common cause, Bethune continued to seek self-fulfillment. The establishment of her school was a significant achievement, since it created an environment where male and female, black and white, could learn together. Long before it was popular to do so, Mary Bethune defied segregation laws by allowing mixed groups to meet on her campus. For many years it was perhaps the only place where integrated meetings were held in the state of Florida.

The birth in December, 1935, of the National Council of Negro Women (N.C.N.W.), which Bethune considered her third child, was important for the same reason. As a federation of national women's organizations, it united the masses of Negro women in America. Moreover, as an effective lobbying agency, the council brought Negro and white clubwomen throughout the country into a closer alliance.[31]

On the whole, Mary Bethune sought self-fulfillment by aligning herself with causes that promoted goodwill. Her association with Moral Rearmament during the later years of her life was her "crowning experience."[32] The organization appealed to Mary Bethune because it transcended race, party, class, color, and nationalism. Its principles were absolute honesty, purity, unselfishness, and love, and its adherents included people from all walks of life throughout the Far East, Africa, and the Americas. From Mary Bethune's vantage point, Moral Rearmament was the greatest unifying force in the world; this idealistic cause summed up the purpose of her total life's work.[33]

Mary McLeod Bethune's faith was grounded in the Judeo-Christian ethic. "Not for myself, but for others. . . . For me to live is Christ," she once wrote.[34] She meant this literally, as indicated by the numerous social causes to which she gave herself and the many loans for social causes which she extended, and frequently wrote off.

Far more than freeing her from the primacy of self-interest, Mary Bethune's faith freed her for the cause of perfecting the range of human freedom for those who, like herself, were denied the rights and privileges of full citizenship. Seen in this light, freedom for Bethune was essentially an experience of being, manifested through the exercise of choice. On the strength of her convictions she derived the power necessary to operate in an oppressive society in such a way that her options were never frozen. Time and again she circumvented protocol and institutional structures, as well as the strictures of convention. Clear illustrations are found in Mrs. Bethune's refusal in many instances to enter buildings in the South by way of the back or side door, her insistence that white people address her as either Mrs. Bethune or Dr. Bethune rather than "Mary," her practice of contacting Eleanor Roosevelt rather than going through proper channels when she wanted to meet with the President, and the range of her activity, which defied the chauvinistic axiom that "a woman's place is in the home."

A demonstrable manifestation of Christian freedom in Mary Bethune's life occurred early in her career. She was involved in a confrontation with her trustee board during the early years of the Bethune-Cookman school's development. Composed almost entirely of wealthy whites who resided in Daytona during the winter, the board was instrumental in the school's initial success. Having established eight grades, Mary Bethune expressed her desire to introduce a high school. At a meeting called to discuss her proposal, one of the white members commented, "Eight grades is enough for Negroes." Realizing that this represented the majority sentiment of the board, she railed, "Before I will let you tie my hands, I will give you what I have done this far, and I will go [elsewhere to] start another." The board agreed to her proposal after considering the matter, convinced that she would not be constrained for another day.[35]

Because Mary Bethune often acted without constraint, her intentions sometimes were misunderstood. According to E. Franklin Frazier, a noted black sociologist and contemporary, she loved power, and the more power she acquired the more arrogant she became.[36] What was seen as a love of power, however, probably was Mary Bethune's great confidence that in her the power of love was at work. Mary

Bethune believed God acted in history as the power of love. She understood love as a liberating force that will make unity in the world possible. Understanding herself as an emissary of providence, "a piece of clay . . . pliable in the hands of the Great God," she regarded her own activity as a labor of love.[37] She believed unequivocally that " 'Love thy neighbor' is a precept which could transform the world if it were universally practiced." In her opinion, to love one's neighbor is "to create a world of fellowship and justice where no man's color or religion is held against him. . . . Loving your neighbor means being interracial, interreligious and international."[38]

Although Mrs. Bethune's intentions were at times misunderstood, her words and actions reflected a level of consistency which justified her actions in the eyes of her supporters and made her a formidable foe to her detractors. In this regard, the following statement by Robert C. Weaver is illuminating: "Mrs. Bethune articulated the needs and aspirations of Negroes. She dramatized the problems they faced and spoke effectively and consistently in their behalf. At the same time she inspired the respect of those who came into contact with her."[39]

The extent to which Mary Bethune was respected, if not esteemed, is indicated by the nationwide reaction to an attack on her which emanated from Senator Joseph McCarthy and the House Unamerican Activities Committee. In February 1943, Martin Dies, chairman of the committee, accused Mary Bethune of being a communist sympathizer. The public outcry was immediate, widespread, and sustained. Walter White, executive director of N.A.A.C.P.; G. Bromley Oxnam, bishop of The Methodist Church of the Boston Area; and Eleanor Roosevelt were among the first to voice their protest. The accusation did not stand, but even years later, Mary Bethune was still haunted by those allegations. In 1952 a resolution of confidence was adopted by the General Conference of The Methodist Church, typifying the way Mary Bethune was regarded, not only by fellow Methodists but by Americans in general.

WHEREAS, an Associated Press dispatch of yesterday's date contains disturbing charges against one of Methodism's best known and distinguished educators, Dr. Mary McLeod Bethune. THEREFORE BE IT RESOLVED, That the General Conference affirms its complete confidence in Dr. Bethune as a patriotic person, a loyal American, and a sincere Christian. We regard the charges of Communistic affiliations made against her as utterly absurd.

We ask the Associated Press to give equal publicity to our expression of confidence and affection.[40]

A person whose experience of freedom was vital to her sense of mission, Mary Bethune was outspoken on many social issues of the day. But she was far more the strategist than the theoretician. Few of her pronouncements against racism and chauvinism were original, but her genius lay in couching them in the language of evangelical social Christianity, which freed her to speak beyond the interests of special groups. For Mary Bethune the unity of women as one under God was a transcendent value enabling her to speak ultimately to the needs of the nation. Her arguments in behalf of integration and greater participation of blacks and women in business and government were thereby difficult, if not impossible, to deny.

In the final analysis, Mary Bethune's religious faith fostered a style of leadership characterized on one hand by a charismatic personality and a spirit of protest, and on the other, by a pragmatic disposition and the politics of compromise. Her charisma emanated primarily from an overwhelming confidence that providence was active in her personal history. Her pragmatism resulted largely from confrontation with the social realities of racism, sexism, and poverty. The conflict between her personal perception of history and the facts of social history sparked her spirit of protest. Such a spirit has characterized black religious leadership, from Henry Highland Garnet and Sojourner Truth, to Martin Luther King, Jr., and Malcolm X. Also characteristic was her tendency, according to the mandate of her faith, to embrace not only the cause of racial equality, but the larger cause of human justice. More peculiar to the pattern of religious leadership among women, perhaps, was

Mary Bethune's Christian witness, which usually was expressed outside the context of the institutional church.

While there existed for Mary McLeod Bethune a conflict between internal and external history, to use Richard Niebuhr's terminology, there also existed a positive relationship, suggested by her willingness to compromise. For her, the politics of compromise was the art of overcoming immediate conflicts of interest to realize a long-range objective. Fulfillment did not mean simply wholeness of self; it also meant living as if she were one with a divine unity which binds individuals into a community of selves. In the interest of achieving and promoting wholeness and unity, Mary Bethune fashioned a way of living that defied custom, protocol, and convention. Founded upon her religious faith, it was a way that enabled her to overcome many barriers of race, sex, and class.

6

GEORGIA HARKNESS

Martha L. Scott

Unlike the ancient minds, few modern thinkers tolerate
cognitive dissonance. This is especially true in theology,
where the need to categorize and reduce all thought to one
category or another dominates. Such theologians argue
about whether God is immanent or transcendent, whether
humans have a free will, whether the new heaven or earth is
in this life or the next. To these thinkers, and to many others,
hermits and social activists seem to be strange bed partners.
Such dichotomized thinking has made it hard to analyze the
theology of Georgia Harkness. How could a woman so well
known for her peace and justice concerns at all levels of
society be at the same time a closet mystic?

As I delved into papers in the Harkness archive at
Garrett-Evangelical Theological Seminary, the issue was put
in a new light. Flipping the pages of her lecture notes on
mysticism, I discovered Harkness' habit of writing on the
backs of discarded paper. Once the puzzle was completed by
putting the backs together, the relationship between her
mysticism and her activism was clarified. Georgia Harkness
had at one point sent a letter to her friends supporting
George McGovern for president of the United States. His
intent to end the war in Vietnam apparently had captured
her pacifist interest. She had torn the extra copies in half and,
turning them over, had scratched out that day's lecture on
mysticism. Was then mysticism merely of academic interest,
or were her devotional life and her social activism
inseparably related—two sides of the same sheet of paper?
Her personal papers, her books, an unpublished autobiography, and the oral history of her friends and colleagues
unanimously indicate that Georgia Harkness was speaking

from her own experience when she declared that "vital, God-centered prayer is not a luxury in our busy lives, it is a necessity. Without it we are lost, for 'Where there is no vision, the people perish.' "[1] Her contemplative life had implications for her faith, her thought, and her ethics.

This essay will first explore Harkness' basic theological principles, including her definition and theology of mysticism, and then her ethical stands on some of the social issues of her day. Finally, it will consider the resolution of the two in her own life.

The idea of God was central to Georgia Harkness. At a conference in St. Louis in 1937, she gave the reasons: "It [God] is the most vital of all concepts because what a person thinks about the ultimate nature of things will color what one thinks about oneself, about one's neighbor, about one's moral task, about one's vocation, about one's earthly future, about the future of society, about eternity."[2] She went on to say that our affirmations about God are always born in tension, for to speak of God is to limit and confine God. But not to describe or name God in some way is never to move beyond the vague oblong blur.

A star student of the personalist school of Boston University, there were three ideas about God which Harkness would later develop: God is Creator, Judge, and Redeemer. In 1943 at a symposium in honor of Albert Knudson, she tied these ideas together with the notion of divine sovereignty and human freedom. Creation, she argued, is a social and dynamic process which takes place in time, for God, the Creator, is still creating. Jesus Christ is the channel betwen God the Creator and his human co-workers, "linking time to eternity and humanity to divinity, revealing to persons the moral will of God and the eternal creativity of love in which God calls persons to share."[3]

Just as God elicits human help in the ongoing creation, so human beings also have a responsibility for justice. When justice does not occur, Harkness believed, it is because of human inability to act responsibly in relation to God's will. God's grace is the "free, loving, personal activity of God in Christ for the salvation of an undeserving humanity." The

theology, faith, and practice of Georgia Harkness that flow
from that stance can be summarized as follows.

The God who is Lord of all life takes the initiative in love. He
discloses himself, in a vision unsurpassed, to those who are formally
free but spiritually bound. By this vision, blind eyes are opened and
dull hearts quickened to new life. In salvation through Christ
revelation and redemption are so linked, the Vision and the Deed
so at one, that no one having truly seen the vision can be free to act
as if God had no claim upon him. One who has seen the Vision and
felt the impact of the Deed is captive to it. Yet one is free—free with
a new power to serve God, "in whose service is perfect freedom."[4]

Having traced Harkness' theological foundation, we will
now attempt to define both mysticism and the mystic—a
difficult task. Mysticism is called many things: personal
prayer, worship, the devotional life, the practice of the
presence of God, the strengthening of the inner life through
communion with God. Harkness herself had difficulty
naming it. In her older manuscripts, the word *mystic* is often
scratched out and the term *devotional writer* inserted. In
later years, she defined mysticism as communion with
God—that is, with a Being conceived as the supreme and
ultimate reality.

But this was not to say that everyone who prays is a mystic.
Rather, it suggests that the possibility of a mystical
experience exists for all. Many mystical experiences, she
asserted, do not include "being lifted up out of oneself and
the world and into a state of ecstasy in which one sees visions
and hears supernatural voices. This is an abnormal and
possibly pathological experience."[5] As Harkness pointed
out on many occasions, this mystical communion with God
need be only sustaining, not startling. Further, one might
also distinguish mysticism by saying, as did Rufus Jones, that
it intentionally puts an "emphasis on immediate awareness
of relation with God, on direct and intimate consciousness of
the Divine Presence."[6]

Basing her conclusions on her personalistic and panentheistic views, Harkness continued to distinguish the true
mystical experience. The encounter should not be described
as union with God, but rather communion. Too often, union

denotes a merging of the self's identity with God's, which in Harkness' view, would be unchristian. "The basic doctrines of a person's creation, judgment, redemption through Christ and their moral imperatives and responsible freedom, center in the unique identity of each human self."[7] Simply stated, union destroys or swallows up the self, whereas communion preserves the self that God created and called good.

Georgia Harkness was critical of a mysticism that summons one into a mystical experience through negation of the self. For Harkness, the source of this error lay in Gnosticism, particularly in the description by Pseudo-Dionysius in *Mystical Theology*. According to this view, God is totally transcendent. There is but one way to encounter God in this life: That is the *via negativa* by which the soul strips off its selfhood and, in ecstatic union with transcendent Deity, both feels and knows its oneness with the infinite. This view of mysticism contradicts Harkness' vital conceptions about God—that God is both transcendent and immanent, that human persons are the glory of God's creation, and that God can be known, at least in part, through Jesus Christ. Harkness sought to clarify this issue by saying that whereas self-discipline is necessary in order to serve others more fully, we are nonetheless called through Jesus Christ to love and serve with the affirmative use of all our powers. A self that has lost its unique identity can no longer qualify as either a self or a servant.

Georgia Harkness believed that mysticism is not an encounter in which God the initiator solely acts upon the subject. The subject is always called to reciprocate. In the same manner, mysticism is not merely a subjective experience. It always presupposes a God transcendent in nature and yet the "beyond within" the believer. Finally, there are marks in the life of the mystic not found in the psychotic: "In the devotional writers of the past whose works have lasted, there is a quality of steadfast reliance on God, concern for others, deep humility and absence of self-seeking, a staying-power and heroic singleness of purpose that enabled them to confront opposition and not quail before it."[8]

In response to those who criticized mysticism as being

outside the mainstream of Christian faith, Harkness answered first by pointing to both the Old and New Testament accounts that give evidence of mysticism. On christological grounds, she argued that although Jesus' life reflects qualities found in the lives of other mystics, Jesus cannot be limited to the role of a mystic. He was teacher, preacher, friend, and healer. Paul, on the other hand, was the first Christian mystic.[9]

Georgia Harkness also stressed certain philosophical presuppositions of mysticism. First, the five senses are not adequate for perceiving or knowing God. Though they are satisfactory for everyday needs, they are not sufficient for insights that lie at a deeper level. Second, this deeper level is within the mystic, though also transcendent. Third, and most basic, there is an Absolute or Supreme God "which is beyond and above the visible world and on which all else depends."[10] Fourth, the human spirit has the capacity for communion with the Absolute. And finally, there are two more tenets not universal to all faiths but present among Christian mystics: The self both does and does not lose its identity in communion with the divine; further, purity of life and heart is necessary in preparation for a mystical experience and, at the same time, is the fruit of the encounter.

Consistently concerned with the import of theology for lay life, Harkness presented a formula for developing spiritual fulfillment in Christian living. First, she stressed the need to overcome the pitfalls of dogmatism, indifference, formalism, infantilism, egocentricity, defeatism, and finally, the evasion of responsibility. By purging oneself of these temptations, she identified a positive way to communion with God. By not totally refuting the way of purgation, illumination, and union, but merely by redefining and clarifying the way, she broke the myth that spiritual devotions or mystical exercises are confined to monasteries. In so doing, she liberated many a closet mystic. The prayerful encounter could happen anywhere; one could "practice the presence of God in all of life, regardless of time, place or activity."[11] This redefinition of prayer was instrumental in her own Christian ethics. Not only does prayer have a place in the life of an individual, but like the individual, it belongs in the world. Given this definition of mysticism, Georgia Harkness, the devotional writer and poet, was a mystic. Though hesitant to describe herself as such for fear of being misunderstood, and though her friends would never have labeled her "pious," she nevertheless practiced daily communion with God.

Throughout her life the primary social concern for Georgia Harkness was peace. Perhaps this was because she lived in the shadow of two world wars and the Korean, Vietnam, and Middle East conflicts. For whatever reason, her concern developed early in her career. Her activities and participation in peace organizations served as a springboard for her writings in this area, and she corresponded with and advised many groups such as the Commission on Relations of the Church to the War in Light of the Christian Faith. She served on the United States delegation to two world conferences, at Madras and at Oxford, and in 1939 was invited to join a provisional committee on church and war, of the organization that later became the World Council of Churches.[12]

During all those years, Harkness stood firmly as a pacifist. She found war incompatible with the Christian faith. Creation is good and related to its Creator. Whether one approached creation as reconciler or as warrior ultimately affected one's relationship to God. She made this point clear in an article entitled "The Churches and Vietnam," which one of her former students, Senator George McGovern, had published in the *Congressional Record*. She acknowledged that there is a place for Christian disagreement, but appealed to that which should be held in common.

Yet we have firm ground on which to stand in the Gospel's imperatives on love and reconciliation, on respect for human life and the need to relieve suffering wherever it is found, on the recognition that every person, whatever their race, nation, social status, or political coloration, is of infinite worth to God and should be viewed as bound to us by ties of common humanity.[13]

Harkness argued that in the United States Christians should be as concerned about the Vietcong dead and suffering as about their own. Nor should Christians support the slaughter of innocent noncombatants, obliteration bombing, or decreased financial support for war relief. She also encouraged nonviolent draft resistance and protest. Finally, she pointed to the responsibility of the church to educate, minister to, and defend those most touched by the decisions of war. Fortunately, she lived long enough to see at least a part of the world's conflict ended.

For Georgia Harkness, peace was a lifelong commitment. Her views on pacifism were deeper than mere political idealism or social humanism; they blended Christian witness with social concern and study. In the early 1920s, she wrote almost prophetically of the probable outcome of the Treaty of Versailles, signed in 1919 to end World War I. She believed that treaty to have been "forced upon a broken nation too weak to resist, but not too much cowed to rankle under its severity, a document which had in it the seeds of future wars." In making this judgment, she clearly stood outside the dominant thought of the church in her day. Most church leaders had supported the war to "crush the Huns" and it took some fifteen years for them to see the negative impact of the treaty on future efforts for peace.[14]

Harkness did not condone the actions of Germany, but neither did she approve the way the Allies left Germans to bear the guilt for their atrocities. She cautioned American nationalists: "But we are so much in the habit of thinking of Germany as the insensate aggressor bringing suffering to the rest of the world that we forget something very important. We forget that we starved the Germans. During the war over three-fourths of a million civilians in Germany died from the effects of the Allied Hunger Blockade."[15]

Other effects, she pointed out, were equally devastating. Germany was not only emotionally and physically crippled from hunger. War greed had stripped her of her colonies and material resources; widespread poverty and unemployment followed. Those who had no money to buy food were comforted in knowing there was no food to buy. At this point, Harkness raised a significant ethical question: Does a punitive response and singling out of nations to bear the brunt of a corporately fought war force them to raise arms?

Her answer: "Instead of placing all the blame for the war on Germany, we better blame economic imperialism, secret diplomacy, and the whole war system. Until we who call ourselves Christians can bury our grudges and learn to love our enemies, there is not much hope of peace on earth, good-will toward all."[16]

Throughout her life, Harkness continued to look for every means possible to oppose war. She actively rejected conscription of both men and women; she opposed military buildup and defense spending. Early in 1941, she wrote the Treasury Department, inquiring whether she could pay her defense tax by a separate check specified for civilian use only, and what penalty would be imposed if she refused to pay. The Treasury Department responded by saying that such tactics are unlawful.[17] She also wrote prolifically on the subject. Nearly 40 percent of her numerous articles, sermons, and books addressed her concern for peace. In fact, her words were influential even after her death in 1974.

In 1976, Charles F. Kraft completed Harkness' manuscript for *Biblical Backgrounds of the Middle East Conflict.* Growing out of her many years spent touring, lecturing, and educating Americans in the depth and sweep of the culture of the Semitic people, this book was impartial, cautioning her readers that there are elements of political and moral right on both sides. Georgia Harkness was not anti-Semitic— indeed, she viewed the racist base of anti-Semitism as abhorrent to all Christians. "Yet," she wrote, "if one is unable to feel sympathy for the dispossessed Palestinians or to see some justice in their yearning for an independent state on the West Bank of the Jordan, one falls into another kind of anti-Semitism. The Arabs also are Semites—as fully semitic in their background as are the Hebrew people."[18]

Though Christians should exert caution in making judgments, they are responsible for taking positions on issues of justice. Harkness employed both rational and reconciling approaches. She called for an understanding of the issue and an ability to sympathize with each antagonist. This, she said, will best be achieved through a knowledge of the background, both recent and in the remote past, which has produced the conflicts. And as a pacifist she argued that military force is not the answer. Armed aggression will only prolong conflict. She contended that a lasting solution to the struggle in the Middle East could be found only through "political and diplomatic effort, and that the policy and diplomacy employed must take into account human values and a basic justice for both sides."[19]

As a Christian ethicist, Georgia Harkness also took stands on a number of other social issues—stands which reflected the depth of her thought and commitment. Her perception of the relatedness of creation and her systemic analyses of society, especially her attack on the economic order, were equally profound. She was one of the few Christian thinkers in the United States who clearly saw the impact of corporate industrialization on the working classes. In an article written in 1925, "The One and the Many," she spoke out against child labor, industrial conditions, and "a society that has driven young girls to prostitution as victims of men's lust in a double standard society."[20] During the middle of the Depression she attacked the impersonal, mechanistic economic theory of capitalism.

The capitalistic system has been reinforced through the giving of intellectual sanction to its processes, with the result that its evils have been accepted as inevitable because of a belief in the inevitable operation of economic forces. The mass production of goods by impersonal corporations has been stimulated. Inequalities of distribution have been accentuated. Attempts to restrict the free operation of the profit have met social and legislative opposition. The result is the present chaos.[21]

She felt, too, that capitalism lowers the value of human life. Exploitation of labor crushes the human personality, but this result is either overlooked or regarded as necessary and inevitable. The destructive effect of capitalism also has a global impact: "Its effect appears again in the tendency to regard economic imperialism, with its consequent wars, as an inevitable effect of economic expansion—to be retarded, perhaps by moral forces, but not to be permanently halted."[22] To Harkness, the connection between an impersonal economic theory and a depersonalized—and disrupted—social order was obvious.

In other articles Harkness attempted to raise class-consciousness in the church. Her queries contain deep implications for Christian dialogues with Marxist thinkers today: Can a society be Christian when it accepts class stratification? Can an individual aristocrat be a Christian?

To answer such questions, Christians need a criterion. For Georgia Harkness, that standard was the practice and teaching of the Jesus of New Testament record. In her mind, Jesus was not an aristocrat. "If ever a person lived and spoke in utter freedom from class stratification, it was Jesus. Our society, democratic though it professes to be, is obviously permeated with the distinctions he refused to make, and by this fact it stands condemned as unchristian."[23] As to whether an individual could be both an aristocrat and a Christian, the answer is less clear. She noted that affluence and prestige set barriers to Christian character, but on the other hand, she quoted John Wesley's "Causes of the Inefficacy of Christianity": "Wherever true Christianity spreads, it must cause diligence and frugality which, in the natural course of things must beget riches, and riches beget pride, love of the world and every temper that is destructive to Christianity."[24] Yes, a Christian can be an aristocrat, Harkness believed—"yes, but under difficulties."

Georgia Harkness strongly denounced racism. It is incompatible with the idea of a God who created the cosmos and called it good, and it directly insults the God who values each individual. Racism also imperils the peace of the world.

Not race, which in the order of nature is ordained of God that there may be variety in the many families that make up the family of God, but racism. Racism is the perversion of this variety by the injection of enmity, superiority and contempt where there ought to be fellowship in diversity. Since this is a moral universe racism cannot go on without peril to all—not to victor and victim, for there are no victors in this struggle—but to those who dominate and those who suffer from the domination of others.[25]

She had the utmost sympathy for black Americans and for Japanese Americans and spoke pointedly of the shortsightedness of the Christian community toward those two groups: "Yet no one needs to be told that church people have often been far more zealous for sending the Christian gospel to Africa than for being Christian toward the Negroes in their own community; for evangelizing Japan than for maintaining good will toward the Japanese in time of national conflict."[26] She tried diligently to counter racist views within her denomination through her work on national boards and agencies of The Methodist Church, and she also took her case to the wider church press.

In a letter to the editor of *Christian Century*, Georgia Harkness registered "her complete agreement" with an article by Benjamin Garrison regarding the Methodist-Evangelical United Brethren (E.U.B.) union. She urged her Methodist and E.U.B. friends to vote against the proposed merger, a surprising stand for a hard-fighting Methodist pioneer in the ecumenical movement. She offered two arguments. First, the merging denominations should not carry two statements of faith and two social creeds into the union. Harkness was even more determined in her second reason for opposition. She believed that all structures of the new denomination must be racially integrated.

The segregated Central Jurisdiction, which has existed in Methodism since 1939, is a clear contradiction of Christian morality. It was voted at the Methodist General Conference of 1964 not to carry this iniquitous structure into the union. It appears about to be carried into it, not by name, but by substance in the continuance of segregated Annual Conferences in some sections. This will deny to our Negro members their present fellowship. Their anguish at this point was dramatically clear at the General Conference of 1966. . . . This injustice I cannot stomach, and I hope my Church can not.[27]

Georgia Harkness also questioned the "democracy" of a nation which fought for freedom around the globe but failed to secure democratic rights at home. In the late 1940s she was one of the few Christian leaders to criticize the internment of Japanese Americans.

The internment of 110,000 Japanese on the Pacific Coast, including more than 70,000 American citizens, will, I am sure, long remain a blot upon our democracy. It is a sobering fact that as war encircles the globe, Germany is the only country outside of the United States that has thought it necessary to intern any considerable number of its own citizens. I do not say that the treatment accorded to the Japanese in the relocation centers is comparable to the German concentration camp. Yet in the loss of economic security and professional opportunity, the uprooting of families and surrender of personal liberty that has been forced upon great numbers of our fellow citizens and loyal neighbors, there is something of which no American can be proud. One wonders whether, in the history books of the future, we shall try as hard to forget it as we now do the Mexican War.[28]

Harkness opposed not only racism, but every form of ethnic prejudice. Ever ahead of her time as a Christian thinker, in 1921 she published *The Church and the Immigrant,* a revision of her master's thesis, to inform religious bodies concerning the immigrant population and to suggest some practical ways the church could be helpful to the new Americans. This work demonstrates her ability to analyze social structures and to empathize with the suffering of others. Harkness understood that immigrants not only were recipients of America's bounty but had much to contribute to the national life and prosperity. Besides their extensive artistic and cultural abilities, they supplied the labor to run American industry. On the lower rung of the economic system, immigrants were forced to live in poor and overcrowded housing, since they lacked the economic means for improvement.

Harkness called on the church to understand the plight of the immigrants, and also to aid in alleviating their condition: "We have applied to him [the immigrant] unpleasant epithets and have frequently placed upon his shoulders the blame for all our present social and industrial unrest."[29] It was the responsibility of the church to help protect those people from the unjust practices of labor agents, both before and after their migration, and it should assist in their relocation in order to prevent the rise of ghettos. To speed up the assimilation of new populations, churches could teach courses in English and provide other services to supplement federal assistance.

On rare occasions, Georgia Harkness slipped back into a more conservative mold. Certain of her views on assimilation of immigrants are ethnocentric.

The American government has generally maintained toward the exclusion of undesirables a sane attitude which the church will do well to support. But whatever the future policy may be, the immigrant of the newer type is here. If we do not like him as he is, we must make him over in the light of our finest American and Christian ideals.[30]

In general, however, she believed the church could assist the immigrant most effectively by providing self-help opportunities—social, economic, and spiritual.

Among many United Methodist women, Georgia Harkness will be best remembered for her stand on women's issues in church and secular society. Yet it would appear that she developed this "full-participation" stand over a period of years. Though she made exceptions for single, professional women like herself, her early basic view of the role of married women reflected the spirit of her times. This double standard emerged in a speech she made in the early 1940s on the topic "Women and Church Unification":

To avoid any misunderstanding, let me say that I too believe woman's primary sphere is the home! If some of us do not talk much about it, it is because there does not seem to be enough negative evidence to get up an argument. But, however much we may agree upon the primacy of the home, there is still a long way to go before we shall have generally the kind of home called for by the ideal of the family of God.[31]

Apparently she grew uncomfortable with this double standard, for by the end of that decade, her support for women of every age and stage of consciousness ranged from participation in their teas for home missions to their struggles for women's ordination.

Georgia Harkness believed that women should assume public leadership in the church and that this leadership should include ordination. She began to argue for ordination in the 1920s and stated her fully developed views in 1939 in an article, "What Price Unity": Women's ordination was biblical, it was practical, and it was spiritually advisable.[32] Much of her thinking on this issue was compiled in her later book, *Women in Church and Society*.[33]

Harkness' contribution to the women's ordination movement in The Methodist Church culminated on May 4, 1956. Debate on the floor of the General Conference focused on the controversial issue of "full clergy rights for women," and arguments for both sides were presented during most of the day. At five o'clock the final vote was taken. "It is carried," stated Bishop King.

Reading the *Daily Christian Advocate* account of that floor debate, one would not realize that Georgia Harkness had any part in gaining ordination for women. She made no eloquent speeches that day, nor was she quoted by any of those who spoke. Thelma Stevens, a friend and a longtime women's advocate herself, stated that Georgia Harkness was intentionally silent that day. Since the 1944 General Conference, Harkness had written and taught and had lectured in her travels. Hundreds of memorials supporting full clergy rights for women had come in from across the nation, due in no small part to the work of the Woman's Society of Christian Service. Harkness felt the church was ready to make its decision. She was sure that the 1956 General Conference would vote to support the issue and that nothing she could say now would change any opinions. Someone else would have to do the arguing.

As it turned out, she was right, and that evening, the whole General Conference recognized it. Lynn H. Corson, a clergy delegate from New Jersey, stepped to the microphone and expressed the sentiments of that assembly.

Mr. Chairman, this is a day of particular triumph and significance to one of the members of this group who for many years has been looking forward to this moment when full clergy rights for women would be voted by this General Conference. I refer to Dr. Georgia Harkness. (Applause)

I think that it is a matter only due her as a courtesy from the General Conference to express the appreciation of the conference for this valiant fight she has waged for this cause for many years and express to her how we know that on this day she must have peculiar satisfaction in the knowledge that this fight has eventuated in final victory for her cause.

Let us salute Dr. Georgia Harkness. (The audience arose and applauded.)[34]

Since those days many feminists in the church have wondered whether Georgia Harkness was a feminist or a feminist theologian. Harkness answered that question best herself: "I believe women should have equal opportunities for leadership, equal pay for the work they do and a much larger place in the officialdom of the Church than in the past."[35] In the secular realm, Harkness certainly leaned toward a feminist ideology.

However, did she develop a feminist theology? The answer would be no, and by her own definition. In 1973 she wrote the editor of the *Christian Century* concerning an editorial which had quoted her as supporting "separate theologies for men and women because of the divergent circumstances of their lives." She clarified her views: "Christian theology is a quest for truth, and this truth is not contingent on sex or race. For this reason I squirm at the idea of either woman theology or black theology, though of course women and blacks may be theologians who, as in all authentic Christian theology, affirm the full equality of persons."[36]

Harkness believed, in regard to sexist language, that inclusiveness should be practiced in official documents of The United Methodist Church. However, she opposed changing biblical material in references to God. Since Jesus called God Father, so should we.[37] Her theological conception neither obstructed nor supported feminist theology.

Georgia Harkness also held mixed opinions about the nature of responsible sexual behavior. She favored birth control. In the United States, it reduced the threat of overpopulation; in other countries, where similar or worse problems existed, birth control should be offered, but never forced upon an unwilling populace. As to abortion, she assumed a more conservative stance: Abortion was not a Christian alternative unless the life of the mother was in danger, or in the case of rape.[38]

Georgia Harkness' sexual ethics also included a Christian view of heterosexism, or what has been more popularly referred to in the United Methodist press as a homosexual orientation. For Harkness, it was necessary to explore two questions in order to develop a responsible ethic for the church in regard to the homosexual life-style. First, is homosexuality intrinsically evil and therefore a sin? Second, what is the obligation of the church? In 1974, she outlined her position in a letter to a retired clergyman.

As for the first question, homosexuals have been far more sinned against than sinning in the way both society and the churches have treated them as moral lepers and outcasts. I regard it more as an undesirable practice than a sin, and in the words of theologian Norman Pittinger, a state of being "different" rather than "deviant."

I do not at all approve homosexual practices in which young boys, or other immature young people, are made the victims of adults. That must be discredited on the grounds of "using" the innocent for the sexual pleasure of the adults.

When it is practiced between consenting single adults, I think it is their own business and less reprehensible than either heterosexual adultery or sexual intercourse outside of marriage. In either of the two latter, it is apt to break up a marriage or make a bad foundation for a later marriage, plus the possibility of an undesirable pregnancy. In a homosexual case, if one or both of the partners is married it might seriously affect their family life, but otherwise it does not need to have these effects.

Another factor in the case is that it is so hard to define precisely. A strong attachment between two persons of the same sex may be mutually supporting and have nothing sexy about it, yet the suspicion arises that they are homosexuals especially if they share a home together.

But as to the second question, what to do about it in the churches, my answer would be homosexuals should be treated charitably and not excluded from the churches' fellowship. However, with the sentiment against it still as strong as it is, one had better not advertise his homosexuality if he wants to be a minister. Just as one may smoke or drink in moderation and still be an effective minister if it is not generally known, so until the current mores change, there are things that are not expedient in the light of one's total influence.

This is as far as I get with it, and definitely do not expect to write a book about it.[39]

Harkness' response to the concerns of homosexuals in the church was, as most of her responses, sensitive, just, and practical. Perhaps because she understood the church's inability to deal with the issue, she chose to keep quiet, or perhaps she feared rumors regarding her thirty-year friendship with her housemate, Verna Miller. It is probably the only question of human justice she did not take to the press and apparently never intended to do so.

Georgia Harkness' final socioreligious concern was ecumenicity. Her role of leadership in the World Council of Churches dated back to its earliest provisional committees of 1939. She confessed that her panentheistic theology often ran head on into the Barthian "sky-God" of the Continent and the "hard, impersonal world of the states."[40] However, the appeal is always made to Jesus Christ, who is the mediator not only between God and humanity, but also between American and continental theologians. Harkness' own feelings about the hope emanating from the cooperative effort of all faiths to address the issues of world peace and human needs are revealed in her poetic verse, "Hope of the World." When these words were put to music by V. Earle Copes, the result was chosen as the most significant hymn written in recognition of the second assembly of the World Council of Churches, which met in Evanston in August of 1954.[41]

In her own life, how did Georgia Harkness combine and balance her theology of mysticism and her social stands? Harkness the poet best expressed this tension in one of her five devotional books, *Be Still and Know*. In a selection based on the story of the Transfiguration, she described the process of movement from the vision to the task.

> Transfigured on a mount the Master stood,
> His raiment white, and dazzling to the sight
> In radiance divine. It would be good
> To stay and dwell forever in that light,
> So Peter thought—but Jesus spake him nay.
> He knew that all about was work to do.
> That in the vale below a sick boy lay,
> And troubled folk they might bring healing to.
>
> I too have seen a vision on a mount—
> Have gazed on dazzling whiteness, and been swept
> By mountain winds, dew-cleansed at morning's fount,
> I yearned to linger there—but downward crept
> A mist, and drove me to the vale below.
> Because He went, I was less loath to go.[42]

Such a harmonious flow between task and vision did not "just happen." Harkness achieved the proper balance only over a period of years.

Georgia Harkness, born in the spring of 1891, was the last child of her parents, who were then residing in a New York town named for her father's family. Their homelife was basically stable and happy, though not without tragedy. Her father was a brilliant man, widely read and multitalented, to whom the community and the church looked for leadership and counsel. Unlike Georgia's college-educated father, her mother had completed only the eighth grade. The death of a daughter, in-law problems, and a lingering illness marked her life with much unhappiness. She seldom verbalized her faith, but nonetheless, Georgia Harkness believed that her mother was a very pious woman. As an adult, Georgia would come to encompass the views of both her parents in her own theological beliefs; she would be recognized as a well-informed religious leader and also as a steadfast, faithful servant who had endured much mental, physical, and spiritual anguish in her lifetime.

Church attendance was compulsory in the Harkness home, and the family's religious interest was a sure foundation for Georgia's future faith. At the age of six or seven, she began to pray. However, her spiritual guide was the hired girl, not her parents or her church.

Like many children in rural churches, she "got the faith" each time a revival came to town and "backslid" just as many times. However, when she was about ten, the seeds of her mystical theology were planted. One Sunday after church she asked her father about angels. "His answer," she recalls, "touched off a chain reaction."

"Some people," he said, "say that when folks die they go to heaven and become angels, but I don't know how they know it."

It was as if the words, "I don't know how they know it," became frozen in her stream of consciousness. His indecisiveness threw her whole faith into flux. How did one know? Could the Bible be just a storybook, and Jesus a mere character? If Jesus were just a storybook creation, how could one know whether God really exists? In the 1950s in her autobiography written for the Pacific Coast Theological Group, she described the remembered childhood feelings: "I felt alone, bereft, queer. I knew of nobody else who did not believe in God, and was too appalled at myself to talk to anybody about it. I clearly remember lying awake alone at night, sobbing because I could not pray and could have no certainty that God existed." Relief came only after she identified with the main character of a book by Edna Lyell, *Donovan,* a young man who had labeled his similar experience a crisis of faith, or atheism. Since Georgia too would turn to academics, it is significant that the young man sought advice from a wise teacher. The teacher told him that nobody could prove the existence of God, but showed him that there were many more reasons for belief than for disbelief and assured him that the greatest and best people of all ages had lived by this faith. The teacher's answer proved sufficient for Georgia, and she began to pray again. She asserted, some years later, "The connection between this painful experience and my present profession I leave you to trace."[43]

When she entered Cornell, she was an extremely shy social misfit. Clearly out of her isolated rural element, she described herself as "the utter antithesis of a Big Shot on Campus." Two events marked her spiritual development and social commitment. She joined the Student Volunteer Band and signed the pledge: It is my Purpose, if God permits, to become a foreign missionary. As it turned out, God led her in another direction, but her concern for others, deepened by the liberal social gospel later impressed upon her in Boston, was never forgotten. The second event was her escape from death by what she called a miracle of God. Having fallen into twelve-foot water and not knowing how to swim, she prayed; her prayers were answered—she was rescued. "Thus," states Harkness, "a miracle of deliverance was wrought, but within the order of God's nature."

Intellectually, her thirst for knowledge, much like her father's, could not be quenched. After teaching for a few years she applied to Boston University School of Theology. In 1918, she began a degree in religious education, and then her interests began to change. After taking a course under

Brightman, she applied and was accepted as a candidate for the doctoral program at Boston University. She extended her academic adventures with a semester's study with Hocking and Whitehead at Harvard, then spent a year writing, publishing, and teaching at Yale and later at Elmira and Cornell colleges. Georgia Harkness had become an accomplished intellectual. This pursuit of academic excellence and achievement continued throughout her career.

However, Georgia Harkness' personal faith was about to be transformed again. In 1937 she went home to attend her dying father. The rest of the story is hers.

I cannot faithfully recount my spiritual autobiography without telling something which he said to me within an hour of his death, and which I took as a directive from an eternal realm. Asking me how many books I had written (by that time seven), he said, "I think they must be good books. Wise men say they are. But I wish you would write more about Jesus Christ."[44]

This experience, as Harkness notes, marked a definite turn in her thinking "toward a more Christ-centered approach." Later she referred to the change that occurred in her life between 1929 and 1939: "More determinative for me than what has happened in the political or theological world have been the events of my private world."[45]

She identified this new element of faith as "a second blessing," although it was not an intense, ecstatic, radical transformation. Over that ten-year span she maintained her activity and interests: She wrote six books and published many more articles; she represented United States religious leaders at two world conferences; she taught in Japan and Manila before receiving an appointment to the Religion Department of Mount Holyoke College. The American Theological Society recognized her contributions and elected her its first woman member.

Yet the results of that progressive "second blessing" colored her outlook and participation in the external world of events.

I have become more of a theologian, probably less of a philosopher. My religion is more Christ-centered. I have rediscovered the Bible; Mysticism and Worship have taken on added richness. I seem in a small way to have become a peripatetic evangelist, speaking often on personal religious living. I was a pacifist and a socialist ten years ago and still am, but my Christian conviction in both spheres has taken on greater clarity and firmness. I am more church-minded. Finally I have seen a new vision of the world mission of the Church.[46]

At the time when she was most involved in the world, she was also most turned inward in contemplation and devotion. New vision and world mission were wed in Georgia Harkness.

Her contemplative life continued to develop side by side with her social concerns. She left Mount Holyoke in 1939 and took a position at Garrett Biblical Institute. She referred to the next eleven years as basically good years, although they were marked by physical, emotional, and spiritual pain. During the fall of 1939, she was hospitalized with a disease similar to undulant fever. This illness was immediately followed by a fall which injured her spine. The spine never healed properly and she was tormented for some time by pain. Colleagues then on the faculty at Garrett remember that she carried a large pillow, enabling her to sit through faculty meetings. Nearly financially destitute from medical costs and having suffered "many things at the hands of my physicians," she plummeted still farther emotionally and spiritually, with resulting acute insomnia and depression. When she related the experience to Harry Emerson Fosdick later, she referred to it as a nervous breakdown.[47] Reaching out for salvation, she reactivated and deepened her devotional life, and it was at this point that she wrote *Dark Night of the Soul,* the title borrowed from John of the Cross.[48] Georgia Harkness now knew that God was present also in pain and suffering. She stated, "In those dark years God taught me much that I should not otherwise have learned."[49] In relating her own pain to that of her readers, she became pastor of a congregation of thousands.

With renewed confidence and faith, in 1947 Georgia Harkness wrote *Understanding the Christian Faith,* in which she articulated the formula for moving from the vision to the task in making ethical decisions. To begin, people must learn the mind of Christ and live with the New Testament until it becomes internalized. Also, they must open themselves to the leading of the Holy Spirit at all times, "If we are not too dull to sense this presence." Then the problem must be solved within its total setting. People do not live as isolated individuals; what one does has a profound effect on others. Therefore, all decisions and their possible consequences need to be checked out within the context of the community. Finally, "We must act then by the light we have."[50] Georgia Harkness no longer held just a theology of ethics; she possessed a faith to live by.

In the final analysis, what can we say about Georgia Harkness? Has not the feminist movement outgrown Harkness' analysis? Did she consider the need for a new ecclesiology? Or had she settled for a spot in the old? In her devotional books, her work appears as surface piety. However, in the effort to find loopholes in her tension between faith and works, one discovers that Georgia Harkness was probably the best Methodist applied-theologian the century has seen. She was not just a pious old woman whose heart was in the right place. With pen and tongue she entered into worlds many men feared, and where still more were uninvited.

She redeemed whole sections of recent church history, speaking especially to the needs of immigrants and working-class people. In her concern for the "justness" of the American socioeconomic system, her analyses and solutions for relief were more than simply adhesive-strip bandages. She believed the church should not only feed the hungry, but should change the whole economic system that makes hunger a possibility. United States Protestant and Catholic theologians beginning their Marxist-Christian dialogues with third-world countries will find a predecessor and a teacher in Georgia Harkness.

Her theology was not limited to the ivory towers of seminaries. It was clear and simple, a theology usable in local churches as well as in institutions of higher learning. It was for lay people as well as for clergy and philosophers.

Harkness' theology has some important ramifications for today's world. As possibilities continue for conflict with other countries, she reminds us of the Christian vision of reconciliation. She calls us to employ every diplomatic and policy formulation for peace. She also raises the question as to whether our own greed might have gotten us into certain situations. She even calls upon us to reexamine our hope in punitive food embargoes. Is it possible to repeat the mistakes of the Treaty of Versailles? Could we incite the people of another country to war by our acts of retaliation? Can we truly fight for democratic principles elsewhere and not hold out those same privileges for the oppressed in this country? These questions are not easy, yet they stand out when we apply Georgia Harkness' theology for peace to the world problems of today.

There is room within today's women's movement for Harkness' emphasis on reconciliation. Because she was a reconciler, she avoided separatism. She dedicated herself to overcoming systems and ideologies that oppress all of us, but she avoided the easy solution of giving up on the tradition altogether. Nor did she believe equality for all people would be created when women gained traditionally male-dominated positions within the existing structure. The positions and the structure of the systems themselves must change, if New Women are to create a New Church or a New World.

Finally, Georgia Harkness offers women spiritual renewal for the 1980s. Many today characterize the 1960s as activist years and the 1970s as passive years. Yet, is this the history of women, or only of men? During the 1970s, women were actively working for women. They were building day-care centers and women's health clinics. They were building shelters for battered women and creating a whole new culture and way of life. Holly Near, a feminist singer and artist asks, "If we weren't doing anything, why are we so tired?" The question is very much on target. All of us know women—superwomen—who have now dropped out of the movement or out of the church. Many are tired, others discouraged, and some disillusioned. The time has come to reevaluate our vision. Let us heed the message of Harkness. Let us not be too busy to pray, to contemplate the evil structures in our world and the hope we are promised. Let us not be too busy to pray, for where there is no vision, women—even strong women—perish.

Who was Georgia Harkness? She was a woman who lived in the best of two worlds. On the mountaintop she saw a vision of a New World. In the world of her day, she made it happen.

III

CONTRIBUTIONS
OF WOMEN
TO CHURCH LIFE

MINISTRY THROUGH MARRIAGE

Julie Roy Jeffrey

Looking back over many years of itinerant ministry on the Trans-Mississippi frontier, the Reverend Andrew Monroe remarked upon one of a Methodist preacher's most fateful choices, that of a wife. He counseled:

How careful young ministers should be in that important step . . . which is to settle their domestic relationships and give coloring . . . to the future of their ministerial history. Passion and fancy in many cases dethrone the judgement. Men hastily and unadvisedly form alliances wholly unsuited to their calling. . . . Many a star with a bright morning has passed noon and evening both under a cloud.[1]

Monroe's concern reflected a new set of conditions that had evolved in American Methodism in the early nineteenth century. Although almost all itinerants once had been single, as the Methodist Episcopal Church moved into the new century and pushed across the Mississippi to new frontiers, more and more Methodist ministers married. Their decisions might be delayed, but marry they did.[2]

Natural urges, the desire for home and family to offset the burdens of itinerancy, doubtless helped to create the new pattern. The notion of the distinctive female character which emerged early in the nineteenth century also played a part in turning the Methodist clergy toward marriage. As Francis Hodgson pointed out, "It . . . often occurs that the female portion of the church embodies the greater amount of piety, intelligence, wealth, and influence."[3] This view of woman helped to establish a climate of opinion where clerical marriage could be seen not just as a necessary evil but, in fact, as a desirable goal. Woman's innate religious nature made her eminently qualified to serve as the preacher's helpmate, especially in an evangelical denomination such as Methodism, which focused not on the head, but on the female domain of the heart. So it was hardly surprising that the Reverend Orceneth Fisher, whose wife aided him in his West Coast missionary work, wrote in 1861 to his itinerant son in Texas that he hoped he would marry. "Surely you can find *one* good religious girl that will help you in God's work."[4]

Sharing these views of female nature, a growing number of young Protestant women were convinced that their duty to God required a commitment to evangelical work. Because the definition of evangelicalism had broadened to include teaching as well as charitable and religious endeavors, single women had some flexibility in realizing their vocation to bring souls to Christ. But as unmarried women, their choices of missionary terrain were limited. They might be sent to foreign or to American Indian missions, but church boards generally were reluctant to send them into the home mission field. Marriage to a frontier itinerant promised new and broad avenues of religious usefulness, and Methodist women, like those in other denominations, accepted matrimonial proposals in order to embark on God's work.[5]

The Methodist missionary courtship pattern, similar to that in other denominations, emerges from scattered sources. Converted and committed young women, eager to broaden the scope of their work, were sought out by Methodist preachers who were looking for wives/missionary assistants. Daniel Poe, a midwestern itinerant, later of Texas, found his future wife, Jane Ingram, teaching and caring for Indians on the shores of Lake Superior; Jacob Adriance, a Colorado missionary, explained, "I went back to New York to visit my parents and friends. There I found a girl [Fanny Rogers] willing to be a missionary's wife."[6] Isaac Beardsley's journal suggests the considerations involved in selecting a bride. Religious qualifications loomed large, and Beardsley's future wife is portrayed as "a seeker of salvation," with whom he prays.[7] Courtships were often quick and to the point. Soon after the wedding, couples set off for western missionary fields. Seventeen days were sufficient for Adriance's courtship, marriage, and departure for Colorado.

Even when marriage and removal to the mission field did not follow in rapid sequence, each partner must have weighed the other's religious commitment seriously before entering the relationship. The mutual decision made by Anne and William Taylor to leave the East for California is instructive of the nature of their marriage. Returning from a meeting with his bishop, who had proposed the assignment, Taylor asked his wife if she were willing to go. Pregnant with her third child, Anne ran upstairs to her room and, in a few minutes, returned with her consent. Explaining her rapid decision, Anne revealed herself as the obvious choice for William. "I went upstairs and kneeled down and said, 'Lord, Bishop Waugh wants to send us to California. Thou knowest, Lord, that I don't want to go . . . but . . . if it is Thy will to send us to California, give me the desire to go.' In a second or two he filled and thrilled my whole being with a desire to go to California."[8]

Such devoted clerical marriages explain James Finley's descriptions of Daniel and Jane Poe as a missionary *pair*, "as noble a couple as ever labored and suffered in the Methodist itinerancy"; both were "devoted missionaries."[9] Just because preachers sought wives as assistants while women accepted proposals in order to enter missionary work does not mean, of course, that genuine affection was not involved. But for many young Methodists, evangelical enthusiasm had become a primary consideration in the selection of a mate.

The transition to a married clergy in effect opened new areas of religious activity to Methodist women. Bishop Asbury had reported that women offered their homes for services, provided hospitality to circuit riders, presented testimony at love feasts, led prayer meetings, and worked together. But marriage to a frontier itinerant offered the possibility of a genuinely shared ministry. The domestic mission field was less colorful than those in foreign lands, but as important in enriching the scope and variety of women's work in the church and in contributing to their changing position.[10]

If matrimony became usual among the Methodist clergy

and offered new opportunities to women, we have seen that Monroe has suggested a few of the hazards. Specifically, an unwise choice of wife could threaten a minister's career. Because the selection of a wife was so crucial and few precedents existed to guide either the choice itself or appropriate female behavior following marriage, it became vital to establish general guidelines. In 1851, H. Eaton's *The Itinerant Wife: Her Qualifications, Duties and Rewards* was one attempt to clarify the characteristics and attitudes of the model clergy wife, to warn away those who might lightheartedly undertake "the great responsibilities" of marriage to a clergyman, and to define the boundaries of wives' religious work.[11]

While acknowledging the serious religious duties of the itinerant's wife, Eaton warned his female readers never to challenge or threaten their husband's professional prerogatives. Since the spheres of male and female activity overlapped in clerical marriage in a way foreign to nineteenth-century views of sexual order, Eaton's insistence on the wife's supportive religious role is hardly surprising. Her most important task, Eaton advised, was to encourage her husband. A wife's prayers and comforting words were vital to evangelical success, for without them a disheartened husband might abandon his ministry altogether.[12]

Yet clergy wives could expect more than a life of prayer and counsel behind the scenes. They were urged to circulate in society and cultivate friends, especially among women. By her example and good works, a clergy wife, Eaton advised, might shape society's character and its standards. Armed with "correct" doctrines, she was to answer the questions of both the curious and the sincere. Other pastoral activities included visiting and being a religious model for the community by her devoted attendance at services. In sum, the good wife was to be ready to "embrace every opportunity to invite sinners to come to the Saviour" and "constantly to promote a growth in grace."[13]

Even as a clergy wife's religious work should never overshadow her husband's, so too, her duties must always take second place to family obligations. Because an itinerant would so often be away, his wife had the grave responsibility of overseeing their children. Eaton told his readers sternly that the wife "will . . . resolve, that whatever else shall be left undone, her duties to her family shall command her first attention."[14]

Implicit in this description of the clergy wife's work were the particular qualities needed to carry it out, but Eaton left nothing to chance. His list of her "qualifications" included common sense, an evangelical but cheerful piety, a sufficient acquaintance with literary and religious sources, and a love of the itinerancy that would enable her to bear its burdens happily. He saw these as closely related characteristics and believed them to be peculiarly female.[15]

In his final chapter, Eaton considered the rewards an itinerant's wife might expect. These meshed neatly with his concept of the clergy wife as her husband's subsidiary. The promise of eternal life might, of course, be anticipated. But little consideration was given to the possibility that a woman might seek more direct satisfaction from her work. Her reward would lie instead in the knowledge that she had served her husband well. For "her husband occupies a conspicuous and very responsible place in the little circle of which he must necessarily be the centre," Eaton gravely reminded readers, "and the duties thus imposed on him render it very desirable that every possible assistance should be afforded him, and for many things he can look only to his wife."[16]

At the same time that Eaton highlighted the common notion of female service at the nuptial altar, he created a distinct model for clerical marriage. He recognized that a woman's evangelical desire to serve was important, but deemed it secondary to her duties as wife and mother. If his insistent points left little room for uncertainty, they also suggested his worries. He studiously overlooked the likelihood that the exact boundaries for a clergy wife's religious work might be apparent neither to herself or to her husband. He was clearly uneasy about this, as well as about potential disagreements between husbands and wives over religious and domestic priorities.[17]

The reality of clerical marriage was both more problematic and complicated than Eaton was willing to admit. This is immediately apparent in numerous accounts of the expansion of Methodism to the frontier. Such historical and devotional documents usually mention clergy wives only in passing, but even fleeting references reveal the limitations of Eaton's model. The qualities exhibited by women in these memoirs were neither typically feminine or subservient. Clerical authors commented on the energy, courage, and perseverance of clergy wives, describing vigorous women with "the courage of . . . their convictions" and "strong mind[s]." True, wives also were remembered as diligent helpmates, but with "driving will-force[s] that overcame most formidable obstacles." The wife who "nothing admitted of compromise when duty to God, the church, or her husband was made plain," was a tower of strength, indeed, but what if her duties were neither plain nor complementary? Finally, most authors saw clergy wives as "producers" who grappled successfully with economic matters. Here was yet another side to Methodist clerical marriage, neglected by Eaton and only awkwardly related to the idea of evangelical mission and to nineteenth-century norms for female conduct.[18]

These narratives indirectly suggest the complexities of those clerical marriages that Monroe had referrred to as "incumbrances." These complexities ranged from the psychological demands of a missionary relationship to its financial exigencies. The sources show a broad new field of usefulness opening for women, but one ill-defined. A strong woman's interpretation of her duty to God could easily clash with the needs of her husband or her children. Each woman had to work out her own delicate balance—for some it tilted toward home; for others, toward religion. Because the frontier was a needy mission field, providing more than enough work for two laborers, it dramatized both the possibilities and the problems faced by clergy wives.[19]

The moving western frontier posed a special and important challenge, of course, to all nineteenth-century Protestants. Many feared that as settlers moved west, they would become cultural and religious barbarians. The American West had to be secured for Christ, for civilization, and for national unity. The frontier was the *home* mission field, even more crucial in terms of the future than remote foreign mission fields. The *Thirtieth Annual Report of the Methodist Missionary Society* emphasized the scope of the task. "The field for missionary enterprise in the West is almost without limits. Its population is increasing with unexampled rapidity. . . . How these multitudes . . . are to be supplied with the Word of God . . . is a question over which the Church cannot slumber without criminality."[20]

Recognition of the frontier's national and religious importance was intermixed with a healthy dose of denominational self-interest. Like other groups, the Methodists hoped to establish ascendancy. When James H. Addison, a Texas itinerant in the 1850s, referred in his journal to "the Baptists and Campbellites stealing your sheep, and the devil triumphing," he revealed a shared frame of reference.[21]

If Methodist frontier preachers did not need to learn to work in an alien culture, as did foreign missionaries, they discovered nonetheless that the home-mission field was not without its problems. At first it was deceptively promising. Initially buoyed up by working within their own culture, ministers were deflated when they discovered frontier indifference. Because settlers' homesteads were scattered and the inhabitants moved frequently, it was hard to establish stable congregations. Coming from different denominational backgrounds and often out of the habit of regular worship, many frontiersmen and women showed little interest in becoming faithful church members. Physical reminders of religious life, such as church buildings and bells, which the nineteenth century considered important in encouraging institutional regularity, were absent. Funds to create physical reminders of the spiritual body proved difficult to obtain in a society where cash was scarce. David Blaine, missionary to Washington state, summed up frontier conditions and missionary disillusionment.

We are low in the scale spirituality [sic]. The people here are different from any class of persons I had even imagined. . . . Observation and experience have taught us since we left home the unwelcome lesson that separation from gospel influences has rendered them quite indifferent to gospel truth . . . while their being far removed from those restraints under which they had previously lived has produced unfavorable and debasing effects upon their morals, habits and views.[22]

The mining frontier was demographically, socially, and economically distinct from the farming frontier, but neither yielded few easy victories for Christ. Early mining society was even more impermanent, and religion there found rivals in gambling, drinking, and prostitution. Mining camps full of men without families often provided larger Sabbath congregations and more ready cash, but no more conversions or serious commitments.[23]

If the home mission field was challenging, then the Methodist approach to it may have created special burdens for its clergy. Because the *whole* church was perceived as a missionary body, little in the way of special home missionary organization evolved in nineteenth-century Methodism. New frontier circuits usually were established by a neighboring annual conference and then gathered into a separate grouping responsible for overseeing its own religious development and much of its monetary sustenance. This process of simply extending circuits meant little continuing financial support for Methodist missionary activity on the frontier, and also little central direction for the church's missionary work as a whole.

By contrast, other Protestant denominations set up independent boards which supervised, coordinated, and assisted their churches' home missions financially for years. The American Home Missionary Society, for example, sent hundreds of Congregational and Presbyterian ministers to settle in the West, paid at least part of their salaries, and offered vital moral encouragement to sustain their efforts. Regular communication with the central mission board was an important psychological link for those clergy, and the financial benefits were a welcome relief. Methodist domestic missionary efforts appear inadequate and poorly organized by comparison. By financial indices, by the end of the century, the American Home Missionary Society and the New and Old School Presbyterians had spent $35 million to organize and sustain western missionary work, while the

Methodist Episcopal churches, North and South, had spent only $18.5 million.[24]

Lacking adequate support, the western Methodist itinerant and his family often lived precariously close to, or actually on a poverty level. Although the quarterly conference established low clergy salaries, preachers often were unable to collect even those sums from church members. More often than not, no parsonage was provided, which meant that the missionary family would either pay rent or build its own house (which it could expect to leave at the end of a year or two). The economic situation of the Methodist clergy was so desperate at times that many itinerants were forced to "locate" and abandon the active ministry altogether. William Roberts, superintendent of the Oregon Mission (one of the few mission areas so designated, and then only for four years), suggested the basic and unresolved nature of this matter of support when he reported in 1849:

My idea is on every circuit let the preacher go and live, if no house can be had otherwise let him build one. . . . Then let there be a barn and a garden. . . . Then whatever time the preacher spends in work at home at house or fence or garden or pasture it is directly promoting the work of the itinerancy and not for private personal interest.[25]

Circuit riding itself had real drawbacks. The American Home Missionary Society encouraged a settled clergy, although most Presbyterian and Congregational ministers did, in fact, travel. The Methodist itinerancy, by contrast, involved constant travel over rough terrain. In the Pacific Northwest, for instance, traveling was so hazardous that the ministers tended to establish themselves in one place, as did the Blaines in Seattle.[26] On the mining frontier, where population was clustered, ministers also tended to "locate." But the missionary thrust of Methodism was based on an itinerating clergy who preached to communities, instructed the faithful, and then departed, leaving the responsibility for maintaining the community religious life to class leaders and local preachers.[27]

Although Methodists have widely praised the itinerancy as the ministerial system best adapted to frontier life and have pointed for proof to the emergence by mid-century of Methodism as the largest Protestant denomination, there is reason to believe that itinerating posed serious problems. An exhausted and impermanent clergy (not only making rounds on their circuits but changing circuits every two or three years) was scarcely able to make forceful and sustained contact with local church members or potential members. Strong lay leaders were essential to the success of the itinerant clergy, but the extraordinary mobility of frontier society made continuous lay support problematical. Indeed, a study of Methodism in Oregon has suggested that growth in membership did not tell the whole story. For most of the second half of the nineteenth century, the Methodist Church's growth failed to keep pace with the increase in the state's population.[28]

Thus frontier ministries were characterized by conditions that drained energy away from spiritual commitment and could easily hinder missionary effectiveness. In 1847, John Fields, a presiding elder in Texas, traveled to Kentucky, where he married Winna Duncan. His journal described their early missionary months in all their emotional and physical impact.

In January . . . we set out for my new home. . . . After wading and swimming mud and water and staying in the most miserable huts at night we reached Kaufman. . . . My poor wife bore it all with uncommon cheerfulness and fortitude. But when we arrived my house was not yet finished. . . . [We] finally moved into a log cabin 16 feet square, without door, shutters, without kitchen or anything to put in it. Thus we lived one year, from hand to mouth, when we could get it. . . . I travelled my district for which I realized about $300. The expense and trouble of moving was great; and the privations after reaching there still greater. The country new—provisions scarce and high, the season extremely wet and sickly. At last my wife and I both took sick and lay for weeks without much attention.[29]

Yet despite the hazards, many wives were determined to do their "duty." As Kate Blaine explained in an 1854 letter to her family, "Our position is a very important one. . . . We are . . . imprinting characters on a blank sheet and as every mark shows, it is important that each should be correctly made."[30] A Methodist preacher made his marks by preaching, visiting, organizing, instructing, examining his flock; by assisting conversions, and if ordained, distributing the sacraments; and by encouraging commitment to a regular Christian life. But what was the path of duty for his missionary helpmate? Few women recorded their activities in the home mission field, and the Methodist picture must be pieced together from scattered references, since Methodists did not send back regular reports to eastern mission boards as did other domestic missionaries. Clearly the Methodist wives' evangelical work was more varied and more important than Eaton had suggested, and the boundary between female "lay" and male "clerical" efforts was, in practice, often hazy. Clearly also, some clergy wives encroached upon what Eaton had held to be male prerogatives.

A woman's evangelical participation varied, of course, according to her individual commitment, domestic situation, and location. Some, perhaps most, wives played a minor role in religious affairs. But a sufficient number of women are glimpsed functioning as active evangelists to suggest their importance in missionary work. Several, for example, traveled the circuit with their husbands. Jane Poe "labored and suffered in the Methodist itinerancy" in Texas, while Fanny Adriance accompanied her husband in Colorado. At the end of arduous trips, women shared whatever primitive accommodations were available. "It is astonishing to see the people from different states," a shocked Kate Blaine remarked. "When Mrs. Swaford was fixing the bed for us to sleep in, she asked me if we slept in sheets."[31]

Pastoral visitation was one of the itinerant's main responsibilities, and riding the circuit meant visiting. It was an opportunity to assess individual spiritual health and denominational vigor and allowed clergy to respond to varied needs. A trip with her husband took Kate to "a family where the man is disaffected and wants to leave the church. . . . We find on going about that there is considerable dissatisfaction existing among the members. . . . Don't know whether it can be removed or whether the disaffected ones will leave the church."[32]

Doubtless Kate, like her husband, tried to mediate discontent and counsel their hosts. Records reveal wives caring for the sick and dying, and even preparing bodies for burial, in the course of itinerant visiting. Summing up the contributions of one California clergy wife, the writer pointed out, "Whatever of success has attended the labors of Iry Taylor, much of it is due to [his wife]. She went with him in his rounds of pastoral visitation, talked and prayed with the people." Few, the account emphasized, "have done more than she in actual work for the salvation of souls."[33]

Wives often played other highly visible evangelical roles. In a setting where religious indifference was rife, their active participation encouraged others to join in. Kate Blaine reported she was being "as Methodistical as I can, Brother and Sister the people . . . always kneel in meeting . . . and if I chose, I could hardly avoid taking part in prayer meeting, as there are so few."[34] Anne Taylor was an even more conspicuous attention-getter as she accompanied her husband in his street preaching. In the primarily male environment of San Francisco, Anne's presence and hymn-singing helped gather crowds and reactivate forgotten faith by recalling pious mothers and early religious practices. Her husband called her his " 'sweet singer in Israel' [who] . . . has stood by me in every battle."[35]

Some wives played even more instrumental roles in facilitating conversions. Not only did Rebecca, Orceneth Fisher's wife, cook at California camp meetings in the 1850s, but she also "would enter the altar at night and point penitents to the world's Redeemer." That Rebecca was an active evangelist able to take advantage of spiritual opportunities and cool under fire was evident in an unexpected incident during one camp meeting. "When the altar was full of mourners, and Sister Fisher was leading in an earnest prayer," an opponent threw an explosive into the crowd. Rebecca realized she could take advantage of the incident. "Instead of confusing her, she became more earnest," the account reveals. "The 'Amens' to her petitions were more hearty, the faith of the Church rose, and as a result they had very many conversions soon after."[36]

Wives who remained at home while their husbands rode

the circuit often sought out spiritual opportunities in the neighborhood. Many established schools and Sabbath schools. Others embarked alone on rounds of pastoral visiting and counseling.[37] The spiritual nature of these activities was evident in Jane Poe's letter to her absent husband. She spoke of "Dr. W.," who was seeking conversion without success. When Dr. W. became ill, he became desperate. Jane reported the sick man had "sent for me both by night and day, to sing and pray with him, and about two days before his death he found peace and died very happy." While Jane claimed no special credit, she clearly had played an important part in bringing about the conversion. "To be made the humble instrument in the hand of the blessed Savior, of plucking that brand from eternal burnings, more than compensates for all the sacrifices we have made," she modestly declared.[38]

Methodist clergy wives also assumed the undramatic but important duty of fundraising, to help create and maintain the symbols that assisted missionary work. When the Reverend Gober arrived in Sacramento in 1851, he found a mortgaged church and a backsliding congregation. His wife walked the streets and collected money to pay off the debt.[39]

Such financial contributions were not unusual, and perhaps Kate Blaine's maintenance work was not either. After much effort, the Blaines managed to erect a small church in Seattle. "The people came in with all the mud on their shoes, and stuck them up on the seats before them," Kate reported. "Mothers let their children stand on the seats, the nasty tobacco chewers squirted their juice around. . . . We have no sexton and cannot afford to hire one . . . so I went at it today and have made it quite tolerable."[40]

As evangelicals and as helpmates, clergy wives participated in the western ministry far more actively than Eaton's handbook sanctioned, but at a price. The physical demands on women were heavy. William Taylor, who helped his wife with housekeeping, frankly called it "drudgery." "The idea of a regular servant in a preacher's family . . . was out of the question," he noted.[41] Another part of the price to clergy wives was psychological. Home missionary work was far more difficult than anticipated. Early hopes for conversion evaporated. Staunch adherents seemed few and far between. Old friends and supporters were hundreds, if not thousands of miles away. So few were the signs of success in the Blaine ministry that Kate asked herself whether they had identified their duty correctly.[42]

Men, of course, also became discouraged, but their wives carried a double burden. Not only did they feel disheartened by their own lack of success, but most thought they were responsible for alleviating their spouses' depression and for encouraging their persistence. One frontier wife sent a revealing confession to *Woman's Home Missions* in 1887. The hardships of missionary work had weakened her faith, she admitted, for "it seemed as if God had deserted us." Self-absorbed, she suddenly realized that her husband "had let go too!" Her response was to feel responsible for him. "Rebellious despair" was replaced by guilt and mortification for thinking of herself before her husband's needs. " 'I've been to blame,' " she told him. " 'I ought to have helped you. We will ask him together to forgive us.' "[43]

And although wives consistently raised money for the church, they worried about the fearful load of debts they were called upon to assume. "The debt of $800.00 to $900.00 on this church [in Steilacoom] strikes terror to my heart," Kate Blaine wrote, hoping not to be assigned to that place.[44] Some women went so far as to wonder whether raising money was not a diversion from their duty. Ellen Briggs responded in agitation to her husband's new assignment, which included a half-completed church and unpaid debts: "My wondering eyes saw it not. In what respect 'fine!' [A church] too large for the demand, crushing in its outlay to members. . . . I felt sure the Master had need of my toiler just then outside of bricks and mortar."[45] Ellen questioned the misuse of her husband's talents; some women must have considered the misuse of their own.

Women also felt the pressures of conflicting domestic and religious demands. At best, any balance established was a delicate one, accomplished after much struggle. Chloe Willson, whose charge of teaching children she considered "small but a very precious one," wrote in her journal of her trials. Her husband was away, she said, "seeking the wandering souls of men." But she had stayed at home. "I had a severe struggle . . . in my mind between duty and affection to my companion, duty to my scholars seems to say stay; affection to my companion, go! After a severe struggle I decided upon denying self and doing duty."[46] Chloe did not say whether her companion had tried to influence her decision, but some men did and protested when their priorities clashed with their wives'. Elkanah Walker (a Congregationalist but an itinerant) felt his wife's duty lay first to him and their missionary work, not to home and children. "To live without you is the greatest earthly sacrifice I have to make. . . . You have no idea how strong is my feeling on this point," he announced. "You gave yourself to be a minister's wife before you became a wife and mother."[47] Such records only hint at the difficulties and anxieties inherent in missionary marriage.

Women entering the mission field as newlyweds found they must reconsider their responsibilities upon the arrival of children. Then some, like Mary Walker, withdrew to devote themselves, at least temporarily, to home duties. Others consciously redefined duty as motherhood. Chloe Willson explained:

Mothers have as powerful an influence over their children as all other earthly forces combined. I feel my need of help from on high that I may work in my family circle blamelessly before God. It is true that those of my sex may sometimes do good in public but the family circle is the place when there is influence once exerted [it] . . . is felt forever.[48]

Not all were content with their choices, however, and even Chloe worked in a Juvenile Temperance Society. "I fear I am not reconciled," one woman flatly declared. "I thought my duties would be almost wholly spiritual. I have felt unhappy because I have not been able to teach. I came here for that purpose . . . but if domestic toiles [sic] are to be my care I will yield obediently."[49]

The decision to reduce activities represented a double loss to wives—the loss of a field of usefulness and also of their life's companion. Husbands left home on church business, leaving wives behind to children and loneliness. It may be that by moving so often, Methodist clergy wives had fewer opportunities to establish local ties to compensate for a husband's absence. In any case, once alone, their thoughts often turned to distant friends. "My feelings, as I muse over our isolated position—far, far away from those to whom my heart is bound by . . . I will not attempt to describe," Mary Deininger declared.[50] Kate Blaine was equally lonesome: "Another Sunday and I alone. . . . I have been alone so much I get homesick, sometimes I can hardly be contented to stay here."[51]

Other women determinedly juggled domestic and missionary responsibilities. Despite having three young children, Anne Taylor accompanied her husband in his street preaching. Rebecca Fisher's pastoral activities continued. There were rewards, and also costs to omnicompetence, in terms of exhaustion, stress, and poor health. It is revealing that the women's husbands remarked on their wives' health. Rebecca's was so bad at times that she abandoned her teaching.[52]

Financial matters presented another burden. Domestic missionary wives often contended with pressures that dragged them down into that material world considered so inappropriate for nineteenth-century women. Niggardly support for Methodist ministers pushed their wives to work for Mammon rather than for God. They ran schools and boarding houses, and sold milk, eggs, vegetables, and butter while husbands itinerated. Only the need to keep up appearances prevented Kate Blaine from taking in washing.[53]

Economic projects threatened to overshadow evangelical concerns. Certainly Kate devoted more space in her letters to economic affairs than to spiritual ones. And although one author insisted that Melinda Stateler, wife of a well-known western missionary, was not guilty of this, he did admit that her "disposition to look after things" led "some who had only a partial acquaintance with her and saw only this side of her character" to think her worldly.[54] But what choice did these wives have but to plunge into economic affairs? Without their contribution, so grim a poverty loomed that even earnest believers could lose faith or desert the ministry, as did Texas itinerant John Denton. He took up the law, explaining, with inexact punctuation: "Circumstances prevent me from doing as I would consequently must do as I can. at present you have never yet my [brother, been] compelled to struggle with the Cheerless gloom of poverty and misfortune. Burdened with a large and helpless family."[55]

When balancing evangelical fervor and economic needs proved impossible, couples such as the Dentons abandoned the itinerancy, although those with the deepest sense of calling and duty resisted this step. But contemporary comments and a few studies suggest that some ministers located, at least temporarily, to recoup their family fortunes. Between 1861 and 1870, thirty-four Methodist ministers entered Colorado; by 1870 there were only eighteen in the field.[56] Though there is no direct evidence that the missing sixteen located or that family pressures were involved, there is some reason to think that both these conjectures are accurate. Some sources show that women, who carried so many of the burdens of missionary life, sought the change. California itinerant Isaac Owens refused to locate, but his journal shows wifely pressure. "At home," he noted succinctly in October 1860. "O how pleasant to spend a few days with my family. My wife has made great sacrifices for the church and the cause of God. . . . Would be pleased if I would consent to locate."[57]

Although such steadfast itinerants as Owens are best remembered, their wives pass swiftly through the pages of Methodist history with cheerful persistence. But here and there are suggestions of greater complexity alongside courage and strength. Curiously, while her husband spent most of his later life roving in the foreign mission field, Anne Taylor remained in California. And an Arkansas presiding elder candidly wrote, "My wife says she is worse off spiritually than before we entered the itinerancy; that I was preaching to save others and allowing my family to go to the devil. If she ever had any sympathy with my itinerancy I cannot perceive it."[58]

Ellen Briggs, by 1908 an elderly clergy wife, addressed the Ministers' Wives Association during the annual conference at Pacific Grove, with lavish praise for the early women in the

California mission field. Fifty-five years earlier, Kate Blaine had written of young Ellen Briggs, "Soon after Mrs. Briggs' arrival . . . she wrote back to her friends, expressing herself dissatisfied with everything and very homesick. . . . She may by this time have become more reconciled."[59] Ellen *had* become reconciled. In 1908 she hinted, however, at the requirements for becoming that steadfast wife, describing herself as "intensely loyal to my church," but one who "dared to question." Of Isaac Owens' wife, she said, "She kept the homefire bright, and gave her husband to church enterprises. All honor to self-denial." But she added, "Who would seek the honor?" Ellen Brigg's words at the end of a full life give a provocative glimpse into the inner world of some clergy wives, when new opportunities, ill-defined and often troublesome, opened up for women on the frontier mission field. The very fragmentariness of Ellen's report spurs us to further investigation of that "unwritten history of . . . parsonage homes" where, she proudly claimed, lay "laurel crowns for their mistresses."[60]

HISPANIC CLERGY WIVES

Clotilde Falcón Náñez

Despite their rich service and significant influence in the church, ministers' wives never have received special training for their vocation. To enter this important path of service to the institutional church and the local community, all that was necessary was love for a man who felt called to be a minister of Christ. No special academic preparation at seminary, no in-service training, no special counseling has been provided to orient new clergy wives. Simply the question, "Wilt thou have this man to be thy wedded husband . . . ?" and the bride's traditional reply, "I will," have initiated them into their demanding womanly and paraecclesiastical roles.

For the first Hispanic clergy wives in the Methodist connection, the challenge was compounded by the fact that they were converts from a religious tradition in which there were no clergy wives. Clerical celibacy was and is the law of the Roman Catholic Church. Therefore, among their own people, they had no patterns to follow, no examples to copy, no one to give them intimate guidance.[1]

In order to grasp the role and contribution of Hispanic clergy wives to Methodism in the Southwest, one first needs to consider the special history of Spanish-speaking people in that region. These Hispanic Americans include descendants of the first white European settlers of the lands that are now part of the United States. Many are descended also from people who had lived across these lands long before 1492—those people whom Columbus misnamed Indians. Many years prior to the landing of the Pilgrims at Plymouth Rock, there were thriving Spanish colonial communities from Saint Augustine, Florida, to New Mexico, and throughout the present Southwest. Santa Fe claims to have the oldest house in the United States, built by Indians about A.D. 1200 and rebuilt by the Spaniards in 1540.[2]

Christianity was first brought to the New World by Spanish settlers and missionaries, and within the first quarter of the seventeenth century, when English settlement was barely begun in Virginia and Massachusetts, fifty churches were built in New Mexico by twenty-six friars. A small organ with gilt pipes was even brought to Santa Fe in 1610.[3]

The type of Christianity brought by the Spaniards was influenced by their historical experience in the Old World. Christians on the Hispanic peninsula had long lived side by side with Judaism and Islam and had carried on a protracted crusade against the latter, developing a militant and fervent version of the faith in the process. When Christian Castile finally conquered Muslim Granada in 1492, the inhabitants of the entire peninsula were forced to adopt Christianity as the state religion. Jews and Muslims either converted or left the country. Spanish Catholicism was patriotic and intolerant.

Columbus discovered the New World for the Queen of Castile in the very year Granada fell. Soon after, when Pope Alexander VI granted Castile all Western lands discovered and to be discovered, he did so with the proviso that the natives should be Christianized.[4] The deep religious feeling of the Spanish colonists is reflected in the names given to their settlements and discoveries: the cities of Corpus Christi, Santa Fe, and Los Angeles; the Sierra Madre and Sangre de Cristo mountains; the Brazos de Dios and Sacramento Rivers. Cities with names beginning with San ("Saint") are almost innumerable: San Augustin, San Antonio, San Francisco. Columbus himself, after kissing the land he had discovered, named it San Salvador.

Spanish influence and action continued dominant in what we call the Southwest into the nineteenth century. On January 21, 1821, King Philip VII of Spain gave Moses Austin permission to bring three hundred families to colonize uninhabited lands in Texas. The settlers were to be Roman Catholic and were to take an oath of allegiance to the sovereign of Spain. After winning its independence from Spain, Mexico revalidated the concession in 1823, adding the specification that the settling families were to be European.

Actual settlements in Texas did not comply with these specifications, however: The immigrants were from North America and most of them were Protestant. Although there also had been some migration of Anglo Americans to other sections of the Southwest, the entire area from the Gulf of Mexico to the Pacific still belonged to Mexico in the first half of the nineteenth century and contained the largest concentration of Spanish-speaking people ever annexed to the United States—a more or less homogeneous group of Mexican descent and Roman Catholic background. The Southwest became a part of the United States with the Treaty of Guadalupe Hidalgo in 1848, which ended the war the United States called the Mexican-American War, but known in Mexico as "the American Invasion."[5]

This Hispanic and Indian past is part of the heritage of the present United States. It is a past usually gone over very lightly, but it gives Mexican Americans pride in their distinctive ancestry and background, and a reluctance to disappear as an ethnic group. We may underscore the fact that the Spanish-speaking settlers in the Southwest did not come to the United States; the United States came to them. Overnight, Mexicans found themselves owing allegiance to another nation, a nation they had but recently fiercely fought. The aftereffects of wars last for many generations. It would have been surprising had invaders and invaded, conquerors and conquered easily embraced one another, while differences in language, customs, ethnic background, and religious sentiments reinforced the results of the original military conflict. These differences were more clear-cut and sharply defined in the nineteenth century, although it would be naïve to say they no longer exist.

From the first, Anglo-American Protestants who settled in the Southwest were appalled at the lack of biblical knowledge among the native population. Itinerant Methodist preachers had been preaching to English-speaking settlers even before freedom of worship had become a reality with Texas independence in 1836. As early as 1834, a Methodist layman, David Ayers, began to distribute Bibles in the Spanish language, and a Methodist minister, James P.

Stevenson of the Mississippi Conference, was appointed to the "Texas Mission."[6]

Mounting tensions over slavery and the ensuing division of the Methodist Episcopal Church in 1844 largely halted Methodist work among Spanish-speaking people, however. In 1850, the Methodist Episcopal Church created a district in New Mexico, commissioning Enoch C. Nicholson to serve primarily the English-speaking population of Santa Fe, with the provision that "the progress of the mission must determine whether its attention will be turned at all to the Spanish-speaking population."[7]

Interest in evangelizing the Spanish-speaking group was not renewed until several years after the Civil War; thus continuous work by antecedent bodies of The United Methodist Church among Hispanic communities in the Southwest has been in effect for just over one hundred years. During the past century, however, these have been among the most progressive and aggressive denominations in this mission field.

The pioneer Spanish-speaking Methodist ministers were natives of Mexico who had been converted from Roman Catholicism. Benigno Cardenas, a "rebellious" Catholic priest who had been suspended by his bishop, was the first Methodist minister in New Mexico. He never married, so there was no clergy wife. Alejo Hernandez, a disillusioned student for the priesthood, was ordained in the West Texas Conference on December 21, 1871, and sent to launch evangelical work in Laredo. The following year, he married a young lady in Monterrey, Mexico. This first Hispanic Methodist clergy wife remains anonymous, however, because her name is not mentioned in any of the church records. Oral tradition of the Hernandez family preserves these details: She married Alejo against her family's wishes, since he was a Protestant; years later, one of their daughters attended the new Laredo Seminary (now Holding Institute) and died there during an epidemic.[8]

The growth of Spanish-speaking Methodism was remarkable. There were three basic reasons for this.

1. There was spiritual hunger among the Spanish-speaking population. When the Roman Catholic Church in the

Southwest passed from control of the Mexican hierarchy to that of the United States, many priests returned to Mexico, and most of their replacements did not speak Spanish.

2. In their former church the liturgy was in Latin, which the people could not understand, but the services of the Methodists were in Spanish. This made Methodism highly attractive.

3. In the religious tradition in which they had been brought up, the Bible was a forbidden book, whereas Methodism provided Spanish Bibles and encouraged the people to read them. This freedom to read and interpret the Scriptures was a strong point for gaining converts and contributed significantly to the rapid growth of Methodism.

In 1874 a Mexican Border Missionary District was organized in the West Texas Conference of the Methodist Episcopal Church, South, with three Mexican ministers and an Anglo-American presiding elder. By 1885, after eleven years, it had become the Mexican Border Mission Conference with thirty-one ministers under appointment. Because of language and cultural affinities, the conference pursued evangelical work in both the United States and Mexico.

Almost simultaneously, educational work began. Both the Methodist Episcopal Church and the Methodist Episcopal Church, South, realized the importance of teaching religion and training a native ministry. Schools were established in strategic cities from California to Texas, as well as in Mexico. Because the Hispanic people did not look with favor on coeducation, separate schools were founded for girls. Harwood School, in Albuquerque; Effie Eddington, in El Paso (later merged with Lydia Patterson Institute); and Holding Institute, in Laredo were three such schools where many young women who later married Methodist ministers received their education. Great emphasis was given to Bible studies and religious services, and many students joined the Methodist church. The teachers and missionaries on these faculties were deeply committed Christians who inculcated in their students high moral and spiritual values and set excellent examples for them to follow.

As has been suggested, little is known of the wives of the

first Spanish-speaking Methodist ministers except for incidents recalled by their descendants, who heard them from parents or grandparents. From these vignettes we deduce, however, that these women contributed much to the expansion of Methodism, both in the United States and in Mexico. They endured many hardships and were true pioneers in the faith. In spite of very limited economic resources, since salaries for Spanish-speaking ministers were meager, these clergy wives gave their homes love, grace, and amenity. Since their daily lives were like an open book in their communities, their example had an impact.

Real courage was required to become an "evangelical": Protestant Hispanics were dubbed traitors to the faith of their parents; they were socially ostracized and became objects of mockery and even persecution. In the United States, Spanish-speaking Methodists constituted a minority within a minority. Genuine conviction and a sense of mission were necessary to withstand the initial trials which, in the long run, however, strengthened their faith.

One courageous Methodist clergy wife of whom we have substantial knowledge was Rosaura Garcia de Grado.[9] She was born in Guerrero, Tamaulipas, Mexico, in 1872 and married a pioneer Methodist minister, Pedro Grado. Pedro had studied jurisprudence and was a highly educated man, very energetic, with a keen sense of justice. After his marriage he was appointed to Durango, Mexico, and in 1891, he and Rosaura made the arduous trip from the border of Texas to Durango in a small cart drawn by a burro. In Durango, Grado held a public debate with a priest, Father Irineo Durán, with the understanding that the loser would join the winner's church. The priest was the loser. He became a Methodist and the Grado family treasured his cassock for many years. This incident, however, created antagonism toward Grado.

The following year Pedro and Rosaura were sent to Cuencamé. There he visited inmates in the penitentiary, distributing tracts and talking about the love of Christ, and succeeded in converting a few prisoners.[10]

The fanatics in Cuencamé, however, resented these conversions. One night while the service in the small

Methodist church in Cuencamé was in progress, two men wearing sombreros and woolen ponchos entered and sat down on the bench near the only door. The congregation was made up mostly of women and children, as was customary at that time. When the service ended and the congregation left, the two men remained seated. When the pastor walked up to greet them, Rosaura Grado was directly behind him, carrying the kerosene lamp and the big iron key to the door of the church. Her sister followed, carrying the Grados' baby in her arms. Suddenly Rosaura saw one of the men pull a dagger from his poncho! She did not lose any time, but gave the man a mighty blow on the hand with the huge key! The dagger fell to the floor and she immediately picked it up. Dumbfounded, the assailant ran out the door, with his frightened companion close behind.

As has been noted, the work of the conference covered territory on both sides of the Rio Grande River. In 1914, at a time of great political unrest, Pedro Grado was appointed to serve La Trinidad Church in Pharr, Texas, in the Rio Grande valley, where Anglo Americans were then settling. At the same time, neighboring Mexico was in the throes of its revolution, and many refugees were crossing the border. Great distrust and fear, intensified by differences in language, culture, and economic well-being, existed between Hispanic and Anglo Americans. Vigilantism broke out, and as one critic bluntly stated, "Killing Mexicans was a sport in parts of the Southwest."[11]

One day a friend sent Pedro Grado word that his name was in the "little black book" which contained those who were shortly to be picked up by Rangers. He had attracted vengeance by preaching openly against the injustices being committed. Grado narrowly escaped to Reynosa, Mexico, just across the Rio Grande. La Trinidad was left without a pastor, but Rosaura Grado substituted for her husband magnificently. She had a beautiful soprano voice and had always sung in the choir. Now she also preached, visited the sick, and carried on the work of the church until the next meeting of the annual conference, when Grado was appointed to Seguin.

At Seguin a different type of problem developed. Texas

schools were segregated, and the one-room public school for Mexican children had only one teacher. Believing avidly in education, Rosaura took her children to nearby San Marcos to attend better schools. In the very cold winter of 1916, she developed pneumonia and died. The memory of her love, tenacity, and courage persists, however, to this day.

Another notable "pioneer in the parsonage" was Isabel Hill de Verduzco.[12] Unlike most Spanish-speaking Methodist clergy wives of the later nineteenth century, Isabel was a native Texan, born in Bandera on February 6, 1873. She also was unusual in that she was a third-generation Methodist. Her mother was the daughter of José Policarpo Rodríguez, one of the first Spanish-speaking converts to Methodism and a very famous Texas pioneer. Her father, James J. Hill, was Anglo American. Isabel was completely bilingual and received her education at the Laredo Seminary and at Colegio Inglés (Colegio Roberts) in Saltillo, Mexico.

In 1900 she married Pablo G. Verduzco and as a clergy wife, began a vocation of Christian service which she declared to be her life's greatest joy. During World War I, Isabel taught in the army school at Fort McIntosh, Texas. In 1934 her husband was appointed to Port Arthur, Texas, where he died in 1937. Mrs. Verduzco, then sixty-four, stayed on in Port Arthur and continued to help the Mexican-American people as she had done from the day of her arrival. Most legal documents were brought to her for interpretation; all Port Arthur's lawyers, and the doctors, personnel directors, and employment supervisors knew Isabel Verduzco, for she worked closely with them on her people's behalf.

Isabel taught citizenship classes for the Bureau of Immigration and Naturalization and frequently served as witness for people seeking citizenship papers. She recalled, "I once felt called upon to tell the inspector at Beaumont that I was a pastor's wife and thus known to so many people, for I felt sure he wondered why I was always the witness." She also related this incident: "One night a man knocked at my door and asked me to give him a passport. I had a very hard time convincing him that I did not issue passports, but that he had to go to the Immigration Bureau."

During World War II, Mrs. Verduzco returned to teaching, holding Spanish classes in her home and counting among her pupils some of Port Arthur's outstanding citizens. She became known affectionately as *la madrina de los Mexicanos* ("the godmother of the Mexicans").

When advancing age forced her to move to Louisiana to live near her only son Paul, the Port Arthur newspaper interviewed Isabel Verduzco and paid her a well-deserved tribute. In the interview this unusual clergy wife summed up her life simply: "I have done almost everything from selling insurance and real estate to teaching, but my main interest has been and always will be helping people."[13]

Because she had given so much of herself without expecting anything in return, Isabel Verduzco was truly loved and respected. She lived to be ninety-nine and died at Hico, Texas, in 1972. Her son caught the sense of the resurrection in her life when he said soon after her death, "She was a great Christian lady, and I know where she and Dad are, and I too will join them there."[14]

In important ways Mexican culture has strengthened the influence and the roles of Spanish-speaking Methodist clergy wives beyond those of their Anglo-American counterparts. Especially among Mexicans, the Hispanic tradition of *machismo* delegates the observance of religion to women. Anticlericalism has long pervaded male culture, and frequent church-going was considered effeminate. It is not strange therefore that Protestants made converts first among women. Even today some local United Methodist Hispanic congregations are made up mostly of women and children.

As a result, a major concern for Methodist ministers and their wives has continued to be the involvement of Spanish-speaking men in the congregations and the recruitment of men for the ordained ministry. At a meeting of the annual conference in the early 1940s, Maria Vidaurri, a minister's wife, was asked to lead the devotions. She was known as a powerful speaker and used the occasion to challenge young men to enter the ministry. She chose as her text the question Samuel asked Jesse in the Old Testament: *"¿Hanse acabado los mozos?"* (literally, "Aren't there any more young men left?" [I Sam. 16:11]).

The tradition of *machismo* has in fact both motivated and allowed women to play a very important part in the Spanish-speaking work of Methodism. The shortage of men opened doors for women workers, although they could not be ordained in full connection. For example, in 1920, upon the unexpected death of the pastor at Mission, Texas, Carolina A. Farias, his widow, was appointed to serve in his stead. Her effective service as her husband's co-worker and her outstanding leadership qualities prompted the superintendent to ask Carolina, who had been left with seven children, to take charge. In the conference appointments for 1920, she was listed as "missionary,"[15] and she served in that capacity until 1929; for the next two years she was assistant to the pastor. At this writing, Carolina Farias is ninety-seven.

In Spanish-speaking Methodism in the Southwest, clergy wives have led the women of the local churches and have worked devotedly to develop women's potential. These wives first organized the Hispanic Methodist women into Sociedades Femenil ("women's societies") which have been a financial mainstay of the Spanish-speaking churches.

In 1933, when the Woman's Missionary Society was originally organized in what is today the Rio Grande Conference, all the elected officers were clergy wives. The first meetings of the Sociedad Femenil were held in conjunction with the meetings of the annual conference so that the ministers' wives and the women delegates could travel with the ministers.

In 1935 the Sociedad Femenil meeting was held at the old El Mesias Church in Mission, Texas, under circumstances which reveal the dedication and bonding of Spanish-speaking clergy wives. Because of illness in their families, neither the president or the vice-president was able to attend. Angelina Moraida, the secretary, presided. She herself had been seriously ill for some time, but because she lived in nearby McAllen, she made a great effort to attend. The afternoon of the meeting was very hot, and one of the members stood by the feverish lady, fanning her with a piece of cardboard. Anxiously, the members urged her to go home to bed. Very emphatically and resolutely, Angelina Moraida replied, "As long as there is breath of life in me, the woman's work of this conference will go on." Her words made a very deep impression upon one newly married preacher's wife who attended that meeting. Without direction or counsel from anyone, lost and disoriented, that young wife was struggling to find her place in the church. Angelina Moraida died just a week or two after the meeting, but her words continued to reverberate. Someone should respond to her challenge! The torch should be picked up so that her sacrificial labor would not have been in vain. This author was that minister's wife who heard Angelina Moraida's challenge and subsequently tried to respond to it. For me, Angelina Moraida occupies a special place of gratitude.

The official organ of the conference, *El Heraldo Cristiano*, in reporting news of the local churches, mentions Mrs. Moraida often with praise. Angelina studied at Colegio Roberts in Saltillo. While she and her husband were serving in Del Rio in 1918, *El Heraldo Cristiano* reported that "Mrs. Moraida is as highly committed as she is educated, as kind as she is enthusiastic. The labor was hard but she worked diligently to prepare a most solemn and beautiful Christmas program."[16] The following year when the Methodist Episcopal Church, South, was celebrating the centenary of Methodist missions, she organized the Del Rio women of the church into the Sociedad Misionera del Centenario-Dorcas. She also wrote the words to a hymn for the conference Woman's Society and asked Vicente Mendoza to compose spirited music to encourage the women to greater effort.

Twelve presidents of United Methodist Women and its antecedent organizations in the Rio Grande Conference have been clergy wives, including the first and the present:

Cerman Luján	1933–35
Jovita O. Ramos	1935–38
Elodia A. Sada	1938–44
May J. Alvirez	1950–52
Minerva N. Garza	1952–56
Enriqueta Ch. Ibarra	1956–58
Esther Paquet	1958–62
Maria de la Luz Salazar	1962–66

Maria V. Valdez	1966–70
Norma T. Vera	1970–72
Clotilde F. Náñez	1975–77
Adela Quintanilla	1977–81

Of these twelve, only Esther Paquet, a victim of cancer, is not living at this time. The first president, Carmen Luján, though her husband has retired, is still very active in church work, especially in United Methodist Women.

Under the leadership of ministers' wives, the women's organization not only has kept abreast of conference needs, but often has helped identify them. In 1939, when three branches of American Methodism united, the two Spanish-speaking conferences in Texas and New Mexico merged to form the Southwest Mexican Conference. When the educational standard for admission of clergy into full connection was raised, many of the young Spanish-speaking ministers could not obtain the required schooling because their salaries were too low to pay tuition. Upon a motion made by a preacher's wife, the conference Woman's Society, recognizing the need, established a ministerial scholarship fund, financed through a special program presented annually in the local churches. The program also served as a challenge to young people to enter Christian service. Sixty-seven ministers in the conference were helped to attend college in order to meet the educational requirements for full connection. This work was taken over by the conference itself in 1969; the women nevertheless continue to contribute to the conference scholarship fund.

Today it would be unworkable to suggest that the women's organization meet in connection with the annual conference. Both groups have become very large. Two hundred twenty-nine women attended the 1979 annual meeting of the Rio Grande Conference United Methodist Women, held at Mt. Wesley in Kerrville, Texas. Only two ministers and four laymen were present. When Eutimio González, Sr., was introduced, he paid his wife a beautiful tribute which contains a seed of truth about the general role of clergy wives: "I thank God for my wife. She is the real pastor. I am her assistant."[17]

The women's group in the now extinct Latin-American Provisional Conference, which included Arizona and California, also was under the leadership of clergy wives, with Celia T. Dominguez and Maria G. Tirre as two outstanding examples.

A separate organization of clergy wives originated in the Rio Grande Conference in 1951. Every summer, a one-week pastors' school is held at Mt. Wesley in Kerrville, and many of the ministers' wives attend with their husbands. At times, there have been special classes on nutrition, budgeting of time and energy, financial investments, first aid, and other such practical subjects. Schedules must be arranged so that the wives can also attend the lectures for the ministers. Excerpts from a report on the women's class in *The Shepherdess,* which at one time was published exclusively for the Methodist minister's wife, reveal the sentiments of this pastors' school.

It is Monday afternoon. The preachers and their wives and children are coming in more rapidly than the registrar can take care of them. It is unbearably hot. Some have traveled 600 miles or more in cars or buses and fatigue can easily be read in their faces. But, oh! the joy of meeting their co-workers! In true Latin-American style the women embrace and kiss each other; . . . the men pat each other on the back and their outbursts of happy laughter resound all over Mt. Wesley.[18]

On the closing day of that year's class for ministers' wives in 1951, the group voted unanimously to organize the Rio Grande Conference Ministers' Wives Association and elected the first officers. The twenty clergy wives present formed a friendship circle and offered prayers for unity and the grace to carry out God's will in establishing his Kingdom on earth.

Now this association meets officially only during annual conference for a special program. The president of the association elected in June 1979, Debbie González, is one of the youngest clergy wives in the conference, but since she brings to her role a veneration for age that is typically Hispanic, she maintains an admirable rapport with the senior members. Mrs. González also teaches in the public schools.

Her husband, Hector González, Jr., plays the guitar, and they sing beautifully together.

In the century since Methodism was planted among Spanish-speaking people, with clergy wives among its leaders, it has brought special gifts to the church and to the Southwest. Some traditions treasured from the Roman Catholic past have been incorporated into Methodist Spanish services, although officially they are not part of the rituals. In the sacrament of baptism, for example, *padrinos* (godparents) are always part of the ceremony. They are not mere witnesses, but become *compadres* ("co-parents") with the parents of the baptized child. The *padrinos* will assume responsibility for the child's upbringing should anything befall the parents.

In the Roman Catholic Church, marriage is a sacrament. In the United Methodist Church, it is not. Two beautiful customs from the Roman marriage service have been incorporated into the Hispanic Methodist ceremony. One is the *arras*—the groom gives thirteen silver coins to the bride as part of his pledge. These she must keep as a sort of nest egg, should he die or should some emergency befall the family. The other is the *lazo*. While the bride and groom are kneeling for the blessing, two joined loops of orange blossoms or ribbon are placed over their heads, symbolizing that they are no longer two, but one.

Among Hispanics the celebration of a girl's fifteenth birthday is called a *quinceañera*. But in Hispanic Methodism, a service of blessing and a reception introduce the young woman to society, rather than the mass and the dance of the old tradition.

A language asset, erroneously dubbed a barrier, exists among Hispanics. In the late nineteenth century children were not taught Spanish in the public schools, and the segregation practiced at the beginning of the twentieth century reinforced the lack of educational advantage. The first year at public school was a traumatic experience for children who had been brought up in homes where the parents did not speak English; and yet after they entered school, the students were not allowed to speak Spanish. It was not until 1948 that the federal court ruled segregation of Mexican children in the public schools illegal.[19]

In the late 1800s many clergy wives started Spanish classes in the churches for both children and illiterate adults so that they could read the hymns and the Bible. Later, the annual conference requested the Women's Division of the Board of Missions to sponsor kindergartens in the Rio Grande Valley to teach the children English before they entered public school. Among the prospective teachers sent to the National College for Christian Workers in Kansas City for special training was Minerva N. Garza, a minister's wife.[20] Of the three kindergartens opened in 1947, two were served by ministers' wives. Similar schools were established by the National Division of the Board of Missions, and in most of these, too, the teacher was the minister's wife. Then Head Start was initiated by the federal government, and the churches' kindergartens became Early Childhood Development Centers, of which there are about ten in the conference now.

In the local churches, ministers' wives teach Sunday school and work in vacation church schools. On the conference level all the directors of children's work have been clergy wives. Eveli Rodríguez presently serves as that director and is also secretary to the program director of the conference.

Six years ago Perkins School of Theology in Dallas initiated a program to train Hispanic lay people as associates in Christian education. Four consecutive two-week summer courses are required for certification. Two ministers' wives, Elisa Gaytán and Rebeca Canales, will become certified in the summer of 1980.

Very early in the beginning of Methodist work in the Southwest, clergy wives learned that money for worthwhile church projects could be most easily raised by staging Mexican dinners, which consist of rice, beans, tortillas, and tamales (or tamales alone, which is the traditional Christmas dinner). On Christmas Eve, the choirs go caroling and return to the churches for a tamale supper and the midnight service. For New Year's Eve watch, the traditional *buñuelos* are served—crisp flour tortillas, fried and powdered with sugar and cinnamon.

175

During Lent, *capirotada,* a bread pudding made with nuts, raisins, sugar, and cinnamon is traditional. This delicious Mexican dish is not as well known as some others; another Lenten dish not yet accepted by Anglo Americans is *nopalitos.* This is prepared from the tender leaves of cactus, cut into small pieces after the thorns have been removed, parboiled, and then fried with egg and red chile.

Most Hispanic clergy wives play the piano and sing well, and many have organized and direct choirs in their local churches. Since most of the hymns are English, these women also have provided some of the translations. Anita G. González, a minister's wife, served on the committee which prepared the *Himnario Metodista.* Her invaluable musical knowledge enabled her to translate hymns which had not previously been printed in Spanish. The *Himnario Metodista* is now used in nearly all Spanish-speaking Methodist churches in the United States, Mexico, and Puerto Rico.

Some clergy wives have degrees in music: Anita N. Soltero majored in voice; Raquel M. Martinez, who until recently was on the staff of the Women's Division of the General Board of Global Ministries, majored in piano. Since 1975 Raquel has been composing hymns and anthems in both English and Spanish. Her latest composition was used with the study on Latin America in the 1980 Schools of Christian Mission, and others have appeared in *response* magazine and in the Program Resources Book.[21]

The Hispanic minority is young and growing. With increasing numbers comes increasing prominence, and in the last two decades Hispanics have made great strides in acceptance and recognition. One of the great assets of the Rio Grande Conference and the other Spanish-speaking churches in the Southwest is that they can assimilate and be served by ministers from Latin American countries. A survey of the 104 clergy wives presently in the conference provides an interesting study: 63 were born in the United States, 25 in Mexico, 7 in Cuba, 2 in Costa Rica, 2 in Guatemala, and one each in Argentina, Colombia, Nicaragua, Puerto Rico, and Paraguay.[22] Most of these women received excellent training in Spanish in their native countries, but because of their lack of proficiency in English, it is difficult for them to find employment comparable to their education. Two were deaconesses—one in Argentina and one in Mexico. Their beautiful delivery of the Spanish language enhances their acceptance by the constituency of the conference. They awaken our church members and the citizens of our country to a new appreciation of the liberties we take for granted and the educational opportunities and advantages we enjoy. They also alert us to the many "isms" which dominate and exploit. Their experience enriches us.

The median age of clergy wives is about forty-four; consequently, most of them will have many years of service ahead. It is interesting to note that in the roll of 32 retired ministers in the conference, only 3 are widowers, while the roll of the Board of Pensions shows 27 clergy widows.[23] Now that The United Methodist Church is ordaining women, it may be that some will enter the ministry, should they survive their husbands. Such was the case of Margarita Verver, who is now serving as a local pastor.

Equal-opportunity legislation has made it easier for women and persons from ethnic groups to gain employment. At least half the clergy wives in the Rio Grande Conference are employed outside the home. Most are teachers in the public schools; others are ministers, social workers, nurses, office workers, laboratory technicians, seamstresses, and teachers' aides. Twenty-five are college graduates, and many hold higher degrees.

The need for Spanish-speaking work in The United Methodist Church is evident. People should hear the gospel in the language they best understand, and Hispanic churches are best suited to reach the many immigrants, both documented and undocumented, who enter our country every year from the Spanish-speaking nations.

The role of "first lady of the church" is not simple or easy. It is a great responsibility, but it offers a glorious opportunity to serve humanity in the name of Christ. In the words of Paul K. McAfee,

> A shepherdess, is she, who is always there,
> Loving the shepherd through dark days and fair.[24]

9

PREPARING WOMEN
FOR THE LORD'S WORK*

Virginia Lieson Brereton

The Chicago Training School for City, Home and Foreign Missions; the New England Deaconess Home and Training School; and the Scarritt Bible and Training School—all Methodist institutions—were founded between 1885 and 1892. They pioneered in a vigorous educational movement; nearly sixty other religious training schools were opened in the United States between 1880 and 1915. Intended primarily for lay people, and most of them for women, these schools emphasized the acquisition of skills and practical experience, particularly in the areas of Bible teaching and missions.[1]

Despite their individual histories, the three institutions explored here were part of a unified educational phenomenon. Their founders were responding to the enormity of the religious tasks facing the churches in late nineteenth-century America, which Protestant leaders addressed with an increased sense of urgency. The crowding of American cities through rapid urbanization and the influx of immigrants, including many Roman Catholics, aroused the churches to the need for drastic evangelistic and humanitarian measures at home. Revivalist Dwight L. Moody warned of "hundreds of families in cities . . . never coming in contact with churches or their representatives"; he anxiously foresaw a "reign of terror such as this country has never known" if churches did not step up their evangelization efforts.[2] In

*Much of the material in this paper is derived from the author's work on Auburn Seminary's history of Protestant theological education in America, in progress and supported by the Lilly Endowment, Inc.

1906, the leaders of the New England Deaconess Home and Training School declared that "A strong effort should be made to change prevalent conditions, which admit of church bells pealing in the ears of hundreds of children who know nothing of the children's best Friend and of God's Work."[3] Other Protestant leaders lamented the woeful lack of knowledge of the English Bible, even on the part of devout Christians. Lucy Rider Meyer, founder of the Chicago Training School, recalled:

During the three or four years of my travelling Sunday-school work in Illinois and other States, I became greatly impressed with the astonishing, and to me alarming ignorance of the Bible on the part of our Church people, Sunday-school teachers, and Christian workers. . . . I realized the great need of more thorough and comprehensive Bible study.[4]

Still other writers and speakers concentrated their sights on the foreign field, unable to blot out images of the millions who had not even heard of Christ. In a typical statement, two hundred women missionaries who met in Shanghai in 1890 sent home "an urgent appeal on behalf of the 100,000,000 women and children who sit in darkness and in the shadow of death."[5]

To cope with the prodigious tasks of teaching and evangelizing at home and abroad, new agencies and organizations came into being: the Salvation Army, the Y.M.C.A. and Y.W.C.A., new and more complex missionary organizations, young people's groups, settlement houses, and city missions. Ordained ministers could not possibly staff these organizations alone; legions of lay people were also required—Sunday school teachers and administrators, pastors' assistants, home missionaries, lay evangelists, settlement workers, "Y" secretaries, and lay foreign missionaries. "This is the age of laic activity in spiritual things," intoned one Protestant leader, and others provided variations on this theme by calling for "gap-men" or "irregulars" to meet the religious emergency.[6]

American women made up the largest single group of potential lay workers, and a part of the appeal to lay people was, in fact, a plea for the mobilization of women. In reality, women long had demonstrated their eagerness to participate in the tasks of the church. In the early part of the nineteenth century, they had begun to organize local missionary societies, which after the Civil War were transformed into powerful national agencies. At that time mission board and missionary society leaders also came to realize the need for single women missionaries who could teach and evangelize women and children in other lands more effectively than could their male counterparts. "Women's work for women," became the rallying cry. In the 1880s, the diaconate emerged as an important channel for service for Methodist, Episcopal, and Lutheran women. Many deaconesses served as nurses; others pioneered as social workers or assistants to pastors. But the areas of religious teaching, evangelism, and social service also beckoned to other women who preferred not to don the deaconess garb.[7]

When they called for lay religious workers, however, most Protestant leaders did not intend to summon the untutored. In common with most other Americans, Protestants of the late nineteenth century had too much respect for schooling to sanction the sending forth of untrained and inexperienced workers, no matter how zealous. But to recruit lay workers and urge them to undertake the traditional ministerial course of high school, four years of college, and three years of theological seminary was out of the question. That span of education cost too much, took too long, was too academic to provide the actual skills and first-hand experience needed, and also would cool the enthusiasm of prospective workers. For women, such a long course was particularly unrealistic and forbidding; they seldom were welcome at theological seminaries and almost never eligible to enter the regular ministerial courses, even if they could have financed the enterprise. Indeed, opportunities for higher education were only slowly opening up to women.

But alternative forms of schooling were at hand. Training schools for nurses, teachers, salesmen, and secretaries, among others, were springing up all over the United States. Why not religious training schools as well? Missionary training institutions had existed in Europe since 1850, and some were well known in American Protestant circles.

PREPARING WOMEN FOR THE LORD'S WORK

The Religious Training Movement
in the United States

American religious training schools answered late nineteenth-century requirements admirably. In response to the emergency at home and abroad, the programs of the schools were brief—usually lasting two years— and did not detain workers unduly. Moreover, students felt free to attend for even shorter periods. In the first decade of Scarritt's history, only 107 out of a total of 264 students stayed the full two years.[8] The schools were practical: Classes were oriented toward the acquisition of skills, and students were encouraged or required to gain experience in city churches, settlement houses, or missions while they studied.

To accommodate all possible recruits, the schools were open to students with varied educational backgrounds. No dedicated soul need be left out. Prospective lay workers were more likely to be turned away for lack of religious zeal than for deficient academic preparation. At the turn of the century, it is true, few colleges or seminaries were as strict in their admission requirements as at present. But the religious training schools, with their emphasis on service rather than academic performance, outdid the more conventional institutions in extending a welcome to all possible students. Most provided English courses for those who fell below high school standards, and they also offered a variety of academic programs. In 1913, for instance, the Chicago Training School provided a "graduate division" for those who already had attended college, a "general division" for high school graduates, and a "special division" for those with less education.[9] The special division in effect served as a preparatory department at a time when most colleges were attempting to phase out such departments or already had succeeded in doing so.

If no student was prevented from attending these training schools because of poor preparation, neither did lack of financial means often stand in the way. Tuition was free and room and board usually minimal. In addition, some students received remuneration for the work they did outside the school.

The schools were relatively inexpensive to run, since they were small and the largely part-time and often heavily female faculties received little or no salary. Until about 1917, the teachers at the Chicago Training School, including the principal, earned only "deaconess allowances"; they regarded their duties primarily as opportunities for Christian service rather than as sources of income.

Within the general group of religious training schools was a large subgroup of institutions intended specifically for women and often founded and run by women. The first, the Baptist Missionary Training School, opened in Chicago in 1881. Lucy Rider Meyer launched the Chicago Training School shortly afterward, in 1885.

The Chicago Training School for City, Home and Foreign Missions

The founder of the Chicago Training School was a remarkable woman, even in a generation of exceptional churchwomen. A native of Vermont, Lucy Jane Rider graduated from Oberlin College and eventually would earn a doctor of medicine degree from Northwestern University. She first attended the Woman's Medical College of Philadelphia to prepare herself to be the wife of a medical missionary. Her intended husband died suddenly during her second year, however, causing her to interrupt her education and plunging her into despondency. The need to turn her affections and energies into other channels may explain the breadth and intensity of her subsequent activities. Before age forty, she had taught and organized Sunday schools, written for Sunday school journals, taught college chemistry, and was a frequent speaker at religious conferences and conventions.[10]

Her most prized project, however, was the creation of a school that would be primarily for the preparation of Methodist deaconesses. The idea of a training school had been broached in the Methodist Episcopal women's foreign and home missionary societies, but nothing concrete had been accomplished before Meyer turned her attention to the task. Though her first efforts went unrewarded, she did not give up. The idea of a school, she said, "colored my dreams and mingled in my prayers. I wrote letters to every one that I thought would be interested in the plan, and spun articles about it out of my brain, both real and fictitious for all the papers that I thought would publish them."[11]

In 1885, assisted by her new husband, a former Y.M.C.A. secretary, Mrs. Meyer went ahead with her plans despite lack of adequate support. With a handful of students, she opened the Chicago Training School on faith: All the teachers, including Lucy Meyer, who served as principal, went unrecompensed; the house in which the school was located was only half furnished; together students and faculty prayed for money to pay for the next meal or to meet the next bill. The first classes were in Bible and Bible history, medicine, singing, church history, and methods of teaching Sunday school. An additional feature of the program, visitation, was an early designation for practical experience; in missions of mercy, students visited the sick, the poor, and the unchurched.[12]

The work of Mrs. Meyer and her associates rapidly expanded. The Chicago Deaconess Home, connected with the training school, was opened in 1887, and the next year the Methodist Episcopal General Conference recognized both the office of deaconess and the existence of the school.[13] The practice of caring for sick people in a few rooms of the school was soon formalized by the building of a hospital.

Within twenty years, the Chicago Training School was turning out a whole range of workers: deaconesses, home and foreign missionaries, Sunday school teachers, specialists in work with children and young people, pastors' assistants, temperance workers, evangelists, pastors' wives, and experts in the new field of "home economy." The curriculum stressed the areas of Old Testament, New Testament, theology, missions, "sociology and social service," religious education, home economics, medicine, and music, in addition to the more basic subjects of English, history, and elocution.

The catalog usually listed at least one offering which chronicled the past and present accomplishments of women and urged them on to greater usefulness—a subject of particular significance in a school devoted to enabling women to take on new roles. The course, The Woman Movement, for example, dealt with the "history and development of woman's social, industrial and political activities," as well as her "domestic, social and civic opportunity." Several years later, a course in the history and genius of the deaconess movement was offered.[14]

A focus on the unique contributions of women to the solution of social and religious problems was an important feature of the training-school movement. But the women's training schools were not hotbeds of feminism. Emphasis was always on woman's responsibility, not her rights; on her service to the cause of Christ, not her leadership of it.

The New England Deaconess Home and Training School

The work of the New England Deaconess Home and Training School, founded in Boston in 1889, began on a similar humble scale. In its second year, two of its ten students died. "The Death Angel twice visited our Home," read the annual report for that year. Prospective students faced no educational prerequisites for entry; it was only necessary that they be between twenty-three and forty years of age and provide recommendations from their pastors and churches and a health certificate from their doctors. The two-year course of study offered two options: one for those planning to become nurses and another for those looking toward some other religious vocation. The faculty, all part-time, consisted mainly of area pastors and teachers. Only a woman superintendent, who had many other duties in addition to teaching, remained at the school full-time.[15]

Though the Boston institution was established by the New England Conference of the Methodist Episcopal Church, rather than by a central animating figure such as Lucy Meyer, it seems to have embarked on its course with the same sense of adventure and pride. A year after its founding, the school's annual report meticulously listed student accomplishments:[16]

Number of religious calls made........................... 6,150
Number of opportunities for singing with sick........... 122
Number of tracts distributed.............................. 1,078
Number of Bibles distributed................................. 42
Number of garments distributed............................857
Number of jars of fruit, etc. distributed.....................49
Aggregate number taught in Mission school............. 917
Aggregate number taught in Industrial school........... 564
Aggregate number taught in Sunday school............ 1,321
Aggregate number taught in children's meetings........ 629
Number of missionary and other meetings addressed.. 110

In all probability the practical work reflected in these statistics constituted as important a part of the total curriculum as the academic work, which initially amounted to little more than a reading list: the Methodist *Book of Discipline,* denominational catechisms, the English Bible, manuals and physiology textbooks for nurses, standard theological works, and books on Bible history and geography and church history. As at the Chicago Training School, New England students were encouraged to delve into the history of Methodist women, especially the deaconess movement. Among required and recommended readings were Lucy Rider Meyer's history of the deaconess movement and biographies of exemplary deaconesses.[17]

Despite limited resources, the work of the school progressed. In 1896 an associated hospital was built, enabling prospective nurses to obtain direct experience. By 1906 the school could boast one female resident teacher, a gift of $50 with which to start an endowment, and an enrollment of twenty-eight. In 1910 the number of students had climbed to thirty-seven, and in 1916, to fifty (with an additional sixty-seven extension students).[18]

The New England Training School curriculum was gradually expanded and modernized to include a mixture of typical theological seminary subjects: introduction to New Testament, life of Paul, life of Christ, Pentateuch, systematic theology, church history; and the usual training school specialties such as methods of work, practical hygiene, kindergarten and Sunday school techniques, psychology and pedagogy, domestic science, and institutional management.[19]

The practical work of the students did not diminish with the expansion of academic courses. In fact, more care than ever was devoted to the supervision of practical experience. Even the academic courses routinely dispatched students outside the school walls, as the description of the sociology class in the 1912 annual report makes clear. In addition to reading and class work, the sociology students "visited different charitable institutions, studying philanthropic activities of the City. Several fine entertainments have been given by this class at the Saturday evening Temperance Meeting at Morgan Memorial."[20]

The Scarritt Bible and Training School

In 1887, just two years after the opening of the Chicago Training School, Belle Harris Bennett, a southern Methodist and a missionary enthusiast, visited Lucy Rider Meyer in Chicago. As the result of a denominational missionary meeting in Kentucky the same year, Bennett had become keenly aware of the need for more and better-trained missionaries. When she heard that the northern Methodist, Lucy Meyer, had started a religious training school, she hastened to confer with her and soon afterward became convinced that the Lord wanted her to establish a training school for women of her denomination.

Belle Bennett did not arrive at such a resolution easily. A timid and retiring woman from a wealthy Kentucky family, she might have remained comfortably at home. A few years before, however, she had been deeply stirred by an evangelist and had dedicated herself to Christ and his service.[21]

So it was that, overcoming her timidity, she became the champion of women of the Methodist Episcopal Church, South. Southern women, she said, "longed to work in the Lord's vineyard," but could not, *"because they did not know how to work."*[22] The Woman's Foreign Missionary Society of the southern church thereupon appointed her to be the school's fund raiser and organizer; the well-known southern evangelist, Sam Jones, allowed her to plead the cause and solicit money at his camp meetings. Nathan Scarritt donated $25,000 and a building site in Kansas City, Missouri, and Scarritt was founded there in 1892. The excitement of this early period is nicely captured in this account:

With the eyes of human wisdom the enterprise seemed one of childish weakness. No money, no resources . . . committed to an earthen vessel, untried and unknown, but I went out as directed in God's strength, committing my works and my ways unto Him. . . . From the old and young and rich and poor, donations have come. . . . Women have taken earrings from their ears, and watches from their bosoms, saying, "Take these, we have no money, but we want to give something for the cause of Christ."[23]

At first Scarritt served largely as a recruiting and teaching arm of the Woman's Foreign Missionary Society. It offered a two-year course, including classes in the English Bible, Christian evidences, church history, missions, personal work, sacred music, bookkeeping, and nurse's training. About a third of the first generation of Scarritt graduates became foreign missionaries, others served as home missionaries or nurses, and some became pastors' wives.

After the first decade, Scarritt leaders devoted increasing attention to home missions. Following the establishment of the diaconate by the General Conference of the Methodist Episcopal Church, South, in 1902, southern Methodist deaconesses began to train at Scarritt in large numbers.[24] That same year, the school's board provided for a special teacher in the emerging field of sociology. The new teacher, Mabel K. Howell, gathered ideas for her post by visiting the best-known settlement houses and institutional churches in the nation. ("Institutional" churches were a recent and chiefly urban innovation; they offered social and educational programs in addition to worship services and Sunday school classes.) Howell's classes studied the social problems of poverty and crime and discussed the church's role in their solution. Under the influence of its active department of sociology, Scarritt expanded the early informal practical work to more closely supervised field work.[25] Many early Scarritt students drew their experience from a small mission in the Italian section of Kansas City, which became the first institutional church in the southern Methodist denomination.

At a time when such subjects were still foreign to many theological seminaries, Scarritt's Department of Religious Pedagogy, introduced in 1909 by a woman graduate of the Hartford School of Religious Pedagogy, offered courses in Bible pedagogy, the modern Sunday school, teacher training, organization of church work with young people and youth, child study and storytelling, and the principles and history of religious education. Gradually the school added other courses applicable to the lines of work students would enter when they graduated: domestic science, missionary languages, phonetics, art, and kindergarten training.[26]

Courses Offered by the Schools

The selection of courses at these schools at any given moment was variable, depending on who was available to teach and where her or his special interests lay. Clergymen, who frequently taught part-time, tended to offer what they themselves had learned in their seminary classes, sometimes several decades before. Once this haphazard element in the training schools' curricula is noted, however, it is possible to generalize about characteristics they shared. In addition to making do with whatever resources were available, school leaders regarded themselves as educational innovators, and certain opinions about the way Christian workers should be prepared were held in common. Their most important objectives were to promote knowledge of the English Bible, provide a high proportion of practical subjects, and expose their students to varied forms of religious work by sending them outside the schools.

Bible study was of first importance in all the schools. The late nineteenth century was a time of renewed Protestant fascination with the Bible, whether in the form of preoccupation with biblical prophecy or enthusiasm for modern biblical scholarship. Training schools differed in their approach, but all were mindful of protests such as that of one bishop: "How often have we heard young missionaries cry out, 'Oh, I cannot teach the Bible; I do not know where to begin. Would that I had been trained before I reached the field!' "[27] School leaders agreed that prospective Christian workers must know their Bible intimately. Thus the first teaching chair at Scarritt was the $25,000 Belle Harris Bennett Chair of the English Bible, for which funds were raised by 1899. In the opening year of the Chicago Training School, the Bible was studied five times a week, more time than was devoted to any other subject. At the New England deaconess school, students traversed the whole of the Old and New Testaments, "book by book."[28]

This intensive study of the English Bible was expected to make a palpable difference for the students. First, it was to guide them in their approach to the unchristian. If only a training school student were acquainted intimately enough with biblical texts, it was thought, she would be able to recall just the right passage to soften the heart of the most hardened sinner.[29] On a more personal level, familiarity with the Bible was expected to improve the worker's own conduct; the memory of a particular verse from Scripture, it was assumed, would safely direct her behavior during difficult times.

In addition, Bible study at all three schools involved learning how to teach it. Storytelling techniques which capitalized on the inherent interest in biblical narratives ranked high. For example, a course at the Chicago Training School entitled Popular Bible Stories offered "subjects selected from both the Old and New Testaments" and was specifically "designed to give not only instruction in subject matter, but suggestions as to methods of presenting Bible addresses and studies to popular audiences."[30] Students even learned to illustrate their stories with simple drawings.

The insistence upon the practical uses of Bible knowledge partially explains the training schools' attention to the English Bible, to the virtual exclusion of the Hebrew, Greek, or Latin texts. Study of biblical languages was considered too time consuming and was thought to lead to a temptation to talk above the heads of ordinary people, a fault not unknown among male ministers.

The curriculum of each school was designed to teach the students, in the shortest possible time, exactly what they needed to know in order to become effective Christian workers. The very word *training* in the school names reflected this emphasis on brevity and practicality.

In espousing these principles, training-school educators participated in the spirit of their times. Late nineteenth-century Americans commonly rejoiced in the practical, the effective, and the efficient, and educators of the period recoiled from what they considered the excessively academic and formal aspects of traditional education. In this climate, classical studies, particularly Latin and Greek, were slowly yielding hegemony to new subjects in the social sciences and the technical fields. These, it was presumed, bore more relevance to the problems of an urban industrial society. The new educational climate gave rise to normal schools, vocational schools, professional schools, and high schools for manual training, all designed to give students useful knowledge.

Religious training schools stood in the forefront of this educational movement; the recital of course listings reveals that the larger part of the curriculum was practically oriented. A significant number of classes under such headings as "religious pedagogy" taught how to teach. Also provided were bookkeeping for pastors' assistants; medicine for nurses, deaconesses, or medical missionaries; "personal work" for those in need of methods to convert the unconverted; domestic science for those anticipating work in settlement houses or institutional churches; sacred music for prospective church musicians; and information on foreign lands and missionary methods for missionaries in training. The word *methods* figured strongly in training-school catalogs; the Chicago Training School even featured a *department* of methods.

The work outside the schools, in churches, missions, settlement houses, hospitals, tenements, and on the city streets fulfilled the demand for a "practical" education. Training-school educators prided themselves on being in step with the best practices of modern medical and scientific education, in insisting that their students acquire what they referred to as laboratory, or clinical experience. The Chicago Training School catalog announced, for instance, that "A Christian training school should be in the heart of a great city for the same reason that a medical school needs to be near a hospital." The city served, of course, as the school's gigantic "laboratory."[31]

As in most schools where the students reside, learning at the training schools did not end with the formal program. Young women learned from the examples of their teachers, who frequently were women and who served as models of piety and consecrated service. They also actively influenced the spiritual lives of their students. Principal Maria Gibson of Scarritt encouraged students who had religious problems to talk with her, and often she and the student would pray together for a solution.[32]

Students learned from each other as well. They traded accounts of their work in city missions and settlement houses, prayed and worshiped together, and avidly followed the accomplishments of those who had graduated before them, particularly those who had sailed as foreign missionaries. Through letters and return visits, alumnae became big sisters in an extended school family.

Students were exposed to steady streams of visitors attracted by the missionary spirit of the schools. Many of these visitors gave lectures: They informed students of "the present missionary situation" in China or India, briefed them on deaconess work in other countries, traced religious themes in English literature, discussed Methodism's past and present, and described the history and purposes of various American Protestant agencies.

The Demise of the Training-School Movement

Between the First World War and 1940, most of the religious training schools for women either closed or were merged into other institutions. Those that merged almost invariably lost their autonomy, and usually their identity as well. Of the three schools in this study, only Scarritt has survived in recognizable form until the present, and its financial base was precarious at the beginning of the 1980s.

Diverse factors explain the almost total disappearance of these schools. Educational standards were rising rapidly, and newly powerful accrediting agencies at the college level, and later at the seminary level, were encouraging institutional uniformity. Schools that did not meet the narrowing definitions of college, professional, or graduate school, and that did not award standard degrees, were beginning to draw criticism from educators and were attracting fewer students. Meanwhile, more colleges and theological seminaries had opened their doors to women. Under "practical theology," seminaries had added a greater number of courses—religious education, missions, sacred music, sociology, and methods of social service—which until then had constituted standard training-school fare and had most appealed to women bent on Christian service. Supervised field work was also becoming a standard item in seminary programs.

In response to the demand for higher standards, most training schools attempted to include at least part of the work of colleges and seminaries. About the time of World War I, some began to admit men for abbreviated pastoral courses, placing themselves, perhaps unwittingly, in rivalry with seminaries. Because of their almost total lack of endowment and their dependence upon the generosity of churchwomen (who began to lose some of their fiscal independence at this time), the schools could neither remain exactly what they were nor compete successfully with better-financed colleges and seminaries.

There were other pressures. Boards of foreign missions echoed the general cry for higher standards in arguing for more and better preparation for their candidates. Particularly after the Edinburgh Missionary Conference of 1910 had published a long list of desirable studies for prospective missionaries, the training schools found themselves increasingly obliged to incorporate a multitude of new subjects, thus severely straining their modest resources.[33]

Lay service in the United States also was demanding more specialized preparation. Increased sophistication regarding complex social and religious problems led to a call for well-trained experts who were masters or mistresses of their respective disciplines. Of particular concern to the training schools, the informality associated with early city mission and settlement work began to yield to the professionalism of social work. Experience and dedication were no longer valued as highly as the proper credentials. Increasingly, preparation for social work meant attendance at a graduate professional school, preferably one associated with a university. The trends in education for social work strongly affected education for home missions. By about 1917, in fact, church leaders were calling for professional training for all types of Christian workers in the United States—religious educators, pastors' assistants, Y.M.C.A. and Y.W.C.A. secretaries.[34] Although training-school leaders attempted to introduce more specialized courses and longer programs in order to turn out more accomplished workers, they rarely had the means to emulate the standards of university professional schools.

Other factors weakened the training-school movement as well. The vigor of the women's movement waned after the high point represented by the passage of woman's suffrage in 1920. At about the same time, the founders and early leaders of the training schools left the scene. Lucy Rider Meyer retired from the Chicago Training School in 1917; Scarritt's first principal, Maria L. Gibson, resigned in 1918; and Belle Harris Bennett, founder of Scarritt, died in 1922. Men took their places, often to preside over drastic changes in the schools' identities. Many of the training schools for women which managed to survive intact until the late 1920s succumbed to the privations of the Great Depression.

The New England Deaconess Home and Training School made an effort to meet the higher and higher educational demands of the times, but it was increasingly difficult for its leaders to distinguish their goals from those of the emerging schools of social work.[35] In 1918 this deaconess training school, by now known as the New England School for Christian Workers, was merged into a new university-affiliated institution called the Boston University School of Religious Education and Social Service. The new school, created as the result of a survey by a committee of the Home Missions Council of the Methodist Episcopal Church in New England, was made up of several previously distinct educational enterprises. Financing for the new school came from the church's centenary fund.

The 1917 report of the New England Deaconess Association explained that the proposed merger of the training school into the new Boston University School satisfied "the present demands" for a "high scholastic standard" and concluded that "the advantages accruing more than offset any embarrassment."[36] The "embarrassment" was not spelled out, but very possibly training-school leaders recognized that the control of the new school would lie in other hands. In fact, a Boston University professor headed the new school, and no influential positions were held by former training-school personnel.

Not surprisingly, the 1924 curriculum of the university school revealed a radical diminution of the deaconess training interest. Although courses on religious education, the city, music, and rural churches remained plentiful, gone were the courses on history of women and deaconesses which had served to develop the students' sense of their uniqueness and identity as Christian workers. Gone also were flexible admissions, since the entrance standards became the same as those of the university.

Any interest that New England Methodist women, and especially deaconesses, still retained in the Boston University School of Religious Education and Social Service was probably weakened in 1934 when the school became the School of Religious and Social Work. By that time the financial pressures of the Depression had nearly depleted the demand for religious educators. By 1940 a further change of name, to School of Social Work, indicated that the university school's interest in religious training had disappeared almost entirely.[37]

By the time of World War I, the Chicago Training School also apparently was ripe for change in policy and administration. Not only was pressure for higher academic standards arising from general cultural and educational conditions, but, as in the case of the New England school, it was issuing also from the Methodist Episcopal Church. One essential for higher standards was a more specialized faculty, holding college and graduate degrees. The academic background of the Chicago Training School faculty was modest, a good number having graduated from the training school itself. Moreover, they were still subsisting on deaconess allowances, and professional pride, if not economic necessity, was rendering such sacrifice increasingly unpalatable to younger, better-educated teachers.

Another necessity for the upgrading of standards was the raising of an endowment. If the school were to attract a more impressive faculty, it would need more generous and reliable funding. But thus far Lucy Rider Meyer had failed in her efforts to gather funds, despite apparent pressure from her bishop.[38] In 1915, to make matters worse, Norman Wait Harris, an important benefactor of the school, died. And conditions during World War I undoubtedly further aggravated attempts to improve the school's financial position.

As if these problems were not enough, the Meyers, husband and wife, disagreed on matters of theology and policy. Mr. Meyer distrusted change:

[He] walked in the old ways and loved the old truths, and felt they were being discredited by modern investigations and research. . . . He could not be convinced that special educational equipment was essential to the work of ministering to the poor, and caring for children, the sick and the aged. [He believed] consecration and the spirit of service were the great requisites.[39]

His wife, on the contrary, was receptive to the new views of the Bible and to modern theological formulations and was of the opinion that good will should be aided by "all the scientific knowledge available, especially a knowledge of child nature and the principles of religious education."[40] Their conflict reflected disagreements in the society at large.

The retirement of Lucy Rider Meyer and her husband in 1917 heralded enormous changes. First, masculine leadership took over. Despite Lucy Meyer's wish to be succeeded in the principalship by a woman, a man was appointed. Other crucial changes were instituted under the designation of reorganization, paid for in part by the centenary fund of the Methodist Episcopal Church. "Reorganization" entailed a larger course offering and more ambitious programs—for instance, a graduate program in conjunction with Northwestern University and Garrett Biblical Institute.

But perhaps most significant was the admission of male students. If their entry had meant simply that they would receive lay training, the move might not have altered the identity of the school as greatly. However, a two-year Ministerial Training Course was introduced for the "many men entering the ministry who are unable or disinclined to take a technical course at a theological seminary, but who nevertheless desire and greatly need practical training for their work as pastors."[41] True, the ministerial program with its emphasis on practicality was apparently in keeping with the spirit of the training school. But there is little doubt that school leaders felt obliged to make the program as much like that of a theological seminary as possible. By 1924, for instance, the course of studies had grown longer; ministerial students were being urged to spend three years in training, rather than the initial two.[42]

In 1935 the Chicago Training School became a part of Garrett Biblical Institute. This event is not well documented, but some of the reasons can be surmised. The drive for ever-higher standards certainly continued, while the means to attain them dwindled. The depletion of sums from the centenary fund was followed by the Great Depression, rendering an already difficult financial situation impossible. Perhaps even more critical, the training school leaders continued to be unclear about their goals. If the principal aim was now to produce ministers, could the Chicago Training School claim to do this better than well-financed Garrett? If, on the other hand, its major objective continued to be the training of men and women as Christian lay workers, could it adequately certify them as "professionals" for the various fields of Christian work? Or could other institutions, such as seminaries and schools of social work, do this better?

Like the other training schools, Scarritt faced a new world after World War I. A man, Jesse L. Cuninggim, assumed the leadership in 1921, a year before the death of Belle Harris

Bennett. He sized up Scarritt's problems: Its academic level was too low; it needed graduate-level study and degrees for women preparing to become missionaries and religious educators and to enter other forms of Christian work. Second, it had "very inadequate facilities, consisting of one large school building in poor repair, and a president's home." Moreover, the school's circle of supporters was too small, made up almost entirely of women of the Methodist Episcopal Church, South, who were interested in missions. The school had "little educational prestige," thought Cuninggim. Because the laws of Missouri would make it difficult to revise the school's charter in that state, a change of location was indicated. Finally, affiliation with "some strong educational institutions"—probably a university— seemed called for, since the "Board of Missions, Men's Division, preferred missionary candidates trained in the Universities or Schools of Theology, rather than in a separate school of missions."[43]

Cuninggim's solution to these problems involved making Scarritt a two-year college and requiring a junior-college diploma for admission. This raised academic standards, but did not limit admission to college graduates only, as many former training schools were attempting to do. He also created a two-year graduate program, recognizing that a graduate degree was becoming virtually necessary in some foreign mission fields. Realizing that a university connection was essential if Scarritt was to enhance its reputation, Cuninggim eventually arranged for the school to associate with Vanderbilt University in Nashville, Tennessee. This affiliation had the further virtue of retaining Scarritt's specialization. Students could take any general courses they desired at the university, while Scarritt concentrated upon "social-religious studies."[44]

Like the Chicago Training School and other training schools for women, Scarritt's leadership decided to admit men. But Cuninggim avoided the pitfall that awaited training schools attempting to educate men for the ordained ministry. He resolved that Scarritt would not undertake ministerial training, but focus upon "the thorough preparation of unordained workers, both men and women, for the many forms of social-religious life and service."[45]

Scarritt moved from Kansas City to Nashville in 1924. A new campus near Vanderbilt was dedicated four years later, built from funds furnished by the Belle Harris Bennett Memorial Fund. In 1940 Scarritt received accreditation from the Southern Association of Colleges and Secondary Schools.

Why Scarritt survived with most of its goals and original character intact, while so many of its sister institutions did not, is a tempting subject for speculation. It was Scarritt's good fortune to make the changes required by the times, without attempting more than was appropriate to its original purpose. Scarritt was blessed with a second-generation leader who understood the value of its founders' accomplishments and endeavored to preseve them amid post-World War I realities. While other training schools were taking advantage of the short-lived financial prosperity of the 1920s for hasty expansion in diverse directions (including the education of ministers), Scarritt held fast to its early goal of training for the laity.

In terms of numbers, size, and longevity, the religious training schools for women constituted a modest movement in the history of American education. Even in their heyday they did not command sufficient prestige to place their graduates in high positions in American Protestantism. College-educated women, rather than training-school graduates, probably assumed most roles of top leadership, many of them voluntary, in Protestant women's organizations. It goes without saying that college and seminary-trained men continued to hold the reins in most of the agencies of Protestantism. Richard Tappan has argued convincingly, if somewhat ahistorically, that the training schools actually prepared women to assume subordinate roles.[46]

This acknowledged, however, it must be remembered that by turning out workers with skill and experience, the training schools performed a substantial service for Methodist and other Protestant churches toward their goals of domestic and worldwide evangelization. The schools performed a notable service for their women students and faculty as well. In addition to teaching actual skills, the training schools gave the first generations of women matriculants sufficient confidence in their own abilities to enable them to leave behind their traditional place in the home.

By pioneering in such fields as religious pedagogy and sociology, the training schools also set an example that helped spur educators to institute far-reaching reforms in other theological education. In the first decades of the twentieth century, theological seminaries began to admit women, give consideration to lay education, and incorporate practical subjects—religious education, music, missions, and field work—into the curriculum. It is difficult to tell to what extent the existence of training schools, particularly those for women, affected the decisions of seminary educators, but there is evidence that seminary personnel were aware of them. Faculty of the Divinity School of the University of Chicago also taught at the Chicago Training School, for instance. Occasionally, indeed, seminary leaders and supporters seemed to fear the training schools as possible competitors.[47]

Now a rapidly expanding revival in the education and mobilization of the laity for ministry is again taking place. In seeking to encourage and guide this movement, church and seminary leaders may find useful instruction in the work accomplished and the lessons learned in the vigorous training-school movement that began a century ago. The experience of the training schools warns of the danger of expanding too hastily the goals of an institution having limited and uncertain funding; it points to the vicissitudes faced by those who relied upon denominational support; and it suggests the difficulties women of the church encountered in preserving the integrity and autonomy of their institutions. On the positive side, however, the existence of the training schools demonstrates that lay education flourished when it responded to a widespread desire for active involvement in the mission of the church and offered effective and practical training directed toward that end.

THE SOCIAL GOSPEL ACCORDING TO PHOEBE

Mary Agnes Dougherty

Introduction

No specific date, event, or movement clearly marks the birth of the social gospel and social Christianity. Some would agree that these were established in the teachings and ministry of Jesus of Nazareth himself in the first century A.D., and that they have been carried out in every generation since by followers who have heard his word and done it. Most church historians, however, agree with C. Howard Hopkins that in its modern American form, social Christianity originated in "the reaction of Protestantism . . . to the ethics and practices of capitalism as brought to point in the industrial situation" following the Civil War.[1] Henry May, for example, claims that "three earthquakes"—the industrial upheavals of 1877, 1886, and 1892–1894—awoke Protestant America's slumbering social conscience from a complacency engendered by the alliance between conservative religion and conservative economics.[2] The first church groups to respond to new social conditions were Unitarians, Congregationalists, and Episcopalians, the last inheriting a "state-church tradition of responsibility for public morals." The Methodists and Baptists only awoke to their social duty later, Hopkins argues.[3] Within all the denominations, it has been commonly supposed that clergymen and professors designed the social-gospel response to the "urban impact."[4]

The essence of social Christianity, however, involved carrying out the gospel, not theorizing about it. Histories that credit its origins to theologians, ministers, and lay*men* usually overlook, slight, or ignore the contribution of churchwomen to the formulation of the social gospel. Yet nineteenth-century clergymen who saw themselves as leaders in a new Christian endeavor were not ignorant of their indebtedness to women. They understood that they were entering a field of service that previously had belonged to women. For example, John R. Commons, secretary of the American Institute of Christian Sociology in Indiana, was perceptive about churchmen's need to be tutored in the elementary techniques of social work. He noted with unconscious androcentrism that Christian men "have hired someone else to love [their neighbors]. They have left it to the women." In an effort to help churchmen catch up with the women, Commons patiently explained the hows and whys of friendly visiting: "It means to go yourself, to get acquainted with your neighbor, to pick out some hard-worked mechanic, some shiftless pauper, some slave of drink, and love him."⁵

And what of the women? Churchwomen, who throughout the nineteenth century had served as the social arm of Protestantism, are largely absent from the accounts of a movement defined by one scholar as "America's most unique contribution to the great on going stream of Christianity."⁶ It seems improbable that women retreated from this work. It is more likely that historians have overlooked or minimized the significance of churchwomen in the rise of social Christianty because they saw nothing unique or unusual in their role as society's servants. Above all else, the social gospel asked its adherents to *love* their neighbors, especially the least among them. Such a demand was considered "natural" to the female personality, making it an improbable source of the new and unforeseen mood in the churches. By contrast, the social gospel demanded a radical change in the attitudes and actions of Protestant men. As a result, for traditional church history, the social gospel was born only when male ministers and professors and laymen began to think and behave in ways which nine-teenth-century American culture considered characteristic of womanhood.⁷

Much like Victorian fathers who assumed an interested

role in rearing their offspring only when the children were well out of infancy, Protestant churchmen assumed full paternal responsibility for the social gospel in 1912, when it already had matured. In that year, the Federal Council of the Churches of Christ in America adopted the "social creed," with each of twelve denominations pledging to promote its sixteen-point program.[8] The years 1911–1912 also saw the creation of the Men and Religion Forward Movement, whose purpose was to enlist Protestant "manhood and boyhood" to carry the social-action message to the churches through a combination of "evangelical fervor and method . . . and the techniques of sociology."[9] In 1912, theologian Walter Rauschenbusch concluded that the Men and Religion Forward Movement had "made social Christianity orthodox."[10] The weight of Rauschenbusch's opinion has led one distinguished historian to estimate that "social Christianity reached its popular peak" in this movement for laymen, but we may conclude that by that date it was respectable enough to be institutionalized, as Rauschenbusch's use of "orthodox" suggests.[11] Prominent theologians and ordinary laymen alike now became votaries of the social gospel.

Deaconesses in the Rise of Social Christianity

A full quarter-century before the "popular peak," certain Methodist churchwomen began to nurture the social gospel by reviving the office of deaconess within Methodist polity.[12] Although Hopkins claims that "in the absence of a well-developed sociology, the 'eighties became a period of discussion rather than practical application of social Christian principles," it was in 1885 that Lucy Rider Meyer founded the Chicago Training School for City, Home and Foreign Missions (C.T.S.).[13] During five years as field secretary for the Illinois Sunday School Association, Meyer had discovered that, as she phrased it, "among women, there was plenty of general intelligence, and personal qualities, plenty of latent power . . . but not the machinery for developing the power and making it effective."[14] To correct this situation, she established her training school. The house-to-house visiting in Chicago's tenements that was part of the school's curriculum opened her eyes to the need for a new Christian approach to urban problems. Within two years, with the encouragement of Mr. and Mrs. Meyer, two C.T.S. students moved to a rented flat at the corner of Dearborn and Erie Streets, not far from the training school, and the first Methodist Deaconess Home in the United States was opened.[15]

For most of Protestantism, the decade of the 1880s was a time of meditation, yet major contributions to social-gospel literature stimulated thought, discussion, and action on the issue of Protestantism's response to industrialism.[16] The revival of the female diaconate within Methodism in 1887 belies Robert Handy's conclusion that social gospel leaders were "not so much activists as they were preachers, proclaimers, and educators."[17] Female social-gospel leaders *were* activists. The work of the early deaconesses also challenges Henry May's conclusion that "only in the early twentieth century when progressive social reform had become a creed of much of the American middle class, did Methodists contribute to the social gospel in proportion to their number, discipline, and fervency."[18] When Methodist women are considered as serious historical actors, the picture of Methodist contribution changes. Upon discovering the latent potential for social good in the ancient and nearly forgotten office of deaconess, a significant number of Methodist women enlisted for active duty in the ranks of social Christianity; and they worked as ardently as the men then engaged, "to change men's views and attitudes, to win them to a new religio-social faith."[19]

Sentiment among some churchwomen for reestablishment of the diaconate, in fact, predated by twenty years its official revival in 1888, the year the Methodist Episcopal General Conference recognized the office in church polity.[20] In Philadelphia in 1868, Annie Turner Wittenmyer organized the Ladies' and Pastors' Christian Union, an organization which "to a great extent" supplied "the want of the order of Deaconesses."[21] Also in 1872, Susan M.D. Fry attempted to arouse interest in the office through a series of historical articles entitled "Ancient and Modern Sisterhoods," in *The Ladies' Repository*.[22] At the time, neither of these proponents found Methodist women receptive, but by the 1880s, when the urban situation in the United States cried out for attention, the idea of a modern diaconate had gained relevance.

The Scriptural Model of Phoebe

The Methodist deaconess obtained her license to minister from Scripture—specifically from Romans 16:1-2, in which Phoebe, a wealthy and cultured woman known for her beneficence, is reported to have served in the primitive Christian church as deaconess to a mission in Cenchrea, near Corinth. Phoebe's *diakonia* was a ministry of service—"a ministry distinguished from other vocations . . . such as prophesying, presiding, teaching, or working miracles."[23] Paul tells us that Phoebe's service was freely and lovingly given; it was not service for pay or such as was required of a slave. At Cenchrea, Phoebe "challenged hunger and disease on the doorstep of the perishing and in Christ's name made them retire." This tradition of Phoebe's *diakonia*—her ability to see "the world's pain" and her desire to overcome it through personal service—was just what nineteenth-century Methodist women wanted to revive.[24]

Methodist Deaconesses in the Metropolis

Phoebe's field of mission work, as well as her active ministry, is relevant to the modern Methodist diaconate. The women from rural America who first attended deaconess training schools like the one at Chicago held fixed and frightening images of the city.[25] Many novices saw parallels between their own work and the work of Paul's Phoebe among the "human flotsom" of the seaport town described by one minister:

As a suburb of licentious Corinth [Cenchrea] received foul drainage of the city-sloughs; panderers out of favor; wastrels amazed at their own self-created ministries; and victims of cruelty, injustice and luck, each with a story that would make angels weep. To some of these Phoebe was the only haven of kindness they ever knew. She presided over their rehabilitation; or, where she could not nurse them back to health and hope, she nursed them on to God . . . "a succorer of many." What histories underlie this superb phrase![26]

For rural women, such dark impressions of urban life only reinforced their fear of the city.

As agents of the emerging social gospel, these modern Phoebes were compelled to make friends with the city or fail in their vocation. William N. Brodbeck urged deaconesses to regard the great cities as a "magnificent opportunity" for the church, rather than as impediments in the path of world evangelization. "There would be no . . . achievement marking the first century of the Christian era," had the apostles confined their labors to the countryside, he reminded them.[27] Aware of the rural loyalties of most American Methodists, another supporter of deaconesses spoke to them boldly, evoking the era's optimistic sense of progress.

While respecting the country and the people who are born there . . . I regard the city as the most moral institution in our Christian civilization, not [as a place] where all the basest passions are developed, but as the theater of the struggle of man to ultimate victory over himself and his surroundings.[28]

This spokesman promised "miracles" to deaconesses who would share his belief in the potential of the city. "He who goes about the city with the vision of the Throne before him will see the city transformed."

Most new students in urban training schools in fact faced a difficult period of adjustment as they adapted to the pulse and rhythm of the city. Provincial impressions of urban life, drawn from rural viewpoints and based on fiction, popular myth, and gossip, predisposed them to distrust the city. The prospect of rubbing shoulders with slum dwellers frightened them. A decision to enter deaconess work was a heroic undertaking for country girls who perceived the city as a "great center of evil," a world of "squalor, ignorance, brutishness," or "an overgrown social and political tumor."[29]

Deaconesses applied their energies to the urban environment more readily than they adjusted their attitudes. In Chicago, Lucy Rider Meyer, principal of C.T.S., helped her students become acclimated by sharing her optimism that the American city had a potential for Christian endeavor equal to that of mission fields in any foreign land. She reminded her students that the religious reformers Martin Luther and John Wesley, the apostle Paul, Augustine, and Jesus himself had worked in cities to bring about the kingdom of God.[30]

In reality, deaconesses accepted the city provisionally—they determined to spend their lives transforming it. They shared their image of a renewed city with the folks back home through their newspapers. For instance, the *Message* of June 1889 described an ideal deaconess home as envisioned by Protestant sisters in Chicago. Located in the city's worst section and surrounded by tenements, their fantasy home was immaculately white and surrounded by a green lawn. The streets in its vicinity were clean and sanitary, free of debris and garbage, thanks to the city fathers. The ideal deaconess home was the center of activity for the people in the neighborhood. This Bit-of-Heaven House, as they named it, suggests the transformation the deaconesses hoped for, as well as betraying their homesickness for a gentler, tidier world. Although settlement houses never became a major arena for their work, the Bit-of-Heaven House indicates that deaconesses considered creating such institutions before they became common agencies of Progressive social reform.[31]

By introducing novice sisters to the city as a "new Jerusalem," offering them hopes and plans for its transformation, the deaconess movement gave rural daughters confidence that the city was not to be feared, but conquered. Thus armed, deaconessses embraced their role as transformers of urban life.

Learning by Visiting

Before any deaconess could see the city transformed, it was necessary to undertake the difficult, unromantic task of visiting the poor. Work in tenement neighborhoods was initially a shocking experience. No amount of rural charity work done on the behalf of hometown congregations prepared young Methodist women for the sights they confronted in the city.

"Visiting" was the modern Phoebe's means of canvassing neighborhoods to discover those who might want or need help. In the slums, a deaconess did not find the needy in separate houses, but in basement hovels, out-shacks, lean-tos, hallways, and alleys. Welcomed by some residents and rebuffed by others, it required determination to overcome shyness and timidity, to let unkind words pass, to brave personal slights. Her evangelistic purpose and the good she might do needed to outweigh her personal fears and anxieties.

Despite the raw and depressing conditions of tenement life that could be unnerving to a novice, the successful visitor was alert to the least encouragement that would grant her entrance into the dwellings of the poor. There she might find a scene such as this:

A Bohemian family was found in two rooms, one a mere shed of an old frame building. The father had been sick for five months with rheumatism. A dead child was lying in the back room, a tiny baby, lacking clothes, was tied up in a pillow. Their destitution was shocking. They lacked clothes, bedding, bread, everything.[32]

While deaconesses visited the poor primarily to help meet their elemental human needs and to evangelize by demonstrating practical love for neighbor, many also functioned in part as students and agents of the new field of quantitative sociology. Like the secular social workers, Protestant sisters gathered information on social conditions during their visits of mercy.[33] In these activities they were guided by the prevailing belief that the scientific study of society was essential to the solution of social problems and the establishment of a just order. A Methodist bishop solemnly voiced this view at a service for the consecration of deaconesses in 1890: "The Deaconess while she visits, may investigate, and with scientific carefulness, collate facts for the use of scientific people, who from facts, draw inferences and are thus able to set at work the great forces which touch society at the center and lift it up."[34]

Students at the Chicago Training School also broadened their educational experiences by visiting institutions such as Graham Taylor's settlement, the Commons. It was reported enthusiastically after such a visit in 1895 that "the Commons is a center of life and light to the neighborhood in which it is located and is an exponent of the real Pauline *charity*."[35]

In turn, the deaconesses themselves were studied as part of the urban landscape by the famous photographer Jacob Riis. In 1911, the *Advocate* printed Riis' photograph of a deaconess at work, with this caption: "I have seen a deaconess through quiet and loving ministry in the chaos of a ghetto transform a street which was a jungle into a spot that breathed of heaven's first law. It is the gentle and noiseless influence that makes mightily for the coming of the Kingdom."[36]

Deaconesses as Analysts of Society

During home visits, while ministering to people's physical needs, deaconesses also heard their explanations as to why they were depressed, sick, drunk, or despairing. The daily repetition of such tales in neighborhood after neighborhood led these Methodist women to look for the underlying causes of the misery they witnessed. The literature of the deaconess movement reveals observations sympathetic to working people and the dispossessed: "The shutting down of a factory, a fit of sickness—and sickness is always lurking about those sunless rooms with their damp walls and leaky sewer pipes—any little unexpected addition to ordinary expenses entails a debt, and a debt is a vampire sucking the very life blood of a family."[37]

In order to finance their work in the city, modern Phoebes needed the support of Methodists elsewhere. To gain this aid, they relied upon the persuasiveness of their press. As the training schools were established, they produced a variety of newspapers to be circulated to friends, families, and neighbors in small-town America, to spread the social-gospel message and enlist material support for their programs. These journals carried vivid accounts, and readers who caught "Glimpses of the City Field" responded by sending canned goods, farm produce, freshly cut garden flowers, and clothing by rail and wagon to stock the shelves of the "poor closet" in the Deaconess Home. Readers also sent money, and gifts were regularly acknowledged in the newspapers.[38]

Deaconesses were not asking fellow Methodists only for expressions of Christian charity, however. As they gained first-hand experience in the slums, Methodist deaconesses raised questions about the causes of urban poverty, decay, and corruption. Since most deaconesses, particularly in the early years of the movement, were not formally educated, it is not surprising that their contributions to social-gospel thinking were more practical than theoretical. Even so, one can be analytical without advancing to theory, and the deaconesses' perceptions of economic injustice were sharp and clear. In probing the sources of poverty and misery, they frequently approached a class analysis. In 1899, one wrote:

When Mr. Van Court, the wealthy merchant needs a little ready money in his business he goes to the bank, where he is treated with the greatest deference. . . . But, when Mrs. Bilinski, who supports her five children by washing, is forced to raise a loan . . . she betakes her to a shop over whose entrance hangs three gilt balls.[39]

If deaconesses' writings lacked the sophistication of academically trained male social-gospel theorists, they nevertheless rang with authenticity. People back home did not doubt the veracity of their daughters.

Deaconesses tried to help impoverished people overcome immediate difficulties caused by lack of food, clothing, fuel, and medical care. But they soon learned that the family they saved from disaster on Monday could be in the same position again on Tuesday. Their experiences challenged older notions that poverty was the result of individual depravity; they disclosed the complacency of "blaming the victim." Isabelle Horton, one of the movement's most perceptive social critics, expressed her views in the *Deaconess Advocate*:

These were not born paupers, but have had pauperism thrust upon them. Perhaps it has been years—perhaps but a few weeks or months since the head of the family failed in health, or in business, or "lost his job." But once down, there is scarcely one chance in a thousand to regain his footing.[40]

Many deaconesses looked into the inequities of the nation's economic system for causes. "Have you ever stopped to think that most foreigners are disappointed in America?" one sister asked deaconess supporters. She argued that the immigrants had expected America to be a land of opportunity, but they had discovered instead "a cruel relentless system of labor."[41]

Solving Urban Problems Through Politics, Prevention, and New Institutions

Deaconesses were sympathetic to those who had been victimized by the economic system, and they tried in their own ways to find jobs for the unemployed, although the magnitude of the labor problem far exceeded their ability to deal with it. Their decision to use the facilities of deaconess homes as employment offices reveals their acceptance of purely political solutions, however. When the state of Illinois established employment offices in 1899, the *Advocate* welcomed them as "a move in the right direction," and in 1908 the paper reported that this work had been taken up by the newly founded Methodist Federation for Social Service.[42] The deaconess movement did not develop a sophisticated critique of the political and theoretical aspects of the labor problem, as did some of the intellectual leaders of the social gospel, but it did give attention to the working conditions of female domestics, a problem ignored by nearly everyone else.[43]

At the turn of the century, Chicago's deaconesses, in particular, actively supported reforms as the lively Progressive movement gained force in their city.[44] Since they worked principally, although not exclusively, with women and children, deaconesses followed with special interest the work of such reformers as Florence Kelley, whose exposés of child labor were reprinted in deaconess literature. In 1902, editors of the *Deaconess Advocate* pointed an accusing finger at New England manufacturers who were being investigated for exploiting children in textile mills. While praised in their own communities as "philanthropists and public-spirited men," manufacturers worked thousands of children twelve hours a day for daily wages of from ten to twenty-five cents.[45] Deaconesses supported legislation to curb such exploitation.

Imbued with Methodism's strong temperance tradition, deaconesses abhorred drink, and their work among immigrant groups who drank beer as though it were water tested their Christian charity. Deaconesses were shocked to witness the consumption of alcohol by children and women and strenuously tried to win the drunkard from his cup. Yet they did not blame the drunkard as much as the salesman and the saloonkeeper. They enthusiastically supported efforts to close the saloons; they opened coffee houses as substitute gathering places. In 1896 the *Deaconess Advocate* endorsed the Prohibition party as offering the "thousands of church members opposed to the liquor traffic . . . an alternative in exercising their vote." The *Advocate* two months later backed the editor of the Methodist *Epworth Herald* in judging the Republican party's statement on temperance "an empty platitude."[46] However, while endorsing the Prohibition party's stance on liquor, the *Advocate* expressed discontent with its silence on free silver and woman's suffrage, both of which the paper favored.

The deaconess movement also perceived prostitution as primarily a social problem, rather than a question of individual depravity, and sought to combat it through prevention—the solution favored by Progressives. Deaconesses did not establish homes for "fallen women" as gospel welfare workers had done in the past. Instead they stationed themselves in railroad depots, where they kept a watchful eye for young women who appeared new to the city and none too sure of themselves, approached them, and directed them to a respectable boarding house if they did not have friends or relatives in the city.[47] Calling themselves Traveler's Aides, deaconesses often competed in this work with procurers of prostitutes, who frequented depots looking for recruits.[48] The aim of the deaconesses was not only to thwart the procurer, but to encourage churchwomen to show more tolerance and understanding toward prostitutes.

Deaconesses and the City Churches

The failure of established Protestant institutions to accommodate the foreign immigrants flooding into the cities was seriously pondered during the 1880s by early social-gospel theorists. In *Modern Cities and Their Religious Problems,* published in 1887, Samuel Loomis marshaled a volume of statistical evidence to show that urban churches were declining in numbers. In what Hopkins has assessed as "probably the most acute anaylsis of the urban religious dilemma," Loomis concluded that Protestantism was failing to win the working classes, who saw the churches as tools of capitalism.[49] In addition, the churches were experiencing a condition that in a later, more racially charged context, would be called "white flight."

The decline of the downtown churches aroused concern in every denomination; conferences were called, papers were written, and criticism was meted out generally. Interdenominational rivalry surfaced, with Methodists and Congregationalists contending over which group was comparatively the greater failure.[50]

In their visiting, the deaconesses saw the truth of Loomis' argument, though probably few had read his book. Through a contributor, the *Advocate* warned, "There is a growing estrangement between the poor and destitute classes and the church of God";[51] and in 1890 it published the following attack by one critic of the churches.

The churches, instead of trying to establish themselves in these strongholds of evil, are removing from them. When asked why they abandon the places, they reply that they want more respectable quarters; there was so much sin in that district they could not stand it any longer. Think of it! The church, pledged to Christ and commissioned of high heaven. Is that not enough to cause angels to weep and devils to laugh?[52]

The deaconesses were seeking to assist "over-taxed city pastors," in the phrase of the C.T.S. catalogue, which pointed out to readers that the female diaconate was thereby contributing to contemporary Methodist Episcopal Church polity.[53]

The Methodist Phoebes came to believe that the church's traditional forms of ministry were simply ineffective with the new city dwellers. They contended that even if the urban churches opened their doors wide, all the immigrants could not be accommodated. In 1888 the *Advocate* reported that in Chicago's thirteenth ward, churches had a combined seating capacity of 1,500 members, while the total population of the ward was 26,000. Mathematics proved, then, that only one in twenty of the ward's residents could find accommodation in the churches.[54]

Deaconesses proposed to create new church institutions in which immigrants could find acceptance and practical assistance. For example, one of the first undertakings of the Chicago Training School was the opening of an industrial school in a room of a downtown church.[55] Over time, the deaconesses developed other institutions to bridge the distance between the church and the unchurched. Thus they not only recognized the weak influence of Protestantism among the growing immigrant population; they took innovative steps to strengthen it.

Moderating Tensions and Christianizing the System

In condemning the churches' departure from the city and in sympathizing with the precarious lot of the poor, the deaconesses did not turn against the rich. Inherent in social-gospel theory was the belief that the prevailing economic system could be Christianized. Deaconesses, like other advocates of the social gospel, accepted this principle. When Walter Rauschenbusch wrote *Christianity and the Social Crisis* in 1907, he asserted that the churches had become servants of "bourgeois culture."[56] Although Rauschenbusch expected chastisement from his ministerial colleagues, his book was highly praised—perhaps because although he had harsh words for Christianity's alliance with capitalism, he nevertheless firmly believed that if the church would repent and rethink, it could Christianize commerce. These hopes were widely held also by deaconesses.

The deaconess movement did not, on the other hand, exonerate the rich. "We have inaugurated missions and movements to reach the *dregs* of society; we ought to inaugurate others to reach the *scums* of society," claimed one *Advocate* writer. "It is not Coxie's deluded crowds that form the greatest menace to society," he added, "it is the idle rich."[57] Social-gospel advocates criticized capitalists, monopolists, usurers, trusts, businessmen, and stony-hearted corporations for their abuse of wealth, and occasionally a deaconess might radically denounce the economic system. Isabelle Horton wrote, in 1899:

If this be true—if under the present system a "righteous distribution" of profits is impossible, let the "moral forces" be brought to bear, though the system be destroyed. Or if "destroyed" savors too much of revolution and anarchy, let us say replaced by a new system which shall not set a man's best self and his business interest over against each other; one in which one man's success shall not mean the failure of hundreds of his weaker brothers, but in which his gain shall mean the good of all.[58]

In the main, however, deaconesses saw themselves as moderating class antagonisms. Their desire was to bring rich and poor Americans together in a common Christian brotherhood, and they encouraged cooperation, rather than competition in the economic sphere. They believed that the businessman could end "poverty, misery, and crime" by dealing morally with the working man, and they praised businessmen who instituted profit-sharing programs.[59] In practice, of course, Methodist deaconesses had little contact with businessmen. Though their leaders appealed to business for funds, the Protestant sisters worked primarily with women and children of the poorer classes.

Conclusion

The Methodist deaconesses' reasoned approach to the church's urban crisis cannot be dismissed as sentimental charity offered in the lady-bountiful tradition. Trained for and consecrated to the order, Methodist deaconesses formed a new breed of churchwomen. They were significant agents of applied Christianity and early exponents of the social gospel about which Walter Rauschenbusch wrote perceptively in 1917, "We *have* a social gospel. We need a systematic theology large enough to match it and vital enough to back it" [emphasis added].[60] The work of helping the "whole needy man, body, soul, and spirit . . . was scarcely touched before our coming," observed one deaconess of her movement's contribution to Methodism; she thoughtfully recalled, "My great mother, the Church, looked askance at first at me, her latest born."[61] When allowed to speak her own lines, the Methodist deaconess claims her historic place in pioneering the social gospel for a chary church.

Adhesion to the social gospel had a different meaning for churchmen than for churchwomen, as suggested by a personal reminiscence of Rauschenbusch. Recalling his early involvement, he wrote from a male perspective:

All whose recollection runs back of 1900 will remember that as a time of lonesomeness. We were few and we shouted in the wilderness. It was always a happy surprise when we found a new man who had seen the light. We used to form a kind of flying wedge to support a man who was preparing to attack a minister's conference with the Social Gospel. Our older friends remonstrated with us for wrecking our careers. We ourselves saw the lion's den plainly before us, and only wondered how the beasts would act this time.[62]

It escaped Rauschenbusch's notice that deaconesses were flourishing at that very time. They were rarely overcome by "lonesomeness" in their work, nor did they worry over "wrecked careers." On the contrary, in their espousal of the social gospel, those venturesome women discovered sisterhood and enough meaningful work for a lifetime. They also achieved significant status in their church, by making themselves trained experts in the field of Christian social service.

IV

THE STATUS OF WOMEN
IN INSTITUTIONAL
CHURCH LIFE

11

LAITY RIGHTS
AND LEADERSHIP

William T. Noll

Near the end of the nineteenth century, women in the Methodist Protestant Church made great strides toward full participation in the church's councils.[1] As late as 1878 there were no laywomen serving on any general boards or agencies. Methodist Protestant annual conference records are incomplete, but again, few women participated on that level of church life. In contrast to the situation in many other denominations, there was no separate organization of women through which they might serve the church and develop independent leadership abilities. Beyond the local congregation, women in the Methodist Protestant Church, with only a few exceptions, were politically invisible, their existence acknowledged, but their contributions never recognized.[2] Church leadership was entirely male; and publicly, no one had expressed any desire to change these circumstances.

But by 1892, just fourteen years later, the entire picture had changed. The Woman's Foreign Missionary Society (W.F.M.S.) of the Methodist Protestant Church was then thirteen years old, and after an extended struggle, had been recognized as an independent agency of the denomination. Members of the society made their own decisions and controlled their own funds. The impact of these women was recognized throughout the church; several W.F.M.S. members were delegates and leaders at their annual conference sessions; and in 1892, four of the society's leaders—one of them a fully ordained Methodist Protestant clergywoman—were elected by their annual conferences as full voting members of the General Conference. Clearly by the 1890s, women's leadership was being acknowledged and legitimated in Methodist Protestantism.

Among Methodist denominations in America, the Methodist Protestant Church was unique in that it granted women the right to be ordained as ministers more or less concurrently with granting them full laity rights. The story of the struggles and achievements of Methodist Protestant laywomen cannot be separated from the successful campaign of their sisters for ordination.[3] Here we will focus primarily, however, on the efforts of laywomen—particularly those working through the Woman's Foreign Missionary Society—to be allowed to do the work they believed God had called them to do, and to that end, to attain full "citizenship" in the church.

While historical attention usually centers on the church at the general level, the movement for laywomen's rights was, above all, a local story—a record of women in countless local congregations who, for more than a hundred years, did work that had to be done, and gradually received acceptance and recognition of their efforts, often grudgingly, from the men who ran the churches. Before churchwomen could serve at a national level, it was necessary to earn support for their wider role from their own congregations and pastors. Every local church of every denomination has such a story to tell. Often these homey struggles were more bitter, protracted—and triumphant—than those that made national headlines. But in almost every case, the local story has gone unrecorded and its memory is lost to history.

In the Methodist Protestant Church, local congregations did not begin to produce women leaders of national standing until the late 1870s. But in retrospect, it has been discovered that laywomen had the potential legal right to hold leadership posts in the general church as far back as 1862. Approved in 1830, the original constitution of the Methodist Protestant Church limited eligibility for ecclesial offices and suffrage to adult white, male members.[4] But when the denomination became divided over the rights of blacks in the late 1850s, this constitutional restriction became a point of contention between the northern and southern members. At the 1858 General Conference, John J. Murray of Maryland proposed a compromise that would "change . . . the constitution, eliminating the offensive word [white] and referring the matter of suffrage and eligibility to office to the annual conferences."[5] Murray's aim was to allow northern conferences to be racially integrated, while southern conferences retained their all-white character. None of the churchmen assembled seemed to have noted that annual conferences might also, by Murray's proposal, allow churchwomen to vote and hold office.

Murray's compromise was defeated by the 1858 Methodist Protestant conference, and the northern conferences pursued their path of withdrawal to form a separate denomination, integrating the compromise proposal into their constitution in 1862.[6] Thus unwittingly, the open possibility of laity rights for women was included.

After the Civil War, negotiations began to reunite the two separate branches of Methodist Protestantism. At the 1877 uniting conference, the constitutional language of the northern branch was adopted for the newly merged church. That is, the 1877 constitution empowered the various annual conferences to decide for themselves who was qualified to vote or hold office right up to General Conference. Whether anyone realized that thereby a door had been opened to the participation of women is unclear, but no evidence exists that the issue was ever officially raised.[7]

No place was provided for women within the overall polity of the church, and no thought was yet given to providing one. Whatever the deeper and unacknowledged cultural connections, the contemporary secular women's suffrage movement did not directly provide the impetus for changing this situation, though churchmen might have harbored such fears. Indeed, Methodist Protestant women leaders in the 1880s specifically disavowed any "Woman's Right's spirit" or even "a mild form of that theory."[8] Instead, crucial changes grew from a meeting in 1879 of some Methodist Protestant women in Pittsburgh who were interested in the religious work of foreign missions.

The Methodist Protestant Church had established a Board of Missions at that time, but still had no missionaries or mission projects of its own. Money raised by the board went to independent or ecumenical mission ventures. Local groups of Methodist Protestant women interested in missions contributed either to the ecumenical Woman's Union Missionary Society or to the Woman's Foreign Missionary Society of the Methodist Episcopal Church, begun in 1869.[9]

The Pittsburgh women dared to hope that the Methodist Protestant Church might develop its own program of missionary outreach, and beyond that, that they might be the ones to initiate it. Therefore, in 1879, they organized themselves as the Woman's Foreign Missionary Society of the Methodist Protestant Church. The question arose as to whether the society should emphasize cooperation with the ecumenical Union Society, or with the Methodist Protestant Board of Missions. Despite the board's undistinguished history and current inactivity, denominational loyalty proved decisive. The women's commitment, combined with their fund-raising ability, made them powerful agents for Methodist Protestant missions. In 1880 the denomination sent its first missionary, Harriet Brittan, to Japan. Brittan's salary was paid by the Woman's Foreign Missionary Society, while the Board of Missions provided transportation and a schoolbuilding.[10]

Though cooperating with the denominational board, Methodist Protestant women were careful to preserve their independence. The society circumspectly declined an offer to become "an auxiliary to [the board], paying all its money into that treasury and having no further responsibility as to its funds or administration."[11] Instead, under the society's constitution, the women retained the right to make their own decisions and to control and manage their own funds. This independent status was confirmed by the 1880 General Conference, which defined the society's purpose as doing "women's work for women" in the mission field, and further, the recording secretary and one other member of the women's society were invited to address the body.[12]

In her history of the women's organization published in 1896, however, Mary A. Miller noted that the society's independence "was not well received by some of the brethren."[13] Indeed, mutual mistrust between the board and the society soon became evident. Shortly after the first missionary was sent out, in conjunction with its purpose of doing "women's work for women," the society began to collect funds for a woman's home in Japan, where the missionaries might work with women and children. Beginning its own building campaign soon after, the Board of Missions looked covetously at the "Brick Fund" the women were amassing. The board's desire was whetted by E. J. Drinkhouse, editor of the weekly *Methodist Protestant,* who asked pointedly whether the two organizations could actually afford separate buildings at such an early stage of their missionary endeavors.[14]

The treasurer of the Brick Fund, Mrs. John Scott, whose husband edited the other denominational paper, the *Methodist Recorder,* replied in its pages that the women of the society expected the board to turn its attention soon to the sending of clergy missionaries and the building of churches. She believed that a separate home for work with women and children was essential and promised, "Every cent of the money received for the Brick Fund will be kept sacred for the purpose for which it was given, namely the Woman's House in Japan." Her husband had editorialized shortly before that "nothing serves so much to destroy confidence as to collect money for one object, and then apply it to another."[15]

Methodist Protestant women cherished the independence of their organization and clearly feared that when the men of the board had raised enough money to send a clergyman to Japan, they would no longer be interested in providing support for a woman missionary. Board members for their part seemed to have nurtured a corresponding fear of being cut out and protested in a letter to the society that the women "seemed to give notice to the Board that [their] Society intended capturing the whole thing, Miss Brittan and all, and sending our Board adrift."[16]

The board defensively claimed the work in Japan as its own mission project. Its leaders' attitude toward the woman's society was clear in its reply in the *Methodist Recorder.*

If the church is able and willing at this time to build two houses for the purposes set forth respectively by the Board and the Woman's Foreign Missionary Society, let it be done. If not, then let the one most needed be built first. In determining this, let the fact be remembered that one party has on its hands a prosperous and growing mission school . . . the entire support of which may at any time be thrown upon its hands. This question settled, each can give [money] intelligently where in his or her judgment, is deemed best.[17]

John Scott could not resist responding in an editorial in the same issue. There he endorsed two separate homes, but added pointedly, "If the thing is impractical, it may be pertinent to ask, Who proposed to build the first Home, the Woman's Society or the Board? . . . Must the women retire because they decline, as they must do to keep good faith with the people, to hand over their funds to the Board?"[18]

Although the dispute resulted in a noticeable decrease in contributions to the Brick Fund, eventually each group purchased its own home in Japan, the board in 1883 and the society in 1889.

The tensions developing over Methodist Protestant women's new self-assertion and competence burst loose at the 1884 General Conference. In its report to the body, the society requested a renewal of its 1880 mandate and a reaffirmation of its independent status within the denomination. The conference's Committee on Foreign Missions instead drafted and approved a set of "Rules for Governing the Woman's Foreign Missionary Society of the Methodist Protestant Church," which amounted to a new constitution for the society. In what can be characterized only as a crude and anxious deployment of power, the men of this committee failed to show the new rules to the three women whom the society had sent as observers to the conference (Mary Miller among them) until twenty minutes before the rules were to be presented on the floor.

These proposed "Rules" of 1884 departed dramatically from the society's original constitution. As Miller later attested, they provided that:

The liberal Constitution under which the Society had been working was to be taken from it, and it was to be placed under the Board of

224

Missions, simply being an auxiliary of that Board. All power was to be taken from it. Even the appointment of its missionaries, the designation of their fields of labor, all appropriations, and all official acts of the Society were to be presented to the Board of Foreign Missions before they could be legally carried out.[19]

It was a form of ecclesiastical sexual politics that would become familiar in other Protestant denominations in succeeding decades, if it was not already well known.[20]

This proposal was not quite as radical as the male Board of Missions' earlier suggestions that all the society's funds go directly into the board's treasury. Nevertheless, the women observers at the 1884 General Conference were understandably aghast. "True, they had heard rumors that certain brethren were displeased with the large amount of liberty given the young Society . . . ," Mary Miller acknowledged later, "but the idea of consenting voluntarily to surrender the rights of the Constitution, under which they had been working successfully, was entirely foreign to their thoughts."[21] With only minutes to spare before the report was to be presented, the representatives of the society had no time to discuss their objections to the proposed rules or to rally support for the minority report favoring their contrary viewpoint. Without speaking privileges and not being allowed on the floor, the women could only watch, wait, and hope that the conference would consider and adopt the minority report.

The question was never debated, however. The chair of the Committee on Foreign Missions preempted discussion by prefacing his introduction with the announcement that the society's representatives had approved the contents of the majority report in full. One female observer charitably assumed that he had misunderstood their intentions. Whatever the case, the women were powerless to point out the error, and the Rules were overwhelmingly approved by the body.[22]

When word of this preemptive General Conference action reached the local Methodist Protestant congregations, members of the societies were outraged. Although the three representatives had been unwitting and powerless pawns, "they narrowly escaped resolutions of censure from the various Branches."[23]

Leaders of the W.F.M.S. had learned a hard but useful lesson. By 1888, they had explored and developed their political leverage. The General Conference of that year overwhelmingly supported their request "that the former freedom of action granted the Society, and of which it had been deprived at the previous convention, be restored."[24] Seven years later in 1895, members of the Board of Missions were again suggesting, off the record, that the board and the society consolidate, but Methodist Protestant women steadfastly and successfully refused such entreaties.[25]

As the Woman's Foreign Missionary Society gained strength, its officers grew in their ability and willingness to exercise leadership. Further, the women's efforts and talents were increasingly recognized and appreciated by the men of the denomination. Annual conferences began to seat women delegates selected by local churches.[26] With the memory of 1884 uppermost in their minds, women planned how they might obtain even more influence on the floor of General Conference to protect their work and authority.

The 1888 General Conference of the much larger Methodist Episcopal Church had refused (after acrid debate) to seat four women delegates elected by annual conferences.[27] When active Methodist Protestant women and their male supporters looked closely at the Methodist Protestant constitution, they realized that the legal objections to women delegates at General Conference apparently already had been removed in their denomination. Thus four women were elected as delegates to the Methodist Protestant General Conference in 1892. Not surprisingly, all were leaders in the Woman's Foreign Missionary Society. Melissa M. Bonnett was a returned missionary from Japan and had organized many local chapters in the West Virginia Conference; Mrs. M. J. Morgan had been an organizer and an officer of the Indiana branch; A. E. (Mrs. J. M.) Murphy was treasurer of the Iowa Conference Board of Missions; and Mrs. Eugenia St. John was a founder of the Kansas branch.[28]

Eugenia F. St. John also had been ordained an elder by the Kansas Annual Conference in 1889, although clergywomen had not yet been officially recognized in the Methodist Protestant Church.[29] She had a famous predecessor in Anna Howard Shaw, originally a member of the Methodist Episcopal Church.[30] When Shaw had realized that her own denomination was not going to ordain women, she had appealed to the New York Conference of the Methodist Protestant Church, which ordained her in 1880.[31] The Methodist Protestant General Conference of 1884 ruled Shaw's ordination out of order, however (in addition to stripping the Woman's Foreign Missionary Society of its independence).[32] Thus the difficult struggle for laity rights for women in the Methodist Protestant Church became bound, at a critical time, with the even more controversial question of women's ordination.

The two issues aroused impassioned responses within the denomination. The *Methodist Recorder* of 1892 gave considerable space to arguments pro and con on both questions, but most of the articles and letters focused on the ordination issue.[33] The celebrated Methodist Episcopal leader of the Women's Christian Temperance Union, Frances Willard, also contributed an article, "Your Sons and Your Daughters Shall Prophesy," urging the denomination to grant ordination to women.[34]

Two other contributors deserve special attention. One was no less than John J. Murray whose compromise proposal of 1858, as later adopted, had opened the constitutional door through which Methodist Protestant women hoped to walk onto the General Conference floor. Murray and his brother J. T. Murray were prominent members of the Maryland Annual Conference; John J. had served as General Conference president of the southern wing. In a letter entitled "Are Women Eligible As Representatives?" Murray noted that the question was one of church law rather than scriptural interpretation. While such arguments raged in other churches, it is interesting that no one in Methodist Protestantism seems to have claimed that scriptural Christianity restricted the laity rights of women. Murray argued that his 1858 proposed amendment could not be interpreted as allowing women delegates, because its original intent was otherwise, and that the subject of women's suffrage and eligibility had never been raised at that time. Murray warned, "If the recognition of women as eligible to a seat in the General Conference had been insisted upon or even proposed the union [of the northern and southern churches in 1877] would not have been consummated."[35]

Thomas B. Appleget, a New Jersey pastor, turned John Murray's argument neatly on its head. Murray "would be equally safe in saying that if the right of a colored man had been so insisted upon, a like result would have been probable," Appleget argued unforgettably. "The union was consummated by leaving the whole question . . . in the annual conferences," he said, striking to the constitutional root of the matter.[36]

The Methodist Protestant constitution did specify that the membership of General Conference should consist of "an equal number of ministers and laymen." Murray had argued that by definition (that is, by gender) "women are plainly excluded" from the category of lay*men*. Pointing out that in some instances the *Discipline* used the inclusive phrase *his and her,* Murray deduced that, whenever *man* or masculine pronouns were used, the framers of the constitution of the church meant to exclude women.[37] Appleget found other instances in the *Discipline,* however, where *man* seemed to be used with clear reference to both sexes, and concluded, "The words 'man,' 'person,' 'layman,' 'believer,' and 'saint' are used without distinction of male or female in our fundamental law."[38]

The struggle over women's rights was easily the central issue of the 1892 Methodist Protestant General Conference, convened at Westminster, Maryland, in Murray's bailiwick. The editor of the *Methodist Recorder,* D. S. Stephens, wrote that Eugenia St. John was the center of attention as the conference opened. Her eligibility and that of the three laywomen were first considered by the Credentials Committee. Chairing this committee was J. T. Murray, John Murray's brother, and among its members was Thomas Appleget.[39] Stephens' reporting of the Credentials Committee's decision left no room for doubt about how tightly drawn was the issue of women's rights.

The Committee on Certificates of the General Conference of the Methodist Protestant Church, on whom devolved the duty of bringing up the much discussed woman question, submitted two reports to-day, one from the majority and one from the minority. The committee of seven was as evenly divided as could be, the majority report being signed by four members and that of the minority by three. By the emphatic tone of these reports all doubts were set at rest, neither side being disposed to yield an inch. It was supposed that those opposed to woman representatives would not oppose the seating of the women lay delegates, and would make their fight on the case of Rev. Mrs. St. John, one of the ministerial delegates from Kansas. On the other hand, it was thought that those favoring the women's cause would yield something in the case of Mrs. St. John, they claiming that she is the only one against whom any constitutional objection can be raised, and that only because of the deliverance of the General Convention [of 1884], which declared [a woman's] ordination void. But neither side did what was expected of them. The opponents of the women declared most positively the election of all the women to be in violation of the constitution. The other side declared in their report with equal positiveness that the credentials of all the delegates, as certified to the secretary, are in order, and that the delegates are entitled to seats.[40]

The General Conference debated the two reports for two full days. Several proposals suggested postponements or constitutional amendments, which would have entailed a four-year process; all substitute motions were defeated, tabled, or withdrawn. Unfortunately, a full record of the debate was not kept, but eyewitnesses report that J. T. Murray reiterated his brother's arguments concerning church law, and Thomas Appleget restated his defense of the women's constitutional and moral case. Thirteen other speeches were made. Perhaps the most dramatic was Eugenia St. John's, in which she laid the matter out boldly in defense of herself and her sisters.

There is a serious question before you. . . . Dare this conference stand before the omen given by God and frustrate his will for the upbuilding of his church by your prejudices? . . . The great question of the future is whether you will have power to conquer the forces of sin, and I tell you it will need every woman that can be found to stand side by side with the good-minded men in this work if the church is to be triumphant.[41]

229

Finally, by a vote of 77 to 48, all four women delegates were seated at the conference of 1892.[42] The women's position had won convincingly, but the debate on the issue of women's laity rights was not yet over.

Three days later, J. T. Murray formally introduced a constitutional amendment to allow women to serve as both lay and clergy delegates to General Conference.[43] Murray knew that several delegates who had finally voted for seating the women had wanted to give the whole church an opportunity to express its will, and he himself had promised to welcome women delegates "when they are made eligible to a seat in this body by the constitution of the church."[44] Not guilelessly, he knew also that approval of two-thirds of the annual conferences was necessary to ratify a constitutional amendment—and that gaining these votes would be a herculean task in the loosely connected denomination.

Appleget and the other supporters of women's rights were not to be led into this trap. Four years before, in 1888, they had observed a similar maneuver to exclude women delegates from the Methodist Episcopal General Conference. Astutely, Appleget parried with a substitute amendment which permitted annual conferences to forbid women to be ordained or to serve as delegates to the General Conference. Appleget's carefully worded substitute passed overwhelmingly.[45] And, as he foresaw, Methodist Protestant annual conferences overwhelmingly ignored it.

The mood of the General Conference of 1892 had already been expressed when, by a two-to-one margin, it voted to remove the word *obey* from the woman's marriage vow.[46] After debate, prayer, and contest, the brethren of the Methodist Protestant Church had decided to take the advice of Eugenia St. John "that this [was] a grand opportunity of giving an example to all the churches and the world of [the Methodist Protestant Church's] broad spirit of liberality to its representatives, of its progress in God's kingdom, of its willingness to live above prejudice in the spiritual kingdom."[47]

After the initial enthusiasm wore off, however, the church faltered in its implementation of these noble sentiments. Equal opportunities for women in leadership and service thereafter were a possibility, but seldom a reality. Only three women were elected delegates to the General Conference in 1896; only one in 1900. The 1896 Conference actually passed a retrogressive resolution (sponsored by J. T. Murray) that the constitution should be clarified in order for women to be ordained or elected as General Conference delegates. The resolution was referred to the annual conferences, and surprisingly, it almost passed as a constitutional amendment. Well over half the annual conferences approved Murray's proposal, despite the fact that several conferences functioned barely or not at all at the time. The necessary two-thirds vote for passage was not achieved, however, and the constitutional language stayed the same. The will of the church was clear: Those Methodist Protestant annual conferences that wished to ordain women or elect them to General Conference were free to do so. Although few women subsequently would be elected, their right to be seated was never again questioned.[48]

Methodist Protestant laywomen and their clergy sisters had been granted a place, small but significant, within the entire governing structure of the denomination. Between the years 1879 and 1892, they had achieved a degree of freedom and equality far beyond that of women in the dominant northern and southern branches of Methodism, and they had successfully protected the nearly autonomous status of the Woman's Foreign Missionary Society. Why were Methodist Protestant women successful in achieving such a rapid change in status, while their more numerous and prominent sisters in the episcopal branches of Methodism could not? Some Methodist Protestant men may have voted favorably out of a desire to upstage the Methodist Episcopal Churches North and South—those ecclesiastical "stars" toward which Methodist Protestants had long felt rivalrous and somewhat morally superior.[49] The contemporary woman's suffrage movement and increasingly more enlightened public attitudes about the "place" of women in society following the Civil War surely receive part of the credit, but this would apply equally to the larger Methodist branches.

Perhaps the key reason for the transformation was the need of the small, struggling Methodist Protestant denomination for the leadership and participation of all its members, women included, while men in the larger, more prosperous Methodist denominations could indulge in the luxury of keeping their women as second-class citizens. Sensing the times, their true usefulness, and the men's welcome, despite its ambivalence, Methodist Protestant women responded. Credit for the changed status of women goes to the vision, sense of organization, self-reliance, and religiously rooted self-respect of the leaders and members of the Woman's Foreign Missionary Society. Without the personal initiative and sense of call of those women, there would have been no specific Methodist Protestant missions. Women began and inspired the work; they learned and grew from it, also. The unusually high recognition which the Methodist Protestant Church accorded to its women in the last two decades of the nineteenth century was a result of both the church's need and the women's own impressive achievement.

"A NEW IMPULSE"

Donald K. Gorrell

The emergence of laywomen in leadership levels and visible service in two denominations, the United Brethren in Christ and the Evangelical Association, occurred during the four decades after 1870. By 1910, the basic roles of leadership and service for laywomen had been determined and remained fixed until these two rather dissimilar churches of German background united in 1946.

It is common today to study the Evangelical United Brethren heritage as one tradition in The United Methodist Church. As this study will reveal, however, the Evangelical and the United Brethren branches were far from uniform. While common motivating stimuli can be identified, the responses in each denomination differed markedly and produced divergent results. Consequently, much of this essay will constitute a study in contrasts. It is noteworthy also that for both the Evangelical Association and the United Brethren in Christ, the period in which women sought a larger role in the work and ministry of the church was influenced by internal schismatic difficulties, as well as by general Protestant emphases on missions and lay leadership.

Given these complexities, the scope of lay leadership studied here has been narrowed to exclude consideration of women as deaconesses and lay preachers. Both these vocations in fact required a full-time commitment to a specialized ministry that was not typical of most laity at the time. Instead, attention has been confined to two areas where women acquired leadership, power, and influence through more typical lay functions—namely, in women's missionary associations and as lay representatives to annual and General conferences, the decision-making levels of both churches beyond the local congregation.

One obvious similarity in the two traditions is the motivation that inspired their women. In both heritages, the terms *a new impulse* or *a new impetus* appeared when the leaders referred to the origins of the women's missionary movement. For instance, recounting the history of the first decade of the United Brethren Woman's Missionary Association, the initial issue of the organization's periodical, *Woman's Evangel,* said in 1882, "Ten short years ago a woman's missionary association was a thing unheard of in our church. . . . About that time a strange awakening occurred, a new impulse was aroused among us."[1] In 1884, Mrs. W. H. Hammer remarked similarly to a convention of Evangelical women, "When our first missionaries to Japan left home and kindred to enter upon this arduous work, this heart-felt desire [to organize for missions] received a new impulse, and Mrs. Dr. Krecker and Miss Hudson carried with them the awakened sympathies of the workers at home."[2] This "new impulse" was the women's keen recognition of the needs for foreign missions—in Japan for the Evangelicals; in West Africa for the United Brethren.

A second similarity is evident in the laywomen's response to this new stimulus: Both denominations soon formed effective all-female organizations. After Lizzie Hoffman, a United Brethren schoolteacher in Dayton, Ohio, had struggled with her soul about going to Africa as a missionary, she found peace finally in the conviction that God would rather that she organize women to support missions, and she was responsible for initiating the United Brethren work in 1872.[3] When Evangelicals such as Emma Yost in Cleveland in 1878 and Minerva Strawman in Lindsey, Ohio, two years later, felt impelled to assist missionaries, they thought immediately of organizing women.[4]

Since women in those days had no channels for such activity, they sought the aid of churchmen involved with denominational mission boards. The support of men, particularly those on the boards, differed greatly in the two churches. Lizzie Hoffman shared her conviction of the need to organize women with John Kemp, a founder and longtime member of the Home, Frontier, and Foreign Missionary Society of the United Brethren in Christ. Kemp counseled her, and together they called a meeting of interested women and ministers in Dayton, Ohio, on May 9, 1872. Those who attended that meeting voted to organize the Woman's Missionary Association of the Miami Conference. When the men of that annual conference met later that year, they adopted the following resolution: *"Resolved,* That we are highly pleased with the interest taken by a number of sisters in the cause of missions in our conference, and gratified to learn of the organization of a Woman's Missionary Society in our midst, and that we will heartily second the efforts of this society in their noble work."[5]

In May 1873, the quadrennial General Conference of the United Brethren heard endorsements of the Woman's Missionary Association in the bishop's address and in the missionary secretary's report, and the delegates commended the "zeal and enterprise" of the women and urged "that all the 'women's missionary associations' be made auxiliary to the branch missionary societies of the conference within whose bounds they are organized."[6]

In contrast, when Emma Yost and friends petitioned the Board of Missions of the Evangelical Association in 1878, they were refused permission to organize.[7] Two years later Minerva Strawman revived the idea, but with a modified form and emphasis. "The propriety of organizing an independent Woman's Missionary Society is questionable," she admitted, "but we find no reason whatever why Woman's Missionary Auxiliaries should not be formed."[8] Men finally recognized the value of having women raise money for missions, but their enabling action stipulated that women's groups could exist only on the local level and must be "under the supervision of the preacher."[9] When the General Conference of the Evangelical Association in 1883 authorized a national Woman's Missionary Society, the wife of one of the delegates explained to the woman who led the campaign for the women's organization: "Mr. Wiest did his utmost to get the petition before the Conference . . . but had much trouble with the German element of the committee . . . as they could not endure the idea of women *usurping so much authority.*"[10] The men's attitude is characteristic of the Evangelical tradition in this study.

Another contrast between the Evangelicals and the United Brethren was the difference in organization. Initially, Evangelical women were allowed to organize only at the local level, while United Brethren women first created missionary associations in the annual conferences. This distinction faded in importance, however, as it became clear in both denominations that churchwide organizations were needed. To achieve that goal, Evangelical women followed a predictable pattern of petitioning the Board of Missions for "permission to organize a Woman's Board of Missions" that would be "auxiliary to the Parent Society" and under its supervision and authority.[11] Even that docile relationship was granted begrudgingly, with the requirement that the women submit their proceedings to the Board of Missions annually "for examination and approval."[12]

In a similar process, some United Brethren women decided, in consultation with male leaders of their board, that a national woman's organization was desirable; they prepared a proposed constitution indicating that their society would be an auxiliary to existing missionary boards. A number of women regarded themselves as "co-workers and co-laborers in the great mission field" and saw no need for "a separate and independent existence." In the thinking of the men, women were needed to carry the gospel to women and children in mission areas and to educate women and children in local churches in order to raise money for such ministry.[13] However, in contrast to their Evangelical sisters, when the United Brethren women met in October 1875, they decided that it was necessary to be related only to the General Conference and that they could be otherwise independent in structure and function. Thus on their own initiative, United Brethren women amended their constitution and voted to create a churchwide Woman's Missionary Association.[14] One of the more militant women wrote in defense of this action, "We do not propose to wait for any 'Board' or for any authority, save that of General Conference. If God shall give us the missionaries and the means, we shall find the field, whether the original Board has found it before or not."[15] When the association sent two women to report to General Conference in 1877, those representatives simply requested recognition of an existing group which had already sent its first missionary to Africa. Upon recommendation of its Committee on Missions, this General Conference recognized the Woman's Missionary Association as an official church agency, approved its constitution, and confirmed its officers.[16] Such independence in organization typified the United Brethren Woman's Missionary Association.

This contrast in organization was the consequence of a difference in style of operation. From the outset, Evangelical women were affected by their dependent and auxiliary relationship to the male Board of Missions. Although the 1883 General Conference had approved their society, Evangelical women were forced to wait a year to begin to function, because the board, which needed to approve the constitution and officers of the woman's society, did not meet officially until October 1884. To save time and facilitate plans, the women met at the same time as the board and twice adjourned their sessions to confer with that body. At last, the board ratified the constitution of the Woman's Missionary Society, and the women could finally elect their officers and begin to function.[17] When they wanted to publish a periodical and when they wanted to support a "special field" of work, it was necessary for them to petition the board, which repeatedly rejected their requests. Both finally were approved in 1899, but the woman's society had first requested them fourteen years earlier, in 1885![18] In fairness, it must be recognized that the women's activities were impeded by a denominational division; nevertheless, support for women's missionary endeavors developed slowly among Evangelicals.

By comparison, United Brethren women enjoyed considerable autonomy and were able to do as much mission work as they could afford to support. When they felt the need of a periodical, for example, they solicited subscriptions; when they had secured the necessary 1,000, they began publication of their own monthly, the *Woman's Evangel,* in January 1882.[19] With that degree of independence, the achievements

237

of the United Brethren Woman's Missionary Association were remarkable. At the 1877 General Conference, it was reported that the association had 3 conference branches, 18 local societies, and annual receipts of $325. Thirty-two years later, the association informed the General Conference that they had more than 20,000 members and that during the past quadrennium they had raised $175,000 to support 42 missionaries in the foreign field, in addition to 60 native workers. In their missions in Africa, China, and the Philippines, United Brethren women had established churches, Sunday schools, schools, orphanages, and dispensaries with a property valuation of $98,000. As the men of the Foreign Missionary Society acknowledged, the women were responsible by that time for half the denomination's overseas mission program.[20]

These achievements gave United Brethren women considerable power. When the church reorganized its entire plan for missions, in 1909, the Woman's Missionary Association was asked to combine its resources with the other mission boards; in return, the women would constitute one-third of the membership of the boards and their executive committees.[21] Mrs. L. R. Harford, president of the association, interpreted the meaning of the proposal to the General Conference.

The plan proposed of joint control is ideal. Men and women, each with their natural characteristics, join in the great work of bringing this lost world to Christ. We firmly believe that this is a great forward movement, and, if it would not seem like egotism, I would say, brethren, that within the last quadrennium you have almost caught up with us, and we are now ready to join with you in the forward work.[22]

Explaining the significance of the action in the *Woman's Evangel*, Mrs. Harford affirmed, "Just as we believe we were divinely called to begin work thirty-four years ago, so we believe we have been led to take the step now in harmony with the spirit of the times." Noting that United Brethren women had received all they had requested and had been elected to the boards, she went on to observe:

By this arrangement we not only have a voice in the administration of our own funds, but in all the funds of the Church; not only in the appointment of missionaries in the three fields we have in the past, but in the five foreign fields of the Church and in all the work in home missions. We not only have an interest in property in the three mission fields where we invested, but in all the property in all fields.[23]

Futhermore, women were given more opportunity to work with young women and with the Junior Societies of Christian Endeavor. They were to continue to publish the *Evangel* and were convinced that "this action does not change our form of organization in the least."[24]

Through this major reorganization and their larger involvement in the management of the church, the Woman's Missionary Association secured a new status and power for women, described by one officer as "epoch-making."[25] That accomplishment marks a fitting place to end the study of women's rise to leadership and power in the missionary work of the United Brethren in Christ.

By the same year, 1909, the Woman's Missionary Society among the Evangelicals also achieved institutional acceptance, although accompanied by far less power and influence. While consistent with earlier patterns in the denomination, the limited status of women was partially the result of the harrowing effects of schism in the Evangelical Association. Whereas the events that had divided the United Brethren Church in 1889 had had little effect upon its women's missionary activities, the contentions among the Evangelicals directly affected the development of their Woman's society. The impact of denominational division thus has provided another contrast in women's rise to power and leadership in the two churches.[26]

As the 1891 Evangelical General Conference approached, contending factions pushed issues to the breaking point, and the executive committee of the Woman's Missionary Society "saw fit to postpone their annual meeting until after the session" of that deliberative body. Angered by the delay, the Board of Missions condemned the action as a violation of the society's constitution, declared its officers displaced, and called for a reorganization meeting in February 1892. The editor of the denominational weekly of the majority party wrote:

> The circumstance which necessitates this reorganization, is to be deplored, but it is only one of the many sad results of the rebellion in our church. The Woman's Missionary Society has been peculiarly unfortunate in having been planned and manipulated for several years largely in the rebel camp. The male rebel leaders were back of certain women who carried out their schemes as far as possible. Loyal officers were frozen out of the general organization; general officers of the society were sympathizers with the seceders.[27]

As a result, the Evangelical Woman's Missionary Society was split in two and continued separately in each branch of the divided church.

Continuity of leadership in the society went with the schismatic group, which called itself the United Evangelical Church when it organized formally in 1894. During the interim from 1891 to 1894, the woman's organization achieved little and became disheartened. When they met in September 1895, the president poignantly noted, "As an organization we are twelve years old, but as the Woman's Missionary Society of the United Evangelical Church we are holding our first meeting." In the new denominational structure, she reported, women would have a larger influence, with representatives on the quarterly conference of each congregation and on the general Board of Missions. Moreover, they would at last be able to publish their own periodical, *Missionary Tidings,* and to support two women in a foreign mission soon to be established.[28]

The initial elation of the United Evangelical women diminished when they discovered that the constitution they had drafted in 1895 had been drastically modified by the Board of Missions, giving the society less representation than promised. Despite protests by the women, Bishop Rudolph Dubs explained to the 1898 General Conference that the constitutional changes had been necessary in order to avoid "conflicts of authority" and "future friction." The changes also did away with the office of corresponding secretary, which functionally deprived the society of its active leadership and thereby weakened its program.[29] At the 1910 General Conference, the men praised the women for their ability to provide missionary funds, for their efficiency in missionary education, and for their insistence on establishing foreign mission work, which had resulted in the denomination's mission in China.[30] In short, the fact that it was a helpful auxiliary to the Board of Missions was seen as the primary accomplishment of the woman's society in the United Evangelical Church.

It will be remembered that in the mainstream Evangelical Association, the Woman's Missionary Society had been ordered to reorganize itself in the wake of the division of the denomination. At the society's reorganization convention in Cleveland, Ohio, in 1892, new officers were elected. The existing constitution was readopted, but a committee was appointed to revise the document and report to the annual meeting in September. At that meeting, the corresponding secretary of the mission board advised the delegates that they should "gather up the scattered portions of the Woman's Missionary Society of our Church and re-unite them under efficient, faithful management." The women sought to do this by changing the constitution to provide for quadrennial, rather than annual, meetings of the whole society, with only the executive committee meeting annually. They also committed themselves to helping liquidate the mission board's large debt.[31]

Within two years the women were praised for successfully overcoming the difficulties caused by reorganization and for efficiently collecting funds to alleviate the financial crisis.[32] Despite such adulation, however, a request by the society to be given sole use of the *Missionary Messenger* was denied by the Evangelical Association's General Conference and their request that a "special field" be designated for their financial endeavors also was rejected as "superfluous" and "impracticable." Given the mission board's directive that the officers of the woman's society should refer all "important measures and methods" to the board's executive committee for "its investigation and approval," the leaders of the women could not fail to see their limited status in the eyes of the men who governed the Evangelical Association.[33]

At the end of the next quadrennium, however, women's work was more positively evaluated. In 1898 the Evangelical Board of Missions noted that the women were "in prosperous condition" in both money and members, and upon its recommendation, the 1899 General Conference amended the board's constitution to enable a woman representative to become a member. Evangelical women were pleased, too, that this General Conference approved two long desired requests: that the monthly *Missionary Messenger* be designated the "organ of the Woman's Missionary Society," with the society empowered to select its own editor, and that the society be permitted to maintain two of its own missionaries in Japan.[34]

As the Woman's Missionary Society of the Evangelical Association entered the twentieth century, its work had achieved stability. At last it was accorded recognition and assigned expanded responsibilities. Institutional acceptance was evident when the categories "W.M.S. Auxiliaries" and "W.M.S. Members" were officially added to the statistical reports of the church in 1903. An editorial in the *Evangelical Messenger* in September of that year indicated the organization's point of arrival: "The Woman's Missionary Society of our Church had a small and troubled beginning, and a slow growth; it had some opposition and more distrust and disinterest to encounter. But it has clearly won the day. It has shown its fitness to survive and take its place in the family of the church."[35] The direction and pattern of the organization as an auxiliary of the Board of Missions was clearly fixed in the first decade of this century and remained so until its eventual reunion with the United Evangelicals in 1922. There is no doubt that Evangelical women exercised less power and influence in missionary work than did their counterparts in the United Brethren Church.

Lay representation was a second area in which women came to exercise leadership. This area, too, affords a study in contrasts between the two traditions, for the United Brethren in Christ enabled women to be seated as lay delegates in both annual and General conferences in the period from 1870 to 1910 while at no time were women in either branch of the Evangelical tradition accorded that right.

Lay representation was requested by United Brethren men as early as 1861, but that was impossible without amendment of the constitution; this in itself was an issue so controversial that a permanent division occurred in the church in 1889. It was decided in 1877 that while the constitution forbade lay representation at General Conferences, it did not specifically deny it at annual conferences, and the following year, some annual conferences admitted laity to membership for the first time. By 1883 in the Miami Conference, and by 1888 in the East Ohio Conference, women were elected as lay delegates.[36] Liberal legislation enacted under the revised constitution confirmed by the General Conference of 1889 gave United Brethren women even more status and power. After the schismatic minority withdrew, new enactments provided that women could be elected as lay delegates at all levels of the church and that they could be ordained as clergy, as well.[37] Of the fifty-two lay delegates seated for the first time at the 1893 General Conference, two were women, and their presence was resoundingly acknowledged by the bishops.

Since the world began, until now, it is not probable that in an ecclesiastical body of such functions and proportions as belong to this General Conference have women been recognized on an equality with their brethren. Several conferences have chosen to send as delegates esteemed women from among them. These Christian women are here to-day accorded this highest representative trust in the Church, and are welcomed to sit with us in the highest council of the denomination.[38]

From this historic beginning, women delegates were elected to every succeeding General Conference of the United Brethren Church. Initially the numbers were small—six in 1897 and two in 1901—but their ranks swelled after 1905, when lay people were allowed to be seated in equal numbers with ministers; there were twenty-four women delegates in 1905 and twenty-two in 1909. While laywomen theoretically were granted full powers and rights, it is obvious in the records of United Brethren General Conferences through

1909 that female delegates seldom spoke and never chaired a committee. When the bishops assigned delegates to standing committees, they apparently were influenced by certain images of women's role, for the first women to be assigned were both placed on the Missionary Interests committee.[39] This at least testified to women's influence in that area. In 1897 women continued to serve on Missionary Interests but also were placed on committees on Sabbath Schools and Young People's Christian Union, and in 1901 a woman was assigned to the Educational Institutions committee.[40] When the number of lay delegates to General Conferences was increased in 1905, the twenty-four women present were assigned to thirteen of the twenty-eight committees; consequently, their influence was greatly expanded.[41]

Thus, in lay representation as well as in missionary activities, women shared at least moderately in the full leadership of the United Brethren Church. While it is doubtful that they exercised the power and influence suggested by the editorial "Woman's Rightful Place," in a 1901 issue of *Religious Telescope,* it is clear that by 1910, women's place in that church was considerably more elevated and powerful than in the Evangelical branches.[42]

By contrast, lay delegation itself, apart from the question of gender, was opposed and delayed in the Evangelical Association. Lay representation became a major issue in the schism that split this denomination between 1891 and 1894, though there were both rebel and loyalist conventions of laymen. From the beginning, lay representation was advocated by the minority group which formed the United Evangelical Church. However, an examination of its lists of lay delegates reveals that women were not represented. In the more conservative Evangelical Association, the issue of lay delegation was delayed into the twentieth century, with the first layman being seated at the 1907 General Conference. No women were seated then, or at any succeeding conference, until union with the United Brethren was imminent in the 1940s. Thus, in the Evangelical tradition, in sharp distinction to the United Brethren, women never had an opportunity to exercise power as lay representatives.

Women in both the Evangelical Association and the United Brethren in Christ felt similar impulses to organize, to assume leadership, and to engage in more visible and recognized service during the years from 1870 to 1910. But the historical evidence contrasts in the implementation of these impulses. The United Brethren were much more appreciative of women's status and role, and much earlier than the Evangelicals; consequently, women were able to exercise increasingly greater power, influence, and leadership in the ranks of that denomination. Finally, this study underscores the fallacy of assuming too easily that the two churches that today comprise the Evangelical United Brethren tradition within The United Methodist Church were alike in origins, practices, and attitudes. In the case of the status and roles of laywomen, the work that began as a study of a single heritage has necessarily developed into an essay tracing women's evolution in two distinct traditions in the four decades from 1870 to 1910.

CREATING A SPHERE
FOR WOMEN

Rosemary Skinner Keller

The "woman issue," in a multiplicity of forms, was the most controversial question confronting the General Conferences of the Methodist Episcopal Church from 1869 until shortly after the turn of the century. The action taken by 399 male delegates (248 ordained ministers and 151 laymen) who met in Pike's Opera House, Cincinnati, for the 1880 convention, was symbolic of a trend which was to continue for almost forty years. The report of relevant legislation stated simply:

An episcopal ruling that the Discipline provides neither for the ordaining nor licensing of women as local preachers was approved; but it was ordered that the masculine pronouns "he," "his," and "him," wherever they occur in the Discipline, shall not be construed as excluding women from the office of Sunday-school superintendent, class leader, or steward.[1]

The decision of that 1880 conference defined, in large measure, the status and role of women in the heritage of The United Methodist Church until the mid-twentieth century. By denying ordination to women and by revoking their rights to local preachers' licenses, the church prohibited them from entering fields of leadership and service in which they could work as colleagues with men and share governing power and clerical functions. However, by sanctioning the service of women as Sunday school superintendents and volunteer workers, the conference determined that females would have an essential, though subordinate role, as "helpers" of men in positions of authority. Finally the delegates tangled, for the first time, with the "language" issue as it related to women in the church. Ironically, because the church could not function as a voluntary organization unless women assumed a variety of service tasks, it disregarded the significance of the male gender when the daily needs of the institution were at stake—when need be, *he, his,* and *him* could apply to women as well as to men.

In the late nineteenth century, another development equally consequential in determining the pattern of female leadership within United Methodist tradition was taking place. The major female service organizations of the Methodist Episcopal denomination—the Woman's Foreign Missionary Society and the Woman's Home Missionary Society—were being formed and given official sanction and support by the same General Conferences which denied women the right to preach, be ordained, or serve as lay delegates in the church's governing councils. These organizations, the first to send unmarried women missionaries throughout the world and deaconesses into the inner-city slums of burgeoning American cities, were forerunners of the present United Methodist Women and its parallel organizations in other denominations.[2]

By the turn of the century, the leadership and the service of women in the Methodist Episcopal Church were simultaneously being constricted and expanded. The legacy from these conflicting trends is complex. Women's activities were channeled into a sphere separate from men's, which precluded the possibility that females could share decision-making authority and clerical rights. However, it also resulted in the development of powerful women's organizations, originally designed to be autonomous and to draw the women of the church together in bonds of sisterhood, but which have trained women for broadening positions of leadership both within and outside the church and have enabled the church to function as a voluntary organization.

This heritage is not limited to the United Methodist tradition. Restriction of women's function to a separate sphere determined the pattern of women's leadership and participation in all mainline Protestant traditions of America—Episcopal, Presbyterian, Baptist, Lutheran, and United Church of Christ denominations.

247

One essential approach in recovering the history of women is to discover and interpret clearly defined movements for freedom and equality—suffrage, education, property, employment, and other concerns within secular society, as well as ordination and laity rights in the church. A second focus is equally essential: to discover the variety of functions females have performed and to analyze the subtle changes in the constriction and expansion of roles that have affected the evolution of women's position in society today.

Using the Methodist Episcopal Church, this paper will combine these two approaches in a study to analyze the patterns of women's leadership in the church. It will focus on two movements which occurred simultaneously, and which resulted in the creation of a sphere for women in the church: the denial to women of the opportunity to lead and work with men on a basis of collegiality, and the founding of the first national women's organization of the denomination, the Woman's Foreign Missionary Society (W.F.M.S.). The W.F.M.S. was an accommodation to the system, the only way possible for women to work within the denomination and at the same time develop their vision and use their talents on behalf of the church. The underlying question for the historian is whether the significance of a separate sphere for women resulted in the containment and isolation of women's activity, or whether its more important aim and consequence was to expand their function and even to liberate them from the constrictions of the church in the late nineteenth century.

A sphere for women in the church resulted both from the denial of equal clergy and lay rights and from the initiative which women took to create their own organizations and to maintain authority in their carefully carved-out domain. Though the struggle for women's rights in the church in the mid-twentieth century has centered on ordination, which was gained in the United Methodist tradition only in 1956, that was not the center of controversy in the late nineteenth century. A sprinkling of women were local preachers in the Methodist Episcopal Church after the highly effective evangelist, Margaret Van Cott, had gained that right in 1869. No woman threatened male domination of clergy rights until the late 1870s, however, when Anna Howard Shaw and Anna Oliver sought to be ordained by the New England Annual Conference, although support for preaching and clerical roles for women was not great enough to arouse much opposition to the strong will of the male majority of the 1880 General Conference.

There was a recurring bone of contention, however. By the 1880s, vigorous support had developed for voting rights for laywomen at the General Conference, which met every four years, and at annual conferences, which covered regional or state areas. The issue involved the election of females as lay delegates to these governing conventions of the denomination. Laity in the Methodist Episcopal Church were usually referred to as lay*men*. The issue took visible and personal form when four duly elected female delegates from the Rock River (Illinois), Nebraska, Minnesota, and Kansas conferences sought to claim seats at the 1888 Convention. The Rock River representative was Frances E. Willard, founder of the Woman's Christian Temperance Union and an ardent advocate of women's suffrage. Seventeen other women had been elected as reserve delegates by their respective conferences.[3]

The minutes stated that "much time was given to the discussion of the 'woman question.' " Debate was intense, contention being so strong that the delegates referred the decision to the membership of the entire church. The tally of votes reported at the next quadrennial conference in 1892 indicated that 235,668 members of individual churches voted for the eligibility of women, and 163,843 against, while 5,634 ministers were in favor of women delegates, and 4,717 against. Though a plurality of the membership and ministers affirmed the change, the necessary three-fourths majority had not been attained. A ruling by the Committee on Judiciary was designed to clarify the meaning of the vote: "The intent of the lawmakers in using the words 'lay delegates,' 'laymen,' and 'members of the Church in full connection,' in paragraphs 55 to 63 inclusive, in the Discipline, was not to apply them to both sexes, but to men only."[4]

The dissension was not a quibble over words, however,

but a question of possession of governing authority and decision-making power in this major Protestant denomination. Once again, the determination was left to the membership and ministers of the entire church. When four more women were elected delegates to the 1896 conference, one male lay representative, deeply fearful of change, alleged that "to seat the claimants would tend to destroy all respect for the constitution of the Church."[5] Conference members, wearied of the challenge, finally agreed that they could not agree and passed a "compromise" plan— that "no formal decision of the question of eligibility be made at this time." Lewis Curts, editor of the conference journal, made a significant commentary on the import of the 1896 decision: "Compromises may sometimes be useful as peacemakers, but more often they end in making more confusion."[6] This lack of clarity and indecisiveness characterized the attitude of the conference until 1906, when the so-called language issue was resolved and women became recognized officially as lay people in the Methodist Episcopal Church.

Failure to grant them lay and clergy rights could have resulted in greater subordination of women and their relegation to increasingly menial tasks, always directed by men. At the same time the General Conferences were constricting their role, however, many women of prominence and capability recognized that opportunities must be developed for leadership and service in the church. They consciously created a sphere for their sex by founding organizations of service to the church and by maintaining their authority within those domains. The Woman's Foreign Missionary Society of the Methodist Episcopal Church was formed in 1869, the year Margaret Van Cott received the denomination's first local preachers' license granted to a woman. Before the society was one year old, it had sent two missionaries to India: Isabella Thoburn, the first unmarried woman missionary of the Methodist Episcopal Church, and Clara Swain, also a single woman and the first female medical missionary to the Orient from the United States.[7] During the next year, the society sent female workers to China and began to develop a broadly based world missionary program.

In 1880, a complementary organization, the Woman's Home Missionary Society, was formed to concentrate on mission priorities within the United States. Five years later, Lucy Rider Meyer founded the Chicago Training School for women missionaries and almost immediately originated the deaconess order, one of the most significant forms of home missionary work in the denomination's history.[8] As prior conferences had sanctioned the Woman's Foreign and Home Missionary societies, so the General Conference of 1888 commended the training school.

A close look at the formation and early development of the Woman's Foreign Missionary Society suggests the far-reaching vision of early missionary-society leaders and missionaries, and points to the significance of a separate sphere in expanding women's role in the church. Founded in March, 1869, by six women who gathered on a stormy day at Tremont Street Church in Boston, three months later the W.F.M.S. began to edit its monthly publication, *The Heathen Woman's Friend*. Directed to all women in the denomination, it began as an eight-page paper, and three years later had doubled in size. The lead article of the first issue stated the purpose of the society concisely and persuasively: "An earnest desire to develop among the ladies of our Church greater interest and activity in our Missions, together with the firm conviction that the pressing needs of our Foreign Missions demand our immediate attention." The founders admitted forthrightly, however, that "apart from all considerations of duty to others, it will be profitable to ourselves to unite together in such associations as are contemplated by this Society."[9] The W.F.M.S. was created not only to liberate women in non-Christian lands from the bondage and insubordination to which custom and religion had subjected them, but to provide outlets for the energy, ability, and leadership of American women in missionary societies, since such avenues were closed to them in the existing structures of the church. Christianity was the faith that promised true womanhood, and the W.F.M.S. was designed to advance the cause of women as well as to meet the needs of the church.

Methodist Episcopal women had participated in antecedent missionary societies such as the Female Missionary Society, founded in 1819, and the Ladies' China Missionary Society of Baltimore, organized in 1847. Both were auxiliaries to the General Missionary and Bible Society of the denomination and were not autonomous women's societies, and both had disbanded several years before. The Woman's Union Missionary Society had been organized in 1860 by women of six denominations, but some of its members felt that societies of separate denominations could better address the needs. Before the end of the decade Congregationalists and Methodists had withdrawn to form their own organizations, and others followed shortly thereafter.[10] When the Woman's Foreign Missionary Society was formed, Jennie Fowler Willing, who was corresponding secretary of the west division and the key leader in the midwestern states, urged women to join this new "avenue of work, that they may think, and plan, and talk, and write, to increase the enthusiasm of the Church, for the salvation of all people everywhere."[11]

The great demand which had called the society into existence was the support of female missionaries abroad. An evangelistic thrust was at the heart of the missionary movement and many missionaries and society leaders stressed that native women must be reached in order to evangelize India and China, the first countries to which the Methodist Episcopal Church sent foreign missionaries. "We know too how inestimable is the value, and how incalculable the influence of a pure Christian home," wrote the editor in the initial appeal of *The Heathen Woman's Friend*.[12] A steady stream of articles presented this goal to missionary society members to gain their support and their identification with the evangelistic cause. The Church need not worry about the conversion of heathen men if it could convert the women. Equally crucial was the influence of the Christian mother over her sons and daughters. The native woman must be taught to order her household and to give her children Christian training.

Because women of India and China were secluded in their homes, they could not be reached by male missionaries. Only female missionaries, sent through the contributions of thousands of members of the Woman's Foreign Missionary Society, could release the 300,000,000 women enslaved in India, wrote the Methodist missionary there, T. J. Scott. Indian women were more superstitious than men and the main support of idolatry. Once enlightened by Christianity, however, the case was reversed, and women were more zealous than men in accepting the gospel. Native opinion recently had turned strongly in favor of female education, missionaries contended in 1869. At that time, 30,000 pupils were being taught in 700 mission schools for girls—one for every 3,000 women. The largest numbers of these women were being reached by the 500 Roman Catholic nuns in heathen India. The Methodists were confronted with a sharp challenge: "Are the women of the Roman Catholic Church to show more zeal, more energy, more self-sacrificing devotedness to the cause of Christ, than the true followers of the Lord Jesus?"[13]

If one purpose in uplifting heathen women was the evangelization of whole dark continents, W.F.M.S. missionaries and leaders also wrote of the education of native women for their own sakes. Christianity was the friend of women, wrote T. J. Scott. Long-held customs of Hinduism and Mohammedism stressed female inferiority and subservience, and where Christianity had not reached, women were ignorant, degraded, and enslaved. These missionaries contended not only that women existed for the sake of advancing Christianity, but that Christ came to save the whole person. The "foundation principle" of the faith, wrote Mrs. E. E. Baldwin, Methodist Episcopal missionary to China, was "the command to give the gospel to every creature." To bring Christ to Indian women meant that they must be given social and mental elevation as well as religious enlightenment.[14]

The education provided Indian girls who attended the orphanage sponsored by the Methodist Episcopal Church at Bareilly indicates that the missionaries were genuinely concerned about the cultural and intellectual development of the natives, as well as about their religious conversion. In supporting the native children, branches of the W.F.M.S. changed the little girls' Indian names to Anglo-American

253

ones. Those adopted by the New England Branch, for instance, were given names such as Susan Hamilton, Hester Poole, Elizabeth Monroe, and Harriet Richardson, for the missionaries' relatives and members of the societies. The assumption that the education of these young women meant their Americanization may be too hasty a response. Isabella Thoburn, the Woman's Foreign Missionary Society's first unmarried woman missionary, describes an eighteen-year-old girl who came to the orphanage with her baby of three months after they had been abandoned by her husband. The young woman wanted to learn English, but the missionaries persuaded her that she must first become fluent in reading and writing her native tongue. Girls were taught to read secular books, as well as the New Testament, in Urdu and Hindu, and were instructed in the geography and history of India. Descriptions of individual students' progress indicate that their course of study which included arithmetic, cooking, sewing, and needlework, was well rounded.[15]

Primarily, the missionaries sought to train the young women to return to their cities and villages, and to aid their native sisters. Many of the girls were members of medical classes taught by Clara Swain, first woman medical missionary from the United States to the Orient, and by various male missionaries. They were educated to be doctors and nurses of practical medicine, and some continued in more advanced work upon graduation. Others were hired to assist the missionaries as Bible readers to women in the zenanas—apartments containing the harems of upperclass Hindus. The goal for students is best described in the progress of Rebecca Pettis, one of the best scholars in the school and a very good teacher himself. After graduation, she married a young native Christian and "went at once with her husband to Nainee Tal, where they both joined Dr. Humphrey's medical class. She is a very useful woman, well fitted in every way to work among the women of this country."[16]

Beyond their vision of evangelizing and educating native women in the mission field, the early missionary-society leaders were equally clear in the goals they sought for their society, and for women generally, in the Methodist

Episcopal Church at home. Their effort to create an autonomous women's organization and to manage their own affairs was a sensitive issue from the beginning. Even before the formation of the society, its leaders were urged by John P. Durbin, secretary of the General Missionary Society, or "parent board," to develop their society in light of these restrictions: "(1) To raise funds for a particular portion of our mission work in India, perhaps also in China; (2) Leave the administration of the work to the Board at home and the missions on the field." In short, Durbin wanted the new women's organization to be an auxiliary of the General Missionary Society. The women, however, carefully delineated their understanding of themselves as co-laborers with the general board and pastors. They regarded the W.F.M.S. as an autonomous agency committed to harmonious relations with the General Missionary Society, "seeking its counsel and approval in all its work."[17]

One fear of the general board was that the woman's society would encroach on potential missionary giving. Describing themselves as an educational arm, the women contended that they would expand missionary donations for the entire church "by increasing the missionary intelligence and enthusiasm of the people."[18] Only once—at the 1876 convention—did the General Conference of the Methodist Episcopal Church recommend a closer financial union of the woman's society and the parent board. The women's response was firm and clear: "We regard closer financial union as prejudicial to our interests, in short, a change would be disastrous." Maintaining the delicate balance as a coordinate, but not subordinate, agency, the W.F.M.S. won the commendation of the General Conference and also gained increased freedom in its work. By the 1890s, its members were taking collections for the women's missionary program in regular church services.[19]

In consciously creating a sphere for women's work, the missionary-society leaders hoped also to give women of the church, with their unrecognized and unused abilities and energies, an expanded purpose for their lives. By developing a sense of responsibility for their sisters on the other side of the world, women could be caught up in a Christ-ordained task of immense proportions; only they, as women whose lives also were restricted and limited to the home, could value this task as being of consuming significance. The cause was presented graphically in an article entitled "Facts for Christian Women."

Suppose that these millions of degraded women were to rise up and pass in review before us, their Christian sisters, marching so that we could count sixty persons each minute. They pass by us at this rate all the day for twelve long hours, and we find that 43,000 have passed us. Days grow to months, and months to years, still the procession moves on. She who started as a pretty, innocent little girl, has grown to womanhood, yet with all that is lovely, noble, and pure in her nature crushed out in her growth. For twenty long years we must stand and count ere we number the last of this sorrowful procession of 300,000,000 heathen women, whom Satan hath bound in such galling chains "lo, these many years."[20]

Not only was it necessary to picture these throngs of women dramatically; it was also necessary to place the burden for their care on the Methodist Episcopal women in an equally intense manner. "It is indeed a fearful sight to see these millions hastening to destruction," the article continued, "but is it not almost as melancholy a sight to see Christian women quietly, carelessly sleeping the while, instead of putting forth the most strenuous efforts to save them?"

The creation of an enlarged purpose for their members' lives was closely tied to the creation of bonds of sisterhood, stretching from the women of the church at home to the native women in the mission field. "Dear sisters! shall we not recognize, in this emergency, God's voice as speaking to us—for who can so well do this work as we?" questioned the executive board in the initial appeal of *The Heathen Woman's Friend*. "Does it not seem as though the responsibility were thus laid directly upon us? And shall we shrink from bearing it?"[21]

Jennie Fowler Willing articulated this theme of sisterhood most persuasively. In articles entitled "Under Bonds to Help Heathen Women" and "Put Yourself in Her Place," Willing challenged members, "If all men are brothers, all women are sisters." She argued that while American women had the opportunity for education, females of Eastern cultures cowered in the gloom of paganism. "We have it in our power to rescue thousands of our Pagan sisters," and, by bringing them Christianity, to insure a better civilization.[22]

The bond of sisterhood which Willing and her colleagues sought to instill in missionary society members included an understanding that they themselves were "missionaries," like those women whom they sent abroad by the contributions of their pennies and dollars. As young ladies nobly qualified to be "Protestant Sisters of the Cross" were waiting to be sent directly to their heathen sisters, so all women of the church must be aroused to organize societies, raise funds, and sponsor orphans in India and China: "Let every lady, who feels that she *would be a missionary,* go to work at home, and she may, by every dollar raised, teach her heathen sisters."[23]

The missionary society urged that a branch be created in every church with a female membership large enough to sustain it. Detailed directions, "How We Formed Our Auxiliary," were given in *The Heathen Woman's Friend,* and resulted in the early success of 130 branches after one year of the society's existence. The whole scheme of fund raising, "based upon a constant and systematic gleaning of small sums," was designed both to raise money for mission projects and to insure that "all women, even the most humble, could have a share in the work." Membership fees in the W.F.M.S. amounted to one dollar a year, attainable by "every Christian woman laying aside two cents a week." Similarly, the price of *The Friend* was only thirty cents a year, designed to be "within the reach of all."[24]

Further, the pages of *The Heathen Woman's Friend* were avenues for companionship and support. Letters to the editor were a means of sharing "most welcome words of encouragement from distant cities and states." One sister wrote from Indiana, "I cannot tell you how delighted I was to hear of the existence of such a Society." From another state, a woman wrote of her long-held desires and prayer for such an organization and the eagerness of three members of her branch to enter foreign mission service. Still another letter, described as "a cheering note from Illinois," symbolized the way the missionary society helped to bridge the loneliness and isolation felt by women in far-flung rural areas and small towns and offered them a unified purpose for their lives.

Dear Madam:—A Copy of "The Heathen Woman's Friend" has reached me here in my prairie home, and wishing to help forward the work in so good a cause, I here enclose to the "Woman's Foreign Missionary Society" ten dollars ($10.00), with the prayer that it may help some poor, benighted sister to know the truth as it is in Christ Jesus our Saviour. I am but a poor music teacher, the daughter of a poor Methodist minister, and it is but little I can give; but my "mite" is given cheerfully, praying that God will bless the missionary cause in *all* its branches, and convert the heathen from their sins.[25]

In addition to their goals of maintaining an autonomous society and developing purpose and sisterhood among its members, the founders gained personal value from the Women's Foreign Missionary Society, since it was an outlet for their own energies and capabilities. It is crucial to consider the identities of the founders and first officers of the society. Primarily, these women were wives of bishops of the church, wives of secretaries of the General Missionary Society, wives of governors and college presidents, wives of leading pastors and missionaries. The first W.F.M.S. president was married to a bishop, and eight of the original forty-four vice-presidents were wives of bishops. Because of their husbands' positions, these women were concerned with maintaining the society as a middle-of-the-road organization—keeping harmony between the women's society and the larger church and being sure that it did not take independent courses of action which would challenge the consituted authority.

But who were these women in their own right? In the past, they had found identity through their spouses; their basic professional roles had been as their husbands' confidantes, supporting and advising informally in their leadership of the church. But they were highly cultured and well-trained women, who needed a sphere in which to express their own commitment to the church and to develop leadership ability. The Woman's Foreign Missionary Society provided such a channel, and it also opened the way for other women to find avenues for self-expression. This emerging sense of their own identity, and the conflicting emotions it must have produced among the women involved, may have been reflected in the various ways correspondents signed articles in *The Heathen Woman's Friend.* Some continued to refer to themselves as Mrs. Bishop Osman Baker, Mrs. Rev. Dr. Patten, and Mrs. Gov. Wright, while others used their own names—Mrs. Annie R. Gracey, Mrs. Emily C. Page, and Mrs. Jennie Fowler Willing.[26]

The Woman's Foreign Missionary Society had been clear about its goals—to evangelize and educate women of non-Christian countries and to create for themselves an autonomous society which could provide purpose, sisterhood, and avenues for leadership and service to its members. By all measurable standards, the cause flourished. When the society celebrated its twenty-fifth anniversary in 1894, the progress report was impressive. Two hundred thirty-one women missionaries had been sent out by the W.F.M.S., and 161 were still serving actively at that time. Strong mission stations had been established in India, China, Japan, Korea, Burma, South America, Mexico, Malaysia, Bulgaria, and Italy. Property holdings in mission countries were valued at $408,666. During the year, 57,000 patients had been cared for at 13 hospitals; 13,000 girls were in day and boarding schools. Almost $3.5 million had been received and spent for missions.[27]

Surely any commentator would have praised the women for their notable service to the church. Bishop Mathew Simpson did so in addressing a public meeting of the New York Branch of the society. He lauded the strides women were making in the late nineteenth century in the attainment of increased rights in education and suffrage. This was a time of culmination for women, he said. "God is intending, evidently, that woman shall do something in this age more than in the past. . . . I think I see in this Society an answer to the great question, 'What shall women do?' "[28]

To Bishop Simpson, the Woman's Foreign Missionary Society appeared to be the fulfillment—even the containment—of women's progress. How would the founders and leaders have evaluated their gains? In looking back, we can conclude that by developing an autonomous organization which opened up expanded purpose, sisterhood, and leadership for women, the founders possessed the enlightened vision and practical know-how to begin a movement which one day would enable women and men together to eliminate a separate sphere for women in church and society.

THE LAITY RIGHTS
MOVEMENT, 1906–1918

Virginia Shadron

The efforts of white southern Methodist women to create a separate sphere of church work for themselves, to enlarge the scope of that work, to establish professional church roles for women, and to secure equal rights as lay members of the church roughly paralleled those of women in other antecedent denominations of the present United Methodist Church. These developments occurred significantly later in the South, however, a fact that reflects conditions peculiar to southern society and the origins of the Methodist Episcopal Church, South, as a separate denomination.[1]

The southern church's defense of slavery, resulting in its formal separation from the main body of American Methodism in 1844, strengthened patterns of racial inequality, social conservatism, and episcopal authority among white southern Methodists in ways that profoundly influenced both church polity and policy in matters of race, sex, and reform, well into the twentieth century. In the post-Civil War period, the church was unable to accept its black communicants as responsible members. As a result, blacks withdrew from the denomination and established a separate Colored Methodist Episcopal Church in 1870.[2] White women, whose attempts to enlarge their church participation were also frustrated, chose to remain within the Methodist Episcopal Church, South. Their efforts to achieve recognition were complicated by the concentration of power in the episcopacy, which inhibited the emergence of progressive elements within the church and also bolstered the resistance of conservative churchmen to female equality.*

An examination of the woman's laity rights movement in the southern Methodist church from 1906 to 1918 offers a striking study in female leadership and illuminates the patterns of compromise and confrontation developed by southern Methodist women in a male-dominated institution. Recognizing that they had no authoritative voice in church affairs, Methodist women in the South were forced to pursue change within certain boundaries. The suffrage issue became not only a question of representation in the church's governing bodies, but one of self-determination. Ultimately these women were forced to realize that winning the right to vote as lay members of the church did not guarantee their equality.

Leadership for women's missionary activities arose from two sources. Although the organization of the Woman's Foreign Missionary Society in 1878 preceded that of the Woman's Home Mission Society (W.H.M.S.) the latter figured more importantly in the development of the churchwoman's suffrage movement. Organized in 1886 as a modest auxiliary to the men's Board of Church Extension, the Woman's Department (later the W.H.M.S.) afforded women a church-sanctioned opportunity to organize and participate within a political structure. Gradually, as they gained greater autonomy in their home mission organization, they developed a more inclusive interpretation of that mission. In the process, they expanded the southern church's social consciousness and, in effect, professionalized women's church work. At the same time, their self-consciousness as a *women's* organization was heightened. Increasingly confident of their ability to deal with church issues and affairs, southern Methodist women grew impa-

---

*In the following discussion, it should be made clear that the terms "southern Methodist," "southern Methodism," and so on, refer to the white Methodist Episcopal Church, South. These terms might be applied appropriately both to the white church and to its black counterpart in the South, the Colored Methodist Episcopal Church, but in this essay, references to southern Methodist women relate exclusively to the experiences of white women, although aspects of that experience were shared by black southern Methodist women as well.

tient with the political realities of the church that frustrated their ability to define their own organization and control its policies.[3]

The W.H.M.S. was painfully reminded of its structural vulnerability when the 1906 General Conference of the Methodist Episcopal Church, South, imposed new restraints on the hard-won administrative authority of the women's foreign and home mission societies. At that same conference, the General Board of Missions, without consulting the women, recommended the unification of all the church's missionary interests. As the first step in this process, the board urged the immediate union of the two women's organizations. To some women, this maneuver indicated the church's absolute disregard of their preferences. Both the home and the foreign society had consistently rejected unification, even when promoted within their own ranks. In response, women of the home mission society submitted a counterproposal to the General Conference. If organizational unification was inevitable, they asked simply that it be based on equal representation on the new mission board. Belle Harris Bennett, president of the W.H.M.S., bitterly reported the reception of this request: "Such measures . . . were so foreign to the time honored policy of Methodism that the mere formal announcement of the bill met with a good-humored ripple of laughter."[4]

Notwithstanding the rejection of their proposal, unification of the women's organizations was temporarily delayed. The southern Methodist College of Bishops appointed a committee to study the question and to report its findings to the next General Conference. This thirteen-member commission included only four women: Belle Harris Bennett and Tochie Williams MacDonell [Mrs. R. W.] of the home society, and Maria Layng Gibson and Alice Culler Cobb from the foreign society. Despite their presence on the commission, these four gifted women were unable to forestall unification or to secure equal representation for their sex on the new mission board. The 1910 General Conference accepted the commission's recommendations, reorganizing all church missionary activity under one Board of Missions, on which women had but one-third representation. Under the new board, women's work was directed by a unified Woman's Missionary Council.

Publicly, Belle Bennett and the other female members of the commission found it expedient to accept the General Conference's mandate. They assured both societies that functionally their work would remain autonomous. According to Bennett and Gibson, the real difference was that women had gained the "power to legislate on the missionary policy of the Church, instead of being restricted to the women's department."[5]

Privately, however, Bennett revealed the extreme difficulties under which the women representatives of the commission had labored and expressed her own reservations concerning the outcome in a letter to Mrs. F. F. Stephens.

I am a unionist, but I did not believe in the union of the Woman's Boards with the General Board on the basis which we were compelled to accept. I accepted what they gave us, fearing something worse—complete subordination. The constitution under which we work was written by the brethren; and while we were given an opportunity to consider and suggest changes, it was not until after we reached the General Conference. Even then a number of suggestions were met with the statement: "Bishop _____ won't stand that." Fifteen women to forty-five men haven't much showing; added to this the power of the Board is really centralized in the hands of the Secretaries in the Publishing House.[6]

Despite these demoralizing and humiliating conditions, Bennett concealed her own feelings rather than risk completely disrupting the organizational strength of southern Methodist women.

Among the unfortunate consequences of unification in 1910 was the loss of *Our Homes,* the independent publication of the W.H.M.S. since 1892. Throughout the years, *Our Homes* had been critically important to the advancement of new lines of church service for white southern Methodist women and to the raising of their social consciousness. Retained only for an interim period, *Our Homes,* along with the three other missionary papers, was consolidated into one publication in 1911. In the new paper, *The Missionary Voice,* the space allocated to women permitted little more than a straight reporting of Woman's

Missionary Council business. While *Our Homes* had provided extensive coverage of the developing church-woman's rights movement, the editorial policy of *The Missionary Voice* precluded any discussion of the issue.

The immediate resignation of Mary Helm as editor of *Our Homes* was equally unfortunate. Though she concealed her reasons from the journal's readers, Helm's resignation represented a personal protest against the way the plan for unification was formulated and against unequal representation for women on the new mission board. In a letter to Nellie N. Somerville, a Mississippi suffragist also active in the church, Helm admitted her private distress and revealed something of the internal politics which had developed among leading Methodist women during the unification crisis.

Helm thought that Belle Bennett, though sincere in her motives, exercised poor judgment in accepting the terms proposed by the commission on unification. In Helm's opinion, the women's missionary societies should have remained unchanged and no plan for unification ought to have been approved. "The Woman's Council, which they say takes the place of the Woman's Boards, is simply an unwieldly committee," Helm argued, with "no authoritative voice." The one-third representation accorded women on the new board was a meaningless gesture, outweighed by the presence of thirteen bishops who were "accustomed to an absolute domination of the Parent Board." By her reckoning, "We are in a helpless minority in a body where the membership is largely made up of men opposed to independence of thought in women." In the long run, Helm believed that the most talented southern Methodist women would seek avenues for self-realization outside the church, thus leaving leadership to those less able to muster the courage necessary for effective organization.[7]

Helm believed that she had been deliberately excluded from every step of the unification process. Though others were invited to meet with the commission, Helm, who as editor of *Our Homes* might justifiably have expected the same courtesy, was not. In addition to this slight, Helm learned of the new officers and personnel of the board through an announcement in the secular press. Then and only then, she learned that Mrs. A. L. Marshall, whom she considered to be "entirely without editorial experience and absolutely ignorant of the women's missionary work," was to be the editorial secretary. Helm considered Mrs. Marshall's election "tantamount to my dismissal."[8]

Despite her profound disappointment, Helm vowed, "I have no personal feeling against any of those who differed from me and do not intend to antagonize the present organization."[9] Testifying to the seriousness of her commitments, Helm continued to be a courageous advocate of woman's rights in the church until her death in 1913.

Faced with the prospect that the 1910 General Conference would impose still greater restrictions on the women's societies, in 1909 Belle Harris Bennett initiated the laity rights movement in a challenging address before the W.H.M.S. board meeting in Savannah, Georgia.

If I know the minds of the missionary women throughout the field, and I think I do, any disturbance of the autonomy of the Woman's Missionary Societies, more especially any annullment of the administrative rights, which have been vested in their Executive Boards for the last thirty-two years, will bring about such a disturbance of relationships in the Church as Methodism has never known.[10]

To Bennett, the woman's laity rights controversy, stirred by the action of the 1906 General Conference, signified "God's [hand] leading to awaken a great body of women in the South to the religious teaching of Christian scriptures concerning the essential equality of man and woman."[11] Upon her recommendation, the W.H.M.S. board prepared a memorial (or petition) to the 1910 General Conference, requesting full lay rights and privileges for women. After twenty-eight years of pioneer efforts in the foreign and home mission fields, southern Methodist women confronted their political impotence in the church. In this sense, the controversy over the unification of mission work, resulting in the curtailment of women's authority in their own organizations, served as the mainspring for the women's suffrage movement within the southern Methodist church.

In the seven months following the Savannah meeting, women flooded their annual conference *Advocates* with careful explanations of the memorial to General Conference. Widely reprinted endorsements by prominent men and women encouraged other members of the church to promote the issue locally. Conference and district societies, city mission boards, and individuals were urged to signify their approval. The results of these efforts were impressive. As many as 148 memorials, 637 petitions, and hundreds of telegrams in support of women's laity rights overwhelmed the 1910 General Conference.

At that conference, the Committee on Revisals' majority opinion, cloaked in characteristic paternalism, recommended nonconcurrence. Two minority reports were filed. The first proposed to let women in through the back door by extending legal recognition to their election as local church officers. Women stewards, trustees, and Sunday school superintendents could then be members of the quarterly Conference (the official quarterly meeting of a local congregation or circuit), and so theoretically they would be eligible for election to annual, and ultimately, General conferences. The second report recommended simply a reinterpretation of the terms *laymen* and *men* to include *women* in the *Discipline* references to the rights and functions of the laity.[12]

At the 1910 General Conference, the woman's laity rights memorial provoked more discussion than at any subsequent conference, inspiring two hours of lively debate.

By special resolution, Belle Bennett was invited to address the conference in behalf of the memorial. It was the first time in the southern denomination's history that a woman's voice had been heard in General Conference. Bennett expressed the resentment of the W.H.M.S. toward the administrative and structural changes imposed upon them by the 1906 conference. She forthrightly challenged her audience to relinquish its unreasonable prejudice against laity rights for women. She assured the conference that granting lay rights to women was not likely to upset the current pattern of male dominance. "Put this measure on its passage, and let it go down to the [annual] conferences and come back to you; and

267

eight years from now perhaps there will be one or two women in the General Conference."[13]

In response to Bennett, George R. Stuart maintained that the woman's emancipation movement in all its dimensions aimed at the destruction of the home. This movement included, in Stuart's estimation, four deadly "ambitions"—deadly, that is, when envisioned by women: financial, social, political, and finally, ecclesiastical.[14]

Despite the attention given the woman's memorial, defeat was not unexpected. Bennett's address at the 1910 annual W.H.M.S. meeting prepared churchwomen for the next round even before the General Conference vote was taken, and she did not minimize the struggle ahead. "There are yet among us and of us many men and women to whom 'the traditions of men have made the Word of God of no effect,' and at every mention of a change or advance movement in the Church they shrink back in blind terror, full of superstitious fear of some awful calamity as a divine judgment."[15] When the memorial lost by a vote of 74 to 188, the women leaders began to prepare for the second round.

Women were better organized in the second stage of the campaign. They continued to distribute leaflets and petitions and agitated in the church press. At the same time, the focus of their appeal shifted to the annual conferences. In 1912, they asked each annual conference to appoint a special committee to evaluate conference opinion on the women's rights memorial. Innocuous as such a proposal would seem, it met fierce male opposition. As Mary Helm reported, "This effort was suppressed in all but six Conferences. . . . In some the introduction of such a resolution was positively forbidden by the presiding Bishop, and no discussion allowed."[16] Accordingly, what might have become the first step in a "state-amendment" approach to woman's laity rights was effectively quashed.[17]

The Kentucky Conference was among the few to cooperate with the women's request for special committees, but the results were disappointing. The committee reported the conference as unequivocally opposed to woman's suffrage in the church. Apparently, however, the committee did not actually poll local church opinion or gather any new information on the subject, but based its findings on views expressed in conference newspapers and on the prior response of General Conference and other annual conferences. From this, the Kentucky report concluded that the woman's laity rights movement "is an effort of some good women to obtain power," but "they do not represent the mass of our women, some of the most gifted of whom are speaking and printing their opposition to it."[18]

Certainly it was true that some women wrote against woman's laity rights. Though these women may have been "some of the most gifted," with rare exception, they were not among the most prominent leaders of women's church work. Furthermore, most women who wrote against laity rights preferred to maintain their anonymity, perhaps in deference to feminine modesty.[19]

While the Kentucky Conference was among the few courteous enough to commission a laity rights study, the selection of John R. Deering, a rabid antisuffragist, as committee chairman makes the conference's motives suspect. A reply by J. W. Harris to Deering's committee report must have heartened the women. Harris published his response in the *Central Methodist Advocate* because "scant opportunity was given to discuss the Report of the Committee on 'Laity Rights' " at the annual conference. Harris' view, plainly stated, was that "God's blessings will not continue to rest upon those church members who led by prejudice . . . purposely unfairly treat their fellow Christians just because they happen to be born of a certain sex."[20] Unfortunately, while the conference committee's report was widely circulated throughout the church, Harris' rebuttal was not accorded equal treatment.

The leaders of laity rights for women decentralized their efforts still further by sponsoring discussions in local missionary societies on the relationship between woman's suffrage and world evangelization. Local women then formulated their own methods for promoting laity rights. As the movement gained momentum, and as southern Methodist women began to acknowledge the connection between their struggle in the church and the political woman's suffrage movement outside, they plainly became more threatening to the forces opposing the memorial. In one Texas conference, women resolved to work to elect to church office only men known to favor laity rights for women.

As the 1914 General Conference approached, the opposition grew more desperate in its attempt to forestall acceptance of the woman's memorial. One antagonist even advocated censorship, and apparently some opponents actually attempted to implement this suggestion. As L. S. Massey, editor of the North Carolina Conference *Raleigh Christian Advocate,* candidly admitted, "The charge has been made in some quarters that the free discussion of the subject in the church press has been smothered. To some extent this may be true, if by the statement is meant only that certain communications offered have never seen the light."[21] Other antagonists either wishfully predicted that the woman's laity rights memorial would not be an issue at the 1914 General Conference, or simply that it would fail to pass.

In fact, however, support for the woman's memorial was growing. Mrs. W. J. Piggott was pleased to inform the editor of her conference *Advocate* in Kentucky, E. G. B. Mann, that despite the failure of the Kentucky Conference to report favorably on churchwoman's suffrage, six conferences had approved this reform. By the time the 1914 General Conference convened, five more annual conferences had added their support. Again, individuals and conference, district, and local missionary societies indicated their support in hundreds of telegrams and letters sent to the General Conference.[22]

Repeating their 1910 position against woman's laity rights, the College of Bishops set the tone for the reception of woman's memorial in 1914.

We have reason to believe that the demand for this kind of equality is not in harmony with the general sentiment of the women of our Church. . . . We believe, furthermore, that the spirit of this movement is against the view which our people at large have held and still hold in regard to woman's place in the Church and in society, and that such a step would not, therefore, make for the greater efficiency of our Church as a whole in any of the regions occupied by it.[23]

Again in 1914, the Committee on Revisals' majority report sustained the bishops' directive and recommended nonconcurrence on the woman's rights memorial. And again, a minority report filed by sixteen dissident committee members recommended changes that would eliminate sex bias in the *Discipline.*

Bennett, speaking before the conference, based her plea for laity rights on the injustice of taxation without representation, repeating her attack on the restraints imposed on women's autonomy by the 1906 General Conference. Laity rights for women were no radical measure, Bennett assured her audience. It had been tried and tested by all the largest bodies of Methodism for some years without disruption of church harmony or government. Admitting that this was not a majority movement, Bennett contended that the church could ill afford to ignore the counsel of those women who were engaged most actively in its mission.[24]

On the other hand, Mrs. T. B. King, speaking against laity rights, presented herself as the representative of "the motherhood of the Church." She urged the men of the church to preserve their manhood against this "suffragette" intrusion.[25]

The defense of the minority report by W. J. Carpenter concluded the discussion of churchwoman's suffrage. Elaborating Bennett's basic argument, Carpenter claimed that a quarter of a million church members directly or indirectly favored woman's laity rights in the southern Church. Moreover, Carpenter reminded his brothers that their own laity rights movement in 1868 had been supported by only a small minority.[26]

Without further debate, the motion to adopt the minority report extending women's rights was defeated in the General Conference by a vote of 105 to 171. The margin of opposition was shrinking.

In its third and final quadrennium, the reorganized campaign for woman's laity rights was conducted primarily through the *Laity Rights Advocate.* Publication of this paper, financed entirely by private donations, probably began in

1912 or 1913. It was not officially church-sponsored, and no copies appear to have survived the movement.[27]

This loss is particularly unfortunate since surviving remnants indicate that the paper's position was more advanced and more militant than that expressed by the movement's leaders in the regular church press. More important, extant fragments suggest the existence of a separate organization of missionary-society women, the Woman's Laity Rights League, which undoubtedly provided the movement's major source of leadership and financial support. Finally, the *Laity Advocate* was apparently the only forum for church suffrage agitation during the lean years from the 1914 General Conference until after the 1918 General Conference, when discussion of woman's laity rights reemerged.

One *Laity Advocate* article, reprinted in the *Baltimore Southern Methodist,* demonstrates a confrontational tone. In it, Mary Helm herself illuminates the need for such an independent publication, charging suppression of the woman's laity rights question in the church press and pulpit.

It has also been proven that in the Methodist Episcopal Church, South not only the women, but laymen and preachers are forbidden the right of free speech. With this has gone the freedom of the press. The Church papers, with few exceptions, will not (or dare not?) allow a discussion of the subject in their columns. Are they afraid that publicity will bring more women to see the justice of the plea and want laity rights? Or were they put "under orders," as were the women when they desired to advocate the subject in the "Missionary Voice" [sic], in which they had at least a legendary ownership, and in their own little Department Bulletins? Because the league was not willing to air church differences in the secular press, the *Laity Advocate* is being sent out with the prayerful hope that it would reach those not hardened against our appeal for a place in the Church.[28]

At the 1918 General Conference, the woman's memorial was reported out of committee favorably for the first time and was adopted after less than thirty minutes' discussion. Ironically, the major speakers were former members of the opposition. Paul H. Linn, who testified that "all the years since I can remember I have been speaking on the other side of the question," was unanimously selected by fellow members to present the Committee on Revisals' report. Linn, reflecting the wartime concerns of these later converts, cast aside old lines of argument and presented woman's laity rights as a movement toward democracy and religious freedom. "We are not going to give the lives and property of this nation to protect democracy from autocracy in civil government and submit like slaves to autocracy in the Church," he declared.[29]

The main debate in 1918 concerned not a defense or a denial of woman's laity rights, but rather the most appropriate method of adjusting sexual injustice in the church, and the constitutionality of those means. The most far-sighted point of the discussion was H. D. Knicker-bocker's recognition that simply changing the church's law would not give its women real equality: "It is a fact that it will be only a technical advantage for some time to come." In the transitional period, Knickerbocker proposed that women be extended "laity rights-plus"; that is, he suggested continuing the number of women representatives on the Board of Missions guaranteed when the southern church consolidated its missionary interests in 1910. This amendment failed primarily because some felt that by imposing quotas, the principle of equal rights was defeated.[30]

Opposition to the woman's memorial was confined to John S. Candler's attempt to delay the vote on a point of order. When he was not sustained, Candler sputtered, "You have choked us and throttled us and not told us what you are trying to do here, and we have had no discussion of this matter."[31] He joined L. D. Hamilton in demanding a roll call vote so that they might go on record against the memorial. Candler was again defeated, and the General Conference proceeded to adopt the committee's report resoundingly.

The College of Bishops also attempted to stall the enfranchisement of southern Methodist women, thereby revealing both its paternalism toward women and its resistance to democratization. The bishops declared the issue a constitutional question and vetoed the conference's action, but the conference reaffirmed its decision in a dramatic roll-call vote. On the morning of May 14, 1918, the delegates accepted the principle of woman's suffrage in the church by a vote of 270 to 50.[32]

In the midst of the enthusiastic celebration of this victory, Belle Bennett issued a call for continued vigilance. As a constitutional question, woman's laity rights required ratification by three-fourths of all members of the annual conferences. The final reckoning indicates that there was little cause for Bennett's concern. Seventeen conferences passed the memorial unanimously, and twenty-three cast more than the necessary three-fourths vote. Only four conferences, including Bennett's own Kentucky Conference, failed to affirm laity rights for women.[33]

In retrospect, it is not surprising that the woman's suffrage issue emerged in the southern Methodist church in the period between 1906 and 1918. The legislation which precipitously led to the reorganization of the women's missionary societies provided an immediate and specific cause, and leadership for a woman's rights movement had already developed among those churchwomen most prominent in mission work. Some advocates, both male and female, of woman's laity rights had long favored woman's suffrage in church and state and by 1909 were willing to move to the forefront of the southern churchwoman's suffrage movement.

But the most decisive component in the success of woman's suffrage in the southern Methodist church in 1918 had to do with changing male leadership in the church. Between 1910 and 1918 there was a substantial turnover in the General Conference, which at the same time became more liberal. In 1918, 50 percent of the 320 delegates voting on the question of woman's rights were serving in the General Conference for the first time. And of the 156 new representatives, only 13 percent voted against suffrage for women in the church.[34]

Securing laity rights in the southern Methodist church and political enfranchisement in the state by no means ended the struggle for equal rights and opportunities for southern women. Neither did it diminish their concern for autonomy in conducting their own affairs. Even after southern men intellectually accepted the appropriateness and justice of woman's legal rights, they failed to accept the full implications of woman's equality.

A study compiled by the Woman's Missionary Council in 1928, ten years after the extension of laity rights to women, illustrated this point succinctly. Summarizing the position of women, the report stated, "Officially their status is that of total inferiority and it is doubtful whether any woman of ability is justified in accepting conditions which deny her power to use her gifts to the fullest." Furthermore, the report reflected these women's understanding of the historical and social significance of separate woman's missionary organizations in the church. "Fifty years ago the time was ripe for an independent organization. The movement met a crying need . . . training [women] for service and for leadership in an unhampered atmosphere where all people were equally inexperienced." More importantly, these southern women leaders recognized a loss of organizational vigor due to the incorporation of their societies by the Board of Missions in 1910. Finally, the document expressed a continuing need for separate woman's organizations.

Until equal opportunity in industry, in public service, in the professions (especially the religious vocations . . .), is secured, not only in America, but for womanhood of all nations, there is a continuing need for united effort for woman by woman, which can best be directed through permanent organizations. . . . When men and women have attained equality, both theoretical and actual, in church, state and society, then the day of the separate organization for women anywhere will be over.[35]

NINETEENTH-CENTURY
A.M.E. PREACHING WOMEN

Jualynne Dodson

In 1816, the African Methodist Episcopal Church (A.M.E.) was officially organized as a connection of independent, predominantly black congregations, subscribing to religious tenets like those of the Methodist Episcopal Church, and following a similar polity. The origins of the Church were deeply rooted in protests against discriminatory treatment of black people in religious affairs.* The first resistance had been staged in 1787, when a group of black Methodists exited from St. George's Methodist Episcopal Church in Philadelphia, never to return. Those protestors established their own independent congregation, and by 1816 the resistance of black Methodists to white supremacy in the middle Atlantic states had produced an independent black denomination.[1]

Initially the A.M.E. Church consisted of 7 churches and 4,900 members. By 1900, the body had grown to include 5,775 churches and 663,746 members.[2] A much overlooked contribution to growth and change in this Church during the nineteenth century was the influence of women's activities. One way to identify the impact of women on Church development is to trace their incorporation into the official organizational structure of the denomination. In the early phase of African Methodism, official ministerial positions included bishop, elder, deacon, pastor, and local or itinerant preacher. None of these positions was open to women, despite their outstanding numerical presence in the early

---

*Throughout this paper *Church* will be used to designate the connectional interstate organization while *church* will refer to an individual congregation.

A.M.E. Church. If the early structure did not provide any official roles, however, by 1900, organizational positions of stewardess and deaconess, specifically designed for women, had been established. Women also had been granted the right to be licensed as evangelists. There is an important question to ask of these changes: How did woman's activities influence the creation of these positions? The question has yet to be asked either of A.M.E. women specifically or of black women in religious organizations in general.

This essay considers the activities of a select category of A.M.E. women as the "cutting edge" of the inclusion of women as a gender into the organizational arrangements—the polity—of the A.M.E. Church in the nineteenth century. The study explores ways in which preaching women, while they varied as to locale, time, and fame, threatened the traditional male authority structure of the Church by direct petition and indirect pressure to allow women to preach and to be ordained to the ministry equally with men. We shall see that rather than concede the full authority of ordination, the A.M.E. Church would accommodate its organizational arrangements to include positions specifically designated for women—namely stewardess and deaconess—and under duress would approve the licensing of women as evangelists. This essay will reveal that in spite of this structural inclusion and women's intensive labors for the Church, their role remained essentially the same throughout the nineteenth century: They were barred from official leadership positions and kept subservient.

Whether consciously or not, nineteenth-century A.M.E. preaching women were the cutting edge of women's activities which pierced the fabric of the Church's male authority structure. These women were not revolutionaries bent on shaking structures, but reformers wishing a more inclusive and just organization. They were devoutly religious and felt supremely ordained to carry out their call to preach the gospel of Christianity. Not feminist claims for the rights of all women, but their sense of their own special call led them to challenge male domination of the Church. In most instances, preaching women were extremely committed to

protesting white racism in the tradition of African Methodism, but they had no broader social program.

Born in 1783, Jarena Lee was the earliest black female
preacher identified with the A.M.E. Church and the first to
seek a public role for women in its structure. She received
her call from God when she was twenty-four and initially
requested permission to preach under the authority of
nascent African Methodism in 1809. At that date the
connectional A.M.E. Church had not yet been organized,
but Richard Allen, its future founder, had been ordained a
deacon by Bishop Francis Asbury of the Methodist
Episcopal Church and was the influential pastor of Bethel
Church of Philadelphia (later Bethel A.M.E. Church) when
Jarena Lee expressd her desire for a preaching license. Allen
denied her the license, but feeling her call, Jarena set out to
preach the Word without it. In 1817, after the A.M.E.
Church had been officially organized and had elected Allen
its bishop, Jarena Lee renewed her request. Bishop Allen
responded that there were no precedents for women
preachers in Methodist tradition but noted that the young
denomination needed all who could increase its numbers.
Therefore he allowed Sister Jarena to hold prayer meetings
in her own "hired house" and to exhort as she "found
liberty."[3]

In her autobiographical journal, Jarena stated that she
held many prayer meetings and found considerable "liberty"
to exhort men and women to accept Jesus. She also recorded
that Bishop Allen gave her speaking appointments in several
Pennsylvania churches and allowed her to travel with him
and other ministers to meetings in New York and New
Jersey.[4]

Research shows that between the founding of the A.M.E.
Church and the publication of Jarena Lee's *Journal* in 1849, a
number of black women were actively preaching across the
land. Sophie Murray did not travel as a gospel preacher and
is almost unmentioned in the historical records of her time.
As an early, if not founding, member of Bethel A.M.E.
Church in Philadelphia, however, her name was recorded in
Bethel Gleanings, Joseph Thompson's account of interviews
with original members of the congregation. Thompson

described Sophie Murray as the "first evangelist of Bethel," a woman whose activities were revered throughout the Philadelphia community. He also discussed another Philadelphia woman of the gospel, Elizabeth Cole, whose evangelistic work increased the church's membership; she "held many glorious prayer meetings, and many souls were brought to the saving knowledge."[5]

In his *Cyclopaedia of African Methodism,* published in 1882, Bishop Alexander Wayman recorded that in the antebellum period, Rachel Evans of New Jersey was also "a preacheress of no ordinary ability. She could rouse a congregation at any time." Bishop James Handy confirmed this picture of Evans, noting that congregations generally considered her a better preacher than her distinguished husband.[6]

Women of the A.M.E. Church appear also to have preached in the Washington, D.C., area prior to the publication of Lee's *Journal.* In 1840, John Francis Cook identified Harriet Felson Taylor, one of the earliest members of the congregation, as a woman who "distinguished herself as the "First Female Exhorter and Local Preacher" of Washington's Union Bethel Church.[7]

The autobiographical *Memoirs* of Mrs. Zilpha Elaw, published in 1846, indicate that though she was not of the A.M.E. Church, Sister Zilpha's preaching activities were directly related to the denomination. She could only have been referring to Bethel A.M.E. Church of Baltimore when she wrote, "I visited Baltimore [1828] . . . and attended a conference of the coloured brethren, by whom I was very kindly received; . . . a great and effectual door of utterance opened to me."[8] Bethel was the only conference of the colored brethren in the city in 1828. Zilpha Elaw was clearly an early preaching woman within the field of African Methodism.

Jarena Lee, Sophie Murray, Elizabeth Cole, Rachel Evans, Harriet Felson Taylor, Zilpha Elaw, and many other women are significant because none were licensed or ordained by the Church, but all preached. These women preached actively because of their conviction of God's call to them and their personal sense of responsibility, not because of official authority granted them by the Church.

The first official response of the male A.M.E. clergy to preaching A.M.E. women came at the General Conference of 1844. A positive petition was brought by Nathan Ward and others, requesting that the General Conference "make provisions for females to preach and exhort." The petition was defeated.[9] Four years later in 1848, however, the Daughters of Zion, one of many women's societies among A.M.E. congregations, boldly petitioned the General Conference that women be licensed to preach in the connection with "ministerial privileges, akin to those of men."[10]

When he published the first official history of the Church in 1891, Daniel A. Payne, bishop and church historian, acknowledged the petitions and preaching of these black women, only to trivialize them. Payne wrote:

The origin of the question (licensing women to preach) is found in the fact that certain women members of the A.M.E. Church, who believed themselves divinely commissioned to preach by formal licenses, subsequently organized themselves into an association with the avowed intention of laying out a field of usefulness for themselves, and making out appointments for such a field after the manner of our Annual Conferences. They held together for a brief period, and *then fell to pieces like a rope of sand.* (emphasis added)[11]

Equally indicative of this outstanding churchman's position regarding women and traditional clerical authority was the protest he is reported to have filed at the 1848 General Conference against "the licensing of females to travel in the connection."[12] However, despite such opponents, women's preaching activities and petitions for licensing persisted, and in 1852 the issue came before the General Conference a third time.

This General Conference firmly enunciated an official position regarding women preachers and evangelists in the A.M.E. Church. In the episcopal address, Bishop William Paul Quinn recommended that the body consider the question of licensing women to preach. He felt the issue was bound to surface at the session and requested peaceably and, as it proved, unrealistically, that "something distinct may be done that will be satisfactory to all, and the question be put to rest." The distinct action which the bishop requested took place on Friday, May 7, 1852, when the licensing of women to preach was defeated by a large majority of the entirely male membership of the General Conference.[13]

The threat that licensing women to preach posed to the entire tradition of male domination in the A.M.E. Church and churchmen's suspicion of female ambition were evident in an editorial in the *Christian Recorder,* the official newspaper of the denomination, following the 1852 General Conference. It is noteworthy that the editor of the *Recorder* was appointed by the General Conference. The editorial reviewed the encroachment of female preachers on male prerogatives.

Four years ago [1848] this subject of licensing women to preach in the church came up for consideration before the General Conference in the form of a petition from the Daughters of Zion. It then went so far in their favor that they were granted permission to preach in our churches, but not to receive licenses from the Conference. They again petitioned this [1852] General Conference to grant their license in all respects as men are licensed, and so to graduate up to the highest office in the church.[14]

Neither petitions for ordaining women or women's preaching activities subsided with the negative responses of A.M.E. General Conferences at mid-century. As the Church expanded its missionary endeavors west of the Allegheny Mountains and into the southern states, women continued their gospel work. In 1864, their persistent requests for formal licensing and ordination again reached the General Conference. There are no indications that the 1864 Conference voted negatively. Rather, the body dismissed the question by not discussing it.[15]

Perhaps because women's preaching did not subside, male leaders sought a structural alternative to ordination for women who desired to serve the Church. In 1868 the General Conference delegates opened the polity of the Church to include women by mandating that the pastor in charge of a local congregation "may" nominate a Board of Stewardesses. The position of stewardess was thus created, becoming the first and only official organizational position for women in the denomination.

The church's establishment of boards of stewardesses did nothing to alter the containment of women, however, because the position of stewardess did not entail ordination and existed under the strict control of churchmen. The legislation of 1868 provided explicitly that when a congregation did not have the requisite "three to nine most influential women," qualified *men* could serve as stewardesses. No such contingency was provided for in the case of an insufficient number of male stewards! More directly threatening to women's leadership as stewardesses was the provision that male stewards could confirm or reject a stewardess's nomination and, together with the male pastor, could remove and replace any female appointee.[16] Stewardesses had no comparable voice in the appointment and retention of stewards.

Indeed, rather than advancing its talented preaching women, the creation of the position of stewardess formalized the subordinate, serving role of women in the A.M.E. Church. Stewardesses were to "look after the females of the church" and to assist the stewards, class leaders, and pastors.[17] The very idea of a "Board of Stewardesses" was a misnomer, as Bishop Henry McNeal Turner argued in a longer treatment of Methodist polity.

The stewardesses are a *collection* of sisters, numbering not less than three nor more than nine, who assist the stewards, class leaders and pastor . . . but cannot always be recognized as a board, as *they have no legislative or judicial discretion,* but are merely *assistants.* (emphasis added)[18]

In addition to structural changes to include stewardesses, the 1868 General Conference affirmed the authority of the positions of exhorter, missionary, and evangelist and recognized them as part of the denomination's ministerial arrangements. Nowhere were women prohibited from performing the duties of these positions; however, there was a consequential difference between the status of women and that of men. Men regularly began their upward mobility in the church structure through one or more experiences as exhorter, missionary, or evangelist. Their ordination to the ministry from any of these positions was a regular and expected occurrence. Women, on the other hand, were never ordained, though their success as exhorters, missionaries, and evangelists might be international in scope.[19] After 1868, the Church continued to forbid women's ordination to the ministry and gave no formal authority for their preaching activities. Consequently, upward mobility in A.M.E. structures was reserved to males.

While the inclusion of women as stewardesses in A.M.E. organization did not change the Church's allocation of authority on the basis of gender, the significance of this step should not be minimized. Prior to 1868, there had been no formal position for women in the denomination, and there are no indications that if left alone, men of the Church would have allowed women any official participation. Had there never been women devout in their ministerial call, committed to their right to preach, and persistent in their challenge to the Church to sanction their role and authority as preachers, the structure of the A.M.E. organization might not have expanded even to include the position of stewardess.

After 1868, A.M.E. women continued to preach and their preaching further challenged church policies which excluded women from formal authority. By the turn of the century their pressure led A.M.E. men to expand the church structures once more, to include the position of deaconess. Although a variety of women's activities influenced the Church to develop deaconess orders by 1900, preaching women were again—as in the antebellum period and immediately after the Civil War—the cutting edge which pierced the consciousness of A.M.E. men.

Amanda Berry Smith was the most internationally known of the A.M.E. preaching women between 1868 and 1900. She was born in Maryland in 1847, but did not unite with the A.M.E. Church until about 1865. By 1869, Smith had been widowed twice and had begun to devote her life to preaching the gospel in New York and New Jersey.[20] As early as 1871, she was credited with having markedly increased the membership of the waning A.M.E. congregation of Mt. Pisgah in Salem, New Jersey, during a three-week stay. Elder Frisby Cooper reported her work to the *Christian Recorder,* concluding, "Sister Amanda Smith . . . is a very useful helper in the vineyard of the Lord, God bless her ever."[21]

Between 1871 and 1878, Amanda Smith traveled and preached throughout the northeast. She became a familiar figure at camp meetings in New Jersey, Ohio, Tennessee, New York, and Pennsylvania. In 1878 the black evangelist exchanged the shores of the northeastern United States for those of England and India. She achieved international renown in those countries and spent considerable time preaching in Africa before she returned to the United States in 1890.[22] Like her forerunner, Jarena Lee, Amanda Smith eventually wrote and published her autobiography, in which she described her travels.

Many less famous A.M.E. women also responded to ministerial calls.[23] Among those was Margaret Wilson of the New Jersey Annual Conference of the A.M.E. Church. Wilson was born in Baltimore, Maryland, and was called to the ministry in 1870. She was reported to have "labored in the field" until the New Jersey Conference appointed her to the Haleyville Mission in 1883.[24] Emily Calkins Stevens, a native of Freehold Green County, New York, was also of the New Jersey Conference. Receiving her third call to preach in 1882, she was licensed locally by Bishop John Mifflin Brown at the 1883 meeting of the New Jersey Conference. The written fact of Emily Calkins Stevens' preaching license has not been verified. It may have been a verbal license similar to that of Jarena Lee and closely related to exhorting or missionary activities. Nevertheless, in the later nineteenth century, women were preaching in the New Jersey Annual Conference of the A.M.E. Church.[25]

In 1889, Harriet A. Baker was reported to have been "appointed by the Philadelphia A.M.E. Conference to take charge of St. Paul's Church on Tenth Street, in the City of Lebanon, Pennsylvania." Like her preaching sisters discussed here, and many more not identified, Baker worked with many ministers and bishops in the A.M.E. connection who informally approved her ministerial activities.[26]

Lena Doolin-Mason was also among those preaching women whose activities followed the institutionalization of the position of stewardess in 1868. Mason was reported to have received her "first call to preach at seven years of age." In January 1872 she joined the A.M.E. Church of Hannibal, Missouri, where John Turner was pastor. Daniel Culp recorded that Lena Doolin-Mason "entered the ministry" at age 23 and "preached in nearly every state in the Union."[27]

In spite of women's increased preaching activities in the missionary fields of the A.M.E. Church after 1868, stewardess remained the only officially sanctioned position open to them. The institution never declined members, money, or other material supports produced by women's activities, but it did not open its structural ranks further to women for three more decades. Nevertheless, A.M.E. women preached publicly and vigorously, well into the Reconstruction era. The level of men's awareness of and opposition to such preaching women increased concomittantly in that period. When Amanda Berry Smith attended the 1872 A.M.E. General Conference in Nashville, Tennessee, she recorded that several ministers identified her with a movement to ordain women preachers.[28]

Twelve years later, at the A.M.E. General Conference of 1884, the issue of licensing women as local preachers was clearly drawn. It seems to have been decided that to exert some control over preaching women was better than official refusal to acknowledge their widespread existence. George C. Sampson presented a resolution to the body that suggests to later readers what had been happening informally, and not so informally, in the A.M.E. connection for some time past, while the Church refused to admit women to the clergy. The resolution stated:

Whereas, Female evangelists are becoming very numerous and, as they are not amenable to anyone, Resolved, that those sisters that have, and who shall receive licenses from the hand of any of our ministers in the future, shall be subject to the same requirements as local preachers, and they shall be amenable to the Quarterly

Conference of the church of which they are members, subject to all the requirements of a local preacher.[29]

Sampson thus acknowledged that some A.M.E. ministers had already given women written licenses, and he sought to have the General Conference sanction these retroactively, while he carefully specified the church's control over the licensing of women preachers in the future. Implicitly this resolution spoke to the anomaly, not to say hypocrisy, of using women evangelists for the purposes of church expansion, but providing no clear positions for them in the formal structure. Sampson's resolution passed. The 1884 General Conference approved licensing women as local preachers.

Nervousness can easily be detected at this step. At the same 1884 conference, W. D. Cook introduced a second, highly defensive resolution, seeking to clarify the boundaries of women's authority. His resolution, which the conference also adopted, stated:

Whereas, We have in [our] Church some female ministers who have been holding pastoral charges much to the detriment of Church, Therefore be it Resolved, that they are hereby prohibited from assignments to any special work, and hereafter shall labor simply as evangelists.[30]

In spite of formidable opposition to the ordination of women and the constraints placed on their licenses to preach, some A.M.E. Church dignitaries saw benefit in having women ministers and approved of them.[31] Indeed, on November 29, 1885, Bishop Henry McNeal Turner of North Carolina ordained one Sarah A. H. and placed her name on the list of male deacons. At the 1887 meeting of the North Carolina Annual Conference of the A.M.E. Church, however, the presiding bishop ruled that the ordination was contrary to Church law, and Sarah's name was stricken from the list.[32] Although the General Conference of 1884 had approved the licensing of women to preach, it had not reversed the prohibition against ordaining women. The Church's official policy stood. Bishop Turner's action not only cost him public reprimand by the Episcopal Committee of the 1888 General Conference; the response to it illustrated the sensitivity of the clergy to the threat that preaching women posed to male dominance. The effort to escalate Sister Sarah's preaching license into a deacon's ordination in fact became an occasion for public declaration on the topic by the General Conference of 1888. The wording suggests the depth of the threat felt to the established gender order.

Whereas, Bishop H. M. Turner has seen fit to ordain a woman to the order of a deacon; and Whereas said act is contrary to the usage of our Church, and without precedent in any other body of Christians in the known world, and as it cannot be proved by the Scriptures that a woman has ever been ordained to the order of the ministry; ,
Therefore be it enacted, That the bishops of the African Methodist Episcopal Church be and are hereby forbidden to ordain a woman to the order of deacon or elder in our Church.[33]

The 1884 A.M.E. resolutions had conceded women's right to preach under license, while limiting women preachers to evangelistic work. The declaration of the 1888 General Conference reinforced the boundaries of this concession, rigidly reaffirming the denomination's prohibition against women's ordination.

The denomination's formal sanctioning in 1884 of customary women evangelists increased their work, and even the 1888 prohibition against women's ordination did not diminish preaching women's activities during the closing decades of the nineteenth century. Lena Doolin-Mason was an A.M.E. preacher whose activities did not wane after the 1888 prohibition. Indeed, Daniel Culp reported that Doolin-Mason was instrumental after 1888 in converting some 1,617 souls and that "her five months work in . . . churches in Minneapolis will never be forgotten." In the Philadelphia Annual Conference, Harriet A. Baker was recorded as leading efforts to build an A.M.E. church in Allentown, Pennsylvania. This was a post-1888 continuation of her ministerial activities. Mary C. Palmer, Melinda M. Cotton, Emma V. Johnson, Mary L. Harris, and others made extensive reports to the Philadelphia Conference on their preaching activities from 1896 to 1898. In the New Jersey Conference, Margaret Wilson had continued preaching beyond 1888 and was listed with other women evangelists in the 1897 annual gathering of the conference.[34]

Southern states, too, had a good number of preaching women. Charlotte S. Riley was identifiably active in the South Carolina Conference after 1873 and was reported continuing her work in the 1897 *Proceedings* of that body. Response to a sermon preached by Lillian Thurman at the November 1896 meeting of the Alabama Annual Conference of the A.M.E. Church might even have been considered a challenge to the 1888 General Conference resolution against ordaining women. At the close of Thurman's sermon, a Brother Wesley Jones was reported to have paid his "compliments" to the "Christian sister." He said, "Heretofore I have not wanted to hear a woman preacher, but now I am convinced that the Lord sends out various instruments to carry his work."[35]

Unquestionably a whole range of A.M.E. women had not found themselves attracted to the organizational position of stewardess and had refused to limit their ministerial activities. They continued preaching beyond 1868 and in so doing continued to challenge the law and polity of the Church. Even the limitations laid down by General Conference in 1884, and its adamant refusal of women's ordination in 1888, did not curb the gospel energies of these women. To accommodate the reality and success of preaching women, to maintain control of those women's activities, and, it was hoped, to deflect women preachers from challenging men's exclusive authority in the ordained ministry, the 1900 General Conference of the A.M.E. Church bent. It agreed that a second structural position of women should be created. This last position established exclusively for women in the A.M.E. Church was the position of deaconess.[36]

Bishop Abraham Grant wrote the *Deaconess Manual of the African Methodist Church,* which states, in part, that to qualify for the "office of Deaconess," a woman "should not be younger than eighteen years nor older than thirty-five, unmarried, or, a widow, possessed of good reputation, good English education, a full membership of at least two years in the AME Church, and general adaptation for the work."[37]

Although the Church developed a Ceremony of Consecration for deaconesses, including episcopal pomp and ceremony, this ritual was not to be confused with such actions as that of Bishop Turner, when he placed a woman's name on his deacons' list. Deaconesses were never ordained when they entered the A.M.E. Church's ministry. Men, on the other hand, were always ordained when they became deacons.[38]

Thus on two occasions, the Church expanded its official structure to include positions for women. However, neither stewardesses nor deaconesses carried the mantle of ordination. Without ordination, the duties performed by A.M.E. women drew many informal accolades but did not result in increased status and authority for women. The difference in the definitions of stewardess and deaconess from the superficially equivalent titles held by men prevented A.M.E. women from sharing the traditional authority of the clergy and their lay helpers. Women's organizational role still was not to lead, but to serve in positions subordinate to men.

In spite of the fact that the A.M.E. Church created positions for women as stewardess and deaconess, the ordination of women remained a chimera in the nineteenth century. Preaching women's persistent petitions for ordination had failed to gain the prize of clerical authority. These women's activities challenged the male power structures sufficiently that formal roles were conceded to women in the Church. But the concessions granted were designed specifically not to alter the exclusively male structure of the Church. No matter what activities and duties they performed or what titles they were awarded, women remained "helpers" to the official masculine leadership. Thus there was no real change in formal authority for women in the nineteenth-century A.M.E. Church. Black churchwomen had achieved limited objectives, but the goal of equal authority still lay before them.

V

THE MOVEMENT
OF CHURCHWOMEN
INTO SOCIAL REFORM

EVANGELICAL DOMESTICITY

Susan Dye Lee

During the winter of 1873–1874, thousands of pious evangelical housewives took to the streets in a protest demonstration of impressive proportions. Throughout the Midwest, bands of self-appointed female crusaders carried the gospel of salvation into the grogshops, beer gardens, and saloons of their communities. These women wanted an end to the sale of intoxicating spirits, and they believed that peace, prayer, and persuasion would convince rum-sellers to forsake the traffic in liquor. Their action initiated a new era in alcohol reform. For the first time since the beginning of the American temperance movement, women assumed front-rank status in the battle against Demon Rum. More important, this wedding of women, temperance, and evangelicalism signaled the emergence of domestic reformers whose concerns were centered in the family and whose aims were to purify society by making it homelike; they became models for the increasing numbers of capable, middle-class women who entered public life as guardians of civic morality in the years following the Civil War. Indeed, temperance advocates, prominent among them Methodist lay workers and other women active in Protestant church societies, were definitive leaders in the broad, postwar drive to politicize domesticity.

The crusade was a woman's temperance revival whose assumptions were defined by evangelical domesticity. The crusaders believed that the world could be made perfect through the redemptive power of women. Emboldened by the strong feelings of moral superiority that these convictions encouraged, the crusaders went out into the community as evangelists for the home. They marched into saloons, held prayer meetings in front of bars, and attempted to convert liquor dealers to new lines of work. The belief that God had ordained women to restore communities to sobriety rationalized even militant tactics of social ostracism and civil disobedience. Crusading women were certain that intemperance could be eliminated by converting individuals, that woman's moral authority would prevail, and that the gift of the Spirit would usher in the kingdom of God on earth. Through this pentecostal experience, the crusaders liberated themselves from second-class status in the temperance movement and formed the Woman's National Christian Temperance Union, an organization that dominated alcohol reform for the remainder of the nineteenth century.[1]

The crusade, however, was a two-edged phenomenon. An account of the feminization of the temperance movement must also be accompanied by a recognition of women's failure to revise the assumptions which underlay their remarkable expansion into new spheres of public activity. As the crusade progressed, the crusaders' actions became increasingly political. Nevertheless, they were not willing to see their behavior for what it was. By failing to accept the implications of their departure from conventional feminine conduct, they not only imprisoned themselves in a set of obsolete gender stereotypes, but vitiated the impact of their social action as well.

The crusade began in Hillsboro, a southwestern Ohio farm community with antislavery roots dating back to the days of Theodore Weld. Agriculture was the mainstay of the economy. In 1873, Hillsboro's grain output supported two distilleries and thirteen saloons amidst a population numbering little more than two thousand. In this environment, part of the town's male population had become heavy drinkers. One resident described stock-sale day as a "drunken hell, with brawls, cutting, and shooting."[2]

At the same time, Hillsboro had its civilized side. It boasted two seminaries for women, and it was thought that the level of female education promoted an "unusually independent order of thought and action" between the sexes.[3] In any case, whether for personal or more objective reasons, some Hillsboro women clearly harbored temperance sentiments. On Christmas Eve of 1873, these sentiments took active form. Prompted by a lecture rousingly delivered by Dio Lewis on the power of woman's prayer in grogshops, seventy prominent middle-aged matrons met to pray. Dedicating themselves to the eradication of saloons, they then marched singing from the Presbyterian church to begin a campaign against rum-selling in Hillsboro.[4]

This revolutionary idea—prayer meetings held in saloons—had widespread appeal in the Midwest states. Ohio took the lead. Two days after the action at Hillsboro, the women of nearby Washington Court House began a similar campaign, and in just eight days they succeeded in closing all their town's saloons. The new year found crusaders in cities across the counties of southwestern Ohio taking up the banner. Newspapers quickly dubbed this "the woman's war against whiskey" and spread news of the movement.[5] By March, 1874, a female insurrection of impressive proportions was underway. In towns with a long history of evangelical activism, thousands of women joined the crusade, forming temperance societies and marching into saloons to conduct prayer meetings. Although it eventually involved women in states from Massachusetts to California, the crusade centered in Ohio, Indiana, Michigan, Illinois, Iowa, western Pennsylvania, and upstate New York, often in former antislavery strongholds. Women in the New England states participated in far fewer numbers than did their sisters farther west. In the southern states, where notions of gentility precluded women from kneeling in the sawdust of saloon floors, the impact of the crusade was minimal.[6]

The action at Hillsboro not only launched the crusade, but set a pattern followed in other communities. Prompted by clergymen or encouraged by news accounts, enthused temperance women gathered in church for an initial meeting of consecration. Thereafter, early each morning the crusaders began their work with devotions before organizing the day's activities. They then marched singing through the streets, entered a saloon, and, if permitted to remain, held a prayer meeting. A newsman in Waynesville, Ohio, described one such scene.

The ladies sang some beautiful hymns, then the leader called on a very nice-looking old lady to pray. . . . Men that had not heard half a dozen prayers in as many years were deeply touched; and as the ladies rose from their knees, there were tears on almost every face. Not a man seemed to have stirred during the prayer, but at its close the band sang with great force and beauty, "Tell me the old, old story," and one by one, reverently and in silence, the men dropped from the room.[7]

Following worship, the leader of the praying band preached from a pertinent Bible text, instructed the liquor dealer in the destructiveness of his business, and with personal entreaty, exhorted him to abandon his profession. The meeting concluded when the dealer was asked to sign a pledge to cease selling liquor.

Saloon visitation was a central feature of the crusade, and it departed radically from temperance tradition in three important respects. First, the approach utilized prayer, exhortation, and soul-saving in a highly unusual setting and for an entirely new purpose. During the antebellum period, evangelical techniques popularized by Charles Grandison Finney had been widely incorporated into temperance practice.[8] During the crusade, however, the locale for preaching gospel temperance was not the church but the saloon, and the object was not primarily reformation of the drunkard, but elimination of the liquor traffic by direct confrontation of the sellers. With intense feelings of immediacy and with sincere appeals to emotion, in their prayer meetings the crusaders sought to create an atmosphere in which the dealer would feel himself convicted of sin and become receptive to the outpourings of the Holy Spirit. By singling out each offender individually, looking him squarely in the eye, and praying for him by name, the crusaders made it seem that this man's salvation was their sole personal concern. Moreover, if a saloonkeeper did not sign the pledge to quit, he found himself the object of a protracted revival campaign. This form of social pressure and the anxiety it was designed to produce often continued for days, or even weeks.

Innovative in its use of evangelical measures to convert sellers, saloon visitation deviated from temperance tradition in a second crucial way. The agency of conversion in these barroom revival meetings was not a minister, but a group of housewives. This development illustrated the extent to which lay leadership, particularly among the "female brethren," had found its way into evangelical practice. Nonetheless, preaching in saloons was a daring tactic; through it, women whose lives were informed by an ethic of innocence exposed themselves to the seamy underside of society. To banish brandy from the domestic sideboard was one thing; to confront the liquor seller in public, on his own ground, was quite another. In this respect, saloon visitation shattered traditional boundaries of the female sphere and replaced them with new definitions determined by the women themselves. This change was put succinctly by the crusader who asserted, "Where my brother goes to drink, I certainly ought to be allowed to go to pray."[9] If saloon visitation disturbed a man's respite in his favorite grogshop, it was because the crusaders no longer felt confined to their customary domain nor recognized the cultural prerogatives of male territory. In this breakdown of gender boundaries, women took the lead and courageously defied convention.

Finally, by evangelizing in saloons, the crusaders chose an ideal place in which to dramatize their position as women. The saloon challenged a female system of values rooted in assumptions of domestic security; the system depended on men's capacity to underwrite that security. In the crusaders' view, the saloon turned men into slaves of appetite—it was an emasculator. And by stripping men of their manhood, the saloon robbed women and children of their providers. The emotional logic underlying the crusaders' attack on saloons was unassailable. No one better personified loss of independence than the intemperate, and nothing represented a more visible counterpoise to female values than the saloon. For wives who cherished the sanctity of conjugal relationships, the saloon ruined husbands and destroyed families. For mothers who nurtured values of purity and piety in their children, the saloon loosened moral restraints and led sons and brothers into paths of sexual indulgence. For homemakers who provided discipline, stability, and continuity in a private retreat from the outside world, the saloon was a public hell where men courted pauperism, debauchery, crime, and violent self-destruction. Thus from a woman's point of view, the saloon upset the delicate balance of male/female arrangements; when it prevented men from functioning in an autonomous capacity, the saloon jeopardized the dependent position of women as well.

During their initial visits, the crusaders trembled, huddled together, and often swooned, but with repeated sallies, they became increasingly brave. The women began to notice their surroundings: in Brooklyn, indescribable pictures on the walls; in Wheeling, West Virginia, striptease dancing in a burlesque theater; in New York City, prostitutes confined in a "shop of the most notorious character."[10] As they discovered the role of the liquor industry in promoting gambling and sex, the crusaders began to view the saloon as the personification of evil. They saw their visitations as contests with sin and placed their experiences in the tradition of familiar biblical stories in which good battled evil. They likened themselves to Hebrew children passing unscathed through the fiery furnace, or to Daniel in the lion's den. Courage replaced fear, and each prayer meeting in a saloon became a life-and-death struggle with the forces of Satan. As the crusaders' determination increased, the battle assumed warlike proportions. Their official accounts were laced with aggressive war imagery. The ladies "enlisted in the ranks," sought out the "fortress of the enemy," engaged in a "hand-to-hand fight with the rum power," and demanded his "unconditional surrender."[11] There was nothing subtle in the message these phrases conveyed; it was the imagery of militant Christian women at war with sin. A song with lyrics written to the tune of the *Battle Hymn of the Republic* emphasized this uncompromising approach to the forces of evil.

> They have sallied forth to conquer,
>   and will never beat retreat,
> While the banner of the rum-fiend
>   is still flaunted on the street,
> And his hellish snares are waiting
>   for the all unwary feet,
> For God will lead them on.[12]

The crusaders' commitment to a spirit free of malice and recrimination usually kept this rhetoric in the background, however, and they dealt with their negative feelings by making the crusade a test of love. Because it furnished the ideal setting for a confrontation with and a triumph over sin, saloon visitation became a means of sanctification. In this process of growth in grace, the crusaders frequently alluded to Christ's atonement. Believing that faith in the atonement made the attainment of holiness possible, they were extremely preoccupied with suffering. If Christ died to cleanse his children of their sins, he surely expected them to undertake soul-saving in a spirit of loving sacrifice. "We knew the blessedness of being reviled for Christ's sake . . . ," said one, "and we all felt it was sweet not only to work, but to suffer for his sake."[13] Accordingly, the crusaders attempted to maintain a posture of humility and self-abnegation; their appearance was one of solemn consecration. "The spirit that produces martyrs had filled their souls," explained a dedicated worker. "It was not enthusiasm."[14]

Many of the hymns sung by the crusaders reflected this desire to experience redemption through suffering.

> I am coming to the cross;
> I am poor and weak and blind;
> I am counting all things dross,
> I shall full salvation find.[15]

Another popular hymn, which the crusaders often chose when their entreaties met with failure, expressed the identification they felt with Christ.

> Must Jesus bear the cross alone,
> And all the world go free?
> No, there's a cross for every one,
> And, there's a cross for me.[16]

Suffering, then, purified the crusaders, made them more holy, and to become more holy was to experience the Christ. One crusader described saloon visitation in just those terms. "Never have we felt ourselves nearer heaven," she explained, "than when kneeling on the floor of a drinking house, praying for the keeper and for the success of the Woman's Crusade."[17]

Identification with Christ not only had its sources in the evangelical quest for holiness, but in the domestic situation of women as well. Thus the need to experience perfect love through suffering served two purposes: It provided the crusaders with a powerful religious rationale, and it allowed them to express their feelings of indignation as women. In addition to invoking the example of Christ, therefore, the crusaders also claimed sisterhood with the drunkard's wife and repeatedly expressed identification with her condition of dependence.[18] Woman as victim was a familiar message conveyed by the praying bands in their visitations. A Springfield, Ohio, teacher who brought her class of young ladies to Gleason's Saloon to sing *Say, Mr. Barkeeper, Has Father Been Here?* asked in prayer, "How long! oh Lord, how long! must we suffer on and on, while we have left the power to suffer? Oh, God, consider the tears of the oppressed, for on the side of the oppressor is power, which Thou alone can crush."[19] The desire for sanctification—the need for deliverance from sin through an experience of Christ—provided the crusaders with a legitimate way to express the grievances of their sex. As Christians they sought holiness; as women they resented their powerlessness. But as Christian women they could, through suffering, achieve holiness for themselves and simultaneously enjoy the power of bringing salvation to others.

From the crusaders' point of view, these others were not women's moral equals; they were men. During their visitations, the temperance evangelists not only saw their efforts as contests with sin, but as contests fought in behalf of sinning men. In this respect, the crusade was a sexual confrontation in which women asserted their moral authority by attempting to impose their values on men. Unable to accept any rationale that sanctioned a direct expression of their own self-interests, the crusaders channeled their energies into the correction of men's behavior. This widely held nineteenth-century assumption—that women were morally and spiritually superior—was reflected again and again in the crusaders' statements. "We do not think we are 'doing alms' when we carry the gospel to our sinful brothers for whom Christ *died,* neither do we expect to gain any glory for having knelt in saloons," one woman told a saloonkeeper. "Yet we are willing to do so *for your sakes,* and the sake of the fathers and sons you are poisoning with alcohol!"[20] Here was a potentially rich evangelical harvest. As women pictured them, men had no moral fiber, no strength of character. The appeal at Washington Court House spoke to precisely this point of view: "We . . . appeal to you to desist from this ruinous traffic, that our husbands, brothers, and especially our sons, be no longer exposed to this terrible temptation, and that we may no longer see them led into those paths which go down to sin and bring both soul and body to destruction."[21]

The implication was that men were weaklings, unable to resist temptation; they needed it placed beyond reach. Crusaders, therefore, directed their prayers at the saloon-keeper, whose traffic was wrecking homes, ruining lives, and destroying souls. They believed that tender entreaty would achieve what force could not. In weakness resided strength; in love, power. One Quaker lady, asserting her superiority through professions of weakness, beseeched a saloonkeeper thus: "Our father in heaven . . . we come again in a sense of our weakness, needing great help from thee. . . . We implore thee to bless this dear family, we ask . . . that thou wouldst send thy word with power into the heart of this dear brother, that he may give up this terrible sin that has so long kept him away from God."[22] The assumptions of moral superiority were thus turned upside down. Piety ceased to require docility on the part of women and instead called for submissiveness on the part of men. In fact, though the crusaders couched their prayers in terms of female weakness, their strong moral convictions gave them a sense of power, and this power was transformed into a mission of spiritual redemption in behalf of fallen brothers.

As the crusaders visited saloons in the role of redeemers, they themselves began to be transformed by the evangelical power of the crusade. Its millennial appeal brought thousands of women out of their homes and into the community, giving them the opportunity to lead groups, formulate plans, and execute goals. Some crusaders stood before an audience and spoke in public for the first time in their lives. "Almost before I had time to think," said one woman, "I was addressing an audience of hundreds. God gave me the power."[23] In short, crusading women discovered dormant talents. They wrote temperance columns for newspapers, preached from church pulpits, formed lecture bureaus, and learned to "give ringing, effective speeches for a right way of living."[24]

In this experience of self-discovery, the crusaders drew strength from their moral convictions. A sense of divine guidance alleviated their feelings of dependence, timidity, and passivity and provided courage and self-assurance. As women proved capable of dealing with unpredictable situations and mastered the struggle to "yield up their preconceived ideas of what was a lady's place," they felt differently about themselves.[25] "I never had . . . such an exalted opinion of woman, her courage and ability to overcome difficulties and master opposing forces of evil," testified one crusader.[26] The women were making an irreversible debut into public life, and they were aware of it. "Many . . . gave it as their experience at the close of the year, that it had been the richest and noblest of their lives," said one woman.[27] Intended as a mission to convert liquor dealers, the crusade became a pentecostal baptism as well; it initiated the crusaders into a world beyond domestic confines and modified their notions of women's capabilities.

The women who were undergoing these changes shared many similar traits. In general, those who joined crusading bands were educated middle-class matrons in their thirties and forties. Kinship ties were strong in small towns, and daughters often marched alongside crusading mothers. Active in church groups and often the wives of ministers, or even preachers themselves, the crusaders came from a broad spectrum of Protestant denominations. Praising the extent to which the women overcame sectarian rivalries, one crusader said, "The time was when our Presbyterian friends thought women should not pray in public, and it was easy to tell the difference between the prayers of the Presbyterians and Baptists and Methodists. But now they all pray alike."[28]

Whatever their other similarities, however, the crusaders' most common characteristic was an evangelical world-view. "The Crusaders felt that 'unity of the Spirit' was the one essential," said Frances Willard. "Enthusiasm—'a God in us'—enabled the Praying Bands to accomplish prodigies." The necessity of full, personal consecration to Christ, the notion of divine immanence, and the idea of glorifying God through an experience of holiness were all powerful forces at work in the crusade. "The baptism of power came upon us," said one crusader; another reported, "When I first opened my lips to pray, my heart grew light, and never before did I experience such a sacred nearness to God." The women were convinced that by sacrificing themselves to God, they could serve as his instruments in the creation of Christ's kingdom on earth. "No woman among us, who entered into the spirit of it, doubts for a moment the Almighty guidance," said a dedicated worker.[29]

The unity of spirit described by Willard had strong roots in women's domestic experience. Evangelical Christianity offered women a set of ideas they could enthusiastically incorporate into their special sphere of influence—the home. These ideas included the centrality of conversion to Christ and the process of sanctification; an emphasis on love, sacrifice, purity, and discipline in achieving a life of holiness; and a belief in the possibility of perfection. In the crusaders' thinking, home was the ideal spot for the creation of a heaven on earth. It was a community whose purpose was the ordering of affection—a place where passions were tamed, emotions purified, and right feeling nurtured. In this spiritual sanctuary, woman's role was that of mediator between heaven and earth, a kind of secular angel. She was the instrument of redemption through which husband and children would be saved from the world's corrupting influences.

This special redemptive role, with home as locus, also encouraged women to believe that the ideas of evangelical domesticity could solve social issues. Because it treated communal problems as personal sins which could be eliminated with religious solutions, evangelicalism subverted the traditional boundaries of women's sphere and enabled the crusaders to define new arenas of action for themselves.[30] Evangelicalism became their bridge into the world. By insisting that indifference to communal sources of imperfection constituted a sin itself, evangelicalism strengthened the crusaders' conviction that they could maintain their standing with God only by redeeming their communities from destruction.[31]

Despite persistent efforts, saloon visitation by no means ushered in the millenium in all the places it was tried. Particularly in such large cities as Cleveland, New York, Chicago, and Cincinnati, opposition from saloonkeepers was nearly universal. Recalcitrant dealers did not always treat the crusaders with the respect they were accustomed to receiving. Many asked the ladies to leave. Some ignored them. Others cursed. One bartender became so angry at the presence of females in his saloon that he began undressing to take a bath.[32] In other instances, the crusaders were harassed, intimidated, or subjected to outright physical abuse. In New Vienna, Ohio, the proprietor of the Dead Fall Saloon "baptised the crusaders with buckets of dirty water," and in Carthage, Missouri, the praying women were pelted with rotten eggs.[33] Other proprietors locked crusaders out of their establishments or took the women to court for legal violations.[34] Even saloonkeepers who appeared cooperative were more honest in expressing their feelings when the women were not around. "They are very kind in their prayers at first," a dealer confided to a newsman. "They pray for a fellow's soul, and then stick a petition before him. If he don't sign, they pray for lightning to strike his shop."[35]

When they were refused saloon visitation, praying bands devised alternative tactics. If ousted from a saloon, for example, the crusaders moved their theater of operation into the street.[36] "It was a sight calculated to melt the stoutest heart," a newsman confessed when the Hillsboro ladies conducted their prayer meeting on the cold flagstones.[37] Crusaders also circulated temperance pledges, held mass temperance rallies, and boycotted groceries and drugstores that sold spirits. If still unsuccessful, the women went to increasing lengths "to exploit the burning eye of the public." They set up mobile tabernacles and held the equivalent of around-the-clock sit-ins.[38] In Bucyrus, Ohio, "the ladies adopted the picket system, which consisted in two or more ladies remaining in front of a saloon, and taking the names of all who entered."[39] In some cities, the names of these patrons were published in the local newspaper or read aloud at mass temperance meetings.

These new forms of social ostracism were often accompanied by an unmistakable spirit of intolerance, and both spirit and tactics betrayed the moral assumptions of the temperance crusade. As the war of attrition continued, ethnic prejudice, particularly toward German immigrants, often surfaced among the crusaders. Their accounts were peppered with cruel anecdotes that featured German proprietors arguing with the ladies in broken English. "Go vay, vimmins, go home; shtay at home and tend to your papies," a beleaguered beer garden owner was reported to have told the Washington Court House women.[40] The crusaders resented immigrants whose views of drinking had no moral cathexis and whose liquor habits publicly affronted temperance mores. To the crusader, the immigrant was not a citizen with legitimate values of his own, but an unpatriotic sinner. Crusaders in Jeffersonville, Indiana, for example, were incensed when the proprietor of a German saloon unfurled an American flag in a symbolic plea that his liberties be respected. The ladies responded by praying that the "flag of freedom might soon wave over a land forever free from the curse of rum."[41] In the most uncharitable instances of all, whenever a saloonkeeper had an accident, became ill, or died, his fate was seen as a token of God's visitation. Upon hearing that a dealer had been blinded by the bung of a beer barrel, for example, a crusader intoned, "We read in the word 'that, though joined hand in hand, the wicked shall not go unpunished!' "[42]

As a result, the German community castigated the crusade for its know-nothing spirit of persecution. They considered saloon visitation a profanation of prayer and blamed the evangelical churches for supporting the "imbecile women." Praying bands were referred to as preying pests. An editor in *Die Gegenwart,* a German-American newspaper, had this to say about the Methodists: "They come together in their churches and conspire. . . . They come forth from their churches in troops, and interfere with the business of our countrymen, threaten them with death, and deprive them of their liberty. They pray that their God may strike the saloonists and their families dead. (Very Christian—is it not?)"[43]

As spring arrived and millennial expectations of success failed to materialize, the crusaders' tactics became distinctly political. "Prayers and pleadings having failed to accomplish our object with them, we felt that they were *below* the reach of moral *suasion,* and must have some *legal suasion,*" explained a crusader whose band had failed to dry up their town.[44] Crusaders then began to take saloonkeepers to court for violations of local temperance law. Use of the petition became a popular tactic as well. Bands petitioned their councils for better enforcement of existing laws or for passage of strict local ordinances.[45] In Ohio, the women held temperance conventions in support of licensing legislation, and when a law favorable to the whiskey interests was introduced into the state legislature, they descended on the capitol to lobby for its defeat. "Moral influence was all they thought to use," said an organizer, indicating the extent to which it was difficult for the crusaders to see their own behavior in political terms.[46] With the coming of municipal elections in April, crusading bands became even more involved in the politics of temperance. They organized lecture bureaus and gave campaign speeches. They wrote newspaper articles, distributed election material, and posted handbills for temperance candidates. In some cities, the crusaders even called on the voters individually to impress upon them the need for electing temperance candidates. They were totally absorbed in securing by law that which prayer had failed to achieve.[47]

The crusaders saw no inconsistency between this behavior and their moral givens. In these campaigns, the women viewed politics in absolute terms; politics existed only to serve the interests of morality. They made no distinction between behavior in the public forum and the kind of right behavior it was their duty as women to uphold in the private realm. What was morally right could not be politically wrong. This assumption was reflected in the religious approach the crusaders brought to campaigning. One leader described her band's political efforts as a religious act. "Quiet, timid women with calm, resolute courage . . . took their places with hearts full of prayer, and hands full of prohibition tickets, and in the drizzling, cold, rain, fought for the cause they loved."[48]

Though the vote was denied them, the crusaders did everything possible to influence the outcome of their municipal elections. They were not able, however, to recognize their own behavior as organized political activity. At a Springfield, Ohio, temperance convention held June 17, for example, the delegates argued far into the evening over a resolution with the word *political* in it; the proposal was finally amended to suggest that the women would be working not as partisans, but as Christian citizens.[49] The women wanted it both ways, then—political action without partisanship. How could the crusaders promote Christian harmony while behaving as political beings? They could not resolve this dilemma.

Nonetheless, gospel politics did teach crusaders the power of association. During August, 1874, the first National Sunday School Assembly, held under the direction of John Vincent, attracted many crusade participants to the shores of Lake Chautauqua. Among those present was Martha McClellan Brown, Grand Chief of the Ohio Good Templars.[50] Although she headed a temperance society in which men and women worked together on a basis of equality, Brown believed that the crusaders distrusted the organization's secret rituals and its Prohibition party connections. Rather than urge the Chautauqua delegates to join the Templars, therefore, she proposed instead an idea for a national temperance organization—a segregated society composed only of women.[51] A notice was read, preliminary meetings held, and on August 15, about fifty women gathered to hammer out the details of Brown's plan. Jennie Fowler Willing, a professor of English at Illinois Wesleyan University, chaired the meeting, and Emily Huntington Miller, a juvenile-fiction writer, served as secretary.[52]

307

A committee on organization, heavily Methodist and midwestern in representation, was approved, and the officers were authorized to issue a circular letter announcing a national convention. This call was well publicized in the press. It asked woman's temperance leagues to hold conventions for the purpose of electing one woman from each Congressional district as a delegate to an organizational convention in Cleveland. Reminding the crusaders that "in union and organization" lay the permanent success of the temperance uprising, the call repeated a familiar theme. It urged women of the land to redeem the nation from the curse of intemperance. "In the name of our Master—in behalf of the thousands of women who suffer from this evil—we call upon all to unite in an earnest, continued effort to hold the ground already won, and move onward together to complete victory over the foes we fight."[53] The circular, restating the crusade assumption that women had been chosen to save America from the evil of alcohol, thus exhorted women of all denominations to unite for its elimination. Organization was seen as the key to success. The crusade was not over, but would continue in permanent form, to fight intemperance through planned, collective action.

As women gathered during the fall to elect delegates to the organizing convention, they continued to extol the crusade even though saloons went on with business as usual. Clearly, the crusade had not abolished the traffic in liquor. Did this represent a failure of woman's moral power? The crusaders did not think so. They rationalized their efforts by emphasizing the change in public opinion wrought by the crusade. To continue the campaign, they prepared to apply ongoing moral pressure through the national organization.[54]

The temperance revival of 1873–1874 did not change the crusaders' view of drinking, the saloon, or the liquor traffic. If anything, the crusade served to reinforce their perception of the saloon as the root of all evil. A single source, the liquor traffic, was responsible for society's problems. A single solution—its elimination—would restore the communal patient to health. The crusaders did not see drinking as the result of complex causes, nor did they perceive it as a manifestation of deep tensions in the social system. They regarded intemperance as basically a moral problem, even though they applied political measures to its solution.

Although the crusade changed women's notions about the boundaries of their proper sphere, it did not change their ideas about the female role within this enlarged sphere. The political experiences of the crusade offered women the opportunity to question the moral assumptions of their behavior. On the whole, they proved unwilling to evaluate these assumptions and revise them accordingly. It did not occur to most crusaders that their failure stemmed from the fact that their political power was not commensurate with the moral authority they were attempting to exert. Although frustration with limitations of the moral approach led them to undertake increasingly political action as the crusade progressed, they did not see this behavior in any but moral terms. Confronted with political impotence on election day, most stopped short of establishing a connection between the temperance issue and their own civic disabilities.

"It is praying first; it will be voting afterward," wrote Henry Blackwell in the *Woman's Journal,* but his conclusion was not one that most temperance women drew from the crusade.[55] Despite practical support of political remedies for intemperance, the crusaders did not, as a result of the spring elections, identify their own lack of rights as a social problem or reformulate their grievances into direct, self-interested demands. They were unable to take a reform position which proposed changes solely for their own benefit. To have done so would have denied the self-sacrifice and altruism required of redeemers. Though feelings of moral superiority, nourished by evangelical domesticity, got women out of the home, they took home with them when they left. In so doing, temperance crusaders entered the arena of social reform with all the strengths and weaknesses that this ideology implied.

FOR GOD AND HOME
AND NATIVE LAND

Carolyn DeSwarte Gifford

The Woman's Christian Temperance Union (W.C.T.U.) was formed in 1874 when American women responded to the battle cry of the Ohio crusaders: Saloons must go! As the "sober second thought" that followed a spontaneous series of praying demonstrations against liquor dealers, the W.C.T.U. eventually mobilized several hundred thousand women under the motto "For God and Home and Native Land."[1] The organization worked for the prohibition of alcoholic beverages by various methods and in many areas of American life, searching for effective ways to persuade people that drinking was evil. Developing strategies and molding a tight, efficient group to implement them, W.C.T.U. leaders projected the image of a woman equal to the tasks before her in the war for the nation's sobriety.

What sort of person was this W.C.T.U. woman? What qualities did she exhibit? What strengths did she possess? What ideals motivated her to enter what promised to be a long, difficult, even dangerous struggle? What beliefs led her to confront powerful adversaries who controlled wealth, were wiser in the ways of the world, and would stop at nothing to gain their ends?

This essay is addressed to these questions. It seeks to describe the W.C.T.U. woman as some of the union's earliest leaders envisioned her and as they embodied, in their own lives, the woman dedicated to the union's cause. It examines speeches and writings of Annie T. Wittenmyer, first president of the National W.C.T.U. (1874–1879); Frances E. Willard, second president (1879–1898); Mary B. Woodbridge, recording secretary of the national union

(1878–1893) and also president of the Ohio union (1879–1886); Mary T. Lathrap, president of the Michigan union (1881–1895); and Sarepta I. Henry, national union evangelist during the 1880s. Of these, Wittenmyer, Willard, Lathrap, and Henry (until late in her life) were active Methodist Episcopal laywomen, deeply imbued with the culture of American Methodism and well connected to its clergy. These officers labored to bring women into W.C.T.U. membership and to keep them working actively toward its goals. Through their words, a portrait emerges of the kind of woman they sought to recruit. As they wrote and spoke, exhorting their membership, the officers' own dreams for women led the union toward new possibilities. These dreams and possibilities did not develop without conflicts among W.C.T.U. leaders as to woman's nature and proper sphere, however, and this essay will explore these tensions as well.

Much research has been done in the past decade on the image of woman in the nineteenth-century United States, but historians have concentrated on the first half of the century and on the woman's suffrage movement in the later part. They are just beginning to recover the lives, ideals, and accomplishments of women in the second half of the century. During that period, W.C.T.U. members were a significant force in American history.[2] They envisioned a "new American Christian woman"—a powerful image, admirable, worthy of emulation, and yet in some ways disturbing. Through this vision, American women, especially churchwomen, have been influenced by their foremothers in the W.C.T.U. more than they may realize. It is time to recall that segment of the past and reclaim it.

Re-visioning the Image of Woman

In the 1860s and early 1870s, most middle-class Protestant women in the United States were encouraged to be devotees of the "cult of true womanhood" that had developed during the first half of the century. They worshiped at the shrine of domesticity, serving their husbands and children. If they left their homes they were often bound for church, where they were preached at by male clergy who expounded the sacred teachings of this cult. Only in extreme situations did a few bold women venture beyond the confines of home and church. The Civil War was such an emergency. It led many women from the relative security of their accustomed sphere into exciting, risky adventures. With risk-taking and movement into the world came authority, power, and the ability to envision broader roles.

Annie Turner Wittenmyer, the first president of the W.C.T.U., worked for the Christian Commission during the war, overseeing two hundred women who provided relief for sick and wounded northern troops. She witnessed the dedication, the self-denial, and the steadfastness with which these women cared for the soldiers' physical and spiritual needs as they bravely accompanied armies onto the battlefields. In the thick of fighting or in the squalid conditions of army field hospitals and prison camps, women ministered to dying men. They comforted and prayed, wrote letters to mothers, wives, and sweethearts, and on occasion accompanied the caskets back home. They were heroines, "mothering" armies. Wittenmyer became convinced through her war experiences that women, by their very nature, were more spiritual, virtuous, faithful, sober, and sympathetic than men.[3] She believed that the image of "true womanhood"—pious, pure, and domestic—was a valid one, rooted in female nature.

It is well known that men who have experienced battlefields and the roving life of armies often find it difficult to settle into civilian rhythms again. After the Civil War, many American women also found themselves changed. They perceived other "emergencies" that were calling them from their homes into the world. In particular, the cities' poor and suffering humanity, swollen through immigration, seemed to need women's ministry as much as the soldiers had. Woman's natural "heart qualities" suited her for peacetime service in the home mission field, an area of church activity then developing in response to the rapid urbanization and industrialization of the late 1860s.[4]

In 1868 Annie Wittenmyer helped to establish the Ladies

and Pastors Christian Union to promote women's evangelizing work among the destitute and unchurched of the cities. The program was modeled on the Lutheran deaconess centers in Germany and sought to create a diaconal ministry parallel to the pastoral ministry, which, in most denominations, was open only to men.[5] Both Wittenmyer and her supporters within the hierarchy of the Methodist Episcopal Church realized that while women made up two-thirds of the church membership, they had very little opportunity for officially recognized ministry. The world was beginning to open up in the face of American women's insistence. Could the church afford to lag behind the world in tapping the enormous potential energy of faithful women for its redemptive work? With the blessings of several male Methodist leaders, among them Bishop Matthew Simpson, Annie Wittenmyer issued a challenge to church members: What can woman do for Christ and humanity? What is "woman's work for Jesus?"[6]

The evangelistic work Wittenmyer proposed, with its home visits to the urban poor and personal witness for Christ, unsettled both the women and the men of the Ladies and Pastors Christian Union. She appeared to threaten the bases of the cult of true womanhood in which they believed so firmly. Churchmen seemed quite satisfied with women in the home and not in the world, typified by the sprawling, noisome cities. Most churchwomen also preferred this division of space. The call for home mission workers, in effect, brought into question the commitment and activities of women who thought themselves pillars of the church, living exemplary Christian lives as wives and mothers. Wittenmyer's call exposed the fastidiousness of churchwomen who would rather not come too close to suffering and poverty. She confronted women too much at ease in their faith; she suggested that their Christianity had not demanded that they witness to others of its saving power. Painting a vivid picture of ladies who were martyrs to fashion rather than for Christ, she blasted middle-class women's idleness, frivolity, and vanity. She insisted that the Scriptures warned against such sinfulness and that instead, they called women to works of charity. In the context of a scathing attack against

313

the snares of fashion, Wittenmyer mentioned the drunkenness of upper-middle-class women who spent their after-
noons gossiping in drinking places made attractive and
inviting for ladies. Other women, she reported, bought
patent medicines, readily available in drugstores, and drank
at home. "There are many women in the church who love
these things more than they would like to confess. . . . The
church must ask: Why this increasing drunkenness among
women and what can it do to stay this terrible tide?"[7]

Wittenmyer's description of churchwomen's drinking is
one of the few passages by W.C.T.U. leaders that deal with
this issue. Usually the leaders preferred to emphasize the
plight of woman as victim—the gentle, innocent female,
crushed by the evil of drinking men, liquor profiteers, and
crooked or spineless politicians. This portrayal, in pointing
up women's relative powerlessness, contained an element of
truth. Theologically, however, it allowed and encouraged
women to identify with Christ "the Sinless Victim," rather
than with sinners in need of salvation. In her most prophetic
critical moments, Annie Wittenmyer did not allow her
followers such an easy identification. She called women's
actual behavior into question. Even though she usually
glorified women as supremely moral and spiritual beings,
Wittenmyer occasionally understood that they, like men,
were liable to sin and temptation. When she did, she shook
woman's pedestal of virtue. She implied that women and
men shared in a particularly awesome equality before God
the Judge. However, much of W.C.T.U. rhetoric secured
woman on her pedestal, insisting that sinful men would be
saved by pure women.

Churchwomen did not rush into the home mission field in
the early 1870s as they did into the crusade against liquor
dealers. Perhaps part of their reluctance to join Wittenmyer
in her evangelistic efforts in the cities could be traced to their
unwillingness to see themselves as sinful or as lacking deep
commitment. This was not what the cult of true womanhood
preached about their nature. Women were not yet quite
ready to give up their familiar cultic roles as guardians of
piety and purity. Both the crusade of 1873–1874 and the early
W.C.T.U. remained narrowly within the prevailing ethos of

American Protestantism which reinforced the conception of women as servants of men, and ultimately their saviors.

The idea of woman as savior was closely linked with the idea of woman as mother. Frances Willard, the outstanding educator and Methodist Episcopal laywoman who succeeded Wittenmyer to the W.C.T.U. presidency, made the connection explicit. "Mother-hearted women," she announced, "are called to be the saviours of the race."[8] Not all biological mothers automatically possessed the quality of mother-heartedness, while many childless women were, nonetheless, mother-hearted. Both Susan B. Anthony and Frances Willard, neither of whom ever married, are notable examples. Proponents argued that the quality manifested itself in an all-embracing sacrificial love for humanity, which had the power to raise the human race to a higher level of life. Thus women's capacity for love became a force for social reform. In revealing the mother heart of God, mother-hearted women were like Christ the Savior, who by his revelation of God's embracing love lifted humanity out of sin.[9]

Individual women already performed this mother-savior function for fathers, sons, and brothers, union leaders noted. How much more effective they could become if they worked together in the saving task of mothering. Perceiving the advantages in cooperation, the W.C.T.U. proclaimed itself "organized mother-love." This slogan originated by Hannah Whitall Smith captured both the style and strategy of the union;[10] Frances Willard identified its basis of organizational strength: "The great power of organization is that it brings [women] out; it translates them from the passive to the active voice; the dear, modest, clinging things didn't think they could do anything and lo and behold, they found they could."[11]

Willard also supplied a theological justification for organized mother love: "To my mind, organization is the one great thought of the creator; it is the difference between chaos and order; it is the constant occupation of God, and, next to God, the greatest organizer on this earth is the mother."[12]

Imitating God, then, the "mothers" of the W.C.T.U.

315

prepared to bring order out of the chaos they found rampant in American life—specifically, chaos owing to brains disordered by drink. Here was an emergency situation as threatening to American life as the Civil War, less than two decades earlier. And women, mother-hearted and organized, responded. In the mobilization against "King Alcohol," enormous numbers of women moved, as Willard had said, "from the passive to the active voice." Sarepta I. Henry described this move: "It was as if a great peril had suddenly overtaken the loved ones without. . . . And what was left for woman to do? Nothing but to hasten to the scene of danger, dragging her work with her, maybe, but *going,* true to the strongest instinct of the human soul."[13] "Without" was the world outside the home; the "scene of danger" was the saloon.

Sarepta Henry, a young widow with three children, was speaking autobiographically. She had gone outside her home to argue for Prohibition in the main streets of Rockford, Illinois, where saloons were tempting her son. Henry proceeded from Rockford's business district to its churches; from the town's leading attorneys, to meetings of the city council, to its parade grounds, where she organized the youth of Rockford into the first Loyal Temperance Legion. Eventually she went on to the National W.C.T.U., where she quickly became superintendent of the newly created Department of Evangelism. Once Henry began to move she did not stop, and in her determination she was typical of many W.C.T.U. women.[14] They left their homes on rescue missions and found themselves in a vast new territory, socially, culturally, and politically. Although at first they might experience the public world as dangerous, help was available to conquer their fears and doubts. The fast-developing organizational apparatus of the W.C.T.U. stood ready to aid women in their "translation" from "modest, clinging things" who "didn't think they could do anything" to independent women who firmly believed they could do everything.

The W.C.T.U.'s "Do Everything Policy" became the concrete expression of Frances Willard's boldest vision for women. In her most daring dreams, which appeared in her volumes of counsel for young women, Willard challenged her readers to shape themselves according to a new image. Victor Hugo's prediction that "the nineteenth century is woman's century" became her trademark. In 1871, even before the W.C.T.U. had been formed, she declared that the time had come for women to define themselves and to cease accepting definitions from traditional sources. Willard implied that this process of redefinition should not continue to focus on the image of women as oppressed. It should address instead the self-determining question, "What manner of women ought we to be?"[15]

Frances Willard was confident that this crucial question was in fact being answered by W.C.T.U. women as they pursued their multifaceted activities. The re-visioning of woman underlay their stated goal of Prohibition:

The W.C.T.U. is doing no work more important than that of reconstructing the ideal of womanhood. . . . In less enlightened days, your ideal woman composed the single grand class for which public prejudice set itself to provide. She was to be the wife and mother, and she was carefully enshrined at home. But happily, this is the world's way no longer. . . . Clearly, to all of you, I am declaring a true and blessed gospel . . . concerning honest independence and brave self-help.[16]

With this feminist "gospel," Willard announced the toppling of woman off the pedestal. The object of veneration for the cult of true womanhood would no longer hold power over W.C.T.U. women.

Furthermore, women must reject the cultic doctrine that men and women possessed inherently different natures and virtues which necessitated different spheres of existence. This was false teaching for Willard. It obscured the deeper truth that men and women should share together in all areas of life. By denying men and women common space and shared actions and labeling some traits male and others female, traditional thinking had robbed both sexes of their greatest potential for good, Willard argued.

Conservatives say: "Let man have his virtues and woman hers." Progressives answer: "Let each add to those already won the virtues of the other. Man has splendid qualities, courage, intellect, hardihood; who would not like to possess all these? What woman would not be greater and nobler if they were hers? And what man would not be grander, happier, more helpful to humanity if he were more patient, gentle, tender, chaste?"[17]

The view Frances Willard ascribed to "Conservatives" was in fact a belief firmly entrenched in the minds of many W.C.T.U. members. There were many things women ought not to do and many places they must not enter. They definitely were not called by God to cast ballots or to run the institutions of government. They were to labor through the church on behalf of suffering people, employing their particularly female spiritual, intuitive, compassionate natures in this appropriate way. Wittenmyer may have shaken woman's pedestal by questioning whether some women really deserved to be placed there; but she did not ask women to redefine true womanhood as Frances Willard did in her most visionary moments.

The New W.C.T.U. Woman: For God and Home and Native Land

Religious faith was an integral aspect of the W.C.T.U. woman's self-definition; W.C.T.U. members were, above all, *Christian* women. They thought in the language patterns and framework of nineteenth-century Evangelical Protestant Christianity.[18] Frances Willard was particularly skillful in couching her most radical thoughts in familiar language that would not alarm her audience. Thus she suggested redefining womanhood in terms of "calling." Each woman had received unique gifts which should be cultivated so that she could become what God called her to be. As part of this process of becoming she must realize that others also had received unique gifts—women were called to honor other people's talents and to allow them to flourish.[19] Willard's model for self-development was Christ, "the prophet and priest of individuality." Jesus' life was God-defined, not dictated by the world, and he encouraged humans to discover and use their talents.[20]

In order to heed God's call, women should develop the mind, one of God's gifts they had neglected. Men must allow and encourage this intellectual pursuit. Willard rallied both sexes under the banner of "the New Chivalry," which proclaimed the "liberation of ideas" for women as well as for men. Women must be educated to understand the passwords to the vast cultural heritage from which they heretofore had been excluded.[21] Willard called on women to seize and use direct power in the shaping of American life; therefore, they must be given the key to that power—education through the college level. Furthermore, they should prepare themselves to enter all the professions, the business world, and institutions of government. Woman "is learning the art of the greatness and sacredness of power, that there is nothing noble in desiring not to possess it, but that to evolve the utmost mastership of one's self and the elements around one's self that can be, is to the individual, the highest possible attainment."[22] Willard was careful to warn that power must be used for good. But her central message for those so long excluded, and so often taught the virtue of powerlessness, was that women must no longer shrink from acquiring power.

Mary Lathrap and Mary Woodbridge were two powerful women of the sort that Frances Willard admired. They seemed to epitomize the new image of the W.C.T.U. woman. The introductions to both women's biographies laud them as examples of the "fact that in intellect there is no sex." Lathrap and Woodbridge each presided over strong state unions and were deeply involved in political struggles for Prohibition. The campaign for a Prohibition amendment, managed by Mary Woodbridge in Ohio during the early 1880s, was an astounding feat of grass-roots political organizing. Willard revered Mary Lathrap of Michigan as "Our Queen of Prohibition Orators"; she persuasively combined appeals to reason and to conscience, thus blending "male" and "female" characteristics.[23]

The W.C.T.U. drew upon biblical models of power as well as those within their own leadership as sources of courage in their struggles. Recalling Deborah, the Old Testament heroine, Mary Woodbridge declared, "God's power through woman is no less to-day than in Deborah's time, and His command to each 'to do whatsoever her hand finds to do,' and His promise 'to be with her always' is the same."[24] The women of the W.C.T.U. could surely rely upon God's help in their battles just as had Deborah and the people of Israel. Union speakers were particularly fond of citing the prophecy of Joel that the Spirit would be poured out on both women and men, since this passage confirmed the availability of God's power to all who believe, regardless of gender.

Almost everyone, from secular reporters to the participants themselves, interpreted the original Ohio crusade as a spritual baptism, a new Pentecost which had filled women with power. The W.C.T.U. women eagerly sought to recapture the early crusade enthusiasm, and the events of that time came to be seen as the union's formative experiences. References to the crusade abounded in W.C.T.U. speeches; rituals were established using biblical texts connected with the crusade days; songs and poems were written; crusade "mothers" graced the platforms of national union meetings; pilgrimages were made to the Ohio towns where the crusade began. With refreshing candor, Mary Lathrap chided a Michigan annual convention about all this glorification:

It is quite the fashion to exhort each other to personal consecration, to earnest evangelism and to prayer for the old Crusade fire, but my sisters, God never repeats himself. . . . Divine power was not exhausted in 1873. God's tomorrows are even greater than his yesterdays. He has gifts and revelations for the temperance hosts they have never yet known.[25]

Her message was that the ladies must stop dwelling on the past and get on with present business; at the same time, she emphasized God's continuing support.

Sarepta I. Henry felt God's persistent call to join the temperance fight and she too believed that God's faithful would be empowered. When news of the crusade of 1873 reached Rockford, Henry felt it was her Christian duty to bring the crusade fire to her city, but she was timid and frightened. As she went about her domestic chores and her writing, she tried to ignore God's challenge; however, she found she could not concentrate on her work, and finally one evening, she fell to the living-room floor and wrestled all night with God's question, "Will you obey or will you not? I saw at once, that this matter involved salvation: that the salvation of my soul was in the balance. If I did not obey I would lose my standing with God. That meant disaster, and I had to say, I will."[26]

Other women reported similar experiences. They were most fearful of speaking before groups, especially from the pulpit, and entering saloons, gambling dens, city council chambers, courtrooms, and halls of state government. They were terrified of becoming public spectacles. The public space was man's space, and women were neither comfortable or welcome in it. But armed with God's might, temperance workers could and did invade that forbidden territory. To persuade their members to move into the public sphere, W.C.T.U. leaders entreated, coaxed, commanded, and shamed them, often using all these rhetorical skills in the same speech. But union women testified that, ultimately, it was the power of the Lord that enabled them to act or speak. What they dared not do by themselves, they would do when God was with them. This interpretation of "calling" was somewhat different from Frances Willard's vision of women's call to self-development. But the similarity of the language, coupled with the women's own experiences of God's call, persuaded them to heed their leader's words. Had God not accompanied them into bars, pulpits, courtrooms, legislatures? Perhaps he also was calling them and their daughters into colleges, professions, and the voting booth. Perhaps they could indeed "Do Everything," since God expected this of them. At least they could try.

This combination of comfortable, familiar language and radical reinterpretation characterized the campaign for the Home Protection Ballot. For many W.C.T.U. members, leaders as well as followers, the idea of woman suffrage was extremely difficult to accept. Annie Wittenmyer could not approve it. Sarepta Henry and Frances Willard disputed the issue for years. Mary Woodbridge prayed about it. Yet Willard, the most radical, kept bringing up the possibility. She insisted that home was "the citadel of everything that is good and pure on earth."[27] It was the place where men as well as women were renewed and strengthened. As such it must be protected against all threats to its stability. But women could not guard their homes effectively by shutting themselves up and keeping the influences of the world out. It was impossible to maintain a barrier between the home and the world, as Henry and others had discovered.

Women must lay claim to the power of the world and use it for their own ends. For many, the phrase "home protection" merely implied that women would petition for men's option to vote for Prohibition and would then persuade men to vote the way they wanted them to. However, Frances Willard did not intend such an indirect exercise of power. She demanded the home protection ballot for women so that they could embark on political housekeeping, to "make the world home-like."[28] The moral influence of the home and of womanhood must be spread abroad in the world. This line of argument seemed, on the surface, to reinforce the traditional understanding of woman's domestic role. That role was no longer to be confined within a limited space, however, and men were urged to share in the "woman's task" of world-home maintenance. "Good men" would see the value of a homelike world and would work alongside women for its establishment, Willard maintained. She was also questioning the rigid division between man's and woman's work, however cautiously. The language of home protection was designed to help women to feel somewhat more at ease in a new environment, and with W.C.T.U. women, it succeeded. If working in the political arena involved housekeeping, surely they knew how to do that.

The term "gospel politics" is still another instance of justaposing familiar, reassuring language with a new demand upon women. Mary Lathrap's phrase originally was intended to indicate that the usual gospel methods of prayer, Bible reading, hymn-sing meetings, and pledges were no longer effective in promoting Prohibition and that it was time to take the fight into the political realm.[29] But gospel politics soon came to mean that the union should widen its commitments to include study and action on a vast array of issues besides Prohibition, if it wished to assume a responsible role in national life. After taking a hard look at the United States, the W.C.T.U. leadership became convinced that the country was in even more serious trouble than they originally had perceived. Indeed it was in imminent danger of losing its "national soul" and thus stood sorely in need of redemption. The W.C.T.U. leaders called for rededication to what they believed to be the country's original ideals.

Since the leadership was overwhelmingly white Anglo-Saxon Protestant, it interpreted the nation's ideals from that framework. Union leaders were alarmed by what they felt to be the undermining of such treasured values as Sabbath observance and Bible reading in public schools. They were uneasy about labor disputes that threatened to become violent. The cities' growth and complex problems frightened them, particularly since many of them came from rural and small-town backgrounds. The rising tide of immigration from Catholic areas of Europe also filled them with anxiety. They were convinced that the immigrants valued neither the republican system of government or the public education system that transmitted allegiance to America's governmental forms. Their response to all these issues was to attempt, through gospel politics, to "place the government upon Christ's shoulders"—to "christianize" the nation. Following the slogan that "law and moral suasion go hand in hand" in such efforts, they saw praying and voting as complementary duties of the American woman.[30] This slogan suggested that there should be no division of labor by sexes—no longer would only women pray and only men vote. All who were concerned about the nation's unredeemed spiritual condition were to join together in every aspect of gospel politics.

Some union leaders and members interpreted the redemptive task narrowly in terms of working toward legislation for Sabbath laws and Bible-reading in public schools, cracking down on labor agitators, and converting Catholics to "Christianity" and Prohibition. For Frances Willard, however, the vision of national redemption was much broader in scope. It entailed radical solutions to national problems, but such visions could inspire only those women who were becoming accustomed to thinking and acting beyond the limited sphere of the home.

Through its national and state conventions and its weekly paper *The Union Signal,* the W.C.T.U. provided an "adult education" program in which the membership could participate in discussing issues of national and global importance. The union became a training ground for widening women's horizons. A conscientious W.C.T.U. member was obligated to answer the call to intellectual self-development that Willard had issued. By the early 1890s she was able to state, "I do not know a White Ribbon woman who is not a Prohibitionist, a woman suffragist, a purity worker, and an earnest sympathizer with the Labor movement."[31] This was hyperbole, but it does suggest that from 1880 to 1895, many W.C.T.U. women participated vicariously, yet enthusiastically, as their exceptional president grappled with some of the most thought-provoking questions of the day. In her public addresses, pamphlets, books, and articles, Willard alerted her audiences to an ever-widening range of issues, many raised by other reform groups, political parties, and labor organizations of the period. And through their beloved president, the W.C.T.U. membership also pondered them.

In her vision of the self-defined independent woman, Frances Willard also advocated a fundamental equality between men and women in their most intimate relationships; this would be the foundation of the equality of the sexes in all areas of life. Willard's phrase "The White Life for Two" referred to a whole complex of sexual equality issues, ranging from marriage to the elimination of prostitution. She was convinced that the institution of marriage was degraded by the laws, customs, and structures that made women dependent upon men; as a result, men became potential tyrants and women lost their self-esteem. Ideally, marriage would be a partnership. For genuine equality, it would be necessary for women to enter marriage from a vantage point of independence. If a woman had a way to support herself, she would not rush into marriage, nor could she so easily be enticed into prostitution.

Once married, the wife should retain the right to her own

body. Most husbands and the legal system of the time still understood wives as *femmes couvertes*. The expectations implied by that phrase and the laws giving substance to those expectations must be removed, Willard asserted. In an egalitarian marriage, she declared:

The wife will undoubtedly have custody of herself and . . . she will determine the frequency of the investiture of life with form. My library groans with accumulations of books written by men to teach women the immeasurable inequity of arrested development in the genesis of a new life, but not one of these volumes contains the remotest suggestion that this responsibility should be equally divided between husband and wife. The untold horrors of this injustice dwarf all others out of sight, and the most hopeless feature of it is the utter unconsciousness with which it is perpetrated.[32]

Using the argument that woman should have custody over herself to justify her work through the W.C.T.U., Frances Willard set out to rescue "white slaves" and also to research more deeply the reasons women became prostitutes. Out of these investigations arose union efforts to establish industrial training schools for women, and attempts to provide congenial, safe living arrangements for young working women in the cities.

During the first quarter-century of its existence, the W.C.T.U.'s "important work of reconstructing the ideal of womanhood" went on continually. The reports of departmental superintendents in the minutes of annual meetings and in *The Union Signal* reflect the many different paths union women chose in their "reconstruction" work under the Do Everything Policy. They also reveal that alternative images of the "ideal woman" coexisted in the organization. Women who still felt most comfortable with the earlier image of true womanhood were represented, as well as those who championed the image of the independent, self-defined woman. Probably most W.C.T.U. members held views somewhere between those two poles.

At times, the management of the organization appeared to be somewhat like a large and complicated juggling act, as Frances Willard and the other leaders tossed and twirled a variety of roles and activities for women. If the roles were unfamiliar or controversial, they were sometimes put to one side. At other times, no juggling was even attempted. But the roles inevitably would be tossed up again and eventually some union women would hold onto them throughout their lives. These are the women who should be rediscovered and reclaimed—women who were inspired by the new W.C.T.U. vision of womanhood and who continued to work out their inspiration in concrete forms, well into the twentieth century. The names and reports of these second- and third-generation members are waiting on the shelves of the W.C.T.U. archives at Evanston.

In the 1890s, in the second decade of her presidency, Frances Willard began to sketch out a "new and magnificent profession for women." She strongly urged independent young women of the future to enter philanthropic work, since it was appropriate for Christians and epitomized the ideals of the W.C.T.U. Philanthropy would seem to be traditional "woman's work," but there were novel elements in Willard's definition. Josephine Shaw Lowell of the Charity Organization Society of the City of New York, and others, were developing the concept of "scientific social work." They attempted to expose the real causes of poverty and were calling for systemic changes to fight the conditions and the collusion of interests that kept people poor. Willard predicted that the new woman would enter this new philanthropic profession. "After women have conquered a firm foothold in the trades and professions, [they] will gradually withdraw from mechanized work and devote themselves to the noblest vocations that life affords —namely motherhood, reform work, and philanthropy."[33]

What was novel about this? Was this not exactly what women had been doing? The new notion was that women should choose their work. Formerly, they always had envisioned and pursued these tasks thought of as the "proper roles" for women—those that fit smoothly into the earlier nineteenth-century image of true womanhood. In the future, if women were to dedicate themselves to reform work, or to philanthropy, or to motherhood, they would elect that activity out of all the possibilities opening before them. They would choose their work, knowing that they could enter any profession, confront any task. For the new W.C.T.U. woman, the motto "For God and Home and Native Land" would imply a call answered by informed, independent women, eager to serve their God and their country with every gift they possessed.

18

KOREAN WOMEN IN HAWAII, 1903–1945

Alice Chai

Early Korean immigration to Hawaii (1903–1924) has produced a body of literature. Not surprisingly, however, both historical and personal accounts until quite recently have concentrated largely on the experiences of immigrant men; they have provided little information about the immigrant women who joined them. Focusing on the historical experiences of Korean immigrant women, this essay will show that beyond absorbing and dealing with the changes wrought by immigration, Korean women contributed actively and creatively to the group's new life in Hawaii. It also will assess the role played by the church—particularly the Methodist Church—in Korean immigrant women's achievements. Not only did the first generation of these women overcome economic hardships and marital difficulties; not only did they succeed in changing the conditions of their lives and thereby increase the life-chances of their children, but from Hawaii they also lent powerful political and financial support to the Korean independence movement—the struggle of the Korean people within and outside Korea to liberate their homeland from Japanese domination.

This article will analyze the way the church, carried to Korea principally by missionaries from several antecedent bodies of United Methodism, provided immigrant women with an organizational basis and the experience of participation in churchwomen's groups which they could adapt to the political activities necessary for the move toward Korean independence.[1] In setting out this analysis, the essay will sketch the historical background of early Korean immigration to Hawaii and explore the factors that contributed to the women's active engagement in the Korean independence movement, which today would be called a national liberation movement.

Sources for this analysis are furnished by the existing literature on the experiences of Korean immigrants and by personal interviews with "first-generation" Korean women who arrived in the islands between 1903 and 1924. Many have been leaders and active members of the Korean Methodist churches and of Korean women's organizations in Hawaii for more than half a century.

The First Wave of Korean Immigration to Hawaii, 1903–1905

During the first major period of immigration, 7,226 Koreans came to Hawaii as laborers in the sugar plantations. Most were young single men, but some were married men with their wives and families—637 women and 541 children.[2]

A number of factors motivated those first Koreans, but the most important was economic. In Hwanghae and in several other northern provinces, from 1898 to 1901 a severe drought had ruined crops, causing widespread famine. As a result, starving farmers moved even farther north, thus overcrowding the cities in those areas. People in those port cities heard stories about Hawaii; it was a place where they could easily become wealthy and where their children could acquire free education. Consequently, the majority of the first group of Korean laborers came from the northern provinces.[3]

Many Koreans also were troubled by their country's political position: The small peninsula was surrounded and in danger of being invaded by any of three great contending powers—Russia, Japan, or China.[4] China's defeat in the Sino-Japanese War of 1904–1905 only made the situation more unstable. Korea became a "protectorate" of Japan, and political pressures from the Japanese government eventually led to the outright annexation of Korea by Japan in 1910. Many foreign-educated and Christian Koreans went to the United States to escape Japanese oppression and to plan resistance activites from abroad.

Religious factors, too, affected the immigration of Koreans. The early immigration movement coincided with the beginning of Christian evangelism in Korea and was pioneered by American Methodist missionaries who encouraged their converts to emigrate to America. In fact, recruiters from the Hawaiian Sugar Planters' Association worked in conjunction with a well-known Methodist Episcopal missionary, George Heber Jones, at Chemulp'o (changed later to In'ch'on).[5] Thus it is not surprising that the immigrant community in Hawaii was deeply tied to Korean Methodism in particular.

Since Korean converts were often poor, the missionaries encouraged the idea of emigration partly for the emigrants' benefit and partly in the belief that their missionary work would prove to be more successful away from the home country, where Christianity still met with some opposition. The missionaries saw in emigration an opportunity for Koreans to improve their economic condition and also to find religious freedom.

Some of the Korean Christians came with their families to settle in Hawaii. Most of the women in this group were wives and daughters of the laborers, but a few came to escape bad marriages. They were from families of good standing and had had comfortable lives but did not agree with their husbands' practice of keeping *kisaeng* concubines (similar to the geisha of Japan).

"My father laughed when my mother announced that she was going to Hawaii with my seventeen-year-old brother as principal laborer," reported one second-generation Korean American, for example. " 'How are you going to live? You never did a day's work in your life,' [my father said]. But she was determined to leave him and his concubines, even if it meant working in the cane fields."[6]

There were also "Bible women." Korean Bible women were quasi-ministers who combined the roles of evangelist, teacher, public health educator, and social worker.[7] As the recollections of their descendants clearly confirm, they were

330

often alienated from their non-Christian families. A third-generation respondent reported:

My Grandmother was 28 years old when she left Korea with her eight-year-old daughter in 1903. Her own family had thrown her out of the house because of her Christian beliefs. She was estranged from her husband. With no future in Korea, she decided to go to Hawaii as a "Bible woman." She helped so many of the immigrant women, counseling them and encouraging them. She was such a strong person. In the church you could see her standing with the men. They respected her convictions. My family often said, "Grandmother should have been a man!" She really believed that America was a place where people had a chance.[8]

Korean Christians generally were more literate than the non-Christians. Nearly all knew how to read and write the Korean language, since they had to be able to read the Bible in order to join the church and be baptized.[9]

Ministers or Bible women were on board almost every ship that brought immigrants to Hawaii. They were a tremendous help to the immigrants who, if they were not Christians when they left Korea, often became Christians on the ships or soon after their arrival. The Hawaii Methodist Mission encouraged the immigrants to organize and establish their own churches in Korean plantation camps on various islands. The church thus became a focal point of every Korean community.[10]

Korean women who came to Hawaii in the first wave from 1903 to 1905 were attempting to free themselves from poverty, Confucian social and cultural constraints, and Japanese political and religious oppression. They looked to Hawaii as a land of economic opportunity, political independence, religious freedom, and personal autonomy.

The Second Wave of Immigration: The Picture Brides, 1910–1924

Since few women had emigrated during the first wave of recruitment, the Korean bachelor laborers on the plantations presented a problem to the Korean community and to the plantation managers. These single men engaged in such undesirable activities as gambling, drinking, and opium-smoking. The managers agreed that the laborers would settle down and work more steadily if they were married.[11] This concern was brought to the attention of a high-ranking Korean official who observed the loneliness of the bachelor workers as he was passing through Honolulu. At his suggestion, the Korean government approved the emigration of young women who would agree to marry after exchanging pictures with potential husbands.

Almost one thousand courageous Korean women came as "picture brides" to Hawaii between the Japanese annexation of Korea in 1910 and the time of the United States Oriental Exclusion Act in 1924.[12] Some of these young women, between the ages of eighteen and twenty-four, came from the farming communities of the more densely populated and poorer southern provinces of Kyŏngsang in order to reduce somewhat the poverty of their families. Other brides came to escape the restrictive Confucian life-style, as well as Japanese political domination and the subsequent suppression of Christianity by the Japanese. Seeking relief from poverty because of flood and famine, desiring education for themselves and their children, and wanting personal freedom from male domination, these women of the second wave anticipated a "dreamland" in Hawaii.

For example, a seventy-five-year-old former picture bride described the circumstances of her decision to leave Korea.

I was born in a small village in the mountains, only about 10 houses. My parents were very poor. One year, a heavy rain came, a flood; the crops all washed down. . . . That time girls in my village can't walk around. . . . Can't go any place, only to Sunday school. When I was eight years old, I became a Christian. My family was not Christian, my parents all Buddhists. I met one Sunday school teacher, so I became a Christian. . . . So, every Sunday afternoon I came to Sunday school. Girls always only were home their whole life before they marry . . . cooking, sewing, working. That time, a girl very seldom went out to a foreign country. Under the Japanese, no freedom. People can't talk. . . . My auntie told me that my cousin was living where picture brides come, Hawaii. Always I heard Hawaii stories, that time. I thinking when I grow up I like going Hawaii. Hawaii's a free place, everybody living well. . . . If you like talk, you can talk; you like work, you can work. I wanted to come; so, I sent my picture.[13]

The picture brides' anticipations were shattered soon after their arrival, however.[14] Upon disembarking, many were bewildered because their grooms did not look like their photographs. The men had lured the maidens with glowing accounts of the plentiful and pleasant life in Hawaii and frequently had sent pictures of themselves taken ten to twenty years before. It was a shocking and frightening experience for the young bride of seventeen or eighteen to meet her older prospective husband for the first time. Many of the picture brides cried bitterly; some refused to marry the old men who had fooled them. A few who persistently refused to marry men twenty to thirty years their senior were sent back home or took refuge with church agencies. Undoubtedly, a number of picture brides were physically abused by the grooms who had paid the passage. Afraid of being shipped back to Korea as if they had been rejected, most were forced to go through with their unhappy wedding ceremonies. Recalled one woman years later:

I saw him for the first time at the immigration Station. . . . He was really . . . old-looking. So my heart stuck. My cousin in Honolulu arranged the marriage, and I was very angry at her. I'm so disappointed, I cry for eight days. . . . I only came out from the room in the middle of the night to drink water so I don't die. But I knew that if I don't get married, I have to go back to Korea on the next ship. So on the ninth day I came out and married him. But I don't talk to him for three months.[15]

Economic and Family Responsibilities of Immigrant Women

Koreans who were laborers on sugar plantations did not live in one place, but were scattered in camps. Within a camp lived thirty or forty single men and three or four married men and their families. Most of the wives ran laundry services and kitchens called *koksang* for the single men. More than six thousand single Korean male laborers obtained most of their meals from these kitchens.

Often a husband's wages alone did not cover all expenses,

so early immigrant women might work ten hours a day in the fields alongside the men and then far into the night, caring for their families and households, while also looking after the basic needs of a dozen or more bachelors.

Since the bridegrooms knew that their young brides came to Hawaii seeking a life of ease and comfort, many were reluctant to impose on them the hard life of the plantation and instead remained in Honolulu.[16] However, immigrant wives in town also worked to supplement their husbands' meager wages. Some opened small dressmaking shops, ran laundry services, or managed boarding houses. Without electricity or washing machines, laundry was done by hand, and hot coals were used to heat the irons.[17]

The most serious difficulty faced by these picture brides was the need to assume economic responsibility for themselves and their children in the event of a spouse's death. Because the husbands usually were much older, many wives were widowed early and were compelled to become business women. They did not have formal education or experience and could not speak or read much English, but with financial help and moral support from their friends, they somehow managed their businesses successfully. They employed the *kye,* a mutual financing association similar to a cooperative, which functioned as their private banking system. A *kye* group was made up of ten to twenty-four women from the same home village, province, or church, who met monthly for fellowship and recreation as well as for economic purposes. The main motive for participating in the *kye* was to have access, when needed, to a large sum of money to buy real estate, invest in business, pay children's tuition, or make other payments too large for regular income. *Kye* money was and, to some extent, still is an important financial resource for Korean-American women and their families.[18] The story of a former picture bride illustrates the decisive role of female friendship and the *kye* in economic self-improvement.

One day a friend told me about a rooming house for sale on Hotel Street. The owner wanted $1,400. That time my husband couldn't find steady work because of the Depression. . . . I worked in a Navy laundry during the day and at night I ironed shirts for a cleaning shop until midnight . . . fifty cents for ten shirts. After five years I could save only $400. How could I get the other $1,000 I needed? My lady friend felt so sorry for me, she loaned me the money. Then I paid her back with cash I got from the *kye*. Now my family had property. We could make money and live better.[19]

Women also were mainly responsible for the maintenance of the second generation's identity as Koreans and for preserving the cohesiveness of the family and community in the face of great adversities. Specifically, the mothers assumed responsibility for teaching the Korean language and culture to the younger generation. Thus picture brides, with their hard work, Christian faith and patriotism became the backbone of the Korean community in Hawaii.[20]

In addition to shouldering major family responsibilities and engaging in gainful employment, first-generation immigrant women worked with enthusiasm and a sense of calling to help finance the Korean independence movement through their churches and women's groups. They were able to endure even longer hours than men and do both outside labor and household chores for lower wages because they were driven by a strong determination to achieve personal freedom. They had an adventurous spirit and the courage to make a better life for themselves, and especially for their children. Through their unceasing Christian faith and hard work, the majority were eventually successful, to varying degrees, in achieving three major goals: economic betterment; the education of the next generation; and the liberation of Korea.[21]

The Role of Christian Women in the Independence Movement in Korea

Some brief background on the historical situation of Christian women in Korea is needed to set the context of their contributions to the Korean independence movement. Traditionally, unless a woman was of a noble and rich family or was a *kisaeng* (a geisha), she rarely received the chance to learn even the fundamentals of reading and writing. Girls of the Yangban (aristocratic) class enjoyed a tutorial education, receiving lessons in Confucian learning for women. They were taught the Korean alphabet, Chinese characters, Confucian morals, and Chinese classics. In all, women's education in traditional Korea was aimed at infusing into their minds the Confucian philosophy of male superiority and its practical aspects; they were trained to be good wives and wise mothers who must be unconditionally obedient to and dependent upon the authority of their husbands and oldest sons.[22]

American women missionaries exercised significant influence on reform in Korean women's education. In 1886, Mary Fitch Scranton, a Methodist, opened the first Western-style girls' school, the Ewha Hakdang, a name given by the Empress Min. The school was founded to spread the gospel and to convert Korean women; the missionaries taught girls to read and write as a means of carrying out their mission work.[23] Christian teaching also introduced the concepts of political, religious, and personal freedom for women. As a consequence, many educated Christian women remained unmarried and, after the Japanese annexation of Korea in 1910, dedicated their lives to help free Korea. Most important, however, unmarried American women missionaries demonstrated to Korean women that there were options other than the role of wife and mother. Thus missionaries played an important part in shaping the destinies of many young women who chose to be evangelists, dedicated teachers, health educators, social workers, and so on, and who worked with the missionaries to enlighten other women about the sense of personal freedom and self-expression they themselves had achieved through Christian education.[24]

In addition to the Bible women, there were other Christian women who were experienced leaders in organized activities. These Bible women and women activists were aware of current issues facing the nation and were concerned with inspiring Korean national consciousness, rather than with increasing the number of churchwomen. They went into the courtyards to speak with women who were not allowed outside their households; but they sometimes spoke less of religion than of resistance to the Japanese.[25] Others went underground or fled to China or America to continue their efforts for an independent Korea. These Christian women became the focal group for the Korean independence movement.

On March 1, 1919, a large number of female students and women in all Korean cities and provinces participated in the nationwide uprising against Japanese domination. Women educated in mission schools acted as a main force in this series of events and in all anti-Japanese activities thereafter, demonstrating for the first time in Korea that Christianity, by raising their consciousness through education, empowered women to engage in large-scale political leadership. Among 2,656 church members arrested after the uprising, 531 (one-fifth) were women.[26] Thus the 1919 revolt marked the beginning of Korean Christian women's public participation in the independence movement. The women of the various churches collected funds for the families of those imprisoned and later, for the exiled government in Shanghai. Inspired by patriotic zeal to liberate their country from foreign rule, the organization of Christian pioneer women was the first group to promote education for women and to provide charity and social services for the patriots in the independence movement.[27]

After the revolt, Korean independence activities became more systematic. Women's organizations regularly took care of political prisoners and their families. Later, these organizations combined and branched out over the whole nation. All these groups fully supported the Korean Provisional Government in Shanghai by contributing considerable amounts. Through the activities of the societies begun by Christian women, greater numbers of women of all persuasions began to participate in political life. Church-originated group activities provided Korean women with know-how and experience, and the Korean church provided an organizational basis that could be easily adapted to political activities necessary for the independence movement.[28]

The Role of Christianity
in the Korean Independence Movement in Hawaii

After the independence movement took hold in Korea, exiled Korean Christian intellectuals and their followers spread its political activities to Hawaii and to the mainland of the United States. The leaders of this movement were men and women who had attended mission schools in Korea and received higher education in the United States. The goal of liberating their nation from Japanese control provided a strong cohesive force, in particular among the Koreans in the Hawaiian Islands, and the Korean churches became deeply involved in the independence movement.[29]

Having left behind intimate social groups such as the extended family, the immigrants to Hawaii found themselves in a more formalized and often alien milieu. Korean churches provided their members with badly needed structural continuity and psychological security by enabling them to associate with fellow Koreans and to participate in worship services in the Korean language.[30]

Two newly created social organizations—*tonghoe,* a self-governing body, and the sworn brotherhood—were introduced to Hawaii by Korean plantation laborers and took the place of clan association. But women were excluded from these organizations. For them, the Korean churches played an indispensable role in providing an organizational basis—first, for the maintenance and perpetuation of Korean culture and second, for the support of the Korean national independence movement. In every plantation camp, a Korean-language school was established within the church to teach children Korean culture, history, and language.[31] In churches in Honolulu, boarding schools were established for boys and girls from plantation camps. Korean social life revolved around the church, and by providing a fellowship with communal bonds, it became a convenient vehicle for the survival of ethnic identity. Of fewer than 8,000 Koreans in Hawaii between 1903 and 1918, there were about 2,800 Christians in 39 churches throughout the islands. Thus the Christian church, functioning as a religious, social, cultural, and political center, formed the core of the organizational structure of Korean communities.[32]

After a significant number had become converts, the church exerted a certain degree of group pressure on non-Christians to unite for Korean independence activities. Thus parents who were not Christians themselves would send their children to church for Sunday school classes and for language and cultural education.[33]

As a consequence, the church was successful in mobilizing its members for fund-raising campaigns to restore Korean independence. The independence movement among expatriates was supported financially by a great number of small contributions, made largely by Korean residents in the Hawaiian Islands, most of whom were members of local churches.[34] Moreover, Korean churchwomen, by their sale of food and crafts and through their energetic and persistent house-to-house calls, contributed significantly. By providing the organizational basis for the independence movement, the church became the unifying force behind the entire Korean community in Hawaii, both Christian and non-Christian.

Korean Christian Women's Contributions to the Movement

By participating in church and women's group activities, Korean women gained organizational knowledge and experience which benefited both the Korean community and the independence movement and also contributed to the development of female leadership and self-esteem.

Korean independence-movement activities accelerated with active participation by the Korean immigrants during World War II. Those who were better educated felt the need to organize themselves for action; their aim was to mobilize all Koreans abroad for the political cause. Those immigrants who did not belong to patriotic organizations were dubbed *yokchŏk* (traitors).[35]

Both before and after Japan's annexation of Korea, the women in Hawaii had been persistently optimistic about the outcome of resistance against the Japanese. The independence movement—the demand for national self-determination—played an epochal role in enhancing the position of women through their active participation in social and relief activities. With the fusing of religious and nationalistic ideals, the liberation of their homeland became the major priority of first-generation Koreans in Hawaii. The money earned by their *p'ittam* (blood and sweat) was used to finance the independence movement.[36]

> After I come to Hawaii, some friends came to talk with me if I am interested going to the church. Somebody told me the Korean Christian Church was for the Korean independence. So, I went, it looked very good, so I was interested. There were lots of people, an old men's home, and the church working for Korean independence. I am so happy, my life relaxed and I am talking that time with my husband. So, even if my old man was too old, I enjoy the church. Every Sunday I go church. I work for the Society. . . . We all worked so hard for the Korean independence. We every night, house to house going, collecting money send to Washington, D.C. office. . . . We make rice cake *(ttŏk)*, sell, bean cake *(muk)*, sell, candy *(yŏt)*, making sell, all kinds of way making money for independence.
>
> Sometimes when I look back on those days when we were trying to help Korea, I think maybe we were a little crazy. We gave money to help the independence when we were poor. We loved Korea so much. We wanted her to be free, like America. We worked hard to educate our children, hoping that someday they would help to rebuild Korea.[37]

Korean Christian women in Hawaii, working alongside Korean men, contributed to the awakening of Korean national consciousness and helped sustain its independence movement through direct participation as well as through financial and moral support to the cause.[38]

Women's Organizations
Engaged in the Independence Movement

In Hawaii, two women's organizations contributed significantly to the Korean independence movement. The first was the Korean Women's Relief Society *(Taehanpuin*

Kujehoe). Some women leaders in Hawaii had felt that there should be a more encompassing women's society to carry out the movement effectively, but no specific action resulted until the 1919 demonstrations in Korea. Upon hearing the news, Korean residents in Hawaii zealously joined in activities to support Korean independence. Dressed in the traditional white *chogori* (blouse) and *ch'ima* (skirt), the Korean women of Hawaii marched in parades and sang patriotic songs.

Within weeks, the first Korean women's assembly was held in Honolulu. Forty-one women representatives from all the Hawaiian Islands met to organize Korean women's activism. After much controversy, the decision was made to form a separate relief society, rather than a branch of the International Red Cross. The second assembly was also held in Honolulu, with members formally resolving to support the Korean independence movement by collecting money and by engaging in relief work under the leadership of the Korean National Association *(Taehanin Kungmin-hoe).* Later the central board of the society was incorporated in the Territory of Hawaii on January 8, 1929, with its directors elected by ballot every two years at a delegates' convention. Local chapters of the Korean Women's Relief Society of Hawaii were formed on each of the four major islands.[39]

The newly elected officers immediately set about raising funds to support the Korean Independence Army and the Korean Provisional Government in China, and especially the families of the thirty-three signers of the Declaration of Korean Independence. They also sent money to the families of some who had been killed and wounded in the 1919 revolt and to the Korean Commission in Washington, hoping that the money could be forwarded to the Korean Provisional Government. Other funds went to the Korean Military Government and to the general headquarters of the Independence Army in Manchuria and in Chungking, China.

Many young Korean girls raised funds by working in sugarcane and pineapple fields, doing needlework, and making and selling Korean delicacies. They called from door to door, carrying their babies on their backs and riding buses all day when necessary. They also reprinted and sold the Declaration of Independence Manifesto that had been read at the March 1 uprising. The funds raised by the society for various patriotic causes amounted to $200,000.

The second significant women's organization working for Korean independence was the Yŏngnam Women's Society (Yŏngnam Puinhoe). In September 1928, immigrant women from Kyongsang provinces formed a new society under the Kyŏngsang-do Hoe (Association of Kyŏngsang Province Women), for the purpose of promoting friendship. This organization continues under its present name, the Korean Yongnam Women's Society. This society's goals were to encourage savings, to promote Korean manufactured goods, to engage in business enterprises, to have fellowship, and to secure mutual assistance and support. Even though not too successful in business enterprises, the members were very active in promoting the progress of community organizations in support of the Korean independence movement.[40]

One picture bride who dedicated her life to the movement reflected upon her life and her role in organizational work:

Korean women in Hawaii wanted to do something for the patriots in Korea who were sacrificing their lives. We thought it was a matter of life and death for all Korean women to unite our forces. . . . The Honolulu Korean women held their general meeting first; in the Island of Maui we had seventy-two women elect officers at our general meeting. Then we met every day to decide on how to organize and what kind of work we should do. We decided to politically awaken other Korean women and mobilize them to collect funds and relief goods. . . . We were trained by male leaders in making speeches to women's groups. . . . In 1922 I was elected as the third president of our groups. I was only twenty years old. I went around to houses to collect money even when I was pregnant, with one child on my back and another holding onto my hand.

When I look back now, the reason that I could come up with such independent ideas and could express my honest opinions even to strange men was that I had learned to express my thoughts in the church groups by having Bible study meetings and by visiting strangers' houses . . . in the villages with ministers and Bible women to discuss the Bible. Because of my Christian faith I could endure the pain and suffering in my life.[41]

Conclusion

Korean women were able to become politically active for national independence through the Korean churches for a series of interconnected reasons.

The church was the organizational basis for political activities. When the American missionaries introduced Christianity in Korea, Korean women of all classes converted to the faith in order to be free from traditional physical, social, and cultural constraints in a Confucian society. At the turn of the century in Korea, young women attended church as a way to escape confinement in the home. Thanks to their desires for personal freedom and to the dedication of American missionaries in educating women, many Korean women were Christians before they came to Hawaii. In Hawaii, moreover, while men had other associations, for Korean women the church was the only association which provided them with a meeting place and gave them an opportunity to organize activities through which they could develop leadership skills.

Education was the means through which personal freedom could be gained. In the process of their conversion to Christianity, many Korean women had an opportunity to learn the written language for the first time. Most educated Korean women began their careers in connection with a church school. The literacy and verbal skills thus acquired enabled them to take up leadership positions in political activities, and they were strongly motivated to discover options other than the role of a wife/mother. Having learned its value, these women sacrificed personal desires to provide their sons and daughters with equal access to education.

The third factor in the development of women's political involvement was the economic self-sufficiency gained through participation in the work force. Korean Christian women in Hawaii were productive workers who contributed significantly toward family support. As picture brides married men much their senior, many women soon became financially responsible for the welfare of their families, and though they were inexperienced in business skills and lacked English language proficiency, they were able to function by relying heavily on other Korean women as sources of support and assistance.

Finally, the experience of Korean Christian women in church activities provided them with the capability of organizing, implementing ideas, and working together for a common cause. Through their women's groups they were able to give emotional and financial support to one another and to the independence movement. Bonds between women were stronger than conjugal bonds, since they had more contact with one another than with their husbands, who preferred to socialize separately and often had little in common with their wives.

Korean women demonstrated their ingenuity in creating survival strategies, first in Korea, where they adopted Christianity and Western education in order to free themselves from oppressive Confucian ideology and social structures, and later in Hawaii, where they developed survival strategies involving economic control, solidarity groups, and networks designed to overcome the harsh conditions of their lives and to enable them to become politically active in the Korean independence movement.

SHAPING A NEW SOCIETY

Mary E. Frederickson

The white southern Methodist women who became part of
the industrial reform movement during the late nineteenth
and early twentieth century possessed a vision of southern
progress which contrasted sharply with that held by male
industrialists and entrepreneurs.* As New South manufacturers and business leaders endorsed an industrial program
which promised riches but delivered low wages to workers
who entered mills and factories, women within the
Methodist Episcopal Church, South, began to define the
outlines of an alternative New South: an industrial society
run by men and women in the name of God.[1]

These Methodist industrial reformers sought to establish
God's kingdom on earth—a beloved community in which
individuals lived, worked, and loved in harmony with one
another. They envisioned a system in which all social groups
would meet on equal footing, without regard to race or sex,
share the region's resources, and receive just remuneration
for their toil. They believed in the necessity of legislative
controls and in the judicious use of human resources.[2]

In the midst of enormous economic and social changes
in their region at the turn of the century, women of the
Methodist Episcopal Church, South, tallied the human costs
of rapid industrial development and decided to play a part in
redressing the resulting economic and social imbalances. As
they pursued this end, they sought for others a life-style
patterned after their own spiritually and materially rich
existences. Through seeking a better life for others, these

*This essay focuses on involvement of white southern Methodist women,
since black women were excluded from the organizations discussed here.
The history of black southern Methodist women needs concentrated study.

women significantly expanded the dimensions of their own lives and found sustaining work in a sphere stretching far beyond the confines of their homes. Involved in meaningful work, these women thrived in a shared sisterhood which confirmed them personally and professionally. In the 1920s and 1930s, Methodist women reformers joined a broadly based spectrum of both religious and secular women's groups concerned with industrial reform throughout the nation. Together these women's organizations brought social and economic conditions to the attention of numerous individuals, government agencies, and reform groups.

To examine the role of Methodist women as critics and reformers of industrial development in the southern United States, one useful point of departure is to compare the working lives and sense of ministry of two individuals—Atticus Greene Haygood (1839–1896) and Laura Askew Haygood (1845–1900)—the children of an influential Methodist couple in Georgia. While Atticus Haygood became a proponent of rapid industrialization, his younger sister Laura questioned its human consequences and ministered to the region's poor and needy, the victims of the industrial progress her brother promoted. Furthermore, as Atticus and his contemporaries enhanced their careers by carrying out the industrial program of the New South, his sister became part of a strong countercurrent within southern society. Through women's work for home missions in the Methodist Episcopal Church, South, she and her followers focused attention on the exploitation and dehumanizing aspects of the economic system.[3]

On Thanksgiving Day in 1880, Atticus Haygood, then president of Emory College, delivered to the all-male student body a sermon entitled "The New South: Gratitude, Amendment, Hope."[4] In this talk he delineated an optimistic picture of the region's future. An ardent admirer of the New South enthusiast Henry Grady, Haygood underscored both the need for an expanded program of public education for the South's illiterates and the need for a program to draw manufacturers into the states of the Old Confederacy by promoting the region's abundant natural resources and cheap labor.[5]

This sermon launched Atticus, age forty-one, on a new career as one of the best known and most widely respected social philosophers of the New South. In 1881 he published *Our Brother in Black, His Freedom and His Future,* which became the basis for the New South's program of racial progress.[6] That same year, he became a bishop in the Methodist Episcopal Church, South. But Atticus Haygood had a sister.[7]

Unlike her brother, whose work was organized for him within the well-established public framework of a clerical career, it was necessary for Laura Haygood to create meaningful and challenging work for herself. Her activities as a pioneer in the Methodist home mission movement, performed under the dignifying mantle of the church, eventually became a career, and publicly admissable as such.[8]

In the beginning, to expand her horizons and influence in the church within the acceptable boundaries of the usual female role, Laura Haygood organized an interdenominational normal-school class for Sunday school teachers. She and her students also established two large Sunday schools which became self-sustaining congregations. In 1882, she looked with new eyes at the poor of Atlanta and helped form the Trinity Home Mission Society, a group of sixty churchwomen whose hearts were filled with "a burning zeal to do something."[9] Between 1882 and 1884, Laura devoted all the time and energy she could spare from paid teaching to develop a viable home mission in Atlanta. In 1883 she also helped lead a much broader movement to organize the women of the Methodist Episcopal Church, South, for home mission work.

Although Laura Haygood's family and friends felt that her principalship at Atlanta Girls' High School and church responsibilities provided her an "ample sphere for doing her best work," she chafed under the constraints placed on her as a churchwoman.[10] Less than a year after her mother's death in 1883, and two years after her brother's election to bishop (for him the culmination of a successful career), Laura Haygood offered herself as a missionary to China. There, thousands of miles from Georgia, she could fulfill ministerial duties, embracing the occupation denied her at home.

Despite her departure for the foreign mission field, Laura expressed her understanding of the important relationship between domestic missions and women's social responsibility most perceptively in her farewell address to the Methodist women of the South: "I verily believe that the poor can do better without you than you can do without the blessings which God gives to those who minister."[11] The roles played by southern women like Laura Haygood provide an example of the complex interaction between religion and reform and offer an opportunity to study the connection between the social gospel and female emancipation within a specific historical context.[12]

As a small band of women throughout the South turned their attention to home mission work in the 1880s, their activities constituted a new form of religious practice which emphasized a pragmatic social gospel focused on the salvation of others ("thy neighbor") more than personal piety and devotion. The growing public commitment of southern women—first to foreign missionary work, and then to local philanthropy—expanded their role in the church.[13] As they undertook missionary work in the South, organized Methodist women sought to imprint their social vision upon a changing society. This process had long-range implications both for the churchwomen who participated in social reform and for the industrializing South.

This shift in emphasis from foreign to home mission work met with opposition from many southern Methodist ministers, laymen, and churchwomen devoted to foreign missions. In part, it was felt that the appropriation of funds for local enterprises endangered the supply of money for foreign missions.[14] Also, however, foreign work was less threatening than local philanthropy. If southern Christians' attention was directed toward the alleviation of poverty and disease in China or India, it was easier for them to ignore the needs of mill workers in Macon or the unemployed in Atlanta.

Gradually, however, the focus changed as some white

southern Methodist women said, "Quietly, watchfully let us do what lies nearest to us."[15] They formed associations to visit the sick and care for neglected children. They sought out people different from themselves, and with a concerned, if parochial and guarded outlook, they began to minister to those they considered the "heathen" of the South: blacks, mountaineers, rural people, and foreign immigrants who came to the region in pursuit of work around the turn of the century.

Increasingly, their attention was drawn to "the unsaved in our own land" and it was declared "pitiable cowardice" not to face "our southern problems."[16] By 1894, Mrs. Nathan Scarritt, general secretary of the Woman's Parsonage and Home Mission Society, who represented more than eight thousand women, had publicly declared a new orientation toward both home and foreign missions when she wrote, "We believe that the strength and efficiency of home missions must ever be the ground of hope for foreign missions, that to reverse this order would be to ravel out with one hand that which is woven with the other."[17]

While it was obvious to these socially secure women that the South's poor required assistance, they also recognized that they themselves needed meaningful work. They expressed this need across the decades in varying language. As early as 1861, during the Civil War, an Alabama woman wrote to Bishop James O. Andrew regarding the role of women in the church's mission work, both domestic and foreign. She pleaded, "Bishop, give us work! We can do it, not at once, perhaps, but let us begin." She closed her long letter with this emphasis: "Forgive me, pray for me, and put my sisters and myself to work."[18]

When requested by the Board of Church Extension in the mid-1880s to prepare plans for a woman's department, Lucinda Helm of Kentucky noted autobiographically, "I knew many of my sisters must feel as I did. An impetus, a light, a propelling power beyond me had lighted a fire within my soul, and was moving with an irresistible force to throw my life into the work . . . of establishing the kingdom of my Lord."[19]

In the early twentieth century, Methodist women concerned about home missions continued to look to the

349

church for meaningful work as they gathered together and sang the hymn *Awake My Soul, Stretch Every Nerve.*[20] In 1922, Bertha Newell, superintendent of the newly established Bureau of Social Service of the Woman's Missionary Council, wrote enthusiastically, "leisure is unknown to the office and the avocation has become an absorbing job."[21] By 1930, a report of the council described the process by which opportunities for service brought women together "in a sisterhood, which in turn became an opportunity for self-development."[22]

Beyond opportunities for service and self-development, southern women turned to home mission work because of the deep sense of sisterhood that had been created in the Woman's Home Mission Society, which after 1910 became the Woman's Missionary Council. As they worked together, Methodist women participated in, as historian Carroll Smith-Rosenberg has put it, "a female world of love and ritual."[23] These women, realizing that "in organized effort there is strength," formed an association consisting of about one-tenth of the female membership of the Methodist Episcopal Church, South.[24] Through their common work over the years, they created a body of rituals, gained strength from communication with one another, and often found kindred spirits with whom they could share their lives.

Each year in the spring, home mission women met together for a week "to enjoy" as they recorded, "the precious privilege of a rare fellowship."[25] At these meetings they ceremoniously consecrated as deaconesses the young, single women who were trained for work in the home mission movement. In local auxiliary and annual conference meetings of the Methodist woman's society, they presented life memberships to honor those women who had served especially well. As Noreen Dunn Tatum has testified, "The tears of humility and joy" that accompanied each presentation "drew members more closely together in their devotion to one another and to the Cause they represented."[26] Devotion and love between individual members of the Woman's Home Missionary Society, while a crucial factor in the cohesiveness of the organization, often became more personal and self-sustaining as women found in one another a "kinship of soul."

A striking example of this bonding can be found in the relationship between Belle Harris Bennett, first and only president of the Woman's Home Missionary Society, and Mary Helm, first editor of the mission society's publication *Our Homes*. These southern Methodist leaders severed their working relationship in 1909 over the issue of uniting the foreign and home missionary organizations. The depth of Helm's suffering over this separation and the extent of her continued love for Bennett were revealed in a letter she wrote the following year.

My Dear Belle: There has not been a day in the months past that I have not thought of you many, many times—always lovingly and with a deep sense of oneness with you despite surface differences. . . . It was a new experience to oppose you, and the pain could only be borne by the unshaken conviction that I was right. You were the victor, and I yielded up my weapon—and you were no longer my opponent but my own beloved friend, bound to me in the close bonds of *fellowship in Christ*, "a bond stronger than friendship and nearer than kinship . . . ." My dear *Soul* Sister we will forget the difference of opinion and the struggle it involved, leaving it as an incident of the past to be remembered only as it increases our loving respect for the other. "What God hath bound together let not man put asunder" applies to other things than matrimony. The soul union that he formed between us cannot be sundered by man, or time or aught else as long as we are true to ourselves, to each other, and to him [emphasis in the original].[27]

In later years Bertha Newell and Jessie Daniel Ames, two southern Methodist women who collaborated in religious and secular organizations, gradually developed a sustaining and satisfying relationship that provided reassurance for both women, since "their spirits met on common ground."[28] In December 1931, Newell responded with deep sincerity to a message from Ames which had touched her "where I live and feel."

I do believe in you and depend upon your gifts and training, and if you have found in me moral support I am very glad. I have liked you from the first and now I love you and have long counted on your companionship as one of the compensations for giving up home life, in the measure that my work demands. Of friends I have many and love them all in different ways and different measure, but few have I who make me think and . . . [t]hat makes me value those few who do so much the more.[29]

Bertha Newell's husband, a Methodist minister himself, did not wholeheartedly endorse her work.[30] For her, an intellectual and emotional bond such as that with Jessie Daniel Ames provided crucial support. Newell empathized with the women who worked with her in the Bureau of Social Service of the Council, and when writing about them, she revealed much about her own situation: "This [work] usually involves action for many [women] quite outside their usual grooves. Often they face the necessity of running counter to public opinion, to popular prejudice, and, hardest of all, in opposition to members of their own households."[31] Thus as southern Methodist women joined together to eliminate "poverty of mind and body" through the establishment of missions in the South—on home turf—they looked to one another for support, and they developed among their membership "the ideal of a Christian community" in which women could enjoy a special comradeship, share inspirational rituals, and openly express their love.

While women involved in home mission work found special individual relationships within the network of their organization, their corporate ministry nurtured a social feminism which defined their constituency and focused their work. As these women sought to help others, their goal was to bring every southern woman, rich or poor, black or white, native or foreign, into the "bonds of Christian sisterhood." The women who led in organizing home missions in the South looked for opportunities to serve individuals across the entire spectrum of southern society, but claimed southern-born women as their special constituency.

Southern white Methodist women believed in "women's work for women," a concept which they declared "spread throughout the churches of the land like a flame." Home mission advocates theorized, even as had proponents of foreign missions, that "there is a work for Christ which only women can do."[32] Accordingly, they set up homes for unwed mothers, boarding houses for women in industrial jobs, mission homes for foreign immigrants in southern cities, and schools for young black and Appalachian women. Their organization grew rapidly, and by 1908, almost 60,000 Methodist women had joined the ranks; by 1940, the southern network included more than 300,000 women.[33]

The Woman's Home Mission Society of the Methodist Episcopal Church, South, saw its task as "ministering through the physical need of the individual to the soul." Its women argued that "Christ did not dissever physical from spiritual needs."[34] Hence they provided materially for young, poor, unemployed, or destitute women, and in the process, attempted to convert them to Christianity. Envisioning prevention as the primary means of controlling social problems, they established day nurseries, free kindergartens, Sunday schools, sewing schools, boys' clubs, cooking schools, cottage prayer meetings, and a savings plan called the Penny Provident Fund. The day nursery, members argued, was a "blessing wisely bestowed" for it "helped women to help themselves" by freeing them to go to work. The free kindergarten also was regarded as a good investment. Its proponents asserted that it "makes an indelible impression on plastic minds," and of those children participating, "only a very small percent afterward were led into a wicked or criminal life." Methodist home missionary women believed that sexually vulnerable girls between twelve and eighteen years of age were "more sinned against than sinning," and they sought to help these "unfortunate victims of environment" by providing a Christian education and industrial training.[35]

During the first quarter of the twentieth century, this Methodist educational network continued to expand throughout southern cities and in rural and mountain communities. Young female students were encouraged both to become evangelical Christians and to learn the skills of cottage industries. Relatively prosperous white Methodist women who viewed the home as their "special realm" ministered to young and destitute women through "home-like institutions." Their publication *Our Homes* reached out to a wider female audience, both rich and poor, with information about important social issues.[36] Methodist women attached great importance to this weekly: "May we not believe that sometimes a seed is sown?"[37]

But home mission work brought numerous southern Methodist women face to face with the ugly realities of an industrializing society. Out of their experiences and observations, they urged the educational, business, and civic leadership of the South to incorporate "the principles of Christ" into the foundation of the region's new industrialism. "We cannot believe," they explained, "that the differences between capital and labor are never to be harmonized." They sought the cooperation of well-meaning employers, and trusted that "the obligation upon every one to make the world a fit place to live in is bound to bring a changed view to both capital and labor."[38] They sent deaconesses to Wesley Houses in industrial communities and founded cooperative homes for young working women.

After the turn of the century, as southern industrialization accelerated and regional manufacturing interests became more powerful, Methodist women expanded their reform program. Gradually their emphasis shifted from the prevention of social problems to a more active political program designed to achieve social change. As they abandoned their narrowly defined concept of home missions, they embraced a more public role in southern political life.

In 1907, the Woman's Home Mission Society of the Methodist Episcopal Church, South, organized a Committee on Social and Industrial Conditions. "Realizing the power of our influence and our duty also to the helpless and outcast," in that year they unanimously adopted a resolution against the widespread convict-lease system.[39] In 1908, with the formation of a Committee on Sociology and Philanthropy, the society began to endorse bills before southern and federal legislatures on issues that affected southern women and children. They sought legal recourse to improve women workers' low wages, unlimited hours, and unsanitary conditions. They also endorsed legislation for compulsory education and called upon employers to stop using child labor.[40]

After the 1910 merger into the Woman's Missionary

Council, much former home mission work was taken over by the council Committee on Social Service and Local Work. Local work continued: the traditional care of parsonages, poor relief, visiting the sick, Bible classes, prayer meetings, gospel services in jails and other institutions, as well as the promotion of temperance, movie censorship, and antigambling campaigns. But more and more southern Methodist women were "deserting the broad and easy way of visits, trays, and flowers for the narrow and difficult path of investigating 'sore spots.' " For them, social service "pointed the way to new ventur[es]" and included the duty to study and investigate social questions and to arouse public concern for issues of social reform.[41]

As southern Methodist women probed their society more deeply and accepted greater responsibility for its "climate," their role became more public. As they began to take political stands on local and regional issues and to move more aggressively into social reform, they adopted the striking motto, "Grow we must, even if we outgrow all that we love."[42] In challenging the status quo of the solid South, white Methodist women gained sustenance from the national social-gospel movement. When men of the stature of Walter Rauschenbusch spoke of the enlargement of the religious sphere, emphasizing that "the social awakening of the Churches is far from complete" and reiterating the church's role in Christianizing industry, they took heart.[43]

In 1913, having worked through its members to abolish child labor and the convict-lease system, the Woman's Missionary Council endorsed the newly revised social creed adopted by the Federal Council of Churches in 1912. That platform supported protective legislation for women workers, occupational health and safety measures, old-age pensions, workmen's compensation, collective bargaining rights, a minimum wage, and "the most equitable division of the products of industry."[44]

By the beginning of World War I, women of the southern Woman's Missionary Council were encouraged by what they had accomplished since 1886, but were sobered by an ever-widening gulf between Christian ideals and community realities. The head of the newly organized Bureau of

Social Service of the Council wrote in 1915, "Utopia is still a dream. There are but few places in the bounds of our Methodism where special study and special stimulus are not necessary before comfortable people become sensitive to the wrong moral and social conditions about them and are moved to put forces in motion to right those wrong conditions."[45]

During World War I, women's work to sensitize comfortable people to moral inequities in southern society continued unabated. The Woman's Missionary Council endorsed the Keating-Owen Child Labor Bill, sought the establishment of a juvenile court system, and studied the issues of racial reform.[46]

After they won the vote as church laity in 1918, and as citizens of the United States in 1920, southern Methodist women entered a yet more intense phase of reform activity. As they attempted to apply Christian service "through an intelligent use of suffrage," their concern for industrial reform still focused to a significant degree on women and children.[47] Bertha Newell, superintendent of the Bureau of Social Service of the Woman's Missionary Council, had studied at the University of Chicago and come under the influence of Jane Addams. When Newell was appointed to the superintendency in 1921, she argued that the role of the southern Methodist Woman's Missionary Council was to educate "our own people" to the needs of women and children. She saw the bureau as a clearinghouse through which facts and figures regarding southern industrialization could be channeled to women throughout the region, and her leadership strengthened the political and research orientation of "woman's work for women." Newell's message in 1926 was typical:

Eight and one-half million women, mothers and future mothers of the coming generation, are at work in stores, laundries, restaurants, canneries and in a great variety of manufacturing industries, many in our Southern States. We need to know the facts concerning the condition of their toil, and when conditions are known to be harmful, where hours are overlong, pay insufficient, or surroundings unsanitary we must spread the knowledge before we can ask for better State laws.[48]

In the decade of the 1920s, as the South's industrial capacity increased rapidly and new waves of women and children sought employment in mills and factories, Newell and the bureau focused on the human costs of industrialization and the responsibilities of regional development. She implored southern Methodist women in 1927,

As women citizens, we have scarcely grasped the import of forces that are changing our agricultural South . . . into an industrial South. . . . Let us not be so proud of our superiority in water power and spindles, in furnaces and furniture, so drugged by the new wealth these forces bring that we sleep when we should be asking ourselves whether the new industrial development is bringing costs and losses as well as work and wages.[49]

In the later nineteenth century and at the beginning of the twentieth, leaders of the southern Methodist home mission movement viewed the national reform movement of the Progressives somewhat ambivalently. They warned church-women not to dilute the power of Christian reform by serving "as volunteers in the forces of others" and feared losing "the well-equipped women of the church to the secular organizations."[50] At the same time, southern Methodist women maintained ties to the national movements with which they shared many common concerns. Jane Addams addressed the annual meeting of the Woman's Home Missionary Society in 1901; Josiah Strong did so in 1908; Harry Ward, in 1917.[51]

The growing hostility of the male church authorities to the independence of southern Methodist women's missionary work, however, pushed the women into broad-based alliances with other groups of women. Following the move in 1908 to merge the woman's home and foreign missionary groups without the women's approval, the Woman's Home Missionary Society joined forces with a secular women's organization, the National Consumers League, as they endorsed their policy on women wage-earners.[52] In 1922, after another attempt by the larger church to usurp the autonomy of the woman's organization (now merged), the Woman's Missionary Council, and especially its Bureau of Social Services, undertook a concerted effort to cooperate with outside groups.[53] Affiliations with other women's reform associations such as the League of Women Voters, the Women's Trade Union League, and the Young Women's Christian Association strengthened the semiautonomous position of southern Methodist women within the church.[54]

Self-interest was not the only motivation for closer relations, however. After 1920, women industrial reformers in the Methodist Episcopal Church, South, consistently looked at secular organizations, especially women's groups, as allies in the fight for industrial justice. The social-service chairman of the Woman's Missionary Council urged in 1920 that "more and more must we come to avail ourselves of the assistance of every ally."[55] She requested that superintendents of the woman's society within each annual conference join the National Child Labor Committee, the Southern Sociological Congress, and the American Association for Labor Legislation. Five years later, Bertha Newell argued, "Truly this is a time for teamwork, for losing our individual preferences and prejudices, and pooling our talents and experience." She warned Methodist women, "We shall be unworthy [of] our good name if we do not make progress in translating what we believe to be a vital Christian experience into social terms."[56]

It was during Newell's tenure as head of the Bureau of Social Services that southern Methodist women became widely recognized as leaders in southern industrial reform. Outside groups, including the Southern Council on Women and Children in Industry, the League of Women Voters, the Y.W.C.A., and the Southern Summer School for Women Workers in Industry looked to organized Methodist women when undertaking grass-roots development in local communities. It was reported to Newell in 1924 "that the Southern Methodist women lead all other Church groups in social insight and method."[57] That same year, Louise Leonard, Y.W.C.A. national industrial secretary of the southern region, who would later direct the Southern Summer School, reported, "[T]his opportunity to work with the women of the Southern Methodist Church is of great importance, since they represent the best organization for carrying out of social service work through the church and a greater willingness to study underlying causes of social problems."[58]

Gradually, southern Methodist women concerned with industrial reform became part of an amalgam of women's groups working for social change in the South. These organizations spanned a broad political spectrum. They included religious reformers such as the Methodists as well as secular reformers oriented to legislating social change. The spectrum encompassed the Y.W.C.A., a group with a religious ideology but a secular orientation, which encouraged the equal participation of middle-class and working-class women in reform efforts. In the late 1920s and the 1930s, the Women's Trade Union League, with labor movement backing; the Southern Summer School, an independent workers' education program for southern women; and women with socialist political affiliations emerged to form the left wing of the women's groups that were fighting for social and economic alternatives in the South.[59]

Contact with other reform groups expanded the vision of southern Methodist women. In 1930, under Bertha Newell's continued leadership, the Bureau of Social Service of the Woman's Missionary Council was transformed into the Bureau of Christian Social Relations, with commissions on industrial relations, interracial cooperation, and rural development. In 1935, the Woman's Missionary Council endorsed the National Recovery Act—primarily because of its benefits for working women, which included a shorter work week and the minimum wage. Council members worked for protective legislation in southern states, supported the ratification of the Federal Child Labor Amendment, and studied unemployment and old-age insurance. Their special interest in working women eventually also led them to question the working conditions outside industry—in domestic employment and in the rural sharecropping system.[60]

In concluding, let us return to forward-thinking Laura Haygood. At the beginning of the period treated here, on the eve of leaving for China in 1884, she spoke on the place of female education in home mission work. "I thank God that there is no longer a question as to woman's having a part in the world's work." Haygood noted with relief, "though we—the women, as well as our brothers—have been slow to understand [this]."[61] Historians of both church and society have been equally slow to comprehend the significance of American women's work within the church and have neglected its importance to the church, to society, and to the women themselves.

These questions deserve serious consideration: What role did southern Methodist women's work for industrial and racial reform play in the development of the Methodist Episcopal Church, South, especially as it moved toward reunification with the northern Methodist and Methodist Protestant churches in 1939 and 1940? How have leading southern women, trained for social reform through the women's societies, influenced and shaped The Methodist Church since unification, and The United Methodist Church since merger?[62]

Viewed objectively, industrial reformers among southern Methodist women had a mixed record of accomplishment. Certainly between 1880 and 1940, they failed by a wide margin to establish God's kingdom in the South. The adoption of the Social Creed of the Federal Council of Churches, with the support of Methodist home missionary women, doubtless mitigated the actions of some individual industrialists. And the legislative controls on industry that southern Methodist women helped institute through the political process did impose some systematic restraints on a region in the throes of industrialization. Nevertheless, differences between capital and labor were not harmonized during those sixty years. If anything, the gulf grew wider in the twentieth century. In the mid-1930s, when someone asked Bertha Newell how useful the protests of church women had been, she answered honestly, "To this we reply that we have been struggling to promote, in our own way, order in a crazy world."[63]

Still, in an essentially traditional and repressive culture, southern Methodist women, with guidance from leaders such as Laura Haygood and Bertha Newell, worked seriously on the most difficult and protracted problems of their society. They gave continuous public expression to their Christian vision of a more just and humane social system. They spoke out for justice when it was extremely unpopular and even dangerous to do so, and the prophetic voice sends disturbing echoes with female accents, no less than male, into situations of exploitation.

Whatever their failures vis-à-vis industrial capitalism, southern Methodist women did create an approximation of the beloved community within their own organization. Home mission work and industrial reform activities went far to emancipate organized Methodist women both socially and occupationally. Moreover, in the process of forging a Christian sisterhood within their missionary societies, these southern women consolidated their collective strength and nurtured their individual aspirations, while shielding themselves from possible social alienation. Through their working relationships as volunteers, the women found "kindred spirits" with whom to share both public goals and private experiences. Bonds of understanding and belonging buffered these female reformers from the tensions of ecclesiastical and familial opposition to their activities and lessened the burden of their second-class status in both church and society. Confronted with hostility to their work, southern Methodist women could count among their great political strengths their capacity for friendship, and the nurturing of it in exclusively female organizations.

As the cleavage between industrialists and workers deepened in the New South during the Great Depression, organized Methodist women saw the goals of southern reformers coalesce into programs closely resembling their own social vision. When thirteen hundred black and white southerners gathered in 1938 in Birmingham, Alabama, to launch the Southern Conference for Human Welfare in response to Franklin Roosevelt's statement that "the South is the nation's number one economic problem," most of the issues on their agenda were those that had been pursued by southern Methodist women during the previous sixty years. The burning concerns of women through three generations were finally acknowledged to be the deepest social and economic issues of their region.[64]

WINIFRED L. CHAPPELL*

Miriam J. Crist

It has been said of Winifred Chappell that "everybody on the left knew her."[1] Yet a generation after her death in 1951, her name scarcely appears in histories of American radical movements, of women, or of the twentieth-century church. In all these fields we are cheated by her absence, since Winifred Chappell was one of the outstanding figures of the Christian left in the United States during the 1920s, 30s, and 40s. The upsurge of anticommunism in the late 1940s and 1950s, and the fear engendered by McCarthyism just at the time of her death have contributed to our ignorance about her contributions.[2] The recovery of Chappell's story opens a window into a relatively unknown chapter of social Christianity and provides a bridge from the past to the current generation of Christians on the left.[3]

"Fritz," as her friends knew her, worked dauntlessly and unflaggingly to realize her firmly held conviction that Christians must be involved in ushering in a new social order. She sought to raise the church's consciousness of the need for such a new order and used her staff position with the Methodist Federation for Social Service (M.F.S.S.), from 1922 to 1936, to that end. Her tools were public education and a socialist critique of the decaying capitalist system. As a well-known progressive journalist, she highlighted especially the situation of women industrial workers and took up their cause. Chappell came to embrace socialism and many communist ideas as being consistent with Christian commitment. With other progressives of her generation, she

*An earlier version of this essay appeared in *Radical Religion: A Quarterly Journal of Critical Thought,* copyright © 1980, 1:22-28. Permission to publish a somewhat altered version here is gratefully acknowledged.

admired the Soviet Russian experiment and viewed as class struggle the social conflicts that were rending American society. For her beliefs and activities, she was eventually marginalized from the dominant society and from the church.

Early Years and Influences

Winifred Leola Chappell was born on November 24, 1879, in Oakland Valley, Iowa, and would spend her first forty years in the Midwest. Her father, Ellis Samuel Chappell, was a Methodist preacher who itinerated with his family from parish to parish in the small towns of northern Iowa and South Dakota. It was not only her father who was a preacher, but her grandfather, her uncle, and her brother, as well. Her grandfather had traveled for fifty-six years as an evangelist, and both her father and uncle inclined to his personalized religion, remaining aloof to the social gospel throughout their lives. Winifred was to approach the matter differently, however, quite possibly influenced by her mother. In raising her eight children, Mary Smorithit Chappell, English by birth, always placed human concerns above material things, a trait her daughter acquired.[4]

The life of a Methodist family in a parsonage was not an easy one, and the Chappells had their share of poverty and hardship. Winifred was sixteen when her father's decision to enter Garrett Biblical Institute in 1895 took the family to the Chicago area.[5] She spent her high school years in Evanston and at age twenty, entered Northwestern University with the intention of becoming a deaconess in the Methodist Episcopal Church.

It was under the tutelage of George Albert Coe, a leading member of the Philosophy Department at Northwestern, that Chappell began to shape her ideas about life and religion. Coe taught that the church should adopt the methods of science into its system of religious education, to build an ideal society that would embody the values of Christianity—a "divine-human democracy" that would be the kingdom of God on earth. Achieving this future would depend on social education, not only in schools, but in the church and the family as well. For example, Coe urged society to "abandon the doctrine and the practice of inequality of the sexes [and] abolish the sex caste in families." He saw private property as "an ancient wall of division within the family . . . a class distinction . . . a fundamental denial of brotherhood."[6]

Chappell graduated Phi Beta Kappa from Northwestern in 1903 and taught school for three years. She still had a great desire to become a deaconess, one of the few church vocations then open to women, and to attend the Chicago Training School for City, Home and Foreign Missions founded by Lucy Rider Meyer. For Chappell this was a progressive, egalitarian, and exciting institution. In 1906 she was able to enroll there, and after graduating, remained for fifteen years as teacher and then as assistant principal.[7]

The Rock River Conference of the Methodist Episcopal Church, which had sent Frances Willard as its delegate to General Conference in 1888, granted Winifred Chappell her consecration as a deaconess in 1908, a status she kept for the rest of her life. Family members recall that Winifred shortly "became a 'revolutionary' . . . [as] one of the first deaconesses to shed her black bonnet and its ribbons for conventional clothing in order to better mingle with ordinary people."[8]

Chappell Joins the Methodist Federation Staff

Winifred Chappell's connections with the Methodist Federation for Social Service began at least as early as 1914, when she was elected to the federation's executive committee, but she did not join the staff until eight years later.[9]

After World War I, she took a leave of absence from the Chicago Training School to attend Columbia University for her master's degree in sociology. Entitled "Industrial Missions," Chappell's thesis, completed in 1920, gave the earliest evidence of her socialist leanings: It contained a class analysis, criticized United States imperialism and overseas commercial exploitation, and demonstrated some sympathy for the international labor movement, of which she was clearly cognizant.[10]

During that period, Chappell also revealed herself an ardent advocate of woman suffrage. In a pamphlet written in 1918 for the federation, she urged churchwomen to agitate for the vote. She suggested also that they learn about the Women's Trade Union League and encouraged them to "organize some action" around the needs of women and children. The synthesis of her political commitments shows in her challenge to Methodist women to be the "socialized church" enthusiastically endorsed by the General Conference, at the prompting of the federation.[11]

Having returned to Chicago after receiving her degree from Columbia, Winifred Chappell unexpectedly left her assistant principalship at the training school, after her dear friend and classmate, Grace Scribner, was tragically killed by a hit-and-run driver in New York City. Grace had left instructions that if she died, her library and typewriter were to be given to Winifred.[12] As it turned out, she also left her job to her highly qualified friend—Chappell came to New York in the fall of 1922 to become research secretary of the M.F.S.S., with primary responsibility for the bimonthly *Social Service Bulletin*.[13]

She took the job with the understanding that she would be working in partnership with Harry F. Ward, chief executive of the federation from 1911 to 1944, and would be relieved of as much office detail as possible, given Ward's many other commitments.[14] Chappell and Ward held weekly conferences to consult about the *Bulletin* and the federation.[15] Thus while many *Bulletin* articles are not signed, we can assume that most of them were actually researched and written by Winifred Chappell.

A principal organizer of the federation in 1907 and a prominent speaker who traveled widely, Ward overshadowed all aspects of federation life. As president from 1912 to 1944, Bishop Francis McConnell also put his mark on it, giving it an air of legitimacy.[16] Even so, in a short time Chappell began to carve out a special place for herself through her editing, writing, speaking, and teaching. She was soon in demand for conferences, as Scribner had been before her. From across the country her former students plied her with invitations. In 1924 she enjoyed a trip to the Pacific coast, conducting Epworth League institutes in Montana and Oregon and leading a Y.W.C.A. conference at Asilomar, California. Her addresses were so well received that pastors invited her to occupy their pulpits on Sundays.[17]

As she became better known, Chappell made field trips whenever she could get away from administrative responsibilities at the M.F.S.S. office in New York. In addition, she sat on numerous committees and councils, including the Federal Council of Churches and the Industrial Committee of the Y.W.C.A.[18]

Key Issues Confronted as a Christian Journalist

Winifred Chappell's writing soon came to be noticed outside M.F.S.S. circles. One of her concerns was the incarceration of political prisoners in the United States. This she gave an ironic twist in "I Saw Seven Flags," her first piece in *The Christian Century* in 1924.[19] Here she mused on the meaning of freedom in the "land of the free" on a Fourth of July with seven flags flying, while her friends who were members of the International Workers of the World (Wobblies) were confined in jail because of their socialist affiliation. That this political question was crucial is shown by the fact that two of the *Bulletin*'s issues on the topic received special distribution by other interested organizations.[20]

Chappell also wrote about the issue of protective legislation for women which would shorten wage-earning women's hours and forbid night work. Protective legislation was so highly controversial that it split the women's movement in the United States. Chappell described the division to her readers: the more radical Woman's Party (the Equal Rights Amendment group) was pitted against more moderate organizations such as the Y.W.C.A., the League of Women Voters, and the National Women's Trade Union League. But though feminist in sympathies, Chappell's vision was of a working-class solidarity in which all workers, male and female, would receive protection.

Here and there . . . is arising a new attitude . . . [which] appears oftenest in the world of industry and . . . where the labor movement develops militancy. . . . Men and women are coming to recognize themselves as comrades in a common cause, sharing with each other and with their children the need for protection and for opportunity which has been denied them by an exploiting society.[21]

As the 1920s unfolded, Winifred Chappell frequently investigated and reported on strikes—strikes that burst the myth that the 20s were a decade of unprecedented wealth for Americans, with a chicken in every pot. She also challenged another myth that the Flapper Era was introducing unprecedented freedom for women. Her exposés uncovered a very different picture—women struggling to keep body and soul together, trying to eke out a living in the factories, standing beside their men on picket lines, and coping with evictions from their company houses in the coal fields.

When labor struggles erupted, she often went to the scene so that she could file first-hand reports. For example, in 1928 she covered the coal strike in Pennsylvania and Kentucky—a strike marked by great physical suffering. She reported that striking miners living in company houses were harrassed, that attempts to evict them included shutting off the water and tearing off the roofs, and also that there was extreme violation of civil liberties by the mine owners. Company towns were guarded by Pennsylvania's "coal and iron police"; visitors needed passes; and sometimes reporters were seized. Companies obtained injunctions against the unions, prohibiting picketing, singing, and posting of signs.[22]

In 1931 Chappell visited the coal fields of West Virginia.

Up at 4:30 A.M. driving over the hills to see and talk with the men, women and children on their early morning picket lines. Here in the pasture the women sit rocking and nursing their babies in their old evicted rocking chairs. Over there one is trying to make a fire in her rusty evicted stove. Some of the men folk have set up the bedsteads and the women have put on the bedding. How queer they look out here in the open field. . . . Employers mean business when they throw women with children in their wombs, children at their breasts, children at their skirts, out of the only homes they have.

. . . There are guns in the present strike, but they are over the shoulders of mine guards, state troopers, even mine superintendents.[23]

Although her journalistic attention ranged over the spectrum of social, political, and economic ills, and she emphasized the common cause of working women and their men, Chappell was particularly sensitive to the concerns of women workers in industry. This was evident in her investigation of the textile strike at Passaic, New Jersey, in 1926. Chappell became deeply involved in this strike, and out of her research came articles for the *Social Service Bulletin* and an issue of *The Christian Century* devoted entirely to the strike. She was especially attentive to women's participation in the Passaic struggle: "Mothers of children, some of them leading kiddies by the hand or even trundling baby carriages in the picket line; middle-aged women; elderly women? They are of the European peasant type; . . . their faces attract one in the strike meetings, more than the faces of the girls who flutter in and out of the halls."[24] Chappell watched women listen carefully at the meeting when a speaker asked, "When the bosses wanted to cut your wages, did they talk it over with you? No, they put up a sign saying that wages would be reduced." The women nodded vigorously. "Who earned the money for them [the Frostmanns] to travel abroad? While they were traveling, you were working in the mills . . . and getting far less than enough to feed your children." She observed the women's class consciousness growing and concluded, "But it is not chiefly pity that one feels as one looks into their faces. Chiefly one feels admiration . . . ! 'Go back to work? . . . Me no scab!' they said. 'Solidarity forever' is their new battlecry."[25]

That issue of *The Christian Century* brought raves from readers, and the supply was exhausted quickly. Paul Hutchinson, the editor, was immensely pleased with Chappell's work. She was establishing herself as an astute and penetrating analyst.

In her reporting, Chappell continually raised the question of the commitment of the church to industrial justice: "How should church people be involved?" In 1926 the Passaic strike provoked her to this reflection:

[One wonders] whether the Protestant churches . . . can possibly in this generation, reestablish any relations of confidence with the workers there. The Passaic situation bears a message to the churches of the nation. . . . [W]hat [will] the churches of Passaic and Northern New Jersey do to repair the breaches which this strike has certainly driven between them and the laboring portion of this industrial community[?][26]

In 1931, from the West Virginia coal fields, she demanded: "In light of the situation described . . . starving families on one side and rich, entrenched interests on the other, what becomes of the stock argument that the church and the preacher should not take sides?"[27]

As a result of her experiences, Chappell ever more radically questioned the ability of the capitalistic economic system to generate any real improvement in the old order. Her vision, and that of the M.F.S.S., was to build a new social order. She believed that the most progressive ideas and programs were advocated by the socialists and communists. She did not shy away from aligning herself with them.

Having covered the Pennsylvania coal strike in the spring of 1928, Winifred Chappell took a summer trip to the Soviet Union. On her return, she traveled to New Bedford, Massachusetts, to observe the strike against the textile mills. Afterward, for the readers of *The Christian Century,* she boldly compared New Bedford unfavorably to a Russian industrial town, concluding, "New Bedford, it happens, offers one of the most unreasonable and arrogant infringements of simple justice that our industrial world has recently seen." The mills arrogantly cut back wages by 10 percent when the average wage was a mere $19 a week. "Impudent!" she reported.[28]

In reporting these strikes, Chappell clearly sympathized with left-wing union leadership. She gave her support to many of the programs offered by the Communist Party at that time, although there is no evidence that she was ever a member of that party.

369

Chappell's skills in sharpening the class analysis of her constituents were demonstrated in a fascinating exposé of the promotion tactics of the women's clothing industry, written in December 1929. When the stock market crashed, dress styles suddenly became longer. She accused dress manufacturers and fabric makers of colluding to use more cloth. "Will women submit?" she asked, and reported that six thousand Hunter College students had protested in New York, as had "YWCA industrial girls," who complained that they also had to buy new corsets to wear the new styles—an affront to their new freedom, as well as to their health![29]

The Depression Years

As the Depression deepened in the 1930s, Chappell maintained her posture of critical dissent as co-editor of the *Social Service Bulletin*. There were no Social Security or unemployment benefits in those days, and she wrote about the people who were enduring hardships. Particularly, she wrote about women who were unemployed, with no money, no food, and no place to stay; women, waiting day after day in employment agencies, hoping against hope for jobs. She challenged the churches by asking if churchwomen would cook for the poor and the unemployed, as they did for their own church suppers? Would they open their doors to provide a place for unemployed men to sleep?

By 1932, Chappell recognized that the developing crisis was making new demands on everyone and that the federation membership would not escape. She had sympathized with Russia's experiment, and many of her articles carried references to its organization and plans. But now the economic crisis in the United States demanded sharper political analysis.

Regarding the distinction between socialism and communism, she wrote:

In general, socialists hope to get control of the present state machinery and use it for the common good. . . . In general, communists believe that the state in origin and history is an instrument of the exploiters and that state power must be seized by workers' soviets. These will represent a new machinery of government which will be used to serve instead of to exploit the masses. . . . [But] members of communist persuasion will need to be prepared to reconcile faiths and programs that on the surface appear irreconcilable. . . . Here is something to test ourselves by: Will we be for or against the downtrodden ones[?] . . . When the test came in Russia, the church was on the wrong side.[30]

In 1932, when the General Conference of the Methodist Episcopal Church declared that the " 'present industrial order is unchristian, unethical and anti-social . . . ' and that the basic assumptions of our social order are unchristian," Chappell and Ward decided to "strike out for deep water," and the *Bulletin* ran a series of issues on fascism, socialism, and communism.[31]

These issues on political theories may have been costly to the federation. The membership, already decimated by the Depression, may have been divided by the frank presentation of these political views and by their critique of the capitalistic economic system.

Even so, Chappell had no qualms in aligning herself with other intellectuals, journalists, artists, and teachers in signing a declaration that in the 1932 national elections, she would vote for the Communist Party candidate for president, William Z. Foster, then in jail. In this she joined forces with such people as Lincoln Steffens, Sherwood Anderson, Theodore Dreiser, and Edmund Wilson, who, in the declaration, justified their action as "the only effective way to protest against the chaos, the appalling wastefulness and the indescribable misery inherent in the present economic system."[32] This was her directive to the federation constituency in September 1932:

Now let's keep ready to move leftward. For the beneficiaries of capitalism are not going easily to surrender their property and the prerogatives it brings; . . . [C]hurch folk have now to face up to the class-struggle, just what it means, and what they are going to do about it. . . . Violence[?] There's no inclination to violence on the part of the disinherited in this country. *They're far too meek.* It's the other side that resorts to force.[33]

It was a spare time for the Methodist Federation. As their finances struck rock bottom, Chappell offered to go on half-salary and supplement her income with free-lance writing. The federation and Chappell squeaked through 1933 only by the grace of a grant from an anonymous donor. Nevertheless, Chappell attended the National Convention Against Unemployment in Washington, D.C., and helped guide the federation's critical evaluation of the New Deal with articles on "The Farmer and the New Deal," "Labor Under the NRA," and "The New Deal in Relief."

At about that time, Chappell made a new connection that was to herald her future. She met Claude Williams, a maverick Presbyterian minister who was organizing the black and white southern tenant farmers and sharecroppers in Arkansas. After a visit there, she devoted an issue of the *Bulletin* to the plight of southern tenant farmers, reporting, "The [union] locals . . . meet secretly, sometimes converting themselves quickly into religious meetings to avoid detection. . . . The plantation owners have been back of an organized reign of terror by night riders and county officials [with] beat[ings], arrest[s] . . . armed . . . vigilantes."[34]

Chappell helped Williams establish the New Era Schools of Social Action and Prophetic Religion to educate workers and their leaders, since Williams had concluded that this would never be done by the mainline churches. The schools traveled to different areas, offering courses on international relations, political science, labor history, dramatics, and the human relations of race, class, and sex. Chappell was named to the New Era Schools' national committee and was listed as a visiting lecturer.

The years from 1933 through 1935 were critical for the federation. They were years of financial distress, dissatisfaction within, and attacks from without. One source of the dissatisfaction within stemmed from tension between the proponents of education and those who preferred direct action. It came to a head when Chicago federation members formed the Chicago Social Action Conference and proposed that they merge with the federation, possibly moving the federation office to Chicago. As their name indicated, they were more interested in action, while until then, the federation had devoted much of its energy to analyses of social conditions.

Chappell felt that she personally was under attack and wrote in a memo to Harry Ward:

I'm sure the Chicago men are dissatisfied because I don't do enough. . . . God knows I'm dissatisfied too! How much more I could do with a little money to turn round with, I don't know. . . . If I ward off suggestions of things to do, it's because for me, as I am and in my restricted circumstances, they are simply not practical. On the other hand when something comes up that I know I can do, I grab it.[35]

It was clear that Chappell envisioned herself "a propagandist of ideas," a role in which she excelled. If funds had been available, she would gladly have let the office move and been responsible only for the *Bulletin*. Her livelihood was at stake, and if the move came, she thought she might teach at Commonwealth College or at Ashland Folk School, or write for the church press. She liked traveling and reporting on vital events that were happening.[36]

The merger never materialized, nor did the headquarters move to Chicago, but the financial crisis continued. Chappell voluntarily went on a part-time basis with less pay and an "opportunity" to do some free-lance writing and teaching. Even in 1935 the federation barely kept alive by raising $4000 to cover the budget.

But 1935 also proved to be a critical time for the federation in other ways. In that year William Randolph Hearst syndicated a series of articles by George Donald Pierce which started a widespread campaign of "red-baiting." The articles contained accusations that the clergy was being used by the "Reds" to destroy the institutions of the United States. "Rid the M.E. Church of 'Red' Incubus" was the title of Pierce's series, in which he attacked the social movement in the churches, collective bargaining, minimum-wage laws, old-age pensions, Social Security legislation, and so on. He hoped that the General Conference of 1936 would "deal with the McConnell-Ward-Chappell radical aggregation without gloves."[37] It is interesting that Pierce was not in doubt about Chappell's importance to the federation.

This red-baiting had its reverberations within the M.F.S.S., with accusations that the federation office was not employing an explicit enough "Christian emphasis" in its program and that the political positions of Ward and Chappell were questionable, particularly regarding the use of violence. A special leadership conference was called in Pittsburgh to deal with this unrest. Chappell and Ward made statements only after it was unanimously agreed that their political views and affiliations were personal matters and that Methodists might be Republicans or Communists, as their consciences might dictate.

The leftward direction of the federation was implicitly affirmed by their conclusion that a planned economy (in effect, a socialist economy) ought to replace the profit system. It was decided that there should be study *and* action in the federation and that it was the duty of the pulpit and educational forces to pronounce judgment on the capitalist system as the enemy of society and religion.[38]

At General Conference that spring, the controversy still raged. An organization of reactionary Methodist laymen aimed to quiet the Methodist radicals. But "the Federation was not defeated," Chappell wrote afterward. They confronted red-baiting with an issue of the *Bulletin* on the subject, and their income actually increased. Quoting Bishop McConnell, Chappell wrote, "We believe in a militant organization, and we do not care a hoot about what the great church bodies think about us."[39]

Then, seemingly without warning, the *Social Questions Bulletin* (as it had been renamed) carried a small notice in June 1936 that the federation was faced with the necessity of temporarily releasing Winifred Chappell for a much needed rest. She seemed to vanish into thin air. For a year the *Bulletin* carried no mention of her.

Chappell never returned to the Methodist Federation staff, despite the expression of that hope in a resolution at the 1937 national meeting.[40] Such a complete and sudden break with all that had been her life for so many years is puzzling. Was Winifred's illness real? Was she tired out? Had the internal and external pressures taken too much toll? Or did she need an excuse to move in a new direction?

A New Commitment

Chappell's deaconess records tell us that in the summer of 1936 she went to Mena, Arkansas, to teach at Commonwealth College. Founded in 1920 by utopian socialists, Commonwealth was organized on a work-study basis, with students and faculty helping in the kitchen and farm work. Because of its participation in contemporary labor struggles and its reputation for teaching labor leaders, Commonwealth College was then experiencing serious difficulties. Its refusal to purge communists from its faculty and student body had made the college a target for anticommunists.[41] In 1937 Claude Williams became director of Commonwealth and served for two tumultuous years, under pressure from the Arkansas State Legislature to rid the college of communists.[42] Thereafter, under a new plan of reorganization, Winifred Chappell became faculty chairman, but her tenure was as short-lived as Williams'.

In 1938, Williams returned to organizing: He set up the People's Institute of Applied Religion, to "train leaders in religion to serve as labor organizers and leaders of struggles against the poll tax, racial discrimination, and other repressive features of the southern social order."[43]

Chappell joined the People's Institute of Applied Religion in 1941 as associate director, sharing the title with Owen Whitfield, a lay preacher and black union organizer. In this capacity she traveled with the itinerant school, teaching courses such as Religion and Racism, True Religion and Prejudice, and True Religion and Brotherhood. Her aspirations to do more writing seem not to have been fulfilled. At the heart of the ideology of the People's Institute was Claude Williams' interpretation of the Bible as a record of struggle against oppression. The religiosity of southern workers had long been the bane of secular union organizers and radicals. Williams had found a way to convert the

375

religious fervor of the workers into a positive force for justice.[44]

The Last Years

After her retirement in 1946, Chappell remained affiliated with the People's Institute, writing fund-raising letters, teaching, and promoting its work. She also continued her connection with the federation. At its Thirty-Fifth Anniversary Conference in 1942, two years before Harry Ward and Bishop Francis McConnell retired, Chappell participated in a symposium, "Putting Into Action the Federation's Wartime Program for the Maintenance and Extension of Democracy."[45] When she retired to Chicago in 1947, she became a member of the Chicago chapter and was active there until she died.

Chappell was not eligible for a pension at her retirement, but at times she did live at the Chicago Deaconess Home. In 1951, when she was in the hospital with cancer, many old friends came to visit her. Jack McMichael, successor to Harry Ward in the Methodist Federation for Social Action, remembered that Winifred exuded a sense of joy and delight in her life during his time with her. Her spirit was lively and unquenchable, even in illness.[46]

At her death, the *Social Questions Bulletin* which she and Ward had edited together for fourteen years ran this death notice:

Miss Winifred Chappell died suddenly on July 21 [1951] in Chicago. Miss Chappell, with [a] rich Methodist deaconess background, was Office Secretary of the MFSA for many years and Assistant to the Editor of the *Bulletin*. In recent years she has been a very active member and officer of Chicago's MFSA Chapter. To all who knew her "Winnie" was an inspiring example of one who dedicated her entire life to bringing in the Kingdom of brotherhood, abundance, and peace for all God's children everywhere. She was utterly fearless and devoted, and will be sadly missed.[47]

The obituary hardly does justice to Winifred's executive partnership with Ward. She was never the "Office Secretary," but indeed was an executive secretary of the federation. She was never an "Assistant to the Editor of the *Bulletin*," but one of the two editors—the one who actually did all the work. One wonders that her invaluable contributions to the Methodist Federation and other left-wing movements in the church were so easily and rapidly attenuated, soon to be dismissed and forgotten.

Why has Chappell been so elusive and unknown to historians? It is historically important to probe the question. Surely a large part of the answer is that she was a woman. Winifred Chappell experienced sexism throughout her life, though the term had not yet been invented. As a deaconess she may have had a foot in the door of the male-dominated church, but her role was perceived by both clergy and laity as a subordinate, helping one—a perception difficult to transcend. At the Chicago Training School, where she was hailed as a "brilliant teacher," Winifred Chappell had excelled in a "woman's sphere"; but when she went to the M.F.S.S. in New York, it was different. Only after twelve years did she feel she was doing as much as when she left Chicago.[48] In New York, it was necessary to overcome the accepted image of woman as office manager, secretary, and assistant, in order to be recognized as an autonomous executive. In addition, Chappell moved into the "public sphere" by pursuing activities in labor unions and strikes. She developed an economic analysis of the American social order that was critical of both capitalism and the New Deal. She was a highly able journalist and thinker in "man's territory," and perhaps it has been easier to forget her contributions than to acknowledge her presence.

Her Christian commitment to the poor and her socialist orientation to the needs of working people brought Chappell into conflict also with dominant feminist concerns. The women's movement was basically middle class in orientation. Chappell, of course, supported suffrage and always had the concerns of working women at heart. But in some ways her loyalty to the poor and exploited took precedence over her loyalty to women as a group. Winifred was not an ideological feminist; she *was* a socialist to her core.

Struggling for her own identity as a writer and a leader on

the left was not easy. She confided to her office associates that "the boss" could be a tyrant at times. Her notes suggest that she worked incredibly hard, turning down speaking engagements and writing assignments outside the federation because of her work load in the office.[49] Against these odds, her professional, evangelical, and political accomplishments appear that much greater. Dorothy McConnell has confirmed that labor leaders respected Winifred as a thorough researcher and sought her out more often than Ward.

Winifred Chappell was a small, slender woman. She is described by those who knew her as charming and soft-spoken. But what she had to say was revolutionary, and she intended to stir up the people, even as Jesus had in the first century. Winifred knew which side she was on. For this she continues to draw admiration from a later generation of Christian leftists who are still fighting on the same battleground.

NOTES

INTRODUCTION

1. *The Message and Deaconess Advocate* ll/ll(1895):3-4.
2. Quaker women, who throughout American history have led in gaining rights for women, were studied at an "Interdisciplinary Symposium on American Quaker Women as Shapers of Human Space" at Guilford College, Greensboro, North Carolina, March 16–18, 1979.
3. Alexis de Tocqueville, *Democracy in America,* Vol. l, ed. Phillips Bradley (New York: Vintage Press, 1945), pp. 313-26.
4. Barbara Welter, "The Cult of True Womanhood: 1820–1860," *American Quarterly* 18/2(Summer 1966):151-74.

CHAPTER 1. Women's History/Everyone's History

1. Lyle Koehler, "The Case of the American Jezebels: Anne Hutchinson and Female Agitation during the Years of Antinomian Turmoil, 1636–1640," *William and Mary Quarterly* 3/31(January 1974):55-78.
2. Richard Allen (1760–1831) was a celebrated black Methodist preacher, the first to be ordained in the Methodist Episcopal Church. Following disputes in Philadelphia over white control of a black Methodist congregation, Allen founded the independent A.M.E. Church in 1816 and was elected its first bishop. See "Richard Allen," *The Encyclopedia of World Methodism,* ed. Nolan B. Harmon (Nashville: Abingdon Press, 1974) vol. 1, pp. 90-91; for more details, see Frederick E. Maser, *Richard Allen,* The United Methodist Biography Series, pamphlet (Lake Junaluska, N.C.: Commission on Archives and History, 1976). James Weldon Johnson (1871–1938) was a poet, teacher, and activist; in *God's Trombones,* he presented the poetry and cadences of Afro-American Christianity in a vivid and powerful fashion.
3. William H. Chafe, *Women and Equality: Changing Patterns in*

American Culture (New York: Oxford University Press, 1977).

4. Barbara Sicherman; E. William Monter; Joan Wallach Scott; and Kathryn Kish Sklar, *Recent U.S. Scholarship on the History of Women: A Report Presented at the XV International Congress of Historical Sciences, Bucharest, Romania, 1980* (Washington, D.C.: American Historical Association, 1980). Professor Scott lent the report in mimeographed form in advance of the congress, for which the author is most grateful.

5. *Ibid.*, pp. 6-18.

6. *Ibid.*, pp. 18-33, 33-47.

7. See, e.g., Nancy F. Cott, "Passionlessness: An Interpretation of Victorian Sexual Ideology, 1790–1850," *Signs: A Journal of Women in Culture and Society* 4(Winter 1978):219-36.

8. Sicherman et al., *Recent U.S. Scholarship,* p. 29.

9. Donald G. Mathews, *Religion in the Old South* (Chicago: University of Chicago Press, 1977), pp. 102-24.

10. It is true, of course, that men officially managed the local as well as the regional churches, just as they officially managed the black congregations of biracial churches. But this control did not necessarily mean that the organizations in their social bonding were "male," any more than black congregations were "white" churches. See *ibid.,* ch. 5.

11. Barbara Welter, "The Feminization of American Religion: 1800–1860," *Problems and Issues in American Social History,* ed. William L. O'Neill (Minneapolis, Minn.: Burgess Publishing Co., 1974); reprinted in Mary Hartman and Lois W. Banner, eds., *Clio's Consciousness Raised: New Perspectives on the History of Women* (New York: Harper & Row, 1974), pp. 137-57. Ann Douglas, *The Feminization of American Culture* (New York: Alfred A. Knopf, 1977). See Welter's review of Douglas's book in *Signs* 4(Summer 1979):785-86: "If nineteenth-century American culture was feminized—and I, along with several others, have long suggested that it was—what is needed is a comprehensive study of the culture itself, as well as of the dynamics of 'feminization,' and that book has not yet been written."

12. Mary Maples Dunn, "Saints and Sisters: Congregational and Quaker Women in the Early Colonial Period," *American Quarterly* 30(Winter 1978):594-95.

13. Linda K. Kerber, "The Republican Mother: Women and the Enlightenment—An American Perspective," *American Quarterly* 28(Summer 1976):187-205; Ruth H. Bloch, "American Feminine Ideals in Transition: The Rise of the Moral Mother, 1785–1815," *Feminist Studies* 4(June 1978):101-26.

14. Mary P. Ryan, "A Women's Awakening: Evangelical Religion and the Families of Utica, New York, 1800–1840," *American Quarterly* 30(Winter 1978):602-23; Ryan, "The Power of Women's Networks: A Case Study of Female Moral Reform in

Antebellum America," *Feminist Studies* 5(Spring 1979):66-85.

15. William Chafe, *The American Woman: Her Changing Social, Economic, and Political Roles, 1920–1970* (New York: Oxford University Press, 1972).

16. Linda Gordon, *Woman's Body, Woman's Right: Birth Control in America* (New York: Grossman Publishers, 1976).

17. There are many studies of Progressivism in which women figure prominently as social workers and theorists, e.g., Allen F. Davis, *Spearheads for Reform: The Social Settlements and the Progressive Movement, 1890–1914* (New York: Oxford University Press, 1967); Clarke A. Chambers, *Seedtime of Reform: American Social Service and Social Action, 1918–1933* (Minneapolis, Minn.: University of Minnesota Press, 1963). But when generalizations are made about "Who were the Progressives?" they are based on the background and characteristics of men.

18. Revelation 3:8, cited in Emily Clare Newby Correll, "Woman's Work for Woman: The Methodist and the Baptist Woman's Missionary Societies in North Carolina, 1878–1930" (Master's thesis, University of North Carolina at Chapel Hill, 1977), p. 33.

CHAPTER 2. The Last Fifteen Years

1. Julia Cherry Spruill, *Women's Life and Work in the Southern Colonies* (Chapel Hill, N.C.: University of North Carolina Press, 1938; reprint ed., New York: W.W. Norton & Co., 1972), p. 245.

2. *Ibid.*, pp. 247-48.

3. Whitney R. Cross, *The Burned-Over District: The Social and Intellectual History of Enthusiastic Religion in Western New York, 1800–1850* (Ithaca, N.Y.: Cornell University Press, 1950), p. 84.

4. Timothy L. Smith, *Revivalism & Social Reform: American Protestantism on the Eve of the Civil War* (Nashville: Abingdon Press, 1957), p. 124. For more on Phoebe Palmer, see Edward T. James et al., eds., *Notable American Women, 1607–1950: A Biographical Dictionary* (Cambridge, Mass.: Harvard University Press, Belknap Press, 1971), vol. 3, pp. 12-14.

5. Barbara Welter, "The Cult of True Womanhood, 1820–1860," *American Quarterly* 18/2(Summer 1966).

6. *Ibid.*, p. 172; reprinted in Welter, *Dimity Convictions: The American Woman in the Nineteenth Century* (Athens: Ohio University Press, 1976).

7. Welter, "Cult," n. 53.

8. Gerda Lerner, *The Grimké Sisters of South Carolina: Pioneers*

for Woman's Rights and Abolition (Boston: Houghton Mifflin Co., 1967).

9. Carroll Smith-Rosenberg, "Beauty, the Beast and the Militant Woman: Sex Roles and Social Stress in Jacksonian America," *American Quarterly* 23(1971):584.

10. Nancy F. Cott, *The Bonds of Womanhood: "Woman's Sphere" in New England, 1780–1835* (New Haven: Yale University Press, 1977), p. 132.

11. *Ibid.*, pp. 147, 141, 156.

12. Kathryn Kish Sklar, *Catharine Beecher: A Study in American Domesticity* (New Haven: Yale University Press, 1973), p. 182.

13. Welter, "The Feminization of American Religion: 1800–1860";*Problems and Issues in American Social History,* ed. William L. O'Neill (Minneapolis, Minn.: Burgess Publishing Co., 1974), reprinted in Mary Hartman and Lois W. Banner, eds., *Clio's Consciousness Raised: New Perspectives on the History of Women* (New York: Harper & Row, 1974), pp. 137-57; also in Welter, *Dimity Convictions.*

14. Ann Douglas, *The Feminization of American Culture* (New York: Alfred A. Knopf, 1977).

15. Smith-Rosenberg, "The Female World of Love and Ritual," *Signs: Journal of Women in Culture and Society* 1/1(Autumn 1975):1-29.

16. Donald G. Mathews, *Religion in the Old South* (Chicago: University of Chicago Press, 1977), p. 110.

17. Mary P. Ryan, "A Woman's Awakening: Evangelical Religion and the Families of Utica, New York, 1800–1840," *American Quarterly* 30/5(Winter 1978):623. This study was based on city directories, church records, and vital statistics (marriages, births, deaths).

18. Hall, *Revolt Against Chivalry: Jessie Daniel Ames and the Women's Campaign Against Lynching* (New York: Columbia University Press, 1979).

19. Jacquelyn Dowd Hall, " 'A Truly Subversive Affair': Women Against Lynching in the Twentieth-Century South," *Women of America, A History,* ed. Carol Ruth Berkin and Mary Beth Norton (Boston: Houghton Mifflin Co., 1979), p. 363. For a longer account of the Memphis conference, see Hall, *Revolt,* pp. 90-95.

20. Mary J. Oates, "Organized Voluntarism: The Catholic Sisters in Massachusetts, 1870–1940," *American Quarterly* 30/5(Winter 1978):680.

21. Frances J. Baker, *The Story of the Woman's Foreign Missionary Society of the Methodist Episcopal Church, 1869–1895* (Cincinnati, Ohio: Cranston & Curts/New York: Hunt & Eaton, 1895; rev. ed., Cincinnati, Ohio: Curts & Jennings, 1898). See also Mrs. T.L. [Laura E.] Tomkinson, *Twenty Years' History of the Woman's Home Missionary*

Society of the Methodist Episcopal Church, 1880–1900 (Cincinnati, Ohio: Woman's Home Missionary Society of the Methodist Episcopal Church, 1903); Christian Golder, *History of the Deaconess Movement in the Christian Church* (Cincinnati, Ohio: Jennings & Pye, 1903).

22. The same might be said of the various discussions of women in Emory Stevens Bucke, ed., *The History of American Methodism*, 4 vols. (Nashville: Abingdon Press, 1964).

23. *Methodist History* 6/2(January 1968):3-16.

24. Reprinted in Carol P. Christ and Judith Plaskow, eds., *Womanspirit Rising: A Feminist Reader in Religion* (San Francisco: Harper & Row, 1979), p. 39. Saiving's reference is to Virginia Woolf, *A Room of One's Own* (New York: Harcourt Brace & World, 1929).

25. (Grand Rapids, Mich.: Eerdmans Publishing Co., 1968); rev. ed., *American Protestant Women in World Mission: A History of the First Feminist Movement in America* (1980). See also Alice L. Hageman, ed., *Sexist Religion ar.d Women in the Church: No More Silence* (New York: Association Press, 1974).

26. Rowe, *Methodist History* 12/3(April 1974):60-72; Mitchell, *A.M.E. Zion Quarterly Review/Methodist History/News Bulletin* 13/3(April 1975):21-44; Dayton and Dayton, *Methodist History* 14/2(January 1976):67-92; Noll, *Methodist History* 15/2(January 1977):107-21. Over a number of years, the present editor, Louise L. Queen, has steadily encouraged research about churchwomen.

See also Nancy A. Hardesty, "Your Daughters Shall Prophesy: Revivalism and Feminism in the Age of Finney" (Ph.D. dissertation, The University of Chicago, 1976); Mary Agnes Dougherty, "The American Deaconess Movement, 1888–1918" (Ph.D. dissertation, University of California at Davis, 1979); Norma Taylor Mitchell, "Methodist Feminism: A Legitimate Child of the Methodist Past" (Paper presented at the meeting of the Northeastern Jurisdiction Commission on Archives and History of The United Methodist Church, Watson Homestead, N.Y., October 14, 1975); Rosemary S. Keller, "The Deaconess Movement: Liberating or Constricting? A Case Study of the Chicago Training School" (Paper presented at the Missouri Valley History Conference, Omaha, Nebraska, March 11, 1978).

27. Donald W. Dayton, *Discovering an Evangelical Heritage* (New York: Harper & Row, 1976), pp. 85-98, esp. pp. 91, 96-97.

28. See "Other Papers Delivered at the Conference," p. 443.

29. In addition, the publication of *To a Higher Glory: The Growth and Development of Black Women Organized for Mission in The Methodist Church, 1940–1968* (New York: Women's Division, Board of Global Ministries, The United Methodist

Church, 1978) was an early indication of the emergence of stage four.

30. Ruether and McLaughlin, eds., *Women of Spirit: Female Leadership in the Jewish and Christian Traditions* (New York: Simon & Schuster, 1979), pp. 279-300; Falk and Gross, eds., *Unspoken Worlds: Women's Religious Lives in Non-Western Cultures* (San Francisco: Harper & Row, 1980).
31. I am grateful to Hilah F. Thomas, coordinator of the Women's History Project, for introducing me to this tripartite division of women's religious experience, originated by Rosemary S. Keller while planning the Women in New Worlds conference.
32. Smith-Rosenberg, "Beauty," p. 580.
33. Berkin and Norton, *Women of America,* pp. 177-201.
34. Note, e.g., the class action suit *McRae et al.* v. *Harris et al.* joined by the Women's Division of the Board of Global Ministries, which, on January 16, 1980, resulted in a United States Federal District Court decision rendering unconstitutional, partly on First Amendment grounds, the restrictions on Medicaid payment for medically necessary abortions. United Methodist Women's role in this landmark decision for poor women kept faith with the reform traditions of Methodist women in particular, and of American churchwomen in general. Indeed, it placed United Methodist Women at the forefront of current social reform and will deserve historians' attention in the future.

CHAPTER 3. Women of the Word

1. In addition to Leslie Church's book noted below, two of the chief works on early Methodist women are Abel Stevens, *The Women of Methodism: Its Three Foundresses, Susanna Wesley, The Countess of Huntingdon, and Barbara Heck, with Sketches of Their Female Associates and Successors in the Early History of the Denomination* (New York: Carlton & Porter, 1866); and Z[echariah] Taft, *Biographical Sketches of the Lives and Public Ministry of Various Holy Women, in Which Are Included Several Letters from the Rev. John Wesley Never Before Published,* 2 vols. (London: Kershaw, 1825 [vol. 1]; Leeds: Cullingworth, 1828 [vol. 2], a rare book). For Susanna, see Rebecca Lamar Harmon, *Susanna, Mother of the Wesleys* (Nashville: Abingdon Press, 1968); Frederick E. Maser, *Susanna Wesley,* United Methodist Biography Series, pamphlet (Lake Junaluska, N.C.: World Methodist Council/Association of Methodist Historical Societies, 1964).
2. Leslie F. Church, *More About the Early Methodist People* (London: Epworth Press, 1949), pp. 136-76.

3. Edward Smyth, ed., *The Extraordinary Life and Christian Experience of Margaret Davidson, as Dictated by Herself* (Dublin: Dugdale, 1782), p. 97.
4. *Ibid.*
5. *Arminian Magazine* 13(1790):329-30. Emphasis mine.
6. Joseph Sutcliffe, *The Experience of Mrs. Frances Pawson* (London: Cordeux, 1813), pp. 104-5. I Cor. 11:5 reads: "But every woman that prayeth or prophesieth with her head uncovered dishonoureth her head: for that is even all one as if she were shaven."
7. William Bramwell, *A Short Account of the Life and Death of Ann Cutler* (Leeds: Newsom, 1798), p. 4.
8. John Wesley, *The Letters of the Rev. John Wesley, A.M.*, 8 vols., ed. John Telford (London: Epworth Press, 1931), vol. 8, p. 190.
9. Bramwell, *Cutler*, p. 8.
10. John Pipe, "Memoir of Miss Isabella Wilson," *Arminian Magazine* 31(1808):461.
11. John Wesley, *The Journal of the Rev. John Wesley, A.M.*, 8 vols., ed. Nehemiah Curnock (New York: Eaton & Mains, 1909), vol. 7, p. 249.
12. Wesley, *Letters*, vol. 4, p. 133.
13. Taft, *Holy Women*, vol. 2, pp. 128, 122.
14. *Ibid.*, vol. 1, p. 20 (emphasis Mrs. Fletcher's).
15. *Ibid.*, p. 44.
16. J. Burns, *Life of Mrs. Fletcher* (London: J. Smith, 1843), p. 148.
17. Taft, *Holy Women*, vol. 1, pp. 84, 79.
18. Henry Moore, *The Life of Mrs. Mary Fletcher* (London: Wesleyan Methodist Book Room, [preface dated 1817]), pp. 427-34. Well over 95 percent of this work is in Mrs. Fletcher's own words.
19. Wesley, *Letters*, vol. 2, pp. 119-20.
20. *Ibid.*, vol. 4, pp. 133, 164.
21. *Ibid.*, vol. 5, p. 130 (emphasis Mr. Wesley's).
22. Sarah Crosby to Mr. Mayer of Stockport, July 13, 1770, Methodist Archives and Research Center, John Rylands Library, University of Manchester, Manchester, England. (Hereafter cited as Methodist Archives.)
23. Wesley, *Letters*, vol. 5, p. 257.
24. *Ibid.*, vol. 6, pp. 290-91.
25. Taft, *Holy Women*, vol. 2, p. 75. Most of Mr. Taft's long article on Mrs. Crosby is an extract from her journal.
26. Moore, *Fletcher*, p. 112.
27. William Mallitt, "An Account of S. Mallitt," *Arminian Magazine* 11(1788):93.
28. Moore, *Fletcher*, p. 50.
29. Burns, *Fletcher*, pp. 164-67.

30. Taft, *Holy Women,* vol. 1, p. 85.
31. Moore, *Fletcher,* p. 125.
32. Wesley, *Letters,* vol. 8, p. 190.
33. William Bennet, *Memoirs of Mrs. Grace Bennet* (Macclesfield: Bayley, 1803), pp. 19, 53.
34. Wesley, *Letters,* vol. 8, p. 44.
35. Taft, *Holy Women,* vol. 1, p. 84.
36. *Ibid.,* vol. 1., pp. 84-85.
37. *Arminian Magazine* 13(1790):441.
38. Ball to Patty Chapman, August 16, 1776, Methodist Archives.
39. Moore, *Fletcher,* pp. 103-4.
40. Taft, *Holy Women,* vol. 2, pp. 76-77, 83.
41. *Ibid.,* p. 63.
42. *Ibid.,* p. 84 (emphasis Mrs. Crosby's).
43. An example is Mrs. Woods of Wakefield, *ibid.,* p. 93.
44. W.J. Townsend, H.B. Workman, and George Eayrs, *A New History of Methodism,* 2 vols. (London: Hodder & Stoughton, 1901), vol. 1, p. 322.
45. Agnes Bulmer, *Memoirs of Mrs. Elizabeth Mortimer* (London: Mason, 1859), p. 141.
46. *Arminian Magazine* 13(1790):612.
47. Smyth, *Davidson,* p. 98; Taft, *Holy Women,* vol. 1, p. 176; Bramwell, *Cutler,* p. 11.
48. *Arminian Magazine* 4(1781):667.
49. Ball to A.E., May 24, 1776, Methodist Archives.
50. Sutcliffe, *Pawson,* p. 104.
51. Crosby to Mortimer [before 1785], Methodist Archives (emphasis in original).
52. *Ibid.,* November 6, 1779 (emphasis in original).
53. Burns, *Fletcher,* pp. 19-20.
54. Moore, *Fletcher,* pp. 29, 45.
55. Wesley, *Letters,* vol. 6, p. 147.
56. Bulmer, *Mortimer,* p. 131.
57. *Ibid.,* pp. 161, 183, 64.
58. Wesley, *Letters,* vol. 6, p. 217.
59. Journal of Hester Ann Roe, May 13, 1776, Methodist Archives.
60. Sutcliffe, *Pawson,* p. 5.

CHAPTER 4. Minister As Prophet? or As Mother?

1. See appendix, Nancy A. Hardesty, " 'Your Daughters Shall Prophesy': Revivalism and Feminism in the Age of Finney" (Ph.D. dissertation, University of Chicago, 1976), pp. 205-7. Forthcoming from Scarecrow Press.
   Works by authors in other denominations include: Sarah

Righter Major (Church of the Brethren), pamphlet (1835), quoted in full in Donald F. Durnbaugh, "She Kept On Preaching," *Messenger* (April 1975): 18-21; Sarah Grimké (Quaker), *Letters on the Equality of the Sexes and the Condition of Woman* (Boston, 1838; reprint ed., New York: Burt Franklin, 1970); Antoinette Brown (Congregational), "Exegesis of I Corinthians xiv:34, 35; and I Timothy ii:12," *Oberlin Quarterly Review* 3(July 1849):358-73; A.J. Gordon (Baptist), "The Ministry of Women," *Missionary Review of the World* 7(December 1874):910-21, reprinted as Gordon-Conwell Monograph #61.

Writers in the Wesleyan tradition include Luther Lee (Wesleyan Methodist), *Woman's Right to Preach the Gospel (A Sermon Preached at the Ordination of the Rev. Miss Antoinette L. Brown, at South Butler, Wayne County, N.Y., September 15, 1853)* (Syracuse: Author, 1853); reprinted in Luther Lee, *Five Sermons and a Tract*, ed. Donald W. Dayton (Chicago: Holrad House, 1975); Catherine Mumford Booth (Salvation Army), *Female Ministry; or, Woman's Right to Preach the Gospel* (London: n.p., 1859; expurgated reprint, London: Morgan & Chase, n.d.), also found in *Papers on Practical Religion* (London: International Headquarters, 1890; reprinted New York: The Salvation Army Supplies, Printing & Publishing Department, 1875); David Sherman (Methodist Episcopal), "Woman's Place in the Gospel," John O. Foster, *Life and Labors of Mrs. Maggie Newton Van Cott* (Cincinnati: Hitchcock & Walden, 1872), preface; W.B. Godbey (Methodist Episcopal; Church of the Nazarene), *Woman Preacher* (Louisville, Ky.: Pentecostal Publishing Co., 1891); B.T. Roberts (Free Methodist), *Ordaining Women* (Rochester, N.Y.: Earnest Christian Publishing House, 1891); Seth Cook Rees (Pilgrim Holiness Church), *The Ideal Pentecostal Church* (Cincinnati: M.W. Knapp, 1897).

2. Palmer, *Promise of the Father* (Boston: Henry V. Degen, 1859); Willard, *Woman in the Pulpit* (Boston: D. Lothrop Co., 1888); reprinted, Women and the Church in America, American Theological Library Association's Microfiche Series. The genesis of Willard's book was an article in the *Homiletic Review* (December 1887).

3. *Holiness* (New York: Piercey & Reed, 1843; reprint, New York: Foster & Palmer, Jr., 1867); *Faith* (New York: Author, 1849).

4. See Richard Wheatley, *The Life and Letters of Mrs. Phoebe Palmer* (New York: W.C. Palmer, 1876); Edward T. James et al., eds. *Notable American Women, 1607–1950, A Biographical Dictionary* (Cambridge, Mass.: Harvard University Press, Belknap Press, 1971), vol. 3, pp. 12-14; Anne C. Loveland, "Domesticity and Religion in the Antebellum Period: The

Career of Phoebe Palmer," *The Historian* 39(May 1977):455-71; Nancy Hardesty, Lucile Sider Dayton, and Donald W. Dayton, "Women in the Holiness Movement: Feminism in the Evangelical Tradition," *Women of Spirit: Female Leadership in the Jewish and Christian Traditions*, ed. Rosemary Ruether and Eleanor McLaughlin (New York: Simon & Schuster, 1979), pp. 225-54; John L. Peters, *Christian Perfection and American Methodism* (Nashville: Abingdon Press, 1956).

5. Palmer, *Promise*, p. 1.
6. S. Olin Garrison, ed., *Forty Witnesses* (New York: Phillips & Hunt, 1888; reprint, Freeport, Pa.: Fountain Press, 1955), p. 73.
7. See Frances Elizabeth Willard, *Glimpses of Fifty Years: The Autobiography of An American Woman* (Chicago: Woman's Temperance Publication Association, 1889); Anna A. Gordon, *The Beautiful Life of Frances E. Willard* (Chicago: Woman's Temperance Publishing Association, 1898); Mary Earhart [Dillon], *Frances Willard: From Prayers to Politics* (Chicago: University of Chicago Press, 1944); Norma Taylor Mitchell, *Frances E. Willard, "Yours for Home Protection,"* United Methodist Biography Series, pamphlet (Lake Junaluska, N.C.: Commission on Archives and History, 1977); Ida Tetreault Miller, "Frances Elizabeth Willard: Religious Leader and Social Reformer" (Ph.D. dissertation, Boston University, 1978).
8. Willard, *Woman and Temperance* (Hartford, Conn.: Park Publishing Co., 1883), p. 30.
9. Willard, *Pulpit*, p. 62.
10. *Ibid.*, p. 23.
11. Palmer, *Promise*, p. 160.
12. Willard, *Pulpit*, pp. 17-18.
13. *Ibid.*, p. 34.
14. Palmer, *Promise*, pp. 57, 107, 109, 117; *Holiness*, p. 618.
15. Wesley to Alice Cambridge, January 31, 1791, *The Letters of the Rev. John Wesley, A.M.*, 8 vols., ed. John Telford (London: Epworth Press, 1931), vol. 8, p. 259; also quoted with heightened emphasis in Willard, *Pulpit*, p. 111.
16. Willard, *Pulpit*, pp. 56-57. Willard at times became so angry and disappointed with the Methodist Episcopal Church that she threatened to withdraw her membership. In her *Annual Report* to the W.C.T.U. in 1877, she spoke of "the germ of a new church in which, as Christ declared, there shall be neither male nor female" (quoted in Joseph R. Gusfield, *Symbolic Crusade* [Urbana: University of Illinois Press, 1963], p. 77). Also see her 1888 presidential address to the W.C.T.U., p. 46.
17. Palmer, *Promise*, p. 98. Adam Clarke (1762–1832) was an Irishman converted under Methodist preaching in 1779 and soon commissioned by Wesley as an itinerant preacher. Noted

as a linguist and biblical scholar, he is best known to Americans for his six-volume *Commentary on the Bible* (abridged and reprinted, Beacon Hill, Kansas City, Mo., 1967). His *Memoirs of the Wesley Family* was reprinted in 1976 by Van Hoosier Publications, Taylors, S.C.

18. E.g., Roberts, *Ordaining Women,* p. 59.

19. Palmer, *Promise,* pp. 25-26.

20. Willard, *Pulpit,* p. 93.

21. These books were among a genre detailing the lives of early Methodist women, of which Abel Stevens' *Women of Methodism* (New York: Carlton & Porter, 1866) had the widest circulation in the nineteenth century. Stevens addressed his dedicatory preface "to Mrs. Bishop Hamline and Miss Frances E. Willard," and his book was distributed as part of the American Methodist Ladies Centenary Association celebration. Willard served as corresponding secretary and raised $30,000 to build [Barbara] Heck Hall at Garrett Biblical Institute.

22. Willard, *Pulpit,* p. 103.

23. Palmer, *Promise,* p. 34.

24. *Ibid.,* pp. 14-18.

25. *Ibid.,* pp. 21-23. It should be noted that while Palmer uses vivid pentecostal language, she antedates by half a century the Pentecostal Movement, which considered speaking in tongues, or glossolalia, a mark of the Spirit's presence in a believer. Though nineteenth-century Holiness writers, including Palmer, led many to expect to receive "the gift of tongues," Holiness denominations today generally oppose glossolalia, while Pentecostal denominations practice it.

26. *Ibid.,* p. 28.

27. *Ibid.,* pp. 313, vi, 159.

28. *Ibid.,* pp. 189, 208, 164, 178, 174.

29. Barbara Welter, "The Cult of True Womanhood: 1820–1860," *American Quarterly* 18(Summer 1966):151-74, and "The Feminization of American Religion: 1800–1860," *Clio's Consciousness Raised,* ed. Mary Hartman and Lois W. Banner (New York: Harper & Row, 1974), pp. 137-57. Both are in Barbara Welter, *Dimity Convictions: The American Woman in the Nineteenth Century* (Athens: Ohio University Press, 1976).

30. Anna Oliver, *Test Case on the Ordination of Women* (New York: Wm. N. Jennings, 1880), pp. 3-4.

31. See Kenneth E. Rowe, "The Ordination of Women, Round One: Anna Oliver and the General Conference of 1880," *Methodist History* 12/3(April 1974):60-72; William T. Noll, "Shall She Be Allowed To Preach? Methodism's Reaction to Women Preachers in Nineteenth Century America" (S.T.M. thesis, Drew University, 1980), pp. 28-43 (available also at General Commission on Archives and History).

32. W.C.T.U., *Minutes* (1888), pp. 48, 1.
33. Willard, *Pulpit,* pp. 122, 120, 116. This chapter first appeared as an article in the *Homiletic Review* (January 1888).
34. Willard, *Pulpit,* p. 65.
35. *Ibid.,* pp. 132-33.
36. *Ibid.,* pp. 104, 97.
37. *Ibid.,* pp. 63, 66, 39.
38. *Ibid.,* p. 110, quoting the editor of *Pall Mall Gazette.*
39. Willard, *Pulpit,* pp. 46, 47.
40. Her adversaries' antifeminist arguments also raised grave theological problems not acknowledged as such by nineteenth-century mainline churches.
41. Willard, *Pulpit,* p. 90.

CHAPTER 5. Mary McLeod Bethune

1. Mary McLeod Bethune, "What My Faith Means to Me," *The Church Woman* (December 1954):14.
2. H. Richard Niebuhr, *The Meaning of Revelation* (New York: Macmillan Co., 1941), p. 58.
3. Avery Dulles, "The Meaning of Faith Considered in Relationship to Justice," *The Faith that Does Justice,* ed. John C. Haughey, Woodstock Studies, no. 2 (New York: Paulist Press, 1977), p. 13.
4. Niebuhr, *Revelation,* p. 58.
5. Dulles, "Faith and Justice," p. 13.
6. Earl Martin, "Mary McLeod Bethune: A Prototype of the Rising Social Consciousness of the American Negro" (Master's thesis, Northwestern University, 1958), p. 100.
7. Charles S. Johnson, interview with Mary McLeod Bethune, transcript (n.d.), Mary McLeod Bethune Foundation, Bethune-Cookman College, Daytona Beach, Fla., p. 5.
8. *Ibid.,* p. 5; also Dan Williams, interview with Mary McLeod Bethune, transcript (n.d.), Mary McLeod Bethune Foundation, Bethune-Cookman College, Daytona Beach, Fla., p. 1.
9. Johnson interview, p. 2.
10. Williams interview, p. 13.
11. Rackham Holt, *Mary McLeod Bethune* (Garden City, N.Y.: Doubleday & Co., 1964), pp. 21-22. This book is the most authoritative biography of Mrs. Bethune in print.
12. Bethune, "A College on a Garbage Dump," *Black Women in White America: A Documentary History,* ed. Gerda Lerner (New York: Random House, 1973), p. 135.
13. Bethune, untitled autobiographical statement (n.d.), Mary McLeod Bethune Papers, Mary McLeod Bethune Foundation,

Daytona Beach, Fla., p. 5. (Hereafter cited as Bethune Papers.)

14. Bethune, "A Yearning and Longing Appeased" (n.d.), Bethune Papers, p. 5.

15. Newsome, interview with Albert M. Bethune, January 1978, Daytona Beach, Fla.; Bethune, "Yearning," pp. 5, 7.

16. Bethune, "Yearning," p. 7. For more on Lucy Croft Laney, see Catherine Owen Peare, *Mary McLeod Bethune* (New York: Vanguard Press, 1951), pp. 75-77.

17. Bethune, "Yearning," p. 8. As a result of Daniel P. Moynihan's *The Disintegration of the Negro Family: A Case for National Action* (Washington, D.C.: U.S. Government Printing Office, 1965), the term *matriarch* has in recent years been regarded by many as a pathological characterization of black female leadership. It is evident from the context of her statement that Mary Bethune sought to use the term positively.

18. Bethune, autobiographical statement, p. 5.

19. *Ibid.;* interview with Albert Bethune. In 1918, Albertus went back to South Carolina to live and died in 1919 of pneumonia at his family's home in Wayland.

20. Bethune, autobiographical statement, p. 6. Mary Bethune often referred to her school as her second child.

21. Bethune, "Faith," p. 15.

22. Bethune, "Garbage Dump," p. 141; "Faith," p. 15; interview with Albert Bethune.

23. Mrs. Bethune's record of participation in the Methodist General Conference:
    1928—Full delegate, served on 4 standing committees: Boundaries, Episcopacy, Temporal Economy, and Education
    1932—Reserve delegate
    1936—Full delegate
    1939—(Uniting Conference) Delegate from Methodist Episcopal Church, served on committees on Ministry and Judicial Administration
    1940—Full delegate, served on 3 standing committees, including Education
    1944—Full delegate, could not attend because of illness
    I am indebted to Willard N. Rose for this information from his untitled sketch of Mary McLeod Bethune's life, prepared for the Office of Church Relations and Development, Boston University School of Theology, September 1980.

24. For a statement on sexism in the church, see Robert H. Handy, *A History of the Churches in the United States and Canada* (Oxford: Oxford University Press, 1976), pp. 183-84; Jackie Grant, "Black Theology and the Black Woman," *Black Theology, A Documentary History, 1966-1979,* ed. Gayraud Wilmore and James Cone (Maryknoll, N.Y.: Orbis Books,

1979). For two firsthand historical accounts, see Jarena Lee, *The Life and Religious Experience of Jarena Lee: A Colored Lady Giving an Account of Her Call to Preach the Gospel* (Philadelphia, Pa.: n.p., 1836), reprinted in *Early Negro Writing, 1760-1837,* ed. Dorothy Porter (Boston, Mass.: Beacon Press, 1971); Amanda Berry Smith, "An Autobiography: The Story of the Lord's Dealings with Mrs. Amanda Berry Smith, the Colored Evangelist," *Black Women in Nineteenth-Century American Life,* ed. Bert J. Loewenberg and Ruth Bogin (University Park: Pennsylvania State Press, 1976).

25. Martin, "Prototype," p. 73; Niebuhr, *Revelation,* p. 58. Niebuhr's definition is very appropriate for Bethune's understanding of God.

26. Organization of the Central Jurisdiction was approved at the 1936 General Conference. Mrs. Bethune is reported to have said, "I have not been able to make my mind see it clearly enough to be willing to have the history of this General Conference written, and the Negro youths of fifty or a hundred years from today read and find that Mary McLeod Bethune acquiesced to anything that looked like segregation to black people." Also see Henry Nathaniel Oakes, Jr., "The Struggle for Racial Equality in the Methodist Episcopal Church: The Career of Robert E. Jones, 1904–1944" (Ph.D. dissertation, University of Iowa, 1973), pp. 432-36.

27. Kwame Nkrumah was a graduate of Lincoln University in Pennsylvania.

28. Holt, *Bethune,* p. 213. One of the few penetrating studies of Mary Bethune's N.Y.A. activity is Joyce B. Ross, "Mary McLeod Bethune and the National Youth Administration: A Case of Power Relationships in the Black Cabinet of Franklin D. Roosevelt," *Journal of Negro History* 60/1(January 1975):1-29. Other helpful studies are Allen Francis Kifer, "The Negro Under the New Deal, 1933–1941" (Ph.D. dissertation, University of Wisconsin, 1961); William E. Leuchtenburg, *Franklin D. Roosevelt and the New Deal* (New York: Harper & Row, 1963).

29. "Black cabinet" refers to the Negroes who held major appointments in the Roosevelt administration. By 1936 the black cabinet numbered between 30 and 40. See George B. Tindall, *The Emergence of the New South, 1913-1945* (Baton Rouge: Louisiana State University Press, 1967), p. 544.

30. Bethune to Eleanor Roosevelt, Mary McLeod Bethune Papers, N.Y.A. File.

31. The N.C.N.W. was a nonpartisan organization created in recognition of "the need for united and cooperative group action among Negro women." Bethune to Julius Rosenwald Fund, May 22, 1943, Mary McLeod Bethune Papers, N.C.N.W. File. Soon after its founding, it affiliated with both

the National Council of Women of the United States and the International Council of Women of the World. The story of the relationship between black and white clubwomen has yet to be written. Although limited in this regard, Eleanor Flexner's *Century of Struggle: The Woman's Rights Movement in the United States* (Cambridge, Mass.: Harvard University Press, 1959), remains one of the best sources. Another good source is Gerda Lerner, *The Majority Finds Its Past* (New York: Oxford University Press, 1979).

32. Bethune, "Statement Concerning Moral Rearmament Conference, Caux, Switzerland, July, 1954," Bethune Papers, p. 1.
33. *Ibid.*, p. 2; Holt, *Bethune,* p. 263.
34. Bethune, "God Leads the Way, Mary," *Christian Century* (July 23, 1952):851.
35. Williams interview, pp. 13-14.
36. Later, Frazier commented that Mary Bethune added to his "joy of being alive." Martin, "Prototype," p. 84, 108.
37. Williams interview, p. 12.
38. Holt, *Bethune,* p. 258.
39. Martin, "Prototype," p. 79.
40. *Journal of 1952 General Conference of The Methodist Church,* ed. Lud H. Estes (Nashville: Methodist Publishing House, 1952), p. 283. For information about this resolution, I am again indebted to Willard N. Rose. For more on the allegation that Mary Bethune was a communist, see Holt, *Bethune,* pp. 246-51.

CHAPTER 6. Georgia Harkness

1. Georgia Harkness, "The Nature and Reality of God" (1937), Harkness Collection, Garrett-Evangelical Theological Seminary, Evanston, Ill., p. 19. (Hereafter cited as Harkness Collection.)
2. *Ibid.*
3. Harkness, "Divine Sovereignty and Human Freedom—Personalism in Theology: A Symposium in Honor of Albert Knudson" (1943), Harkness Collection, p. 141.
4. *Ibid.*, p. 151.
5. Harkness, *Mysticism, Its Meaning and Message* (Nashville: Abingdon Press, 1973), p. 17.
6. Rufus M. Jones, *Studies in Mystical Religion* (London: McMillan & Co., 1909), p. xv.
7. Harkness, *Mysticism,* p. 23.
8. *Ibid.*, p. 31.
9. See, e.g., Ps. 139:7-10, where the soul, be it imagined in either heaven or hell, cannot flee from God's presence; Luke 17:21; Matt. 28:20. On Paul, see Acts 9:1-9 and 22:6-18; I Cor. 9:1,

15:8; Gal. 1:15-16; II Cor. 4:6. According to Harkness, the Gospel of John contains a wealth of Christian mysticism: 1:5-7, 1:15-16, 3:3, 4:8, 4:24, 5:24.

10. Harkness, *Mysticism,* p. 57.
11. Harkness, "Prayers and Life," *The Intercollegian and Far Horizons* (February 1937):87-88; Harkness' lecture notes on prayer and mysticism, Harkness Collection.
12. Harkness, "Ecumenicity Marches On," *Zion's Herald* (August 9, 1939):800.
13. Harkness, "The Church and Vietnam," U.S. Congress, Senate, *Congressional Record,* February 3, 1966.
14. Harkness, "Germany and the War–Peace," *Zion's Herald* (January 7, 1925):11-12; Sydney E. Ahlstrom, *A Religious History of the American People* (Garden City, N.Y.: Image Books, 1975), vol. 2, p. 378.
15. Harkness, "Germany's Place in the Shadow," *The Christian Advocate* (January 22, 1925):111.
16. Harkness, "Germany and War–Peace," p. 12.
17. U.S. Treasury Department to Harkness, February 26, 1941, Harkness Collection.
18. Harkness and Charles F. Kraft, *Biblical Backgrounds of the Middle East Conflict* (Nashville: Abingdon, 1976), p. 11.
19. *Ibid.*
20. "The One and the Many," *Zion's Herald* (February 25, 1925):239-40.
21. "Ethical Values in Economics" (1933), p. 372, Harkness Collection.
22. *Ibid.*
23. Harkness, "Is There A Christian Aristocracy?" Harkness Collection.
24. *Ibid.,* p. 4.
25. Harkness, "The Racial Issue and the Christian Church," Harkness Collection, p. 2.
26. *Ibid.,* p. 6.
27. Harkness to the editor, *Christian Century* (March 7, 1967), p. 2.
28. Harkness, "Racial Issue," p. 11.
29. Harkness, *The Church and the Immigrant* (New York: George H. Doran Co., 1921), p. x.
30. *Ibid.,* p. 18.
31. Harkness, "Women and Church Unification," Harkness Collection, p. 9.
32. Harkness, "What Price Unity?" *Zion's Herald* (June 7, 1939):27.
33. Harkness, *Women in Church and Society: A Historical and Theological Inquiry* (Nashville: Abingdon Press, 1972).
34. *Daily Christian Advocate* (May 4, 1956):534.
35. Helen Johnson, "Georgia Harkness: She Made Theology

Understandable," *United Methodists Today* (October 1974):56.
36. Harkness to the editor, *Christian Century,* November 16, 1973, Harkness Collection.
37. Johnson, "Georgia Harkness," p. 56.
38. Harkness, "Christian Social Concerns, Planned Parenthood," Harkness Collection.
39. Harkness to a retired minister, May 18, 1974, Rosemary Radford Ruether, Garrett-Evangelical Theological Seminary, Evanston, Ill.
40. Harkness, "Ecumenicity," p. 800.
41. Hymn 161, *The Book of Hymns* (Nashville: Methodist Publishing House, 1966).
42. Harkness, "Transfiguration," *Be Still and Know* (Nashville/New York: Abingdon-Cokesbury Press, 1973), p. 44.
43. Harkness, autobiography written for the Pacific Coast Theological Group (1950s), Harkness Collection, p. 11.
44. *Ibid.,* p. 23.
45. Harkness, "A Spiritual Pilgrimage," *Christian Century* (March 15, 1939):348.
46. *Ibid.*
47. Fosdick to Harkness, February 13, 1957. Fosdick acknowledges a letter from Harkness in which she spoke of her own nervous breakdown; he compares it to the one in his book, *For the Living of These Days.*
48. Harkness, *Dark Night of the Soul* (New York/Nashville: Abingdon Press, 1945).
49. Harkness, autobiography.
50. Harkness, *Understanding the Christian Faith* (Nashville: Abingdon Press, 1974), pp. 162-63.

CHAPTER 7. Ministry Through Marriage

1. Andrew Monroe, *Recollections of the Rev. Andrew Monroe (1792–1871),* microfilm, General Commission on Archives and History, Lake Junaluska, N.C., p. 9.
2. William Warren Sweet, *Religion on the American Frontier, 1783–1840: The Methodists,* vol. 4 (Chicago: University of Chicago Press, 1946), p. 46.
3. Francis Hodgson, *The Ecclesiastical Polity of Methodism Defended: A Refutation of Certain Objections to the System of Itinerancy in the Methodist Episcopal Church* (New York: Lane & Scott, 1848), p. 21; Winthrop Hudson, "The Methodist Age in America," *Methodist History* 12(April 1974):8-9.
4. Sweet, *American Frontier,* p. 496.
5. Sidney E. Mead, "The Rise of the Evangelical Conception of

the Ministry in America (1607–1850)," *The Ministry in Historical Perspective,* ed. H. Richard Niebuhr and Daniel D. Williams (New York: Harper & Brothers, 1956), p. 229; Jerald C. Brauer, *Reinterpretation in American Church History* (Chicago: University of Chicago Press, 1968), pp. 52-53, 141-42; R. Pierce Beaver, *All Loves Excelling* (Grand Rapids, Mich.: Eerdmans Publishing Co., 1968), pp. 59-62, 71; Barbara Welter, "She Hath Done What She Could: Protestant Women's Missionary Careers in 19th-Century America," *American Quarterly* 30(Winter 1978):632; Janice C. Clarke, "Women of the Oregon Missions" (Seminar paper, Reed College, Portland, Ore., 1963), pp. 1-32. For a general discussion of the feminization of American religion, see Welter, "The Feminization of American Religion: 1800–1860," *Clio's Consciousness Raised: New Perspectives on the History of Women,* ed. Mary Hartman and Lois W. Banner (New York: Harper & Row, 1974), pp. 137-57; Ann Douglas, *The Feminization of American Culture* (New York: Alfred A. Knopf, 1977).

6. James B. Finley, *Sketches of Western Methodism: Biographical, Historical, and Miscellaneous Illustrations of Pioneer Life* (Cincinnati, Ohio: Methodist Book Concern, 1857), pp. 499-500; David Marquette, *A History of Nebraska Methodism: First Half-Century: 1854–1904* (Cincinnati, Ohio: Western Methodist Book Concern, 1904), p. 108.

7. Isaac Haight Beardsley, *Echoes From Peak and Plain: or, Tales of Life, War, Travel, and Colorado Methodism* (Cincinnati, Ohio: Curts & Jennings, 1898), p. 61.

8. Leon L. Loofbourow, *In Search of God's Gold: A Story of Continuing Christian Pioneering in California* (n.p.: The Historical Society of the California-Nevada Annual Conference of the Methodist Church and The College of the Pacific, 1950), p. 141; see also Edward Land Mills, *Plains, Peaks and Pioneers: Eighty Years of Methodism in Montana* (Portland, Ore.: Binfords & Mort, 1947), p. 28.

9. Finley, *Western Methodism,* p. 508.

10. Wade Crawford Barclay, ed., *History of Methodist Missions, Early American Methodism 1769–1844: To Reform the Nation,* vol. 2 (New York: Board of Missions & Church Extension of The Methodist Church, 1950), pp. 40-41; Welter, "She Hath Done," *passim;* Sandra Thomson, "Women's Work for God: The Nineteenth-Century Mission Experience," and Jesse G. Lutz, "Foot Soldiers in the Kingdom of God: Backgrounds, Motivations and Expectations of Female Missionaries" (Papers presented at the Third Berkshire Conference on the History of Women, Bryn Mawr, Pennsylvania, June 11, 1976).

11. H. Eaton, *The Itinerant's Wife: Her Qualifications, Duties, and Rewards* (New York: Lane & Scott, 1851), p. 4.

12. *Ibid.*, pp. 10, 32-36.
13. *Ibid.*, pp. 12-27.
14. *Ibid.*, pp. 40-47, 53.
15. *Ibid.*, pp. 7-29.
16. *Ibid.*, pp. 86-96.
17. In the Methodist Protestant Church, women actually became itinerants. See William T. Noll, "Women as Clergy and Laity in the 19th Century Methodist Protestant Church," *Methodist History* 15(January 1977):109.
18. Charles V. Anthony, *Fifty Years of Methodism: A History of the Methodist Episcopal Church Within the Bounds of the California Annual Conference From 1847 to 1897* (San Francisco: Methodist Book Concern, 1901), p. 35; John L. Simmons, *The History of Southern Methodism on the Pacific Coast* (Nashville: Southern Methodist Publishing House, 1886), pp. 28, 37; The Rev. E. J. Stanley, *Life of Rev. L. B. Stateler or Sixty-Five Years on the Frontier* (Nashville: Publishing House of the M.E. Church, South, 1907), pp. 310-18; Glenn Dora Fowler Arthur, ed., *Annals of the Fowler Family with Branches in Virginia, North Carolina, South Carolina, Tennessee, Kentucky, Alabama, Mississippi, California, and Texas* (Austin, Tex.: Author, 1901), p. 140; Monroe, *Recollections, passim.*
19. For a picture of delicate balancing, but not on the frontier, see Anne C. Loveland, "Domesticity and Religion in the Antebellum Period: The Career of Phoebe Palmer," *The Historian* 39(May 1977):455-71.
20. Wade Crawford Barclay, ed., *History of Methodist Missions, The Methodist Church 1845–1937: Widening Horizons, 1845–1895*, vol. 3 (New York: The Board of Missions of the Methodist Church, 1957), p. 113.
21. Macum Phelan, *A History of Early Methodism in Texas 1817–1866* (Nashville: Cokesbury Press, 1924), p. 341.
22. For general conditions, see Julie Roy Jeffrey, *Frontier Women: The TransMississippi West 1840–1880* (New York: Hill & Wang, 1979), ch. 3; Richard A. Seiber, ed., *Memoirs of Puget Sound, Early Seattle 1853–1856: The Letters of David and Catherine Blaine* (Fairfield, Wash.: Ye Galleon Press, 1978), p. 90.
23. Jeffrey, *Frontier Women*, ch. 4 and its references.
24. Colin Brummitt Goodykoontz, *Home Missions on the American Frontier with Particular Reference to the American Home Missionary Society* (Caldwell, Idaho: Caxton Printers, 1939), pp. 181-85, 206-7, 259-61, 286; Emory Stevens Bucke et al., *The History of American Methodism*, Vol. 2 (Nashville: Abingdon Press, 1964), pp. 466-67; C. C. Goss, *Statistical History of the First Century of American Methodism: With A Summary of the Origin and Present Operations of Other*

Denominations (New York: Carlton & Porter, 1866), pp. 125-27.

25. Thomas D. Yarnes, *A History of Oregon Methodism,* ed. Harvey E. Tobie (Nashville: Oregon Methodist Conference Historical Society, n.d.), pp. 117-18. See also Barclay, *Widening Horizons,* pp. 42, 49; Erle Howell, *Methodism in the Northwest* (Nashville: Pacific Northwest Conference Historical Society, 1966), p. 206; William Wallace Youngson, *Swinging Portals: An Historical Account of One Hundred Years of Religious Activity in Oregon and Its Influence on the West* (Portland, Ore.: Privately published, 1948), p. 22.

26. Seiber, *Puget Sound.*

27. Peter French, "The Home Mission in Oregon: Individual Failure and Organizational Success" (B.A. thesis, Reed College, Portland, Ore., 1968), pp. 48, 60; Howell, *Methodism in Northwest,* p. 183; William Hanchett, "The Question of Religion and The Taming of California, 1849–1854," *California Historical Quarterly* 32(March 1953):51-54; T. Scott Miyakawa, *Protestants and Pioneers: Individualism and Conformity on the American Frontier* (Chicago: University of Chicago Press, 1964), pp. 45-51.

28. Myron Jean Fogde, *The Church Goes West* (Wilmington, N.C.: McGrath Publishing Co., 1977), p. 158; Barclay, *To Reform the Nation,* p. 11; Yarnes, *Oregon Methodism,* pp. 234-36. See also Robert Norton Peters, "From Sect to Church: A Study in the Permutation of Methodism on the Oregon Frontier" (Ph.D. dissertation, University of Washington, 1973), pp. 38-64, 85-87, 248.

29. Phelan, *Methodism in Texas,* p. 282.

30. Seiber, *Puget Sound,* p. 93. For one woman's record of the New England frontier, see [Mary Tucker], *Itinerant Preaching in the Early Days of Methodism. By A Pioneer Preacher's Wife,* ed. Thomas W. Tucker (Boston, Mass.: B.B. Russell, 1872).

31. Finley, *Western Methodism,* p. 508; Marquette, *Nebraska Methodism,* p. 109; Seiber, *Puget Sound,* p. 193; Stanley, *L. B. Stateler,* p. 311.

32. Seiber, *Puget Sound,* p. 180.

33. Arthur, *Fowler Family,* p. 129; Simmons, *Southern Methodism,* p. 227.

34. Beardsley, *Echoes,* p. 246; Seiber, *Puget Sound,* pp. 109-10.

35. William Taylor, *Seven Years of Street Preaching in San Francisco, California; Embracing Incidents, Triumphant Death Scenes, Etc.,* ed. W.P. Strickland (New York: Carlton & Porter, 1857), p. 12.

36. Simmons, *Southern Methodism,* pp. 144-46.

37. Chloe Aurelia Clark (hereafter cited as Willson), *Diary,* microfilm UM-87, (General Commission on Archives and History, Lake Junaluska, N.C.), p. 25.

38. Finley, *Western Methodism,* pp. 503-5.
39. Simmons, *Southern Methodism,* pp. 25-28, 143-44.
40. Seiber, *Puget Sound,* p. 137.
41. William Taylor, *California Life Illustrated* (New York: Carlton & Porter, 1858), p. 118.
42. Seiber, *Puget Sound,* p. 150. Mary Deininger penned a parallel picture of unforeseen trials in J. Russell Davis, *From Saddlebags to Satellites: A History of the Evangelical United Brethren Church in California 1849–1962* (San Diego, Cal.: Keystone Agency, 1963), pp. 66-67.
43. "A Prayer Answering God," *Woman's Home Missions* (Woman's Home Missionary Society of the Methodist Episcopal Church, Delaware, Ohio) 4/9(September 1887):136-37, quoted in H. T. Davis, *Solitary Places Made Glad* (Cincinnati, Ohio: Cranston & Stowe, 1890), pp. 273-76.
44. Seiber, *Puget Sound,* p. 138.
45. Ellen Briggs, *Our Pioneer Wives,* [Paper] *Read before the Ministers' Wives Association of the Annual Conference of the Methodist Church, Pacific Grove, California, September, 1908,* microfilm (University of California, Los Angeles), p. 6.
46. Willson, *Diary,* pp. 21, 23.
47. Ruth Karr McKee, ed., *Mary Richardson Walker: Her Book* (Caldwell, Idaho: Caxton Publishers, 1945), pp. 338-39.
48. Willson, *Diary,* p. 28.
49. Clarke, "Women of Oregon Missions," p. 48.
50. J.R. Davis, *Saddlebags to Satellites,* p. 66.
51. Seiber, *Puget Sound,* pp. 145-46.
52. Taylor, *California Life, passim;* Sweet, *American Frontier,* p. 495.
53. Monroe, *Recollections, passim;* Walter N. Vernon, *Methodism Moves Across North Texas* (Dallas, Tex.: Historical Society, North Texas Conference, Methodist Church, 1967), p. 71; Taylor, *California Life,* pp. 44, 48-49; Phelan, *Methodism in Texas,* p. 188; Seiber, *Puget Sound,* p. 88.
54. Stanley, *L. B. Stateler,* p. 312.
55. Vernon, *Methodism Across North Texas,* p. 44.
56. Alice Cowan Cochran, "Miners, Merchants, and Missionaries: The Role of Missionaries and Pioneer Churches in the Colorado Gold Rush and Its Aftermath, 1858–1870" (Ph.D. dissertation, Southern Methodist University, Dallas, Tex., 1975), p. 120.
57. Loofbourrow, *In Search of God's Gold,* pp. 133, 140.
58. Deane G. Carter, *Methodists in Fayetteville 1832–1968* (Fayetteville, Ark.: Central United Methodist Church & Washington County Historical Society, 1968), p. 46.
59. Seiber, *Puget Sound,* p. 44.
60. Briggs, *Pioneer Wives,* pp. 5, 7.

CHAPTER 8. Hispanic Clergy Wives

1. Their situation was parallel to that of women who married priests and ministers in the first generation after the Protestant Reformation in Europe in the sixteenth century.
2. "The Oldest House in the U.S.A.," *American Anthropologist* 7/3(July/September 1905).
3. Paul Horgan, *The Heroic Tryad* (New York: Holt, Rinehart & Winston, 1954), pp. 105, 112.
4. Sturgis E. Leavitt and Sterling A. Stoudemire, *Por los Siglos* (New York: Henry Holt & Co., 1942), p. 24.
5. Alfonso Toro, *Historia de Mexico,* Vol. 3 (Mexico City: Editorial Patria, S.A., 1969), p. 262.
6. Walter N. Vernon, Alfredo Náñez, and John H. Graham, *One in the Lord* (Bethany, Okla.: Cowan Printing & Litho., 1977), p. 51.
7. *Ibid.,* p. 54.
8. As told to the Reverend Alfredo Náñez many years ago by a member of La Trinidad Methodist Church in Laredo.
9. These biographical details were heard from Elida G. Falcón, the author's mother, Rosaura's sister, and also have been verified through Rosaura's daughter, Luisa Garcia, now living in San Angelo, Texas.
10. In the author's possession is a strip of lace made by the inmates and given to Pedro Grado.
11. Stan Steiner, *La Raza: The Mexican Americans* (New York: Harper & Row, 1970), inside book cover.
12. Paul Verduzco (son of Isabel), to Alfredo Náñez, October 6, 1972, in the possession of the author.
13. " 'Godmother' of Port Arthur Mexicans Leaves After Many Years of Service," *Port Arthur News,* n.d., in the possession of the author.
14. Paul Verduzco to Alfredo Náñez, October 6, 1972.
15. *Actas de la Décima Reunión Anual de la Misión Mexicana de Texas* (Chihuahua, Mexico: Imprenta Palmore, 1923), p. 6.
16. "Notas del Campo," *El Heraldo Cristiano* 82/4(January 15, 1919):8.
17. Heard by the author at the annual meeting of the Rio Grande Conference U.M.W. at Mt. Wesley, October 22, 1979.
18. "Report on the Class for Pastors' Wives," *The Shepherdess* 2/2(Winter 1952):17.
19. Jane Pinchot, *The Mexicans in America* (Minneapolis, Minn.: Lerner Publications, 1973), p. 61.
20. Minerva Garza has prepared a history of women's work in the Rio Grande Conference, *Historia de la Sociedad Femenil de Servicio Cristiano, 1933–1970, Conferencia del Rio Grande, La Iglesia Metodista Unida,* mimeographed (available at General

Commission on Archives and History, Lake Junaluska, N.C.).
21. E.g., see *response* 12/5(May 1980):46.
22. These statistics include wives of members in full connection as well as those of associate and local pastors, but wives of retired ministers are not included.
23. Information obtained from Eubaldo Ponce, Board of Pensions, Rio Grande Conference.
24. Paul K. McAfee, "A Real Shepherdess," *The Shepherdess* 2/2(Winter 1952):back cover.

CHAPTER 9. Preparing Women for the Lord's Work

1. For a list of training schools, see Warren Palmer Behan, "An Introductory Survey of the Lay Training School Field," *Religious Education* 11(1916):47-49.
2. Quoted in *An Annotated Bibliography of D.L. Moody,* ed. Wilbur M. Smith (Chicago: Moody Press, 1948), p. 78.
3. *New England Deaconess Association Annual Report* (hereafter cited as *NEDAAR*), 1906, p. 32. All bulletins, annual reports, and journals cited are available at General Commission on Archives and History, Lake Junaluska, N.C.
4. Lucy Rider Meyer, *Deaconesses, Biblical, Early Church, European, American* (Chicago: Message Publishing Co., 1889), p. 90.
5. Cited in Mabel K. Howell, "The Service Motive—Scarritt College," manuscript (Scarritt College, Nashville, Tn., n.d.). The author is grateful to Robert W. Lynn for providing a copy of this manuscript and also for sharing his informal memorandum on the history of Scarritt.
6. J.N. Murdock, "Missionary Training Schools—Do Baptists Need Them? A Discussion," *Baptist Quarterly Review* 12(January 1890):81. Also see Gene A. Getz, *MBI: the Story of Moody Bible Institute* (Chicago: Moody Press, 1969), p. 36; A.B. Simpson, "The Training and Sending Forth of Workers," *Christian and Missionary Alliance* (April 30, 1897):419.
7. For an overview of the movement of American Protestant women into church service, see Virginia Lieson Brereton and Christa Ressmeyer Klein, "American Women in Ministry: A History of Protestant Beginning Points," *Women of Spirit: Female Leadership in the Jewish and Christian Traditions,* ed. Rosemary Ruether and Eleanor McLaughlin (New York: Simon & Schuster, 1979), pp. 301-32.
8. Howell, "Scarritt College," p. 70.
9. *Bulletin of the Chicago Training School* 10(January 1913):15.
10. For Meyer's biography see Isabelle Horton, *High Adventure; Life of Lucy Rider Meyer* (New York/Cincinnati: Methodist

Book Concern, 1928); also Edward T. James et al., eds., *Notable American Women, 1607–1950: A Biographical Dictionary* (Cambridge: Harvard University Press, Belknap Press, 1971), vol. 2, pp. 534-36.

11. Meyer, *Deaconesses,* p. 91.
12. *Ibid.,* pp. 90ff.
13. "Report of the Committee on Missions," *Daily Christian Advocate* 8(May 23, 1888):163.
14. *Bulletin of the Chicago Training School* 12(October 1915):26; 24(March 1923):49.
15. *Third Annual Report of the New England Deaconess Home and Training School, 1891–92,* p. 8; *Second Annual Report of the New England Training School, 1890–91,* p. 91.
16. *Second Annual Report of the New England Training School, 1890–91,* p. 10.
17. *Ibid.,* pp. 18-19.
18. *NEDAAR,* 1906, p. 15; 1910, p. 9; 1915, p. 15.
19. *Ibid.,* 1910, pp. 9-10; 1912, pp. 13-14; 1916, p. 16.
20. *Ibid.,* 1912, p. 14.
21. Howell, "Scarritt College," pp. 19-21, 24, 26-28. See also Mrs. Robert W. MacDonnell, *Belle Harris Bennett: Her Life Work* (Nashville: Board of Missions, Methodist Episcopal Church, South, 1928); James, *Notable American Women,* vol. 1, pp. 132-34.
22. Quoted in Howell, "Scarritt College," p. 35 (emphasis in original).
23. *Ibid.*
24. For conference action, see *Journal of the Fourteenth General Conference of the Methodist Episcopal Church, South,* Dallas, Texas, May 7–26, 1902, pp. 184, 217-18.
25. Scarritt's chair in sociology has had a succession of distinguished occupants, including Louise Young, Ina C. Brown, and Alice Cobb.
26. For Scarritt's history from 1892 to 1918, see Howell, "Scarritt College," pp. 58-111.
27. *Ibid.,* p. 47.
28. *Ibid.,* p. 67; Meyer, *Deaconesses,* p. 115; *Second Annual Report of the New England Deaconess Home and Training School,* pp. 18-19.
29. Reflecting this approach, for example, a class at the New England deaconess school was billed as "preparing the students for personal work and emphasizing the great value of knowing their Bible well in order to deal with all classes of people" (*NEDAAR,* 1910, p. 9).
30. *Bulletin of the Chicago Training School* 10(January 1913):29.
31. *Ibid.,* 28(March-April 1926):17; "Laboratory Work Done by the Students," pamphlet (n.p., n.d.).
32. Howell, "Scarritt College," pp. 68-69.

33. For list, see *The Training of Teachers* (Edinburgh/London: Oliphant, Anderson & Ferrier; New York/Chicago/Toronto: Fleming H. Revell, n.d.).

34. See, e.g., Henry F. Cope, "The Professional Organization of Workers in Religious Education," *Religious Education* 16(1921):163.

35. *NEDAAR*, 1916, pp. 14-15.

36. *Ibid.*, 1917, pp. 36-37.

37. Richard Morgan Cameron, *Boston University School of Theology, 1839–1968* (Boston: Boston University School of Theology, 1968), p. 116.

38. Horton, *Lucy Rider Meyer*, p. 319.

39. *Ibid.*, p. 312.

40. *Ibid.*, p. 322.

41. *Bulletin of the Chicago Training School* 24(March 1923):20.

42. *Ibid.*, 26(October 1924):9.

43. Jesse L. Cuninggim to Merrimon Cuninggim, typescript, Scarritt College, Nashville, Tn., pp. 12, 15.

44. For Cuninggim's analysis, see *ibid.*, pp. 11-17.

45. *Ibid.*, p. 16.

46. Richard E. Tappan, "The Dominance of Men in the Domain of Women: The History of Four Protestant Church Training Schools, 1880–1918" (Ed.D. dissertation, Temple University, 1979).

47. See, e.g., William Rainey Harper's praise of the Moody Institute, at that time classed among religious training institutions, *The Trend in Higher Education* (Chicago: University of Chicago Press, 1905), p. 219; also Murdock, "Missionary Training Schools—Do Baptists Need Them?" and "The New Missionary Training Schools," *Baptist Quarterly Review* 12(January 1890): 101-108.

CHAPTER 10. The Social Gospel According to Phoebe

1. Charles Howard Hopkins, *The Rise of the Social Gospel in American Protestantism* (New Haven: Yale University Press, 1940), p. 319.

2. Henry F. May, *Protestant Churches in Industrial America* (New York: Harper & Brothers, 1949; reprint ed., New York: Octagon Books, 1963), p. 91.

3. Hopkins, *Social Gospel*, p. 318.

4. Aaron Ignatius Abell, *The Urban Impact on American Protestantism, 1865–1900* (Cambridge: Harvard University Press; London: Oxford University Press, 1943; reprint ed., Hamden, Conn.: Archon Press, 1962).

5. John R. Commons, *Social Reform and the Church* (New

York/Boston: Thomas Y. Crowell & Company, 1894), p. 12.

6. *A Dictionary of Religion and Ethics,* ed. Shailer Mathews, (New York: Macmillan & Co., 1921), pp. 416-17.

7. Women's contributions have not been totally ignored. E.g., Abell, *Urban Impact,* and Winthrop S. Hudson, *Religion in America* (New York: Scribner & Sons, 1965) note women's work, although they assign it little significance.

8. See Sidney E. Mead, *The Lively Experiment: The Shaping of Christianity in America* (New York: Harper & Row, 1963: paperback ed., 1976), p. 121. Hopkins called the program the council's "first outstanding pronouncement" and includes the text in *Rise of Social Gospel,* pp. 316-17. Harry F. Ward's *Social Creed of the Churches* (New York: Eaton & Mains; Cincinnati: Jennings & Graham, 1912) is an exposition designed for the instruction of church people. The council's social creed rested on a fourteen-point creed adopted by the Methodist Episcopal Church in 1908. See Donald K. Gorrell, "The Methodist Federation for Social Service and the Social Creed," *Methodist History* 13/2(January 1975):3-32.

9. Men and Religion Forward, *Messages* 2: *Social Service* (New York: 1912), pp. 1-108, quoted in Hopkins, *Rise of Social Gospel,* pp. 296-98. Hopkins argues forcefully that 1912 marks the "official recognition" of the social gospel in the United States, the moment of its maturity.

10. Walter Rauschenbusch, *Christianizing the Social Order* (New York: Macmillan & Co., 1912), p. 20.

11. Mead, *The Lively Experiment,* p. 182. Robert T. Handy has described the Men and Religion Forward Movement as the "high tide of the general Protestant interest in the social gospel" (Handy, ed., *The Social Gospel in America* [New York: Oxford University Press, 1966], p. 11).

12. See Jane Marie Bancroft Robinson, *Deaconesses in Europe and Their Lessons for America* (New York: Hunt & Eaton, 1889); Methodist Episcopal Church, Woman's Home Missionary Society, *The Early History of Deaconess Work and Training Schools for Women in American Methodism, 1883–1885* (Detroit: Speaker-Hines Press, [1913?]); Mary Agnes Dougherty, "The Methodist Deaconess Movement, 1888–1918" (Ph.D. dissertation, University of California at Davis, 1979); and Elizabeth M. Lee, *As Among the Methodists: Deaconesses Yesterday, Today and Tomorrow* (New York: Woman's Division of Christian Service, Board of Missions, The Methodist Church, 1963).

13. Quote from Hopkins, *Rise of Social Gospel,* p. 54.

14. Isabelle Horton, *High Adventure: Life of Lucy Rider Meyer* (New York: Methodist Book Concern, 1928), p. 78. For Meyer's life, also see Edward T. James et al., eds., *Notable*

American Women, 1607–1950: A Biographical Dictionary (Cambridge, Mass.: Harvard University Press, Belknap Press, 1971), vol. 2, pp. 534-36.

15. For the founding of C.T.S., see Lucy Rider Meyer, *Deaconesses, Biblical, Early Church, European, American* (Chicago: Message Publishing Co., 1889; 3rd ed., rev. and enl., Chicago: Cranston & Stowe, 1892); Dougherty, "Deaconess Movement."

16. E.g., Josiah Strong, *Our Country; Its Possible Future and Its Present Crisis* (New York: American Home Missionary Society, 1885); Washington Gladden, *Applied Christianity; Moral Aspects of Social Questions* (Boston/New York: Houghton Mifflin & Co., 1886); Samuel Lane Loomis, *Modern Cities and Their Religious Problems* (New York: Baker & Taylor Co., 1887); Richard Theodore Ely, *Social Aspects of Christianity* (Boston: W.L. Greene & Co., 1888).

17. Handy, *Social Gospel in America,* pp. 11-12.

18. May, *Protestant Churches,* pp. 189-90.

19. Handy, *Social Gospel in America,* pp. 11-12.

20. *Daily Christian Advocate* (May 19, 1888):131.

21. Christian Golder, *History of the Deaconess Movement in the Christian Church* (Cincinnati, Ohio: Jennings & Pye; New York: Eaton & Mains, 1903), p. 307. On Wittenmyer, see Tom Sillanpa, *Annie Wittenmyer, God's Angel* (Hamilton, Ill.: Hamilton Press, 1972); James, *Notable American Women,* vol. 3, pp. 636-38.

22. The first of the series appeared in *The Ladies Repository* 32(October 1872):242.

23. Edward R. Hardy, "Deacons in History and Practice," *The Diaconate Now,* ed. Richard T. Nolan, (Washington, D.C.: Corpus Books, 1968), p. 12.

24. James Dunk, "Phoebe, a Servant of the Church," *Message and Deaconess Advocate* (May 1900):9.

25. I have traced the geographic origins of 164 of the 509 women who served as deaconesses between 1887 and 1914. Of the group researched, 107 (62.5%) came from towns with a population of 2,500 or less. At the zenith of the deaconess movement in 1910, 76.6% of Americans lived in towns designated as rural by the federal census.

26. Dunk, "Phoebe," p. 9.

27. Brodbeck, "Deaconesses and the City," *Deaconess Advocate* (September 1890):3.

28. W.E. McLellan, "The Open Door of the City," *Deaconess Advocate* (September 1898):4.

29. Brodbeck, "Deaconesses," p. 3; Isabelle Horton, "The Crisis in the Cities," *Deaconess Advocate* (September 1906):9; and "The City Problem," *Deaconess Advocate* (July 1896):15.

30. Editorial, *Deaconess Advocate* (October 1911):8.
31. "Our Bit-of-Heaven House," *Message* (June 1889):1-2. In February 1891, the Chicago deaconesses opened a house of this name located "a stone's throw from one of the worst and neediest localities in the city." Three deaconesses there served a predominantly Italian and Jewish neighborhood.
32. *Message and Deaconess World* (June 1893):11.
33. Some deaconesses entered the ranks of the Progressive movement. A novel vocation as a regularly commissioned policewoman in Ottawa, Ill., was reported for deaconess Viola Miller. She is said to have worn a "*star* along with the deaconess bonnet and worked the night shift, 4–11 p.m., especially among the city's youth" (*Deaconess Advocate* [August 1913]:12).
34. *Message* (October 1890):7.
35. *Message and Deaconess Advocate* (December 1895):9. For Taylor, see Louise Wage, *Graham Taylor: Pioneer for Social Justice, 1851–1938* (Chicago/London: Chicago University Press, 1964).
36. *Deaconess Advocate* (September 1911):1.
37. Isabelle Horton, "The Bad Lands of Chicago," *Christian Cosmopolitan* (n.d.), reprinted in *Deaconess Advocate* (March 1904):4.
38. See, e.g., "Acknowledgments," *Deaconess Advocate* (December 1891).
39. "At the Sign of the Three Gilt Balls," *Deaconess Advocate* (January 1899):1.
40. "What Deaconesses Say to the Churches," *Deaconess Advocate* (March 1896):10.
41. *Deaconess Advocate* (January 1906):9.
42. *Ibid.* (September 1899):2; for M.F.S.S., see *ibid.* (October 1908):8.
43. E.g., "Our Sister in the Kitchen," *Message and Deaconess Advocate* (June 1896):5-6.
44. Literature on the Progressives, especially in Chicago, is extensive. For the Christian perspective, see two contemporary writings, Lucy Rider Meyer, "The Italians of Chicago; their religious susceptibility," *Northwestern Christian Advocate* 39/30(July 29, 1891):2; William T. Stead, *If Christ Came to Chicago! A plea for the union of all who love in the service of all who suffer* (Chicago: Laird & Lee, 1894). Also see Ernest P. Bicknell, "Problems of Philanthropy in Chicago," *Annuals of the American Academy of Political and Social Science* 21(May 1903). More recent works include Kenneth Kusmer, "The Functions of Organized Charity in the Progressive Era: Chicago as a Case Study," *Journal of American History* 60/3(December 1973):657-78; Bessie Pierce, *A History of*

Chicago, 1871–1893; Rise of the Modern City (New York: Alfred A. Knopf, 1957); Davis Thelen, "Social Tensions and the Origins of Progressivism," *Journal of American History* 56(September 1969):323-41; Robert Wiebe, *The Search for Order, 1877–1920* (New York: Hill & Wang, 1967); and Allen F. Davis, *Spearhead for Reform: The Social Settlements and the Progressive Movement, 1890–1914* (New York: Oxford University Press, 1967).

45. *Deaconess Advocate* (August 1902):5. The article took its position on the basis of studies conducted by Jane Addams' investigators.
46. *Ibid.* (July 1896):4; (September 1896):13.
47. *Ibid.* (January 1911):10; (June 1897):5.
48. Deaconesses in this work ran certain risks. Confessed one, "I make mistakes still . . . and sometimes get well laughed at for my trouble. I accosted a little bride once and I'll never forget the air of resentful pride with which she drew herself up and replied, 'He's my husband' " (*Deaconess Advocate* [March 1914]:5).
49. Cited by Hopkins, *Rise of Social Gospel,* p. 103.
50. John Atkinson, "Methodism in the Cities of the United States," *Methodist Quarterly Review* 59(July 1877):481-505, defended the status of Methodism in America's fourteen largest cities. The Congregationalist *Independent* had run "seven full editorials, besides minor articles" in February and March, 1877, arguing that Methodists were losing ground in the cities.
51. A.F. Pierson, *Message* (November 1889):7.
52. Brodbeck, "Deaconesses," *Deaconess Advocate* (September 1890):3.
53. Chicago Training School Catalogue (1888), p. 12.
54. *Message* (March 1888):2.
55. See Meyer, *Deaconesses* (1889 ed.), p. 86, for the opening of a school on November 28, 1885, at Douglas Park Mission in Chicago.
56. Rauschenbusch, *Christianity and the Social Crisis* (New York, Macmillan Co., 1920), esp. ch. 7.
57. *Deaconess Advocate* (January 1895):14.
58. "The Coming Billionaire," *ibid.* (January 1899):6-7.
59. See, for example, *Deaconess Advocate* (May 1900):4; (March 1911):7; (March 1912):4; "Wanted: a Mission for Business Men" (February 1896):7; "Save the Business Man" (January 1907):10.
60. Quoted in Mead, *Lively Experiment,* p. 178.
61. Quoted in *Deaconess Advocate* (February 1901):10.
62. Rauschenbusch, *Christianizing the Social Order,* p. 9.

CHAPTER 11. Laity Rights and Leadership

1. Founded in 1830 by Methodist Episcopal dissidents who would not tolerate domination of the church by bishops and clergy to the exclusion of laymen, the Methodist Protestant Church existed as a separate denomination until 1939, when it reunited with the northern and southern Methodist Episcopal branches to form The Methodist Church.

2. For exceptions, see William T. Noll, "Women as Clergy and Laity in the 19th-Century Methodist Protestant Church," *Methodist History* 15/2 (January 1977):109-10, esp. n. 11, 12, 13.

3. Reasons women in Methodist Protestantism were successful in their bid for ordination, while women in other Methodist branches were blocked, are explored in my aritcle "Women as Clergy," pp. 107-21.

4. *Constitution and Discipline of the Methodist Protestant Church* (Baltimore, 1830), art. 12, p. 29.

5. The sole record of this action is found in John J. Murray, "Reply to Reverend Thomas B. Appleget," *Methodist Recorder* (May 7, 1892):3.

6. The northern wing, known as the Methodist Church, was in existence until reunification in 1877. *Constitution and Discipline of the Methodist [Protestant] Church* (Pittsburgh, 1866), art. 12, p. 29. See Edward J. Drinkhouse, *History of Methodist Reform,* 2 vols. (Baltimore: Board of Publication of the Methodist Protestant Church, 1899), the most complete and accurate work on the nineteenth-century Methodist Protestant Church.

7. Murray, "Reply to Rev. Appleget," p. 3. For traces of women's rights sentiments in Methodist Protestantism as far back as 1828, however, see Noll, "Women as Clergy," pp. 109-10.

8. See Mary A. Miller, our most informative eyewitness source, *History of the Woman's Foreign Missionary Society of the Methodist Protestant Church* (Pittsburgh: W.F.M.S., 1896), p. 37 (hereafter cited as *History*); Elaine Magalis, *Conduct Becoming to a Woman: Bolted Doors and Burgeoning Missions* (New York: Women's Division, Board of Global Ministries, United Methodist Church, 1973), p. 24.

9. Drinkhouse, *Methodist Reform,* vol. 2, p. 575; Magalis, *Bolted Doors,* pp. 24-28. For early M.E. women's foreign mission work, see Theodore L. Agnew, "Reflections on the Woman's Foreign Missionary Movement in Late 19th-Century American Methodism," *Methodist History* 6/2(January 1968):3-16; Patricia R. Hill, "Heathen Women's Friends: The Organization and Development of Women's Foreign Missionary Societies

among Methodist Episcopal Women, 1869–1915," *Methodist History* 19/3(April 1981); Magalis, *Bolted Doors, passim.*

10. Miller, *History,* p. 35. See also John W. Krummel, "The Union Spirit in Japan in the 1880's," *Methodist History* 16/3(April 1978):152-68.

11. Miller, *History,* p. 35. In the absence of extant records for either body, we are dependent on Miller for details of these negotiations.

12. *Journal of Proceedings of the General Convention of Methodist Protestant Church* (Pittsburgh/Baltimore, 1880), p. 15 (hereafter cited as *Journal*). Delegates to the General Conference of the Methodist Episcopal Church reacted differently to the presence of women in their midst (Magalis, *Bolted Doors,* p. 116).

13. Miller, *History,* p. 35. Rosalie Porter [Mrs. E.C.] Chandler's *History of the Woman's Foreign Missionary Society of the Methodist Protestant Church* (Pittsburgh: Pierpont, Siviter & Co., 1920) is useful but glosses over many early struggles.

14. Drinkhouse, editorial, *Methodist Protestant* (December 17, 1881).

15. Mrs. John Scott, "The Woman's Home in Japan," *Methodist Recorder* (January 7, 1882):6; John Scott, "Woman's Home in Japan," *Methodist Recorder* (December 31, 1881):8.

16. "Report of the Corresponding Secretary, Mrs. M.A. Miller," *Third Annual Report of the Woman's Foreign Missionary Society [of the Methodist Protestant Church]* (Tiffin, Ohio: Locke & Brothers, 1882), pp. 29-35. There may have been some basis for the men's fears. Chandler, *History of Missionary Society* (p. 55) and Magalis, *Bolted Doors* (p. 28) both quote a reminiscence of Mary A. Miller that "the Society's wish to be independent of the Board of Missions . . . was that it might be able to push its work abroad with more rapidity than the policy of the Board seemed to favor."

17. C.H. Williams, "Our Mission Home in Japan," *Methodist Recorder* (February 4, 1882):3. Indeed, the board even proposed that the society terminate its work in Japan and begin afresh in India (Magalis, *Bolted Doors,* p. 28).

18. John Scott, "Our Mission Work," *Methodist Recorder* (February 4, 1882):8.

19. Miller, *History,* pp. 52, 53-55. Published after adjournment, conference journals of the period contain resolutions passed, but not all that were presented. Reports of the daily activities were carried in the *Methodist Protestant* and the *Methodist Recorder* (available at Wesley Theological Seminary, Washington, D.C.), but in 1884 these newspapers did not consider the squabble over the status of the society important until a storm arose afterward.

20. See Magalis, *Bolted Doors,* esp. pp. 11-40.

21. Miller, *History*, p. 53.
22. *Journal* (1884), pp. 57-58; Magalis, *Bolted Doors*, p. 28.
23. Miller, *History*, pp. 54-55.
24. *Journal* (1888), pp. 46-48, 48-52.
25. Miller, *History*, pp. 79, 32.
26. See extant annual conference journals, 1888–1892, Wesley Theological Seminary, Washington, D.C., and General Commission on Archives and History, Lake Junaluska, N.C.
27. See Magalis, *Bolted Doors*, pp. 119-20; Agnew, "Reflections," pp. 3-5; for interesting texts of the debate, Saranne P. O'Donnell, "The Question of the Eligibility of Women to the General Conference of the Methodist Episcopal Church—1888," *"Woman's Rightful Place": Women in United Methodist History*, ed. Donald K. Gorrell (Dayton, Ohio: United Theological Seminary, 1980), pp. 11-26.
28. *Methodist Protestant* 62/21(May 25, 1892):1.
29. For the stages of this refusal, see *Journal* (1871), pp. 26-28, 32-33; Drinkhouse, *Methodist Reform*, vol. 2, p. 518; *Journal* (1884), p. 44. For details of St.John, see Lyman E. Davis, *Democratic Methodism in America: A Topical Survey of the Methodist Protestant Church* (New York: Fleming H. Revell, 1921), pp. 79-80; Don W. Holter, *Fire on the Prairie* (Nashville: Abingdon Press, 1969), p. 149.
30. See Anna Howard Shaw, *The Story of a Pioneer* (New York: Harper & Brothers, 1915; reprint ed., New York: Kraus Reprint Co., 1972), pp. 122-30; Nancy N. Baumueller, "My Ordination: Anna Howard Shaw," *Methodist History* 14/2(January 1976):124-31; Edward T. James et al., eds., *Notable American Women, 1607–1950: A Biographical Dictionary* (Cambridge, Mass.: Harvard University Press, Belknap Press, 1971), vol. 3, pp. 274-77. In Noll, "Women as Clergy," it is shown that the first woman elder in Methodist Protestant history was Helanor M. Davidson, ordained by the Northern Indiana Conference of the northern branch of the Methodist [Protestant] Church in 1866 (pp. 110-11).
31. See Kenneth E. Rowe, "The Ordination of Women, Round One: Anna Oliver and the General Conference of 1880," *Methodist History* 12/3(April 1974):60-72. For the full story of the struggle to ordain women in nineteenth-century Methodism, see Noll, "Shall She Be Allowed to Preach? Methodism's Response to Women Preachers in Nineteenth-Century America" (S.T.M. thesis, Drew University, 1980); also available at General Commission on Archives and History, Lake Junaluska, N.C.
32. *Journal* (1884), p. 44. For resistance to this decision in the New York Annual Conference, see Noll, "Women as Clergy," p. 113.
33. See Noll, "Women as Clergy," pp. 114-15.

34. Frances E. Willard, "Your Sons and Daughters Shall Prophesy," *Methodist Recorder* (May 14, 1892):3.
35. J.J. Murray, "Are Women Eligible as Representatives?" *Methodist Recorder* (April 9, 1892):3.
36. Thomas B. Appleget, "Men, Persons, Members," *Methodist Recorder* (April 23, 1892):3.
37. Murray, "Are Women Eligible?" p. 3; "Reply to Appleget," p. 3.
38. Appleget, "Men, Persons, Members," p. 3.
39. D.S. Stephens, "Sixteenth General Conference of the Methodist Protestant Church," *Methodist Recorder* (May 28, 1892):1; 53/23(June 4, 1892):1.
40. Stephens (June 4, 1892):1. The minority report appears in *Journal* (1892), p. 64.
41. Quoted in Stephens (June 4, 1892):8.
42. *Methodist Recorder* 53/23(June 4, 1892):8.
43. *Journal* (1892), p. 113.
44. Quoted in Stephens (June 4, 1892):1.
45. *Journal* (1892), pp. 113-14.
46. *Ibid.,* p. 113.
47. Eugenia St.John, "Some Reflections on the Question," *Methodist Recorder* (May 14, 1892):3.
48. *Methodist Recorder* 57/22(May 30, 1896):4; *Journal* (1896), pp. 28-32; *Journal* (1900), p. 14.
49. For a fuller assessment of the "Cinderella complex" and reform calling of Methodist Protestantism within wider American Methodism, see Noll, "Women as Clergy," pp. 120-21.

CHAPTER 12. "A New Impulse"

1. *Woman's Evangel* (Dayton, Ohio), (January 1882):4.
2. *Evangelical Messenger* (Cleveland, Ohio), (October 21, 1884):244.
3. *A History of the Woman's Missionary Association of the United Brethren in Christ* (Dayton, Ohio: United Brethren Publishing House, 1894), pp. 6-7.
4. *Evangelical Messenger* (May 23, 1878):1; (September 14, 1880):1.
5. *Minutes of the Miami Conference of the United Brethren in Christ,* 1872, p. 9.
6. *Proceedings of the General Conference of the United Brethren in Christ,* 1873, pp. 15, 23, 76 (cited hereafter as *Proceedings of the U.B.*).
7. *Evangelical Messenger* (May 23, 1878):1; (October 17, 1878):4.
8. *Ibid.,* (September 14, 1880):1.
9. *Ibid.,* (October 19, 1880):4.

10. Mrs. S.L. Wiest to Mrs. W.H. Hammer, October 25, 1883, quoted in *The Abiding Past; Or Fifty Years With the Woman's Missionary Society of the Evangelical Church, 1884–1934* (n.p.: The Woman's Missionary Society of the Evangelical Church, 1936), pp. 18-19.

11. *Evangelical Messenger* (June 12, 1883):190.

12. *Proceedings of the General Conference of the Evangelical Association*, 1883, p. 59 (cited hereafter as *Proceedings of the E.A.*).

13. *Religious Telescope* (Dayton, Ohio), (July 28, 1875):345; (August 11, 1875):364.

14. *Ibid.,* (October 27, 1875):36.

15. *Ibid.,* (November 24, 1875):66.

16. *Proceedings of the U.B.,* 1877, pp. 83, 112-18.

17. *Evangelical Messenger* (October 21, 1884):242, 244-47, 250.

18. *Ibid.,* (October 6, 1885):628-29; (October 1, 1889):629, 634; (October 15, 1889):660-61; (October 16, 1894):660; (September 18, 1895):597; (October 19, 1898):660; (September 13, 1899):580; *Proceedings of the E.A.,* 1887, p. 80; 1895, pp. 26, 71, 88; 1899, pp. 88, 101.

19. *Religious Telescope* (May 18, 1881):533, 536; (June 29, 1881):633; *Woman's Evangel* (January 1882):1-2, 5-6; (February 1882):20-21.

20. *Proceedings of the U.B.,* 1909, pp. 185, 425-28.

21. *Ibid.,* pp. 429-32.

22. *Ibid.,* p. 433.

23. *Woman's Evangel* (June 1909):164-65.

24. *Ibid.,* pp. 165-66.

25. *Ibid.*

26. See J. Bruce Behney and Paul H. Eller, *The History of the Evangelical United Brethren Church,* ed. Kenneth W. Krueger (Nashville: Abingdon, 1979), pp. 181-87, 221-23, 283-85, 296; Raymond W. Albright, *A History of the Evangelical Church* (Harrisburg, Pa.: Evangelical Press, 1956), pp. 326-33; A.W. Drury, *History of the Church of the United Brethren in Christ* (Dayton, Ohio: Otterbein Press, 1953), pp. 487-504.

27. *Evangelical Messenger* (November 3, 1891):692, 696, 698.

28. *Missionary Tidings* (Harrisburg, Pa.), (October 1895):1-4.

29. *Ibid.* (November 1897):1-2; *Proceedings of the General Conference of the United Evangelical Church,* 1898, pp. 19-20.

30. *Proceedings of the General Conference of the United Evangelical Church,* 1910, pp. 45-46, 110.

31. *Evangelical Messenger* (September 20, 1892):602; (October 4, 1892):633.

32. *Ibid.,* (October 16, 1894):660-61.

33. *Ibid.,* (October 16, 1894):660; (September 18, 1895):597; *Proceedings of the E.A.,* 1895, pp. 26, 71, 88.

34. *Evangelical Messenger* (October 19, 1898):660; (September 13,

1899):580; *Proceedings of the E.A.*, 1899, pp. 88, 101.

35. *Evangelical Messenger* (September 2, 1903):552; *Proceedings of the E.A.*, 1903, p. 106.

36. *Minutes of the Miami Conference of the United Brethren in Christ,* 1883, p. 29; 1884, p. 24; 1885, p. 18; 1886, p. 24; 1889, p. 26; *Minutes of the East Ohio Conference of the United Brethren in Christ,* 1888, unpaginated.

37. *Proceedings of the U.B.*, 1889, pp. 241, 440, 446. See also Donald K. Gorrell, ed., *"Woman's Rightful Place": Women in United Methodist History,* (Dayton, Ohio: United Theological Seminary, 1980), pp. 27-40.

38. *Proceedings of the U.B.*, 1893, pp. 6-7, 16-17.

39. *Ibid.*, p. 33.

40. *Ibid.*, 1897, pp. 53-55; 1901, pp. 59-62.

41. *Ibid.*, 1905, pp. 45-47.

42. *Religious Telescope* (January 16, 1901):1.

CHAPTER 13. Creating a Sphere for Women

1. Lewis Curts, ed., *The General Conferences of the Methodist Episcopal Church from 1792 to 1896* (Cincinnati: Curts & Jennings, 1900), p. 201.

2. For details of these developments, see Elaine Magalis, *Conduct Becoming to a Woman: Bolted Doors and Burgeoning Missions* (New York: Women's Division, Board of Global Ministries, United Methodist Church, 1973); Patricia R. Hill, "Heathen Women's Friends: The Organization and Development of Women's Foreign Missionary Societies among Methodist Episcopal Women, 1869–1915," *Methodist History* 19/3(April 1981).

3. Curts, *General Conferences,* pp. 209-11; Magalis, *Bolted Doors,* p. 119.

4. Curts, *General Conferences,* pp. 214, 219.

5. *Ibid.*, p. 223.

6. *Ibid.*, p. 351.

7. For more details, see Edward T. James et al., eds., *Notable American Women, 1607–1950: A Biographical Dictionary,* (Cambridge, Mass.: Harvard University Press, Belknap Press, 1971), vol. 3, pp. 411-13, 443-44; Clara A. Swain, *A Glimpse of India, Being a Collection of Extracts from the Letters of Dr. Clara A. Swain, First Medical Missionary to India of the Woman's Foreign Missionary Society of the Methodist Episcopal Church in America* (New York: J. Pott & Co., 1909).

8. For more on the Chicago Training School, see Rosemary S. Keller, "The Deaconess Movement: Liberating or Constricting? A Case of the Chicago Training School" (Paper presented

at the Missouri Valley History Conference, Omaha, Nebraska, March 11, 1978). On the deaconess movement, see Lucy Jane Rider Meyer, *Deaconesses, Biblical, Early Church, European, American, with the Story of the Chicago Training School for City, Home and Foreign Missions and the Chicago Deaconess Home,* 3rd ed., rev. and enl. (Chicago: Cranston & Stowe, 1892).

9. *The Heathen Woman's Friend* 1/1(June 1869):1, 2.

10. Frances J. Baker, *The Story of the Woman's Foreign Missionary Society* (Cincinnati: Curts & Jennings, 1898), pp. 9-14; Mary Isham, *Valorous Ventures: A Record of Sixty and Six Years of the Woman's Foreign Missionary Society, Methodist Episcopal Church* (Boston, Mass.: Methodist Episcopal Church, 1936), pp. 7-9.

11. *Heathen Woman's Friend* 1/2(July 1869):12-13, For Willing, see James, *Notable American Women,* vol. 3, pp. 623-25.

12. *Heathen Woman's Friend* 1/1(June 1869):1.

13. *Ibid.,* pp. 5-6; 1/2(July 1869):10-11; 1/4(September 1869):28; 2/8(February 1871):86; 2/9(March 1871):98; 2/12(June 1871):134, 139; Isham, *Valorous Ventures,* pp. 11-12.

14. *Heathen Woman's Friend* 1/2(July 1869):9; 1/3(August 1869):18; 2/12(June 1871):135.

15. *Ibid.* 1/2(July 1869):10; 1/8(January 1870):59; 2/9(March 1871):97; 2/10(April 1871):112-14; 2/11(May 1871):123-25.

16. *Ibid.* 3/1(July 1871):146, 151; 2/10(April 1871):110-13.

17. *Ibid.* 1/1(June 1869):3-4; Isham, *Valorous Ventures,* pp. 15-16.

18. *Heathen Woman's Friend* 1/4(September 1869):29-31.

19. Isham, *Valorous Ventures,* pp. 32-33.

20. *Heathen Woman's Friend* 1/7(December 1869):52-53.

21. *Ibid.* 1/1(June 1869):1.

22. *Ibid.* 1/3(August 1869):20; 1/6(November 1869):46.

23. *Ibid.* 1/1(June 1869):7; 1/5(October 1869):37.

24. *Ibid.* 1/3(August 1869):21; Isham, *Valorous Ventures,* pp. 20-25; Baker, *Woman's Foreign Missionary Society,* pp. 27-28.

25. *Heathen Woman's Friend* 1/3(August 1869):21; 1/2(July 1869):13.

26. *Ibid.* 1/1(June 1869):4-5; Isham, *Valorous Ventures,* p. 15.

27. Isham, *Valorous Ventures,* p. 43.

28. *Heathen Woman's Friend* 2/7(January 1871):77-78.

CHAPTER 14. The Laity Rights Movement

1. See Anne Firor Scott, *The Southern Lady from Pedestal to Politics, 1830–1930* (Chicago: University of Chicago Press, 1970); Sam S. Hill, Jr., ed., *Religion and the Solid South* (Nashville: Abingdon Press, 1972); and Hunter Dickinson

Farish, *The Circuit Rider Dismounts: A Social History of Southern Methodism, 1865–1900* (Richmond, Va.: The Dietz Press, 1938).

2. William B. Gravely, "The Social, Political and Religious Significance of the Formation of the Colored Methodist Episcopal Church," *Methodist History* 18/1(October 1979):3-25. See also Sara Jane McAfee, *History of the Woman's Missionary Society in the Colored Methodist Episcopal Church* (Jackson, Tenn.: Publishing House of the C.M.E. Church, 1934).

3. For a more detailed discussion, see Virginia Shadron, "Out of Our Homes: The Woman's Rights Movement in the Methodist Episcopal Church, South, 1890–1918" (Master's thesis, Emory University, 1976). For early foreign mission work, see Mrs. F.A. [Sarah Frances Stringfield] Butler, *History of the Woman's Foreign Missionary Society, M.E. Church, South* (Nashville: Publishing House of the M.E. Church, South, 1904). Also see Kenneth E. Rowe, *Methodist Women: A Guide to the Literature* (Lake Junaluska, N.C.: General Commission on Archives and History, United Methodist Church, 1980).

4. Belle Harris Bennett, "The President's Annual Message to the Board," *Our Homes* (June 1907):4. For Bennett, see Mrs. R.W. [Tochie Williams] MacDonell, *Belle Harris Bennett: Her Life Work* (Nashville: Board of Missions, Methodist Episcopal Church, South, 1928); Edward T. James et al., eds., *Notable American Women, 1607–1950: A Biographical Dictionary*, 3 vols. (Cambridge, Mass.: Harvard University Press, Belknap Press, 1971), vol. 1, pp. 132-34.

5. Bennett and Maria Layng Gibson, "A Message to Our Colaborers," *Our Homes* (July 1910):1. See also Mabel Katherine Howell and Esther Case, compilers, *The Facts with Reference to the Organization and Administration of the Woman's Missionary Council in its Relation to the Board of Missions* (Nashville: Woman's Missionary Council, Methodist Episcopal Church, South, n.d.).

6. Bennett to Mrs. F.F. Stephens, quoted in MacDonell, *Belle Harris Bennett*, p. 143.

7. Mary Helm to Nellie N. Somerville, August 29, 1910, Somerville-Hopworth Collection, Schlesinger Library, Radcliffe College, Cambridge, Mass. See Mary Helm, *Why and How: A Descriptive Narrative of the Work of the Woman's Home Missionary Society of the Methodist Episcopal Church, South* (Nashville: Woman's Missionary Council, M.E. Church, South, 1912). Mary was the sister of Lucinda Helm, a founder of the W.H.M.S. For Mary Helm, see Lilly Hardy Hammond, *Memories of Mary Helm* (Nashville: Woman's Missionary Council, Methodist Episcopal Church, South, n.d.). For Lucinda Helm see Arabel Wilbur Alexander, *The Life and Work of Lucinda B. Helm: Founder of the Woman's Parsonage and Home*

Mission Society of the M.E. Church, South (Nashville: Publishing House of the M.E. Church, South, 1898). Both sisters were early exponents of interracial work for white southern Methodist women. See May Helm's work, *From Darkness to Light: The Story of Negro Progress* (New York: Fleming H. Revell Co., 1909) and *The Upward Path: The Evolution of a Race* (New York: Young People's Missionary Movement of the United States & Canada, 1909).

8. Mary Helm to Nellie N. Somerville, August 29, 1910.
9. *Ibid.*
10. Belle Harris Bennett, "The President's Message," *Our Homes* (December 1909):8-9.
11. MacDonell, *Belle Harris Bennett,* p. 246.
12. "Committee on Revisals, Report No. 2," *Daily Christian Advocate* (May 11, 1910).
13. *Daily Christian Advocate* (May 20, 1910).
14. *Ibid.*
15. Belle H. Bennett, "Message to the Woman's Board of Home Missions, 1910," *Our Homes* (May 1910):7.
16. Mary Helm, "Do the Women Want It?" *Baltimore and Southern Methodist* (March 26, 1914).
17. See Aileen Kraditor, *The Ideas of the Woman Suffrage Movement, 1890–1920* (New York: Columbia University Press, 1965); Eleanor Flexner, *Century of Struggle: The Woman's Rights Movement in the United States,* rev. ed. (Cambridge, Mass.: Harvard University Press, Belknap Press, 1975).
18. John R. Deering and E.L. Southgate, "Report on Laity Rights," *Central Methodist Advocate* (October 2, 1913).
19. A notable exception was Mrs. J.W. Perry, second vice-president of the Woman's Home Mission Society, who wrote "Why the Women of the Church Do Not Want the Rights of the Laity," *Southern Christian Advocate* (February 24, 1910) and "The Memorial of the Woman's Home Missionary Board," *Nashville Christian Advocate* (April 14, 1910) in opposition to woman's laity rights.
20. J.W. Harris, "Laity Rights for Women," *Central Methodist Advocate* (October 23, 1913).
21. L.S. Massey, "The General Conference," *Raleigh Christian Advocate* (May 7, 1914).
22. Mrs. W.J. Piggott, *Central Methodist Advocate* (February 12, 1914).
23. "Bishops Address to the General Conference," *Daily Christian Advocate* (May 7, 1914).
24. *Daily Christian Advocate* (May 21, 1914). See Donald K. Gorrell, ed., *"Woman's Rightful Place": Women in United Methodist History,* (Dayton, Ohio: United Theological Seminary, 1980), pp. 11-26.
25. *Daily Christian Advocate* (May 21, 1914).

26. *Ibid.*

27. References to this publication, also known as the *Laity Rights Bulletin,* can be found in MacDonell, *Belle Harris Bennett,* p. 247, and in Mrs. T.I. Charles, *Woman's Status in the Church* (Nashville: Department of Education and Promotion, Woman's Section, Board of Missions, Methodist Episcopal Church, South, 1936), pp. 4-5, 10. Deering and Southgate also make reference to the existence of the *Laity Advocate* in their "Report of Laity Rights," and reprints from the *Laity Rights Advocate* appeared in several conference newspapers.

28. Helm, "Do the Women Want It?" This article undoubtedly appeared in the *Laity Advocate* some time before Miss Helm's death on November 12, 1913.

29. *Daily Christian Advocate* (May 13, 1918).

30. *Ibid.*

31. *Ibid.*

32. *Journal of the General Conference,* 1918, M.E. Church, South, pp. 147-50; *Daily Christian Advocate* (May 15, 1918). Figures totaled from roll-call lists are 270 in favor and 50 opposed, but both publications report 265 to 57.

33. *Journal of the General Conference,* M.E. Church, South, 1922, p. 70.

34. These figures are based on a comparison of the membership lists of the 1910, 1914, and 1918 General Conferences with the roll-call vote on the woman's laity rights memorial. For changing leadership in General Conference, see Robert Watson Sledge, *Hands on the Ark: The Struggle for Change in the Methodist Episcopal Church, South, 1914–1939* (Lake Junaluska, N.C.: Commission on Archives and History, United Methodist Church, 1975), esp. pp. 11-72.

35. *Report of the Commission of Woman's Place of Service in the Church,* Mrs. J.C. Handy, chairman (Nashville: Methodist Episcopal Church, South, 1930), pp. 26, 33.

CHAPTER 15. A.M.E. Preaching Women

1. See Richard Allen, *The Life, Experiences and Gospel Labors of the Rt. Rev. Richard Allen* (Philadelphia: F. Ford & M.A. Riply, 1880); Daniel A. Payne, *History of the African Methodist Episcopal Church* (Nashville: Publishing House of the A.M.E. Sunday-School Union, 1891), pp. 1-45; Charles Wesley, *Richard Allen, Apostle of Freedom* (Washington, D.C.: Associated Publishers, 1935). In the 1787 incident, the group was protesting specifically the attempt of a white church official to remove black members bodily from prayer. Wesley notes that "the house of Sarah Dougherty was used from May

to December 1788" as a meeting place for the protestors (p. 60).

2. Daniel A. Payne, *The Semi-Centenary and the Retrospection of the African Methodist Episcopal Church in the United States* (Baltimore, Md.: Sherwood & Co., 1866), pp. 21-25.

3. Jarena Lee, *Religious Experiences and Journal of Mrs. Jarena Lee: Giving an Account of Her Call to Preach the Gospel* (Philadelphia, 1849), pp. 7-15.

4. Lee, *Journal,* pp. 15-17; corroborated by Payne, *History,* p. 41.

5. Joseph Thompson, *Bethel Gleanings* (Philadelphia: Robert L. Holland, 1881), pp. 34-37.

6. Alexander W. Wayman, *Cyclopaedia of African Methodism* (Baltimore: Methodist Episcopal Book Depository, 1882), p. 57; James A. Handy, *Scraps of African Methodist Episcopal History* (Philadelphia: A.M.E. Book Concern, n.d.), p. 345.

7. John Francis Cook, "Outstanding Members of the First Church—September 1, 1840," manuscript, box 1 (ca. 1841), Cook Family Papers, Moorland Spingarn Research Center, Howard University, Washington, D.C., p. 2.

8. Mrs. Zilpha Elaw, *Memoirs of the Life, Religious Experience, Ministerial Travels and Labours of Mrs. Zilpha Elaw: An American Female of Colour* (London, 1846), p. 62.

9. Charles Spencer Smith, *A History of The African Methodist Episcopal Church* (Philadelphia: Book Concern of the A.M.E. Church, 1922), p. 422.

10. *Christian Recorder* (July 1, 1852), ed. page; Benjamin Tucker Tanner, *An Outline of Our History and Government for African Methodist Churchmen* (Philadelphia: Grant, Faires & Rodgers, 1884), pp. 185-86; Payne, *History,* p. 301.

11. Payne, *History,* p. 237.

12. Benjamin W. Arnett, ed., *Budget of 1885–86, Ninth A.M.E. Church* (n.p.: [ca. 1888]), p. 170; Tanner, *Outline,* pp. 185-86.

13. Quotation in Payne, *History,* p. 237. For vote, see Handy, *Scraps,* pp. 189-90.

14. C.S. Smith, *History of A.M.E. Church,* pp. 476-96.

15. *Ibid.*

16. Wayman, *Cyclopaedia,* p. 56; C.S. Smith, *History of A.M.E. Church,* p. 80.

17. Henry McNeal Turner, *The Genius and Theory of Methodist Polity, or the Machinery of Methodism* (Philadelphia: Publication Department, A.M.E. Church, 1885), pp. 165-66.

18. *Ibid.*

19. Amanda Berry Smith achieved an international reputation.

20. Amanda Berry Smith, *Amanda Smith the Colored Evangelist* (Chicago: Christian Witness Company, 1921), p. 47; also see Edward T. James et al., eds., *Notable American Women, 1607–1950: A Biographical Dictionary* (Cambridge, Mass.: Harvard University Press, Belknap Press, 1971), vol. 3, pp.

304-5. For the date of her A.M.E. membership, see "Alphabetical Record of Members in Full Connection of Bethel A.M.E. Church, Philadelphia, Pennsylvania," in Augustus H. Able III, *The Holdings of Mother Bethel African Methodist Episcopal Church Historical Museum in Manuscript and Print*, microfilm (Philadelphia, n.d.).

21. *Christian Recorder*, 9/509(March 18, 1871).

22. Marshall W. Taylor, *Life, Travels, Labors and Helpers of Mrs. Amanda Smith, The Famous Negro Missionary Evangelist* (Cincinnati: Cranston & Stowe, 1887).

23. Smith was not the only A.M.E. female evangelist who went to Africa. Like their white counterparts, dedicated A.M.E. women chose foreign missions as fields for evangelism and professional self-expression.

24. Joseph Morgan, *Morgan's History of The New Jersey Conference of The A.M.E. Church from 1872 to 1887* (Camden, N.J.: S. Chew, 1887), p. 51; *Minutes of The Tenth Session (After Division) of The New Jersey Annual Conference of The African Methodist Episcopal Church* (Philadelphia: Christian Recorder Printer, 1883), p. 17.

25. Morgan, *Morgan's History*, p. 45.

26. John H. Acornley, *The Colored Lady Evangelist, Being the Life Labors and Experiences of Mrs. Harriet A. Baker* (Brooklyn, n.p., 1892), p. 46.

27. *Centennial Historical Souvenir of "Mother" Bethel AME Church* (Philadelphia: Church Historical Society [ca. 1916]), p. 38; Daniel W. Culp, *Twentieth Century Negro Literature* (New York: Arno Press, 1969), p. 444.

28. A.B. Smith, *Amanda Smith*, pp. 199-200.

29. *Journal of the 18th Session and 17th Quadrennial Session of The General Conference of The African Methodist Episcopal Church in The World* (Philadelphia: James C. Embry, General Business Manager [ca. 1884]), p. 253.

30. *Ibid.*, p. 256.

31. See *A.M.E. Church Review*, esp. 1/2(October 1884) and 2/4(April 1886). Only Bishop Campbell's article in the 1886 issue favored women preachers.

32. Edward W. Lampton, ed., *Digest of Rulings and Decisions of the Bishops of the African Methodist Episcopal Church from 1847 to 1907* (Washington, D.C.: Record Publishing Co., 1907), p. 189.

33. C.S. Smith, *History of A.M.E. Church*, p. 159.

34. Culp, *Twentieth Century Negro Literature*, p. 444; *Journal of Proceedings of the Eighty-Second Session of the Philadelphia Annual Conference of the A.M.E. Church* (Philadelphia: A.M.E. Publishing House, 1898), pp. 91-99; *Journal of Proceedings of the Eighty-First Session of the Philadelphia Annual Conference of the A.M.E. Church* (n.p., 1897), pp.

73-74; *Journal of Proceedings of the Twenty-Fifth Session of the New Jersey Annual Conference* (Philadelphia: A.M.E. Publishing House, 1897), p. 4.

35. *Journal of Proceedings of the Thirty-Third Session of the South Carolina Annual Conference* (Philadelphia: A.M.E. Publishing House, 1897), pp. 4, 22; Winfield Henri Mixon, *History of The African Methodist Episcopal Church in Alabama* (Nashville: A.M.E. Church Sunday School Union, 1902), pp. 109-11.

36. John T. Jenifer has contended that A.M.E. delegates "followed the example of the Mother Church"—i.e., imitated the white M.E. Church, in adopting deaconess orders in 1900 (*Centennial Retrospect History of The African Methodist Episcopal Church* [Nashville: Sunday School Union Print, 1912], pp. 251-52). The northern, predominately white church had officially sanctioned the Order of Deaconess at the General Conference of 1892, while continuing to forbid women's ordination. However, the mimetic argument ignores the crucial internal dynamic shown in this essay, in which A.M.E. preaching women contributed significantly by continually pressing the fathers of the A.M.E. Church for full acceptance into the polity and ministry of the Church.

37. (N.p., 1902), p. 23.

38. *Ibid.*

CHAPTER 16. Evangelical Domesticity

1. See Helen E. Tyler, *Where Prayer and Purpose Meet: The WCTU Story, 1874–1949* (Evanston, Ill.: The Signal Press, 1949); Susan Dye Lee, "Evangelical Domesticity: The Origins of The Woman's National Christian Temperance Union Under Frances E. Willard" (Ph.D. dissertation, Northwestern University, 1980).

2. See Gilbert H. Barnes and Dwight L. Dumond, eds., *Letters of Theodore Dwight Weld, Angelina Grimke Weld, and Sarah Grimke, 1822–1844*, 2 vols. (Gloucester, Mass.: Peter Smith, 1965), vol. 1, pp. 201, 208, 224, 228, 235-36, 239, 270; Hugh S. Fullerton, "The Crusade," *Everybody's Magazine* (June 1919):60-61; Elsie Johnson Ayres, *Hills of Highland* (Springfield, Ohio: H.K. Skinner & Son, 1971), pp. 249-52.

3. Mrs. Eliza Jane Trimble Thompson, Her Two Daughters and Frances E. Willard, *Hillsboro Crusade Sketches and Family Records* (Cincinnati: Cranston & Curts, 1896), p. 64.

4. *Highland Weekly News* 1(January 1874), 8(January 1874); Mary F. Eastman, *The Biography of Dio Lewis, A.M., M.D.* (New York: Fowler & Wells Co., 1891), p. 154. Lewis had given a temperance speech in Fredonia, New York, the

previous week and women there had begun marching; however, his lecture in Hillsboro touched off saloon visitation on a mass scale in southwestern Ohio.

5. Mathilda Gilruth Carpenter, *The Crusade: Its Origin and Development at Washington Court House and Its Results* (Columbus, Ohio: W.G. Hubbard & Co., 1893), p. 47; "Ohio Women's Whiskey War," *Frank Leslie's Weekly* (February 28, 1874); J.H. Beadle, *The Woman's War on Whiskey: Its History, Theory, and Prospects* (Cincinnati: Wilstach, Baldwin & Co., 1874).

6. For geographical distribution of crusade activity, see Lee, "Evangelical Domesticity," pp. 121-28. For general reference, see Mrs. Annie Wittenmyer, *History of the Woman's Temperance Crusade* (Philadelphia: Office of the Christian Woman, 1878); Mother [Eliza] Stewart, *Memories of the Crusade, A Thrilling Account of the Great Uprising of the Women of Ohio in 1873, Against the Liquor Crime* (Chicago: H.J. Smith & Co., 1890); Jane E. Stebbins with T.A.H. Brown, *Fifty Years' History of the Temperance Cause* (Hartford, Conn.: L. Stebbins, 1874); Rev. W.C. Steel, *The Woman's Temperance Movement*, with intro. by Dr. Dio Lewis (New York: National Temperance Society & Publication House, 1874); Rev. W.H. Daniels, ed., *The Temperance Reform and Its Great Reformers* (New York: Nelson & Phillips, 1878); Rev. James Shaw, *History of the Great Temperance Reforms of the Nineteenth Century* (Cincinnati, Ohio: Walden & Stowe, 1875); Carpenter, *Crusade;* Beadle, *Women's War.*

7. Steel, *Woman's Temperance Movement*, p. 12. Also see Carpenter, *Crusade*, pp. 46-49.

8. See, e.g., Lorenzo D. Johnson, *Martha Washingtonianism, or A History of the Ladies' Temperance Benevolent Societies* (New York: Saxon & Miles, 1843); George Farber Clark, *History of the Temperance Reform in Massachusetts, 1813–1833* (Boston: Clark & Carruth, 1888); John Allen Krout, *The Origins of Prohibition* (New York: Alfred A. Knopf, 1925).

9. Wittenmyer, *History*, p. 170.

10. *Ibid.*, pp. 351, 381, 444, 538; Frances E. Willard, *Woman and Temperance: Or, The Work and Workers of the Woman's Christian Temperance Union* (Hartford, Conn.: Park Publishing Co., 1883), p. 529.

11. Wittenmyer, *History*, pp. 264, 208, 224, 176.

12. Beadle, *Women's War*, p. 113.

13. Wittenmyer, *History*, p. 352.

14. Carpenter, *Crusade*, p. 38.

15. Stewart, *Memories*, p. 194.

16. Thompson, *Hillsboro Crusade*, p. 83.

17. Daniels, *Temperance Reform*, p. 294. For themes of sanctification and perfection, see John L. Peters, *Christian Perfection*

and American Methodism (Nashville: Abingdon Press, 1956).
18. Wittenmyer, *History,* pp. 339, 737.
19. Stewart, *Memories,* p. 214.
20. Wittenmyer, *History,* p. 142.
21. Carpenter, *Crusade,* pp. 35-36.
22. Steel, *Woman's Temperance Movement,* p. 11.
23. Wittenmyer, *History,* p. 226. See also pp. 232, 331-32; Aaron Merritt Mills, *Life and Labors of Mrs. Mary A. Woodbridge* (Ravenna, Ohio: F.W. Woodbridge, 1895), p. 57; Julia R. Parish, *The Poems and Written Addresses of Mary T. Lathrap* (n.p.: Woman's Christian Temperance Union of Michigan, 1895).
24. Carpenter, *Crusade,* p. 152.
25. Stewart, *Memories,* p. 164.
26. Carpenter, *Crusade,* p. 150.
27. Wittenmyer, *History,* p. 289. See *Union Signal* (December 20, 1883) for the crusaders' perspective ten years later.
28. Beadle, *Woman's War,* p. 66.
29. Wittenmyer, *History,* pp. 20, 106, 217, 99.
30. Timothy L. Smith, *Revivalism & Social Reform: American Protestantism on the Eve of the Civil War* (New York: Harper & Row, 1957), p. 144. I am deeply indebted to Smith's work in the development of my ideas.
31. Mary Henry Rossiter, *My Mother's Life: The Evolution of a Recluse* (Chicago: Fleming H. Revell, 1900), p. 135.
32. Wittenmyer, *History,* pp. 152-68, 533-44, 399-412, 228-44; *New York Tribune,* February 26, 1874.
33. Wittenmyer, *History,* pp. 81, 685.
34. Thompson, *Hillsboro Crusade,* pp. 100-10.
35. Steel, Woman's Temperance Movement, p. 72.
36. *Ibid.,* p. 26; Stewart, *Memories,* pp. 136, 188; Wittenmyer, *History,* pp. 295-96 and *passim.*
37. Stebbins, *Fifty Years' History,* pp. 324-25.
38. Carpenter, *Crusade,* pp. 46-145 *passim.*
39. Wittenmyer, *History,* p. 193.
40. Daniels, *Temperance Reform,* pp. 257-58.
41. Steel, *Woman's Temperance Movement,* p. 78. Also see Wittenmyer, *History, passim.*
42. Wittenmyer, *History,* p. 792.
43. Stebbins, *Fifty Years' History,* p. 492.
44. Wittenmyer, *History,* p. 131.
45. *Ibid.,* pp. 46-293 *passim;* Stebbins, *Fifty Years' History,* pp. 378-80; Stewart, *Memories,* p. 231; Carpenter, *Crusade,* p. 67.
46. Stewart, *Memories,* pp. 234-35; Carpenter, *Crusade,* pp. 105-106, 135-38, 59.
47. Stewart, *Memories,* pp. 302-306; Wittenmyer, *History,* pp. 7-305 *passim.*
48. Wittenmyer, *History,* p. 422.

49. Stewart, *Memories,* pp. 390-93; *Cincinnati Commercial,* June 19, 1874.
50. Willard and Mary E. Livermore, eds., *A Woman of the Century* (New York: Charles Wells Moulton, 1893), pp. 127-29.
51. Brown to *Union Signal* (October 31, 1895).
52. Willard, *Woman and Temperance,* pp. 121-26; *Woman of Century,* pp. 505-506, 785.
53. Willard, *Woman and Temperance,* p. 126.
54. Katherine Lente Stevenson, *A Brief History of the Woman's Christian Temperance Union* (Evanston, Ill.: The Union Signal, 1907), ch. 3.
55. *Woman's Journal* (February 28, 1874).

CHAPTER 17. For God and Home and Native Land

1. Quote is from Frances E. Willard, *Home Protection Manual: Containing an Argument for the Temperance Ballot for Woman and How to Obtain It as a Means of Home Protection* (New York: The Independent Office, 1879), p. 6. The W.C.T.U.'s membership stood at 143,973 in 1890 (Helen E. Tyler, *Where Prayer and Purpose Meet: The W.C.T.U. Story* [Evanston, Ill.: Signal Press, 1949], p. 105).
2. See Gerda Lerner, "Placing Women in History: A 1975 Perspective," *Liberating Women's History,* ed. Bernice Carroll (Urbana: University of Illinois Press, 1976); Mary Ritter Beard, *Woman as Force in History: A Study in Traditions and Realities* (New York: Macmillan Co., 1946).
3. See Annie T. Wittenmyer, *Woman's Work for Jesus* (New York: Nelson & Phillips, 1873); Wittenmyer, *Under the Guns: A Woman's Reminiscences of the Civil War, with an Introduction by Mrs. General U.S. Grant* (Boston, Mass.: E.B. Stillings & Co., 1895). For Wittenmyer's life, see Tom Sillanpa, *Annie Wittenmyer, God's Angel* (Hamilton, Ill.: Hamilton Press, 1972); Edward T. James et al., eds., *Notable American Women, 1607–1950: A Biographical Dictionary* (Cambridge, Mass.: Harvard University Press, Belknap Press, 1971), vol. 3, pp. 636-38.
4. Wittenmyer, *Woman's Work,* p. 55. For Methodist home mission work, see Ruth Esther Meeker, *Six Decades of Service, 1880–1940: A History of the Woman's Home Missionary Society of the Methodist Episcopal Church* (Cincinnati: Woman's Home Missionary Society, 1969); Arabel Wilbur Alexander, *The Life and Work of Lucinda B. Helm, Founder of the Woman's Parsonage and Home Missionary Society of the M.E. Church, South* (Nashville: Publishing House of the Methodist Episcopal Church, South, 1898).

5. Jane Marie Bancroft Robinson, *Deaconesses in Europe and Their Lessons for America* (New York: Hunt & Eaton, 1889).
6. Wittenmyer, *Woman's Work*, pp. 5-6.
7. *Ibid.*, p. 214.
8. Frances E. Willard, "The Dawn of Woman's Day," *Our Day: A Record and Review of Current Reform* 2/11: 345.
9. *Ibid.*, p. 347.
10. Willard, *Glimpses of Fifty Years: The Autobiography of an American Woman* (Chicago: Woman's Temperance Publishing Association, 1889; reprint ed., New York: Hacker, 1970), p. 331. Hannah Whitall Smith was a national evangelist for the W.C.T.U. in the early 1880s.
11. Willard, "Organization," *Report of the International Council of Women, Assembled by the National Woman Suffrage Association, Washington, D.C., United States of America* (Washington, D.C.: Rufus H. Darby, 1888), p. 223.
12. *Ibid.*, p. 224.
13. Sarepta M. Irish Henry, *The Pledge and the Cross: A History of Our Pledge Roll* (New York: National Temperance Society & Publication House, 1879), p. 14 (emphasis in original).
14. Margaret Rossiter White, *The Whirlwind of the Lord: The Story of Mrs. S.M.I. Henry* (Washington, D.C.: Review & Herald Publishing Association, 1953); Mary Henry Rossiter, *My Mother's Life: The Evolution of a Recluse* (Chicago: Fleming H. Revell, 1900).
15. Willard, "The New Chivalry," speech given March 3, 1871, typescript. See Mary Earhart Dillon, *Frances Willard: From Prayers to Politics* (Chicago: University of Chicago Press, 1944); James, *Notable American Women*, vol. 3, pp. 613-19.
16. Willard, *A White Life for Two* (Chicago: Woman's Temperance Publishing Association, 1890), p. 6.
17. Willard, "Woman's Cause Is Man's," *Arena* 5:715.
18. See Susan Dye Lee, "Evangelical Domesticity: The Origins of the Woman's National Christian Temperance Union under Frances E. Willard" (Ph.D. dissertation, Northwestern University, 1980).
19. Willard, *Occupations for Women* (New York: Success, 1897), p. 24.
20. Willard, *Woman and Temperance* (Hartford, Conn.: Park, 1883), p. 310.
21. Willard, "New Chivalry," pp. 1-2.
22. Willard, "Woman's Cause," pp. 715-16.
23. See Julia R. Parish, ed., *The Poems and Written Addresses of Mary T. Lathrap with a Short Sketch of Her Life* (n.p.: Woman's Christian Temperance Union of Michigan, 1895); Aaron Merritt Hills, *Life and Labors of Mrs. Mary A. Woodbridge* (Ravenna, Ohio: F.W. Woodbridge, 1895).
24. Hills, *Life of Mary Woodbridge*, p. 155.

25. Parish, *Addresses of Mary Lathrap*, pp. 386-87.
26. Rossiter, *My Mother's Life*, p. 135.
27. Willard, "Temperance," *Report of the International Council of Women* (1888), p. 114.
28. Willard, *How to Win: A Book for Girls* (New York: Funk & Wagnalls, 1888), p. 54.
29. Parish, *Addresses of Mary Lathrap*, pp. 322ff.
30. Willard, *Home Protection Manual*, p. 27.
31. Willard, *Do Everything: A Handbook for the World's White Ribboners* (Chicago: Woman's Temperance Publishing Association, 1895), p. 45.
32. Willard, *White Life for Two*, pp. 14-15.
33. Willard, *Do Everything*, pp. 181-82.

CHAPTER 18. Korean Women in Hawaii

1. Churches sending missionaries to Korea in the 1880s and 1890s were the Methodist Episcopal, the Methodist Episcopal, South, the northern and southern Presbyterians, the Baptist, and the Protestant Episcopal. See Hyo-chae Lee, "Protestant Missionary Work and the Enlightenment of Korean Women," *Korea Journal* 17/11(November 1977): 33-50; L. George Paik, *The History of Protestant Missions in Korea, 1832–1910*, 2nd ed. (Pyeng Yang, Korea: Union Christian College Press, 1929). A Series of Reprints of Western Books on Korea, No. 6 (Seoul: Yonsei University Press, 1971).
2. Warren W. Kim, *Koreans in America* (Seoul: Po Chin Chai Printing Co., 1971), p. 10.
3. Esther K. Arinaga, "Contributions of Korean Immigrant Women," *Montage: An Ethnic History of Women in Hawaii*, ed. Nancy Foon Young and Judy R. Parrish (Honolulu: General Assistance Center for the Pacific College of Educational Foundations, University of Hawaii, 1977), pp. 73-74; Linda Shin, "Koreans in America," *Roots: An Asian American Reader*, ed. Amy Tachiki et al. (Los Angeles: Continental Graphics, 1971), p. 200.
4. Arinaga, "Contributions," p. 73.
5. Kingsley K. Lyu, "Korean Nationalist Activities in Hawaii and the Continental United States, 1900–1945," Part I: 1900–1919, *Amerasia Journal* 4/1 (1977): 38-42. Also see Lee Houchins and Chang-su Houchins, "The Korean Experience in America, 1903–1924," *The Asian American: The Historical Experience*, ed. Norris Hundley, Jr. (Santa Barbara, Cal.: Clio Press, 1976), pp. 130-32.
6. Arinaga, "Contributions," pp. 73-74. Persons involved in Arinaga's study requested anonymity. Only their generational

position is indicated.

7. See R. Pierce Beaver, *American Protestant Women in World Mission: A History of the First Feminist Movement in America,* formerly *All Loves Excelling* (Grand Rapids, Mich.: Eerdmans Publishing Co., 1968, rev. ed. 1980), pp. 121-22.

8. Arinaga, "Contributions," p. 74.

9. Hwang-kyung Ko, "Korean Women and Education," *Korea Journal* 4/12(February 1964):11.

10. Mary Cooke, "Korean Women Toiled in Camps," *Honolulu Star-Bulletin and Advertiser,* January 1973.

11. Bernice B.H. Kim, "The Koreans in Hawaii" (Master's thesis, University of Hawaii, 1937), p. 120.

12. Harold H. Sunoo and Sonia S. Sunoo, "Heritage of the First Korean Women Immigrants in the United States," *Koreans in America, Korean Christian Scholars Journal,* no. 2, ed. Byong-sur Kim et al. (Fayette, Mo.: Association of the Korean Christian Scholars in North America, 1977), p. 145.

13. A picture bride interviewed by the author in 1978.

14. B.B.H. Kim, *Koreans in Hawaii,* p. 121.

15. Arinaga, "Contributions," p. 75.

16. B.B.H. Kim, *Koreans in Hawaii,* p. 122.

17. Arinaga, "Contributions," pp. 75, 77.

18. Hyo-jae Lee, "Life in Urban Korea," *Transactions of the Royal Asiatic Society, Korea Branch* (1971):47; B.B.H. Kim, *Koreans in Hawaii,* pp. 164-65.

19. Arinaga, "Contributions," p. 78.

20. Sunoo and Sunoo, "Heritage," pp. 165-68; Lyu, "Korean Nationalist Activities," Part I, p. 29.

21. Arinaga, "Contributions," p. 78.

22. Ko, "Korean Women and Education," p. 10.

23. *Ibid.,* p. 11.

24. See Beaver, *American Protestant Women,* pp. 119-29.

25. *Ibid.*

26. Yŏng-ock Park, "The Women's Modernization Movement in Korea," *Virtues in Conflict: Tradition and the Korean Woman Today,* ed. Sandra Mattielli (Seoul: Royal Asiatic Society, Korea Branch, 1977), p. 105.

27. Yung-Chung Kim, ed., *Women of Korea: A History from the Ancient Times to 1945* (Seoul: Ewha Woman's University Press, 1976), pp. 261, 266.

28. Park, *Women's Modernization Movement,* p. 106; Yung-Chung Kim, *Women of Korea,* p. 249.

29. Hyung-Chan Kim and Wayne Patterson, *The Koreans in America, 1882–1974: A Chronology and Fact Book,* Ethnic Chronology Series, no. 16 (Dobbs Ferry, N.Y.: Oceana, 1974), pp. v-vi.

30. Hei-Chu Kim, Won-Moo Hur, and Kwang-Chung Kim, "Ethnic Role of the Korean Church in the Chicago Area,"

mimeographed (Western Illinois University, Macomb, Ill., n.d.), p. 3.

31. Kim and Patterson, *Koreans in America,* pp. v-vi.
32. Hei-Chu Kim et al., "Ethnic Role," p. 3; Shin, "Koreans in America," p. 201.
33. Kim and Patterson, *Koreans in America,* p. 127.
34. *Ibid.,* pp. 136-37.
35. Shin, "Koreans in America," p. 204; Lyu, "Korean Nationalist Activities," Part 1, p. 24.
36. Sara Lee Yang, "75 Years of Progress for the Koreans in Hawaii," *The 75th Anniversary of Korean Immigration to Hawaii: 1903–1978* (Honolulu: 75th Anniversary of Korean Immigration to Hawaii Committee, 1978), p. 17.
37. A picture bride interviewed in 1976.
38. Yŏng-ho Ch'oe, "The Early Korean Immigrants to Hawaii: A Background History," *Korean Immigrants in Hawaii: A Symposium on Their Background History, Acculturation and Public Policy Issues,* ed. Myŏngsup Shin and Daniel B. Lee (Honolulu: University of Hawaii, 1978), p. 2.
39. Lyu, "Korean Nationalist Activities," Part 2: 1919–1945, *Amerasia Journal* 4/2 (1977): 59-60; W.W. Kim, *Koreans in America,* p. 233.
40. W.W. Kim, *Koreans in America,* pp. 238-39.
41. A picture bride interviewed in 1975.

CHAPTER 19. Shaping a New Society

1. See *Twelfth Annual Report, Woman's Parsonage and Home Mission Society* (Nashville: Publishing House of the Methodist Episcopal Church, South, 1898), p. 47 (hereafter cited as numbered *Report*); 21st *Report* (1907), p. 8; 22nd *Report* (1908), p. 41; Mrs. R. W. MacDonell, *Belle Harris Bennett, Her Life Work* (Nashville: Board of Missions, Methodist Episcopal Church, South, 1928), pp. 88-91; Noreen Dunn Tatum, *A Crown of Service: A Story of Woman's Work in the Methodist Episcopal Church, South from 1878–1940* (Nashville: Board of Missions, Women's Division of Christian Service, 1960), pp. 349-62.
2. 22nd *Report* (1908), p. 41.
3. The woman's home missionary organization formed in 1886 as a result of the vision of Laura Haygood and others was originally simply a department within the southern Board of Church Extension called the Woman's Department of Church Extension. Its assigned duty was to collect funds for purchasing and securing parsonages for southern Methodist ministers. In 1890 they were granted increased authority—to build parson-

ages as well as raise funds for them—with the name of the organization changed to the Woman's Parsonage and Home Mission Society. In 1898 the deaconess program was inaugurated and the name became the Woman's Home Missionary Society. See Sara Estelle Haskin, *Women and Missions in the Methodist Episcopal Church, South* (Nashville: Publishing House of the M.E. Church, South, 1925), pp. 27-33; Tatum, *Crown of Service,* pp. 21-28.

4. Elam Franklin Dempsey, *Atticus Green* (sic) *Haygood* (Nashville: Methodist Publishing House, 1940), pp. 200-219. Also see Harold Wilson Mann, *Atticus Greene Haygood: Methodist Bishop, Editor, and Educator* (Athens, Ga.: University of Georgia Press, 1965), p. 235.

5. See Paul M. Gaston, *The New South Creed, A Study in Southern Mythmaking* (New York: Alfred A. Knopf, 1970).

6. (New York: Phillips & Hunt, 1881.)

7. In comparing Atticus and Laura Haygood, my inspiration comes from Virginia Woolf, who, in *A Room of One's Own,* approached the question of the limited literary achievement of women in past history through the differential advantages traditionally offered brothers over sisters. "Let me imagine, since facts are so hard to come by, what would have happened had Shakespeare had a wonderfully gifted sister, called Judith" ([New York: Harcourt, Brace, & World, 1929], p. 48).

8. Mann, *Atticus Haygood,* pp. 7, 68; Oswald Eugene Brown and Anna Muse Brown, *Life and Letters of Laura Askew Haygood* (Nashville: Publishing House of the M.E. Church, South, 1904), pp. 1-98. See Anne Firor Scott, "Women, Religion and Social Change in the South, 1830–1930," *Religion and the Solid South,* ed. Sam S. Hill, Jr. (Nashville: Abingdon Press, 1972), p. 109: "Church work was the essential first step in the emancipation of thousands of southern women from their antebellum image of themselves and of woman's sphere." Donald G. Mathews has contended that like southern blacks, white southern women used evanglicalism "to fend off oppression, secure their personal and group identity, and assert themselves in new and sometimes surprising ways" (*Religion in the Old South* [Chicago: University of Chicago Press, 1977], p. 102).

9. Brown and Brown, *Laura Haygood,* p. 69.

10. *Ibid.,* p. 32.

11. *Ibid.,* pp. 82, 76.

12. See Scott, *The Southern Lady: From Pedestal to Politics, 1830–1930* (Chicago: University of Chicago Press, 1970), esp. pp. 142-43, and "Women, Religion and Social Change," pp. 92-121. Also see Jacquelyn Dowd Hall, *Revolt Against Chivalry: Jessie Daniel Ames and the Women's Campaign Against Lynching* (New York: Columbia University Press,

1979), esp. pp. 59-106.

13. See Scott, "Women, Religion and Social Change," pp. 105, 110.

14. See Tatum, *Crown of Service,* p. 27; Haskin, *Women and Missions,* p. 29; Scott, "Women, Religion and Social Change," p. 106; MacDonell, *Belle Harris Bennett,* p. 85; Brown and Brown, *Laura Haygood,* pp. 87, 96.

15. 7th *Report* (1893), p. 38.

16. 21st *Report* (1907), p. 7.

17. 8th *Report* (1894), pp. 19-20.

18. Tatum, *Crown of Service,* pp. 16-17.

19. *Ibid., p. 26.*

20. *21st Report* (1907), p. 19.

21. *Report of the Thirteenth Annual Meeting, Woman's Missionary Council* (Nashville: Publishing House of the Methodist Episcopal Church, South, 1923), p. 128 (hereafter cited as *Report of Council).*

22. *21st Report of Council* (1931), p. 80.

23. Carroll Smith-Rosenberg, "The Female World of Love and Ritual: Relations Between Women in Nineteenth-Century America," *Signs* 1(Autumn 1975):1-32.

24. Brown and Brown, *Laura Haygood,* p. 87.

25. 13th *Report of Council* (1923), p. 7.

26. Tatum, *Crown of Service,* p. 69.

27. MacDonell, *Belle Harris Bennett,* pp. 264-65.

28. *Ibid.,* p. 264. For Ames, see Hall, *Revolt Against Chivalry.* For Newell, see Hall, pp. 312-13.

29. Newell to Ames, December 31, 1931, Jessie Daniel Ames Papers, Southern Historical Collection, University of North Carolina, Chapel Hill, N.C.

30. See correspondence between Newell and Ames, Jessie Daniel Ames Papers, 1925–1934. Also see correspondence from North Carolina in the League of Women Voters Papers, Box 123, Biennia Series, 1926–28, Manuscript Division, Library of Congress, Washington, D.C.

31. 18th *Report of Council* (1928), p. 139.

32. Tatum, *Crown of Service,* prologue, p. 394.

33. 22nd *Report* (1908), p. 41. See also 6th through 24th *Reports* (1892–1910).

34. 12th *Report* (1898), p. 38.

35. *Ibid.;* 22nd *Report* (1908), p. 112.

36. 11th *Report* (1897), p. 28. *Our Homes* (Nashville) 1–18 (1892–1910) was the organ of the Woman's [Parsonage and] Home Mission Society.

37. 18th *Report* (1904), p. 126.

38. 9th *Report of Council* (1919), p. 82. See also James Cannon, III, *History of Southern Methodist Missions* (Nashville: Cokesbury Press, 1926), pp. 318-24.

39. 21st *Report* (1907), p. 20.
40. 22nd *Report* (1908), p. 163; Tatum, *Crown of Service,* pp. 349-55. See also Mary Noreen Dunn, *Women and Home Missions* (Nashville: Cokesbury Press, 1936), pp. 74-79.
41. 22nd *Report of Council* (1932), p. 108.
42. Tatum, *Crown of Service,* p. 36.
43. 3rd *Report of Council* (1913), pp. 293-94. Quote is from O.E. Goddard and Mrs. R.W. MacDonell, *Making America Safe, A Study of the Home Missions of the Methodist Episcopal Church, South* (Nashville: Centenary Commission M.E. Church, South, n.d.), p. 58. Also see Alva W. Taylor, *Christianity and Industry in America* (New York: Friendship Press, 1933).
44. 3rd *Report of Council* (1913), p. 294. See Donald K. Gorrell, "The Methodist Federation for Social Service and the Social Creed," *Methodist History* 13/2(January 1975):3-32.
45. 6th *Report of Council* (1916), p. 135.
46. 5th *Report of Council* (1915), pp. 26-27, 96-101; 8th *Report of Council* (1918), p. 7.
47. 12th *Report of Council* (1922), p. 148.
48. 17th *Report of Council* (1927), p. 117.
49. 18th *Report of Council* (1928), p. 140.
50. 7th *Report* (1893), p. 38; 18th *Report* (1904), p. 18.
51. 15th *Report* (1901), p. 51; 22nd *Report* (1908), p. 8; 8th *Report of Council* (1918), p. 7.
52. 23rd *Report* (1909), pp. 46-49; Tatum, *Crown of Service,* pp. 30, 390.
53. 15th *Report of Council* (1925), p. 125; 17th *Report of Council* (1927), pp. 116-17.
54. 28th *Report of Council* (1938), p. 148; Scott, *Southern Lady,* pp. 141-42.
55. 10th *Report of Council* (1920), p. 97.
56. 15th *Report of Council* (1925), p. 125.
57. 15th *Report of Council* (1925), pp. 125-154.
58. "Report of Louise Leonard, Secretary, Southern Region, March, 1924," *Industrial Department Reports* (1924), Y.W.C.A. National Archives, New York City.
59. For activities between 1925 and 1940, see Mary S. Simms, *The YWCA, An Unfolding Purpose* (New York: Woman's Press, 1950), pp. 72-73; Gladys Boone, *The Women's Trade Union Leagues in Great Britain and the United States of America* (New York: Columbia University Press, 1942), pp. 176-81; Mary E. Frederickson, "A Place to Speak Our Minds: The Southern Summer School for Women Workers," in *Working Lives: The Southern Exposure History of Labor in the South* (New York: Pantheon Press, 1980), pp. 155-65.
60. Tatum, *Crown of Service,* p. 350. Newell retired in 1938 and was succeeded by Thelma Stevens. In 1939, as part of Methodist reunification, the bureau's work was taken over by

the Department of Christian Social Relations and Local Church Activities of the new Woman's Division of Christian Service. Lodged within the Board of Missions and Church Extension of The Methodist Church, the Woman's Division consolidated the work of six previous women's mission organizations in the three uniting denominations. For the transition, see Thelma Stevens, *Legacy for the Future: The History of Christian Social Relations in the Woman's Division of Christian Service, 1940–1968* (New York: Women's Division, Board of Global Ministries, United Methodist Church, 1978); 25th *Report of Council* (1935), p. 148.

61. Brown and Brown, *Laura Haygood*, p. 89.
62. There is evidence that organized women of the southern church had a cooperative relationship with northern Methodists throughout the period (e.g., Tatum, *Crown of Service*, p. 393; 22nd *Report* [1908], p. 33; 5th *Report of Council* [1915], pp. 96, 101; 30th *Report of Council* [1940], p. 13). See also Thelma Stevens, oral history tapes, Southern Historical Collection, University of North Carolina, Chapel Hill, N.C.
63. 25th *Report of Council* (1935), p. 102.
64. 29th *Report of Council* (1938), p. 124. See also Thomas A. Krueger, *And Promises to Keep: The Southern Conference for Human Welfare, 1938–1948* (Nashville: Vanderbilt University Press, 1967).

CHAPTER 20. Winifred L. Chappell

1. Dorothy McConnell, interviewed by author, New York City, August 1978. Daughter of Bishop Francis J. McConnell, long president of the Methodist Federation for Social Service (M.F.S.S.), McConnell was editor of *World Outlook*, the magazine of the Methodist Board of Missions, from 1948 to 1964, and associate general secretary of the Woman's Division of Christian Service from 1965 to 1968.

The M.F.S.S. (renamed in 1948 the Methodist Federation for Social Action [M.F.S.A.]) was and still is an unofficial Methodist organization dedicated to speaking out on social issues and to pushing official church bodies to act prophetically. See John Milton Huber, *A History of the Methodist Federation for Social Action* (Ph.D. dissertation, Boston University, 1949), microfilm; also George D. McClain, "Pioneering Social Gospel Radicalism: An Overview of the History of the Methodist Federation for Social Action," *Radical Religion: A Quarterly Journal of Critical Thought* (hereafter cited as *Radical Religion*), 5/1 (1980):10-20. (That issue of *Radical Religion* is devoted entirely to the history of the federation.)

For the story of the founding of the federation in 1907 and its connection to passage of the social creed of the Methodist Episcopal Church, see Donald K. Gorrell, "The Methodist Federation for Social Service and the Social Creed," *Methodist History* 13/2 (January 1975):3-32.

2. Beginning in 1947, the M.F.S.A. came under virulent attack because its leaders, including Chappell, had worked with and respected known communists and refused to disavow these long-time associations (Alan Thomson, "Prophetic Religion and the Democratic Front: The Mission of Harry F. Ward," *Radical Religion* 5/1[1980]:34-36). Both in the press and in The Methodist Church, from an unofficial coalition called the Circuit Riders, Inc., the attack on the M.F.S.A. was unrelenting. Chappell died during the year preceding the 1952 Methodist General Conference, which was to participate in the McCarthyist wave of "guilt by association" to the extent of asking the Federation to "remove the word 'Methodist' from its name" and endorsing the move to evict it from its rented office space in the Methodist building in New York City (*Daily Christian Advocate* [May 1, 1952]: 308-9).

Finally, the chief executive of the M.F.S.A., Jack R. McMichael, was interrogated by the House Un-American Activities Committee (H.U.A.C.) in July 1953 (McClain, "Pioneering," pp. 17-19). The transcript of this encounter reveals that H.U.A.C. attempted to smear Chappell's name posthumously, apparently granting her some importance, but McMichael adroitly refused to allow officials to make charges against her (see *Hearings before the Committee on UnAmerican Activities, House of Representatives, Eighty-Third Congress, First Session, July 30 and 31, 1953: Hearings regarding Jack R. McMichael* [Washington, D.C.: U.S. Government Printing Office, 1953]; brief excerpts are reprinted as "From Hearings before the Committee on Un-American Activities . . . July 31, 1953," *Radical Religion* 5/1 [1980]:53-54).

Seven years after the H.U.A.C. hearings, the 1960 Methodist General Conference explicitly repudiated the Circuit Riders, regretting "that any Methodists contribute either money or leadership to such organizations . . . which utilize the 'guilt by association' and 'fellow-traveler' approaches as they . . . develop unfounded fears" (*Daily Christian Advocate* [May 6, 1960]:429).

See Robert Justin Goldstein, *Political Repression in Modern America: 1870 to the Present* (Cambridge/New York: Schenkman Publishing Co., Two Continents Publishing Group, 1978); Ralph Lord Roy, *Communism and the Churches* (New York: Harcourt, Brace & Co., 1960), pp. 291-324.

3. Aware of this author's research, George McClain also has

recently broken the long silence on Winifred Chappell and Grace Scribner. In "Pioneering," he credits Chappell as "a very astute activist and publicist . . . and a primary factor in moving the Federation to a more radical advocacy of a new social order" (p. 12); also McClain, "No Illusions About Capitalism: The Federation on the Eve of the Great Depression," *Radical Religion* 5/1(1980):39-40.

4. The author wishes to thank Faith C. Callahan (Mrs. Wm. E.) of Des Moines, Washington, for providing rich biographical information about her cousin, Winifred Chappell. Additional sources were interviews with Dorothy McConnell, Jack McMichael, Richard Morford, and Willard Uphaus in New York City during 1978 and 1979; Harry Earl Chappell, Winifred's brother; Alumni Records, Northwestern University, Evanston, Ill.; the Archives of the Methodist Federation for Social Action, Rose Memorial Library, Drew University, Madison, N.J. (hereafter M.F.S.A. Archives). For more on Chappell, see Miriam J. Crist, "Everybody on the Left Knew Her" (M. Div. thesis, Union Theological Seminary, New York City, 1979).

5. Whatever her father's reasons for obtaining further education, relocation in a university town affected all his daughters. "One of her sisters married a seminary professor, another held prestigious teaching positions yet it was Cousin Winifred who employed both mind and heart to the fullest" (Faith C. Callahan to Norma Taylor Mitchell, October 20, 1977, files of the Women's History Project, General Commission on Archives and History, Lake Junaluska, N.C.).

6. George A. Coe, *Social Theory of Religious Education* (New York: Charles Scribner's Sons, 1977), pp. 211, 217-18.

7. Elizabeth Meredith Lee, *As Among the Methodists: Deaconesses Yesterday, Today and Tomorrow* (New York: Woman's Division of Christian Service, 1963), p. 34. Also see Lucy Rider Meyer, *Deaconesses, Biblical, Early Church, European, American, with the Story of the Chicago Training School for City, Home and Foreign Missions and the Chicago Deaconess Home,* 3rd ed. rev. and enl. (Chicago: Cranston & Stowe, 1892); Isabelle Horton, *High Adventure: Life of Lucy Rider Meyer* (New York: Methodist Book Concern, 1928).

8. Callahan to Mitchell, October 20, 1977.

9. Since George Coe was associated with the Federation in its earliest years, Chappell may have followed it from its start in 1907. Also see William McGuire King, *The Emergence of Social Gospel Radicalism in American Methodism* (Ph.D. dissertation, Harvard University, 1977), (Ann Arbor, Mich., University Microfilms).

10. "Industrial Missions" (Master's thesis, Columbia University, N.Y., 1920), esp. p. 6.

11. Chappell, *Social Service for Church Women* (New York: Methodist Federation for Social Service, 1918), p. 10.
12. From the books left her, Chappell created the circulating M.F.S.S. Grace Scribner Memorial Library. Winifred also created a posthumous collection of Grace's letters. First serialized in *The Christian Century,* the collection was later published with a preface by Ward as *An American Pilgrimage: Portions of the Letters of Grace Scribner,* ed. Winifred L. Chappell (New York: Vanguard Press, 1927). Also see Crist, "A Story of Two Women: Grace Scribner and Winifred Chappell" (Paper for church history course at Union Theological Seminary, New York City, 1978), pp. 2, 11; McClain, "No Illusions," p. 39; Ward, "Grace Scribner," [M.F.S.S.] *Newsletter* (May 1, 1922).
13. The *Social Service Bulletin* was the federation's organ from 1911 through June 1933. In October 1933 it was renamed the *Social Questions Bulletin* and continues to the present (hereafter cited as *Bulletin*).
14. Chappell to Ward (datable to 1934 from internal evidence), reminding him of elements of their original agreement and citing a letter of that period (M.F.S.A. Archives).
15. A brief entry in the *Bulletin* in the early 1930s notes that after a period of illness, Dr. Ward was resuming his weekly meetings at the M.F.S.S. office.
16. See Francis J. McConnell, *By the Way: An Autobiography* (New York: Abingdon Press, 1952). See McClain, "Pioneering," pp. 11, 17, and "No Illusions," p. 38. Also see Harry F. Ward, *The New Social Order: Principles and Programs* (New York: Macmillan Co., 1919); *Our Economic Morality and the Ethic of Jesus* (New York: Macmillan Co., 1929); *Democracy and Social Change* (New York: Modern Age Books, 1940). For Ward's impact, see Thomson, "Prophetic Religion . . . The Mission of Harry F. Ward," pp. 29-36; Robert H. Craig, "Introduction to the Life and Thought of Harry F. Ward," *Union Seminary Quarterly Review* 29 (Summer 1969):331-56 (reprints by Church Research and Information Projects).
17. *Bulletin* (September 15, 1924):3.
18. These two organizations linked Chappell to the most progressive women of the Methodist Episcopal Church, South, in its Woman's Missionary Council.
19. *The Christian Century* (February 21, 1924):238-39.
20. These distributions were noted in the quadrennial report of the activities of the M.F.S.S. in a *Bulletin* of 1924.
21. "Shall Women Workers Have Special Protection?" *Bulletin* (September 1, 1926):4.
22. "The Present Coal Strike," *Bulletin* 18/1(January 1, 1928):2, 4.
23. Chappell, "Embattled Miners," *The Christian Century*

(August 19, 1931):1044. Also see Philip S. Foner, *Women and the American Labor Movement from World War I to the Present* (New York: Macmillan Co., The Free Press, 1980), pp. 244-55.

24. "Women of Passaic," *The Christian Century* (May 6, 1926): 582.
25. *Ibid.*
26. Special issue of *The Christian Century* (August 5, 1926):987.
27. "The Revolt of the Miners," *Bulletin* 21/3(September 1, 1931):4.
28. "The Strike in New Bedford," *The Christian Century* (October 4, 1928):1191. Also Foner, *Women and American Labor Movement,* ch. 11.
29. "Women's Clothes," *Bulletin* (December 1, 1929):2. See also Chappell, "Women's Dresses and Coats—Backstage: An Impartial Story of a Fighting Industrial Situation," *World Tomorrow* (July 1929):300-304.
30. "Classifications," *Bulletin* (May 15, 1932):1.
31. See *Daily Christian Advocate* (May 24, 1932):594, quoted in *Bulletin* 23/1(January 1, 1933):1.

   The phrase "strike out for deep water" appears in a messy but revealing typed memo, Chappell to Ward, "Re Chicago Meeting Feb. 16 [1933]: The desire of Chicago men to have out-of-New York headquarters is sound. . . . This may be the turn we have been looking for to get work onto someone elses [sic] shoulders—with McConnell not happy with us and the rest of Ex. Com. clucking after us as we strike out for deep water" (M.F.S.A. Archives).

   The issues in the *Bulletin* were "Fascism," 23/7(April 1, 1933); "Socialism," 23/9(May 1, 1933); "Communism," 23/10 (June 1, 1933).
32. Declaration quoted in *The Christian Advocate* 107 (September 29, 1932):1026, mentioning Chappell as a signatory.
33. "'The Social Gospel Crowd': And Now What?" *Bulletin* 22/14 (September 15, 1932):1.
34. *Bulletin* (May 1935):3. On Williams, see Cedric Belfrage, *South of God* (New York: Modern Age Books, 1941), p. 164; Mark Naison, "Claude and Joyce Williams: Pilgrims for Justice," *Radical Religion* 4/2(1978); Papers of Claude Williams, Walter Reuther Labor Library, Wayne State University, Detroit, Mich.
35. "Fritz" to H.F.W., two-page undated typescript memo, M.F.S.A. Archives.
36. Previously cited typescript memo, Chappell to Ward, "Re Chicago Meeting Feb. 16 [1933]."
37. Chappell, "The Red Baiters and the Methodists," *Bulletin* (May 1936):1.
38. See issues of the *Bulletin* from October 1935 through May 1936 for the unfolding and resolution of this debate.

39. Chappell, "Methodist Federation Strengthens Labor Program after Conference," news release to Federated Press Eastern Bureau, May 27, 1936, M.F.S.A. Archives.
40. *Bulletin* (May 1937):4.
41. Naison, "Claude and Joyce Williams," p. 11. Some Commonwealth College archives are in the Tamiment Collection, Elmer Holmes Bobst Research Library, New York University, New York City.
42. "Announce Reorganization: Claude Williams Elected Director," *Fortnightly,* a publication of Commonwealth College (August 15, 1937):1.
43. Naison, "Claude and Joyce Williams," p. 11.
44. *Ibid.,* p. 12.
45. *Bulletin* (June 1942).
46. Interviewed by the author, Brooklyn, New York, July 1978.
47. "Winifred Chappell," *Bulletin* (June 1951):23.
48. Chappell to Ward (1934), M.F.S.A. Archives.
49. M.F.S.A. Archives.

CONTRIBUTORS

VIRGINIA LIESON BRERETON is an educational consultant for the Lilly Endowment, Inc., and a researcher and writer for the collaborative Auburn History of Protestant Theological Education in America. She received her doctorate in American history and education from Columbia University in 1981. Her publications on women and education include the chapter "American Women in Ministry," of which she is co-author, in *Women of Spirit,* edited by Rosemary Ruether and Eleanor McLaughlin (Simon & Schuster, 1979). At the present time, Dr. Brereton is teaching at the University of Michigan at Ann Arbor.

EARL KENT BROWN is professor of church history at Boston University School of Theology and received his doctorate from the same university. He has also taught church history at Union Seminary in Manila, the Philippines; at United Theological College in Bangalore, India; and at the University of Manchester, England, as well as at several schools in the United States. Methodist Church history has been the chief subject of his many articles. He is an elder in the East Ohio Annual Conference, under special appointment.

ALICE CHAI, a native of Korea, is assistant professor in the Women's Studies Program at the University of Hawaii at Manoa and has taught at universities in Korea and Hawaii. She received her Ph.D. in sociology and anthropology from Ohio State University, with a dissertation entitled "Kinship and Mate Selection in Korea." She is lay leader of Christ United Methodist Church in Honolulu and a member of the Committee on Higher Education of the Hawaii District of the church. She also participates in various cultural organizations and sits on the Committee on Education of the Commission on the Status and Role of Women of the state of Hawaii.

MIRIAM J. CRIST is pastor of the United Methodist churches in East Quogue and Flanders, Long Island, New York. She received the M.Div. degree in 1979 from Union Theological

Seminary in New York City, where her thesis was on the life and work of the Methodist reformer and deaconess, Winifred L. Chappell. The Rev. Ms. Crist has been an advocate of women's causes and a participant in struggles for social justice in The United Methodist Church for many years, and is an ordained deacon in the New York Annual Conference.

JUALYNNE DODSON is associate professor and has directed the Research and Demonstration Center at the School of Social Work, Atlanta University. She has been project director for grants on Child Welfare Curriculum Development and Multi-Cultural In-Service Education, funded by H.E.W. and the Georgia Department of Human Resources, respectively. She also has been visiting associate professor at Garrett-Evangelical Theological Seminary in Evanston. She is completing her Ph.D. in sociology at the University of California at Berkeley, writing her dissertation on "Women's Collective Power in the African Methodist Episcopal Church." She has written and lectured frequently on aspects of black culture and black families. Her civic involvements include membership on the Advisory Board, Institute of the Black World, and the Public Broadcasting Council of Atlanta.

MARY AGNES DOUGHERTY received her Ph.D. in history in 1979 from the University of California at Davis, where she periodically teaches United States history. Her dissertation was entitled "The Methodist Deaconess, 1885–1918." She has held the Chancellors Patent Fund Research Grant and a Regents Fellowship at Davis. Her affiliations include membership in the Institute for Historical Study at San Francisco and the Center for Women and Religion of the Graduate Theological Union in Berkeley.

MARY E. FREDERICKSON received her doctorate in 1981 from the University of North Carolina at Chapel Hill. The research for her dissertation, "A Place to Speak Our Minds: The Southern School for Women Workers," was supported by a Rockefeller Foundation Dissertation Fellowship. At the same university, she has worked as assistant and acting director of the Southern Oral History Program of the Department of History. In her numerous articles and lectures, she emphasizes the history of women, especially in the southern labor force, and is currently teaching a course on "Women and Work" at Rhode Island College in Providence.

CAROLYN DESWARTE GIFFORD holds a Ph.D. from Northwestern University. Her dissertation was entitled "Spirituality in Slavonic Christianity and in the Philosophy of Nicolas Berdyaev." She has taught at Mundelein College and in the Religion and Philosophy Department of Mount Union College,

Alliance, Ohio. Her section in *Women and Religion in America, Vol I: The Nineteenth Century* (Harper & Row, 1981) , edited by Rosemary Ruether and Rosemary Keller, dealt with the participation of women in social reform movements. Her interest in Eastern Orthodoxy has been expressed in travel to the U.S.S.R. as a member of a study seminar and in the translation from the Russian of an article by Berdyaev, "Salvation and Creativity: Two Understandings of Christianity," for a volume on forms of spirituality (Paulist Press).

DONALD K. GORRELL is professor of church history at United Theological Seminary in Dayton, Ohio. He holds an M.Div. degree from Yale University and a Ph.D. from Case Western Reserve University, and was awarded the Faculty Fellowship of the Association of Theological Schools. In 1972 he was a fellow at the Case-Study Institute in Cambridge, Massachusetts. An elder in The United Methodist Church, Dr. Gorrell has been active in the work of that denomination and of the Evangelical United Brethren Church in Ohio since 1955. He is secretary of the United Methodist General Commission on Archives and History, and sits on the board of trustees of United Seminary. He has contributed articles to encyclopedias and professional journals, including *Methodist History*.

NANCY A. HARDESTY is a former assistant professor of church history at Candler School of Theology, Emory University. Before receiving the Ph.D. in the history of Christianity from the University of Chicago, she worked on the editorial staffs of *Eternity* magazine and *The Christian Century*. Her dissertation was entitled " 'Your Daughters Shall Prophesy': Revivalism and Feminism in the Age of Finney." She is the author of "Women in the Holiness Movement: Feminism in the Evangelical Tradition," in *Women of Spirit,* edited by Ruether and McLaughlin (Simon & Schuster, 1979).

JULIE ROY JEFFREY is associate professor of American history, director of the degree program in Historic Preservation, and director of faculty development at Goucher College, where she has taught since 1972. She holds the Ph.D. from Rice University. She is the author of *Frontier Women: The Trans-Mississippi West, 1840–1880* (Hill & Wang, 1979) and *Education for the Children of the Poor: A Study of the Origin and Implementation of the Elementary and Secondary Education Act of 1965* (Ohio State University Press, 1978) and has participated in and coordinated conferences on women's history, historic preservation, and faculty development. In recognition of the impact of the preservation program she directs, Goucher College received the Calvert Prize for the greatest contribution to historic preservation in Maryland in 1979.

ROSEMARY SKINNER KELLER, co-editor of this volume, is an associate professor of religion and American culture at Garrett-Evangelical Theological Seminary. She holds a doctorate in American history and the history of women from the University of Illinois at Chicago Circle. Her dissertation, "Abigail Adams and the American Revolution: A Personal History," is forthcoming from Arno. She is currently at work with Rosemary Ruether on a three-volume documentary history, *Women and Religion in America* (Harper & Row). She has held dissertation fellowships from the Newberry Library, the American Association of University Women, and the University of Illinois. Dr. Keller is a member of the United Methodist General Commission on Archives and History and currently chairs that agency's committee on Women's History and Status. A clergy wife and diaconal minister, she has long been active in the church.

SUSAN DYE LEE earned her Ph.D. in history at Northwestern University in 1980, with a dissertation entitled "Evangelical Domesticity: The Origins of the Woman's National Christian Temperance Union Under Frances E. Willard." She has taught in the Department of History at Northwestern, as well as at the elementary and high school levels. She is the author of articles on American history for children and an article in the *Supplement* to *Notable American Women,* and has been consultant to and author of a range of audio-visual materials, with an article on this field in *Signs: A Journal of Women in Culture and Society.*

DONALD G. MATHEWS is professor of history at the University of North Carolina at Chapel Hill and previously taught at Princeton. He holds a B.D. degree from Yale University and a doctorate in history from Duke University. He has received many fellowships and awards, and his numerous books and articles have made important contributions in the fields of United States social history, religious history, and women's history. The University of Chicago Press published his *Religion in the Old South* in 1977. His current research includes a study of opposition to the Equal Rights Amendment in North Carolina, with Jane DeHart Mathews, and a major study of "Society and Religion in the South, 1845–1956."

CLOTILDE FALCÓN NÁÑEZ holds an M.A. in Ibero-American civilization from Southern Methodist University. She taught Spanish at Trinity University and in the School of Continuing Education at Southern Methodist University, and headed the Spanish Department at Saint Mary's Hall, San Antonio, for fourteen years. She has taught English to non–English-speaking students in the Division of International Education at Pan American University, Edinburg, Texas, and was recently awarded a certificate of appreciation for her promotion and development of divisional programs. She is married to Dr. Alfredo Náñez, a member of the Rio Grande Annual Conference, and has long been active in conference women's work. For twenty-six years she and her mother translated the Program Book for the Woman's Division into Spanish. She has served as secretary of literature and publications for the Woman's Society of Christian Service in the South Central Jurisdiction and was a member of the Woman's Division of the Board of Missions, The Methodist Church, from 1964 to 1968.

CLARENCE G. NEWSOME is an assistant professor at Duke Divinity School. He holds the M.Div. and Ph.D. degrees from Duke University, where his dissertation was on "The Revelation and Liberation of Mary McLeod Bethune: A Biographical Study of the Black American Religious Experience." While studying at Duke he has held administrative positions and teaching assistantships and was awarded the James B. Duke Dissertation Fellowship. He is currently consultant on a film about Mary McLeod Bethune. He has lectured on black American religion, the family, and education, and in November 1979 he delivered a paper on Mary McLeod Bethune at the First National Scholarly Research Conference on Black Women, "Black Women: An Historical Perspective," sponsored by the National Council of Negro Women.

WILLIAM T. NOLL is pastor of Belvidere United Methodist Church in Belvidere, New Jersey. He earned the S.T.M. degree in 1980 at the Theological School, Drew University, with a thesis entitled "Shall She Be Allowed to Preach? Methodism's Response to Women Preachers in Nineteenth-Century America." An earlier essay on the movement to ordain women in the Methodist Protestant Church won the 1975 Seminary Award of the General Commission on Archives and History and was printed in *Methodist History.* He has co-chaired the Commission on the Status and Role of Women in the Northern New Jersey Annual Conference, drawing on his experience as a clergy spouse.

MARTHA L. SCOTT holds the M.Div. and is presently working on her Ph.D. in contemporary theology and American culture at Garrett-Evangelical Theological Seminary and Northwestern University. Her awards include the Georgia Harkness Scholarship and the Garrett-Evangelical Doctoral Fellowship of the Women's Institute. She is an ordained deacon in the Northern Illinois Annual Conference and is serving as pastor of McKinley Park and Lincoln United Methodist churches in Chicago.

VIRGINIA SHADRON holds the M.A. in history from Emory University and is working on her Ph.D. in American studies in the Graduate Institute of Liberal Arts there. Her thesis examines the woman's rights movement in the Methodist Episcopal

Church, South, from 1890 to 1918, and the relationship of that movement to the woman's suffrage movement in the South. Her interest in southern history, especially women's history, is reflected in extensive research in primary sources in that field. She has been photo/historical researcher for a major exhibition on the history of women in Atlanta, sponsored by the Atlanta Historical Society. She was co-compiler of *Women's Records: A Preliminary Guide (Georgia Department of Archives and History, 1978), a model guide* to a state collection of manuscript holdings about women, and is presently employed by the Georgia Archives.

KATHRYN KISH SKLAR is associate professor of history at the University of California at Los Angeles. She received her Ph.D. from the University of Michigan, where she taught previously. In 1973 she published *Catharine Beecher, A Study of American Domesticity* (Yale University Press), and she has since lectured and published prolifically on women's history. In 1973-1974 she was a fellow at the Radcliffe Institute, and she has won many other fellowships and prizes, including the annual prize of the Berkshire Conference of Women Historians. She is on the editorial board of the *Journal of American History* and has chaired the Committee on Women Historians of the American Historical Association. Dr. Sklar was one of the United States' representatives who delivered a report on *Recent U. S. Scholarship on the History of Women* at the 15th International Congress of Historical Sciences at Bucharest, Romania, in the summer of 1980. The report has been published by the American Historical Association.

HILAH F. THOMAS, co-editor of this volume, was project coordinator of the Women's History Project of the General Commission on Archives and History, The United Methodist Church, from 1978 through 1980, and gave leadership to the Women in New Worlds Conference. She holds the M.A. and M.Phil. degrees in modern European history from Columbia University, where she held Woodrow Wilson National and Kent fellowships, and has done research toward her Ph.D. dissertation at Columbia on the founding of the twentieth-century French review, *Annales d'histoire economique et sociale.* She is author of "The Era," in *The American Book of Days,* 3rd ed. (H. W. Wilson Co., 1978). She has taught in the History Department of Brooklyn College, City University of New York, and in 1975-76 she was instrumental in founding The Institute for Research in History, New York City, whose board she has chaired. Currently she is consultant for the oral history project of the Women's Division, United Methodist General Board of Global Ministries, and co-chairs The Coordinating Committee on Women in the Historical Profession, New York Metropolitan Chapter.

OTHER PAPERS DELIVERED AT THE CONFERENCE

Janet F. Asteroff, "Frontiers of Faith: Mattie Cone Sleeth, Methodism, and the W.C.T.U., 1865–1919."

Mary Lou Santillán Baert, "Clay, Rock, and the Morning Mist: The Quests and Achievements of Notable Hispanic-American Women of the Rio Grande Conference."

Frank Baker, "Susanna Wesley: Puritan, Parent, Pastor, Protagonist, Pattern."

Anne L. Barstow, "The Position of Anglican Clergy Wives after the Reformation: Ambiguous Legacy for Early Methodist Clergy Wives."

Adrian A. Bennett, "The Southern Methodist Woman's Missionary Society's China Mission, 1878–1898."

Emora T. Brannan, " 'Let Us Give Them Equal Advantages in the Business of Life': John and Mary Goucher Found the Woman's College of Baltimore."

H. Myron Braun, "Women as Hymnodists in the United Methodist Tradition: Crescendos and Diminuendos."

Joan Jacobs Brumberg, "Missionary Hagiography and Female Popular Culture: The Case of Ann Hasseltine Judson, 1812–1850."

Mollie C. Davis, "The Old World Connects with the New: The Countess of Huntingdon's Enthusiastic Efforts for New World Settlers and Indians."

Donald W. Dayton, "Prophesying Daughters: The Ministry of Women in the Holiness Traditions."

Joan Chamberlain Engelsman, "The Legacy of Georgia Harkness."

Thomas W. Fassett, "The History and Role of Methodism and Other Missionary Churches in the Lives and Culture of Native-American Women."

Minerva N. Garza, "The Influence of Methodism on the Hispanic-American Woman Through the Women's Societies."

Joanna Bowen Gillespie, "The Mother in Early Nineteenth-Century Methodist Sunday School Lore: 'The Sun in Their Domestic System.' "

443

Alan L. Hayes, "The Thwarted Romance of John Wesley and Sophy Hopkey in Frontier Georgia (1736–1737): A Case Study of Clergy Attitudes towards Marriage."

Patricia R. Hill, "Heathen Women's Friends: The Organization and Development of Women's Foreign Missionary Societies among Methodist Episcopal Women, 1869–1915."

Sylvia M. Jacobs, "A.M.E. Women Missionaries in Africa 1882–1904."

James L. Leloudis II, "Methodist Women and White Male Morality in the Antebellum South: *The Lady's Southern Companion,* 1847–1854."

Odette Lockwood-Farley, "Anna Howard Shaw and Her Critics: The Controversial National American Woman's Suffrage Association Presidency, 1904–1914."

Sarah R. Mason, "Women's Roles in Two Korean United Methodist Congregations in Minnesota, 1976–1980: Shaping the Church for Mutual Support and Ethnic Solidarity."

Harriet L. Miller, "Status and Images of Women in Christian Education in the Evangelical United Brethren Church, 1948–1968."

Ida Tetreault Miller, "Frances Elizabeth Willard's Religious Thought: Gospel Basis for Social Action."

F. Joseph Mitchell and Norma Taylor Mitchell, "Supporting, Sharing, Shaking the Patriarchy: Women and Bishops in United Methodist History."

Rosa Peffly Motes, "The Changing Role of the Pastor's Wife in the Pacific Northwest, 1840–1979."

Saranne P. O'Donnell, "Distress from the Press: Anti-Feminism as Expressed in the Editorial Opinions of James Monroe Buckley, Editor of *The Christian Advocate* (New York), 1880–1912."

Carol A. Page, "Charlotte Manye Maxeke: A.M.E. Missionary and Educator in South Africa."

Amanda Porterfield, "Phoebe Palmer and Spiritual Perfectionism."

Catherine M. Prelinger, "The Sometime Model: Fliedner's Deaconessate at Kaiserswerth and the Methodist Deaconess Movement in America."

Vivian U. Robinson, "C.M.E. and United Methodist Women's Missionary Training Institutes: A Quarter Century of Cooperation."

Alice B. Scott, "The Helm Women: Methodist Women in a Political Family."

Arnold Shankman, "Methodist Women in the South and Civil Rights: The Roles Played by Carrie Johnson, Jessie Daniel Ames, and Dorothy Tilly."

Anastatia Sims, "Women and Social Service: A Comparative Study of Methodist Missionary Societies and Women's Clubs in North Carolina, 1890–1930."

OTHER CONFERENCE PAPERS

Ralph W. Spencer, "Anna Howard Shaw, 1915–1919: The Evangelical Feminist's Final Years."

Carolyn L. Stapleton, "Belle Harris Bennett (1852–1922): Model of Holistic Christianity."

Virginia R. Stewart, "Voices from the Past: What Is Real and Valuable in Historical Records?"

Marilyn Richardson Truesdell, "Jarena Lee (1783–185?), First Woman Licensed to Preach in the A.M.E. Church: Her *Journal* and Her Life."

Mari Watters, "Nez Perce United Methodist Women and the Establishment of Methodism on the Nez Perce Reservation (Idaho), 1890 to the Present."

David W. Wills, "Womanhood and Domesticity in the A.M.E. Tradition: The Victorian Era."